Rust for C++ Programmers

Learn how to embed Rust in C/C++ with ease

Mustafif Khan

www.bpbonline.com

First published: 2023

Published by BPB Online
WeWork
119 Marylebone Road
London NW1 5PU

UK | UAE | INDIA | SINGAPORE

ISBN 978-93-55513-595

www.bpbonline.com

Dedicated to

My beloved Parents:

Yousuf Khan

Fouzia Sultana

&

to my amazing family and friends for their support

About the Author

Mustafif Khan is a Canadian student majoring in Financial Mathematics and minoring in Computer Science. Some of his hobbies are programming, gaming, and writing. He has been writing his books since he was a kid, with a few self-published poetry books in his catalog. His interest in programming began with his wish to write his own website. Soon after, Khan became interested in systems programming with his change to using Linux distributions. He has been programming Rust for the last three years and has learned a lot from books, documentation, and building projects, such as TexCreate (a LaTeX project creator) and TexCore (a library to write LaTeX using Rust types). Before Khan found Rust, he was writing projects in C++ and Golang, although after using Rust, he has not been able to go back except for C.

About the Reviewer

Pooya Eimandar is the leader of PlayPod, the first cloud gaming in the Middle East. He has developed many games and real-time applications in C/C++ and Rust with GPU APIs, mostly Vulkan and DirectX. He is also the author and technical reviewer of quite a few books in the game development area. Moreover, he is Co-Founder and CTO at RivalArium cloud gaming.

This work is dedicated to the brave and courageous people of Iran who have become the source of inspiration for many around the world. Let us amplify their voice, their message and their hope for a brighter future;

Women, Life, Freedom!"

Acknowledgement

There are a few people I want to thank for the continued and ongoing support they have given me during the writing of this book. First and foremost, I would like to thank my parents for their continuous support as an author and programmer. Secondly, I would like to thank my best friends Catherine Xiao and Diane Zaide, who have been there to encourage me whenever I would have writer's block. They have given me continuous support when things would get stressful, and without them, I do not know how I would have been able to complete this book.

My gratitude also goes to the team at BPB Publications. This is my first experience writing a book for a publisher and with the support from BPB, the experience was way less scary as it may have seemed. I am grateful for the opportunity given to me and the experience I was able to gain from writing this book.

Preface

This book is a beginner to advance guide for the Rust programming language. Still, since Rust has a notoriously steep learning curve, we are targeting C++ programmers who can use their pre-existing knowledge to help learn Rust easier. In this book, we will go through how to write simple programs in Rust, look at different topics such as networking, concurrency, and metaprogramming, and to better align our goals with C++. We will also look at unsafe Rust and Foreign Function Interface (FFI) to integrate Rust into a C project and vice versa.

A neat approach taken in this book is dedicated project chapters that will give you a better experience writing programs in Rust to better cram in the knowledge you will be learning. We will build things such as command line applications to desktop apps (GTK and Tauri) and also write a standard library in Rust for the toy language, Mufi, with a bytecode compiler written in C.

This book is divided into **11 chapters**. The **first 6 are beginner to intermediate level**, while the **last 5 are more advanced topics** containing more complex, messy code. Within the 11 chapters, there will be seven dedicated to Rust content and four chapters dedicated to building projects.

Chapter 1 will cover an introduction to the Rust programming language and how we can use it and C++ to flatten the learning curve of the language better. We will look into the fantastic package manager Cargo to create applications, libraries, benchmarking, and testing. The goal of this chapter is to have the reader be able to write simple programs in Rust, so beginner topics like bindings, conditionals, loops, functions, and structures will be discussed as well as trying to understand Rust's ownership model and what it means to borrow a value.

Chapter 2 will cover how to apply object-oriented concepts to structures and enumerations using implementations, traits and generics. These techniques will allow developers take full advantage of structures and enumerations while also being able to see how things such as bounded methods, polymorphism and templates in C++ can be translated into Rust easily.

Chapter 3 will cover how to handle errors in Rust, whether it means to handle them gracefully or panic. We will see Rust's dedicated types toward error handling, instead of using a try-and-catch method. While we will learn how to handle errors, and will also look into creating our custom error type that can be applied in your projects for personalized error handling, which becomes a big part of a Rust project.

Chapter 4 will cover how to create a command-line interface application in Rust using the amazing structopts crate. We will also learn how to write a simple web server so we can have our CLI act as the client, which will involve an introduction to asynchronous programming in Rust. After we create our application, we will go through the process of publishing it using the package manager Cargo.

Chapter 5 will cover how to create concurrent programs in Rust using a combination of threads, smart pointers and locking types. We will discuss the importance of concurrency and how Rust guarantees thread safety in programs to avoid data races with the Send and Sync traits.

Chapter 6 will cover the basics of networking in Rust in both synchronous contexts using the standard library and asynchronous contexts with the tokio crate. We will look into both kinds of contexts by creating IO models that can help us understand how to bind an address as well as reading/writing to data streams.

Chapter 7 will cover how to create desktop applications for native Linux systems using the GTK framework. We will discuss the pros and cons on developing desktop applications using Rust types exclusively and how to write different type of applications using the family of GTK crates.

Chapter 8 will cover what unsafe Rust is and how to integrate other languages in a Rust program; our focus will be C/C++ using Rust FFI. We will discuss what it means to be safe and unsafe in Rust, and when it is appropriate to consider performing an unsafe operation. After discussing unsafe operations, we will look at adding raw C bindings to our Rust programs and using a Rust shared library in a C program.

Chapter 9 will cover metaprogramming in Rust and how to utilize Rust syntax and token trees to generate code. We will discuss when it is appropriate to use metaprogramming compared to normal functions, traits, among others, and whether to choose declarative or procedural macros.

Chapter 10 will cover how to integrate Rust into a bytecode-compiled toy language written in C called Mufi. In this chapter, we will look into developing a standard library in Rust for the language Mufi and creating a batch benchmark using native functions written in C, Rust, and an interpreted Mufi program.

Chapter 11 will cover how to write cross-platform desktop applications using the Tauri framework. Like developing applications in GTK, we will look at the pros and cons of Tauri development and when to consider using it to create an application. We will discuss using Rust alongside a Svelte frontend to create responsive applications that functionally work similarly to Electron.

Code Bundle and Coloured Images

Please follow the link to download the
Code Bundle and the *Coloured Images* of the book:

https://rebrand.ly/dj5r16a

The code bundle for the book is also hosted on GitHub at **https://github.com/bpbpublications/Rust-for-C-Plus-Plus-Programmers**. In case there's an update to the code, it will be updated on the existing GitHub repository.

We have code bundles from our rich catalogue of books and videos available at **https://github.com/bpbpublications**. Check them out!

Errata

We take immense pride in our work at BPB Publications and follow best practices to ensure the accuracy of our content to provide with an indulging reading experience to our subscribers. Our readers are our mirrors, and we use their inputs to reflect and improve upon human errors, if any, that may have occurred during the publishing processes involved. To let us maintain the quality and help us reach out to any readers who might be having difficulties due to any unforeseen errors, please write to us at :

errata@bpbonline.com

Your support, suggestions and feedbacks are highly appreciated by the BPB Publications' Family.

Did you know that BPB offers eBook versions of every book published, with PDF and ePub files available? You can upgrade to the eBook version at www.bpbonline.com and as a print book customer, you are entitled to a discount on the eBook copy. Get in touch with us at :

business@bpbonline.com for more details.

At **www.bpbonline.com**, you can also read a collection of free technical articles, sign up for a range of free newsletters, and receive exclusive discounts and offers on BPB books and eBooks.

Piracy

If you come across any illegal copies of our works in any form on the internet, we would be grateful if you would provide us with the location address or website name. Please contact us at **business@bpbonline.com** with a link to the material.

If you are interested in becoming an author

If there is a topic that you have expertise in, and you are interested in either writing or contributing to a book, please visit **www.bpbonline.com**. We have worked with thousands of developers and tech professionals, just like you, to help them share their insights with the global tech community. You can make a general application, apply for a specific hot topic that we are recruiting an author for, or submit your own idea.

Reviews

Please leave a review. Once you have read and used this book, why not leave a review on the site that you purchased it from? Potential readers can then see and use your unbiased opinion to make purchase decisions. We at BPB can understand what you think about our products, and our authors can see your feedback on their book. Thank you!

For more information about BPB, please visit **www.bpbonline.com**.

Table of Contents

CHAPTER 1
Introduction to Rust

Introduction

Rust is a fairly new language that was developed from the ground up to be memory safe and has zero abstractions. Compared to other systems programming languages like C or C++, Rust offers close performance while avoiding memory issues like leaks, double free, or segmentation faults.

How you may ask? We will delve into detail later in this chapter, but Rust manages memory using binding's lifetimes and ownership. Within the compiler, we have something called the borrow checker. Its role is to check ownership for each binding, and when out of scope, it is dropped. Ownership, in this case, means that each binding or variable owns its value, and when another binding takes that value, the previous is dropped.

If this seems overwhelming, do not worry; we will fight the borrow checker together, and we will learn how to love it. The compiler teaches us how to be smarter programmers, and thus make safer decisions when it comes to memory management.

This book assumes you have a fair knowledge of C++. We will compare code between Rust and C++ at certain points in the book and hope that it helps flatten the learning curve.

Structure

In this chapter, we will discuss the following topics:

- Installing Rust
- Getting started with Cargo
- Bindings and Mutability
- Ownership
- Control Flow
    - Logic and conditional operators
    - If/Else statements
    - Match statements
- Loops
    - While loops
    - For loops
    - Loop
- Functions
- Structs and Enums

Objectives

By the end of this chapter, the reader will be able to understand how to write simple programs in Rust using C++ as a translation layer, as well as get a general understanding of concepts like ownership and what it means to borrow a value. We will look into Rust's package manager Cargo, which will help us create projects throughout the book, and see how the package manager can be used for benchmarking and unit testing.

Installing Rust

To install Rust, we will use the rustup tool, which allows us to change toolchains, update to stable, beta or nightly, and so on.

For Unix systems like Linux or macOS, you can enter the following command on your terminal:

```
$ curl --proto '=https' --tlsv1.2 -sSf https://sh.rustup.rs | sh
```

On Windows systems, you will need to visit **https://rustup.rs** and install the setup file. However, make sure that you have C++ Build tools installed from Visual Studio.

Getting started with Cargo

Cargo is Rust's package manager, and it allows developers to build projects and publish them. It is similar to **pip** for Python or **npm** for Node.js. Packages in Rust are referred to as crates and can be publicly found at **https://crates.io**. Let us create a project for our next section so we can see what Cargo offers us.

Bin versus Lib

Cargo has two types of projects that can be built: a binary or a library project. A binary project is a project that creates an executable and has a **main.rs** file, while a library is a collection of code that can be used in different projects and has a **lib.rs** file.

For our purposes, we will create a binary project. Run the following command on your terminal:

```
$ cargo new bindings_and_mut --bin
# for lib: cargo new <name> --lib
```

You will find a new directory named **bindings_and_mut**. Let us enter the directory and we will notice the following structure:

```
bindings_and_mut/
            Cargo.lock
            Cargo.toml
            src/
                main.rs
```

Let us look at what each of these files does in a Cargo project, so we are not confused when we create projects throughout the rest of the book:

- **Cargo.lock**: Keeps a cache of the dependencies of a project.
- **Cargo.toml**: Contains all the metadata of the project, as well as dependencies.
- **src/**: The directory that contains all the source code for the project. If the project is a binary, the folder will contain a **main.rs** file while a library will contain a **lib.rs**.

Let us edit our **Cargo.toml** file so we can add the **rand** crate, and we can create a guessing game for the next section.

```
[package]
name = "bindings_and_mut"
version = "0.1.0"
edition = "2021"
```

```
# See more keys and their definitions at https://doc.rust-lang.org/cargo/
reference/manifest.html
```

```
[dependencies]
rand = "0.8.5" # add rand here
# generally it's crate = "version"
# version is in form of major.minor.patch
```

Bindings and mutability

To begin this section, let us first look at a simple C++ program that shows variables of different data types. We will then follow with the same program but written in Rust:

```
// C++
int main(){
        auto varOne = 76; //inferring integer
        char* varTwo = "var Two"; // C String
        int varThree = 69; // integer
        double varFour = 42.0; // floating point
        return 0;
}
```

How can we create this program in Rust? First of all, how do we declare bindings?

We will use the **let** keyword. It is used to declare a binding. Binding's data types in Rust are implicitly inferred but can be explicitly declared using the separator operator (a semicolon or ':'). So, let us recreate the program:

```
// Rust
fn main(){
        let varOne = 76; // inferring integer
        let varTwo: &str = "var Two"; //borrowed string
        let varThree: i32 = 69; // 32-bit integer
        let varFour: f64 = 42.0; // 64-bit floating point
}
```

You may be a bit confused with the data types but that is fine. *Table 1.1* shows each data type:

Data Type	Description
i8	Signed 8-bit integer
i16	Signed 16-bit integer
i32	Signed 32-bit integer
i64	Signed 64-bit integer
i128	Signed 128-bit integer
isize	Signed arch-sized integer(32/64)
u8	Unsigned 8-bit integer
u16	Unsigned 16-bit integer
u32	Unsigned 32-bit integer
u64	Unsigned 64-bit integer
u128	Unsigned 128-bit integer
usize	Unsigned arch-sized integer (32/64)
f32	32-bit floating point
f64	64-bit floating point
&str	Borrowed String
String	Owned String

Table 1.1: Rust data types

Note: When a value is inferred and it is an integer, its type will be an i32. If the value is a floating point, the value is an f64 and string literals will be a borrowed string &str.

Strings seem confusing at first because there are two string types: borrowed (&str) and owned (String). We will go through this in detail when we discuss ownership, but the basic reason is that strings are heap-allocated values. Moreover, since their size cannot be determined during compile time, a borrowed string is essentially a reference to that heap value.

Guessing game

In our Cargo section, we conveniently created a project **bindings_and_mut**. Let us open it and start our simple guessing game. The game will first ask the user to enter a number. We will compare the number to the randomly generated answer and reveal the output if it is too high/low or correct. Let us begin with asking and getting user input:

```
fn main() {
// Ask the user for input
println!("Please enter a number from 1-20: ");
// Create a new empty string instance
let mut input = String::new();
// read the input from standard input
std::io::stdin()
.read_line(&mut input)
.expect("Couldn't get input.");
```

Wait for a moment here. There's a lot of mystery in these five lines of code. Let us resolve each mystery one line at a time.

println! is what we call a declarative macro, and it is defined by a "!". It acts as a way to add formatting and arguments into **println!**. We will see these in a more detailed view when we discussed in *Chapter 9, Metaprogramming*.

In Rust, bindings are immutable by default. To make a binding mutable, we place **mut** beside **let** followed by the identifier. After that, we create a new string instance to allow us to mutably borrow it for the standard input. This can be seen in the code here:

```
let mut input = String::new();
```

Why are Rust bindings immutable? Immutable Rust bindings improve security and safety in applications since values just can't be changed. Apart from that, most of the time bindings don't need to be mutable.

To read the input, we use the standard library's standard input (**std::io::stdin()**). With this, we use the method **read_line(&mut input)** that requires a mutable reference to our binding. When we place the **expect ("Couldn't get input.")** at the end of our binding, **input** prints a message if the program panics:

```
std::io::stdin()
.read_line(&mut input)
.expect("Couldn't get input.");
```

Now, let us continue with the next snippet:

```
// trim and parse the input to an int
let guess: i32 = input.trim().parse().expect("Couldn't convert to
integer");
// make random number with range 1 to 20
let mut rng = rand::thread_rng(); // random generator
let answer: i32 = rng.gen_range(1..20); // creates number from range 1 - 20
```

```rust
// use match to compare the value
match guess.cmp(&answer){
// if guess is greater it's too high
Ordering::Greater => println!("Too high!"),
// if guess is lower it's too low
Ordering::Less => println!("Too low!"),
// if guess is equal it's correct
Ordering::Equal => println!("Guess Correct!!!")
}
```

Before we continue with the explanation, we have some imports to do at the top of the file:

```rust
use rand::Rng; // random number generator
use std::cmp::Ordering; // compares each value to compare
fn main() {

    ...

}
```

First, let us look at how we convert our input to guess:

```rust
let guess: i32 = input.trim().parse().expect("Couldn't convert to integer");
```

First, we trim the string. This means removing any extra white space, and after that, we use **parse()**. When using this method, a type must be specified, either explicitly as we did here or using the turbo-fish method **.parse::<i32>()**. Then, we have **expect()** at the end since parse returns an error if the conversion goes wrong.

After having our guess, we need to start getting our answer ready. To do that, we use a random generator using the **rand** crate. To create a random generator, we use **thread_rng()** and then pass in a range **1..20** to generate the answer:

```rust
let mut rng = rand::thread_rng();
let answer: i32 = rng.gen_range(1..20);
```

To compare the guess to the answer, we rely on the **cmp()** method that returns the **Ordering** enum. We utilize the match statement to look at each case (Less, Greater, Equal), similar to how one would towards a switch statement. We can see this being done as follows:

```rust
match guess.cmp(&answer){
// if guess is greater it's too high
Ordering::Greater => println!("Too high!"),
```

```
// if guess is lower it's too low
Ordering::Less => println!("Too low!"),
// if guess is equal it's correct
Ordering::Equal => println!("Guess Correct!!!")
}
```

This project gives us a good outlook on what we expect to see in this chapter. You may now run **cargo run** that will execute the binary or **cargo build** that will build the binary at **target/debug/bindings_and_mut**.

Ownership

Let us now look at the various aspects of ownership in Rust.

How Rust manages memory

Rust manages memory differently compared to other languages such as Python or Java that rely on garbage collectors. While Garbage Collectors nicely take care of memory management for the user, it creates an overhead during runtime to mark and blacken objects (a technique used for the garbage collector for Mufi-Lang). Rust being a zero abstractions language, having a garbage collector is unacceptable, so how do we manage memory? Do we do it manually like C/C++? Well yes and no; it is called the borrow checker!

Rust uses the notion of ownership to manage memory and utilizes the borrow checker during compile time. This may increase the time during compilation, but if it does compile, it will most likely work during runtime (take it with a grain of salt).

Before we dive any deeper, let us consider how Rust's memory management compares to C++. Well, Rust and C++ both use a form of **Resource Acquisition is Initialization (RAII)**. In Rust's case, since bindings are stored on the stack, to allocate any value from the heap we need to use a smart pointer. The smart pointers all have different purposes; whether it is heap allocation (Box), **reference counter (RC)**, Cell (Internal Mutability), and so on.

Owning and borrowing values

Owning or borrowing a value has the same goal of having a binding value, and the difference only lies in whether you want to take over it or not.

Borrowing a value is to have a reference to a value, whereas taking ownership of a value is becoming a new owner. To borrow, we use the **&** operator, which can also be considered a safe pointer (where * is a raw pointer). So, let us jump into some examples of borrowing and owning values:

```
let string = "Hi, who owns me?".to_string();
```

```
// makes &str to String
let borrowed_string = &string; // type: &str
println!("{}", &string);
println!("{}", borrowed_string);
```

If we run this code, we can see the output as follows:

Hi, who owns me?

Hi, who owns me?

Let us recreate the example but instead of having **borrowed_string**, we will have **owned_string**. Will we be able to print both bindings? (spoiler alert: no!):

```
let string = "Hi, who owns me?".to_string();
// makes &str to String
let owned_string = string; // type: String
println!("{}", &string);
println!("{}", owned_string);
```

If we run this code, we can see the following error, as follows:

```
error[E0382]: borrow of moved value: `string`
 --> test.rs:5:16
  |
2 |     let string="Hi, who owns me?".to_string();
  |         ------ move occurs because `string` has type `String`, which
does not implement the `Copy` trait
3 | // makes &str to String
4 | let owned_string=string; // type: String
  |                  ------ value moved here
5 | println!("{}", &string);
  |                ^^^^^^^ value borrowed here after move

error: aborting due to previous error

For more information about this error, try `rustc --explain E0382`.
```

This is because once a new owner takes ownership of a value, the old binding is dropped. But what if we want to keep it? Well, that ties into our next topic, the Copy and Clone traits.

Copy and clone

The copy and clone traits are used to copy a binding's value, while copy only does this by taking a reference to the value and can be done implicitly or by borrowing a value. Clone is explicit by using the **clone()** method and creates a duplicate owner to a binding.

While we look at using the **clone()** method, let us shoot two birds with one stone and discuss scope. For this example, we will use a Reference Counter (**std::rc::Rc**) that counts the number of references made for a binding, and once it reaches 0, the binding is dropped.

In this example, we will create clones of binding and show the count of owners when we create the new clone and when we are about to leave it. Since **Rc** is a strong reference compared to **Weak** (which is a weak reference, hence the name), we will use **std::rc::Rc::strong_count()** to count the number of strong references of the owner:

```
use std::rc::Rc; //import reference counter
fn main(){
let owner = Rc::new(8); //create a new reference counter
println!("Owners: {}", Rc::strong_count(&owner));
{ // create a closure using {}
println!("New closure");
let owner2 = owner.clone(); // clone of owner
        // to access value within, you can use *owner2
println!("Owners: {}", Rc::strong_count(&owner));
{ // new closure
println!("New closure");
let owner3 =owner.clone(); // clone of owner
println!("Owners: {}", Rc::strong_count(&owner));
println!("Leaving closure, owner3 dropped");
} // owner 3 drops out of scope
println!("Owners: {}", Rc::strong_count(&owner));
println!("Leaving closure, owner2 dropped");
} // owner 2 drops out of scope
println!("Owners: {}", Rc::strong_count(&owner));
} // owner drops out of scope
```

As you can notice, once we leave the closure, the binding is dropped and the strong count will decrease. If we run this code, we will see the following output:

```
Owners: 1
New closure
Owners: 2
New closure
Owners: 3
Leaving closure, owner3 dropped
Owners: 2
Leaving closure, owner2 dropped
Owners: 1
```

> **Note: Values don't always implement Copy; some only implement Clone or Copy & Clone (since Copy depends on Clone). This will make more sense when we discuss structures and enums in OOP, where we will discuss deriving traits from them.**

Borrowing rules

To help avoid fighting against the borrow checker, it is best to know the rules of borrowing. To start off, we will talk about the different syntaxes for immutable and mutable borrowing:

- **&T:** Immutable Borrow
    - o Cannot change values of borrowed values
    - o Simply a reference to a binding's value

- **&mut T:** Mutable Borrow
    - o Can change the values of a borrowed value
    - o Requires the binding to be mutable

Rules

- A reference may not live longer than its owner.
    - o For obvious reasons, if the owner is dropped, the reference of the value points to deallocated memory; in other words, to invalid memory (segmentation fault).
- If there's a mutable borrow to a value, no other references are allowed in the same scope.
    - o Best way to think of this is as a sort of Mutex lock to a value.
- If no mutable borrows exist, any number of immutable borrows can exist in the same scope.

    o Since the value isn't mutably changing, this immutable borrow cannot affect the owner.

By following these rules, you should be able to get along with the borrow checker better, and someday, you will be best friends forever as segmentation faults give you death stares.

Pointer types

We will give an overview of the different pointer types, and these will be explained in greater detail in the latter chapters of the book.

- **&: Reference or Safe Pointer**
  - Used to borrow a value

- ***: Dereference or Raw Pointer**
  - Used to dereference a pointer
  - Mainly used in unsafe code

- **Box<T>**
  - Used to allocate values on the heap
  - Owns the value inside

- **Rc<T>**
  - Used for reference counting
  - Creates strong references of a value
  - Can be downgraded to provide a weak reference to a value
  - Value drops once reference count reaches 0

- **Arc<T>**
  - Atomic reference counting
  - Thread safe unlike Rc

- **Cell<T>**
  - Gives internal mutability to types that implement Copy
  - Allows for multiple mutable references

- **RefCell<T>**
  - Gives internal mutability without requiring the Copy trait
  - Uses runtime locking for safety

Control flow

This section on control flow will be very familiar since Rust follows a C syntax. So, as a reminder, logic operators are used to evaluate a Boolean expression. Conditional operators are used to compare values, and these two operators come in the following forms.

Logic operators

- **&& (and)**
    - true && true = true
    - true && false = false
    - false && false = true

- **|| (or)**
    - true || false = true
    - true || true = true
    - false || false = false

- **! (not)**
    - !false = true
    - !true = false

Conditional operators

- **== (Equal Equal)**
    - Compares values if they are equal to each other

- **<= (Less than or Equal to)**
    - Compares values if they are less than or equal to each other

- **< (Less than)**
    - Compares values if they are less than each other

- **>= (Greater than or Equal to)**
    - Compares values if they are greater than or equal to each other

- **> (Greater than)**
    - Compares values if they are greater than each other

If/Else Statements

If statements evaluate a block of code if the condition is true. Unlike in C++ or C, **if** statements in Rust do not require any parentheses:

```rust
if 5 > 3{
    println!("TRUE");
}


// Output: TRUE
// 5 is greater than 3
```

Unlike **if** statements, **else** statements evaluate if the condition is false. Else can be thought of as a default option, but its use cases depend on the context of the control flow:

```rust
if 5 < 3{
    println!("TRUE");
} else {
    println!("FALSE");
}

// Output: FALSE
// 5 is not less than 3
```

An **else if** statement is used to add another clause after the **if** statement, it will only execute as long as the other statements are false and it is true:

```rust
if 5 < 3{
    println!("TRUE");
}
else if 7 > 5{
    println!("ALSO TRUE");
}
else {
    println!("FALSE");
}
// Output: ALSO TRUE
// 7 is greater than 5
```

Match statements

Match statements are the replacements to switch statements, and they say goodbye to adding a **break;** to the end of each case. They follow a simple pattern-matching syntax without the unnecessary **case** keyword as shown in the following example:

```
match Foo{
        Bar => {...},
        ...
        _ => // default option
}
```

As much as Foo Bar shows us the general idea of the syntax, it is better if we dive into a deeper example:

```
// ask for favourite colour
let mut input = String::new();
std::io::stdin()
                .read_line(&mut input)
                .expect("Couldn't get input");
// trim and make it lowercase
input = input.trim().to_lower();
// match input
match &input{
        "purple" => println!("Good choice"),
        "blue" => println!("Close to purple"),
        "red" => println!("Close to purple as well"),
        _ => println!("Why have you not picked purple?");
}
// this program might be biased
```

Depending on what you input, a case will be printed.

Loops

Loops are used to execute code repeatedly until a condition is met. In Rust, we have three main loop statements, **while, for,** and loop. While the first two are quite familiar, the last isn't commonly used, so we will not look into it in greater detail, compared to the others.

While loops

While loops execute until a condition becomes true. They work the same like in C++ and can be used in a simple example like this:

```
let mut sum = 0;
let mut i = 0;
while i < 50{
        sum += i;
        i += 1;
}
```

In Rust, we have no increment operator (**++**) like in C++, so to increment, we use **+=**. This **while** loop will keep running until i becomes 50, and we can also use keywords like **continue** or **break** to add special conditions inside the loop.

For loops

For loops are closer to how they work in Python than C++. We can either iterate through an iterable object (**for i in &list**) or through a range (**for i in 0..20**). Let us see this in practice and introduce vectors while we are doing this:

```
// Create a vector list
let vector = vec![1, 3, 5, 7]; // type: Vec<i32>
// Iterate and print each element
for i in &vector{
        // i is type &i32
        println!("{}", i);
}
// Output:
1
3
5
7
```

So, what's going on? First, let us talk about how Rust implements vectors or dynamic arrays. You can either declare a vector with elements like the above (**vec![...]**) that uses the **vec!** macro which simply pushes each of the elements into the vector, or we create a new empty vector using **Vec::new()**.

To push or pop values in a vector, you must make the binding mutable. To explicitly declare a type for the vector, we use the syntax **Vec<type>**.

When we iterate through the vector, we borrow it so **i** becomes an **&i32** type and goes through each value in the vector.

Let us switch things up and use for with a range and push elements into a vector and create another for loop to print each element. This is completely inefficient, but we are doing this for learning purposes:

```
// Create the vector
let mut vector: Vec<i32> = Vec::new();
// Push values from 0..10
for i in 0..10{
        vector.push(i);
}
// Create loop to print each element
for i in 0..vector.len(){
        println!("Element => {} : Value => {}", &i, &vector[i]);
}
//Output:
Element => 0 : Value => 0
Element => 1 : Value => 1
Element => 2 : Value => 2
Element => 3 : Value => 3
Element => 4 : Value => 4
Element => 5 : Value => 5
Element => 6 : Value => 6
Element => 7 : Value => 7
Element => 8 : Value => 8
Element => 9 : Value => 9
```

Similar to Python, we declare a variable and assign it to a range using **in**. Instead of using **range(0, T)**, we use **0..T** which defines the range from 0 to T - 1. To get the length of the vector, we use the method **.len()** that is implied in the vector instead of using something like **sizeof(vector)**.

Loop Statements

Sometimes, we do want an infinite loop and instead of using **while true** or **for(;;)** in Rust, we use **loop**. This isn't popular to use (since infinite loops aren't recommended), but it is still useful to know just in case it matches your needs.

So how do we declare it? Since loop statements are infinite loops, there are no conditions and are just followed by a block expression. It is up to the code in the loop to break or return at some point:

```
// initialize our count
let mut count = 0;
// declare loop
loop{
// when count is greater than 10, we get out
if count>10{
println!("GET OUT!!!!");
break;
}
println!("Count at {}", &count);
count += 1;
}
```

Functions

Let us now discuss functions in Rust.

Declaring functions

Finally, we get to have some fun with new materials; functions in Rust are different enough from C++ that we will look at translating a C++ function into Rust.

To declare functions in Rust, we use the **fn** keyword followed by an identifier to name the function, parameters in parentheses, an arrow then a return type if present. To put it simply, follow this general syntax:

```
fn foo(bar: &type, baz: type, laz: &mut type) -> return_type{}
```

Even if that doesn't look the most pleasant, let us look at a C++ Fibonacci function and then recreate it in Rust:

```
// C++
int fib(int n){
        if(n <= 1) return 1;
        return fib(n-1) + fib(n-2);
}

// Rust
```

```
fn fib(n: u32) -> u32{
        if (n <= 1) {
                1
}
fib(n-1) + fib(n-2)
}
```

You're probably wondering where the return statement is. In Rust, the last statement in a function implicitly returns; you can use **return** explicitly but it is more common to use implicit returns. In this book, we will use implicit returns a lot, but I will make sure to add a comment that we are returning the value in case you get lost in the code. In modern C++, this can also be replicated using the **auto** keyword which will infer a variable's data type:

```
auto fib(auto n) -> int{
    if (n <= 1) return 1;
    return fib(n-1) + fib(n-2);
}
```

Note: Implicit returns must be the same type as the function; if not, there will be a compile error.

In parameters, you must specify if you are taking ownership, immutable borrow, or mutable borrow. For example, if we were to do the following:

```
fn take_ownership(s: String){
        println!("Now we have ownership of {}", s)
}


fn main(){
        let s = "I am bob the string".to_string();
        take_ownership(s);
        // attempt to print s
        println!("{}", s);
}
```

If we run the program, we get the following error, as follows:

```
error[E0382]: borrow of moved value: `s`
 --> test.rs:9:20
  |
6 |     let s = "I am bob the string".to_string();
```

```
 |              - move occurs because `s` has type `String`, which does not
implement the `Copy` trait
7 |       take_ownership(s);
 |                      - value moved here
8 |       // attempt to print s
9 |       println!("{}", s);
 |                      ^ value borrowed here after move
 |
 = note: this error originates in the macro `$crate::format_args_nl`
(in Nightly builds, run with -Z macro-backtrace for more info)


error: aborting due to previous error


For more information about this error, try `rustc --explain E0382`.
```

Modules and publicity

In Rust, you can organize code in modules, and when importing code from other files, they are considered modules. To create a module, use the keyword **mod**, followed by an identifier and then a block statement. Inside the block, all functions, structs, and so on. are part of the module.

By default, functions in Rust are private and publicity must be explicitly stated using the keyword **pub**. This improves security since it allows fine control of what the user can and cannot access.

Super versus self

How do you access functions within the module? To do that, you can use **self** to access functions. To do this, we use the syntax, **self::<idenitifier>**. You can see this in the example as follows:

```
pub mod test{
// adds hello to string
fn add_hello(str: &str)->String{
let mut owned = str.to_owned();
owned.push_str(" hello");
owned
}
// adds world to string
fn add_world(str: &str) ->String{
```

```
let mut owned = str.to_owned();
owned.push_str(" world");
owned
}
pub fn hello_world(s: &str){
// adds hello
Let with_hello = self::add_hello(s);
// adds world
let hw = self::add_world(&with_hello);
// print the masterpiece
println!("{}", hw)
}
}


fn main(){
let s = "I am Bob!!!";
// access test using test::<method>
test::hello_world(s);
}
```

We create our public module **test**. Here, we have two private functions called **add_hello** and **add_world** that simply push "hello" or "world" into the string, respectively. In our public function **hello_world**, we can be seen accessing the functions using **self::add_hello** or **self::add_world**. To access the module inside our main function, we use **test::hello_world**.

If we run the code, we get the following:

I am Bob!!! hello world

Modules can be nested inside each other. That is where **super** comes in! Let us change our previous example a bit, so we have **hello_world** inside a nested module **best_quotes**:

```
pub mod test{
        // adds hello to string
fn add_hello(str: &str)->String{
let mut owned = str.to_owned();
owned.push_str(" hello");
owned
        }
```

```rust
                   // adds world to string
fn add_world(str: &str) ->String{
let mut owned = str.to_owned();
owned.push_str(" world");
owned
        }
pub mod best_quotes{
pub fn hello_world(s: &str){
// adds hello
let with_hello = super::add_hello(s);
// adds world
let hw = super::add_world(&with_hello);
// print the masterpiece
println!("{}", hw)
        }
}
}


fn main(){
let s = "I am Bob!!!";
// access test using test::<method>
test::best_quotes::hello_world(s);
}
```

As you can see, not much has changed except that instead of using **self**, we use **super** and when using **hello_world**, we instead need to put **test::best_quotes::hello_world**.

Testing and benchmarking

Testing and benchmarking functions are very useful when performing changes or optimizations. For this section, we will have two implementations of a Fibonacci function, and we will have tests on it, then benchmark, and compare the two. For this topic, we will create a library for our testing and benchmarking. Let us open up our terminal and get started:

```
$ cargo new —lib test_and_bench
$ cd test_and_bench
# Create file for our fib functions
```

```
$ touch src/fib.rs
# Create benches directory for benchmarking
$ mkdir benches
# Create our fib bench file
$ touch benches/fib_bench.rs
```

Let us edit our **Cargo.toml** and add the following changes under **[dependencies]**:

```
# For benchmarks
[dev-dependencies]
criterion = "0.3"


[[bench]]
name = "fib_bench"
harness = false
```

Our Fibonacci functions will differ quite a bit: one will follow a concurrent model by using thread spawning, while the other will just be a regular if/else statement. These functions will be written in **src/fib.rs** while we will write the tests in **src/lib.rs**.

Here is how our first Fibonacci function, **fib_one** looks like:

```
// import threads from standard lib
use std::thread::*;
pub fn fib_one(n: u32)->u32{
// spawn a thread
Let thr = spawn(move || {
// match n
match n{
// if n <= 1 = 1
0 =>1,
1 =>1,
// else fib_one(n-1) + fib_one(n-2)
_ =>fib_one(n-1) + fib_one(n-2)
}
});
// join the thread to get the result
    thr.join().expect("Coudln't join threads.")
}
```

We will not go into greater detail about using threads as that will be explained in Chapter 5: Concurrency in Rust, but essentially, we spawn a thread to do our job. Once it is done, we join it with our main thread to get the value. Now, let us look at our simpler Fibonacci function, **fib_two**:

```
pub fn fib_two(n: u32) ->u32{
if n<= 1{
    1
      } else {
    fib_two(n-1) + fib_two(n-2)
      }
}
```

The tests we want to conduct are fairly simple and straightforward:

- Test if **fib_one** equals the right value
- Test if **fib_two** equals the right value
- Test if **fib_one** equals **fib_two**

In these tests, we will utilize the macro, **assert_eq!**. This checks whether the right value equals the left value: if so, the test passes, and if not, it fails.

This is a simple example of using it:

```
assert_eq!(1+2, 3); // passes since 3 == 3
assert_eq!(5, 2+4); // fails since 5 != 6
```

Clear everything from **src/lib.rs** and we will write the test module from scratch. We need to configure it for testing, and then we can start writing our test functions in it; the layout looks like the following:

```
// import fib.rs by declaring module
pub mod fib;
// import the functions using "use"
pub use fib::*;
// pub use is so other crates can use it

// Testing module
#[cfg(test)] // configures for testing
modtests{
// import functions use super
use super::*;
```

```
/* to make a test function
#[test]
fn foo(bar) {
// test
}
*/
}
```

Let us start writing our tests:

```
// 1. Test if fib_one equals the right value
#[test]
fn test_fib_one(){
assert_eq!(fib_one(5), 8)
}


// 2. Test if fib_two equals the right value
#[test]
fn test_fib_two(){
assert_eq!(fib_two(7), 21)
}


// 3. Test if fib_one == fib_two
#[test]
fn test_one_eq_two(){
let n = 10;
assert_eq!(fib_one(n), fib_two(n))
}
```

These tests are quite straightforward. Thus, if we run **cargo test**, we should see all the test passing. But what if one fails? Let us try that by changing test #3 a bit:

```
// 3. Test if fib_one == fib_two
#[test]
fntest_one_eq_two(){
let n = 10;
        // to fail
assert_eq!(fib_one(n), fib_two(n+1))
}
```

If we run **cargo test** now, we can see the results as follows:

```
running 3 tests
test tests::test_fib_two ... ok
test tests::test_fib_one ... ok
test tests::test_one_eq_two ... FAILED


failures:

---- tests::test_one_eq_two stdout ----
thread 'tests::test_one_eq_two' panicked at 'assertion failed: `(left ==
right)`
  left: `89`,
 right: `144`', src/lib.rs:23:9
note: run with `RUST_BACKTRACE=1` environment variable to display a
backtrace


failures:
    tests::test_one_eq_two


test result: FAILED. 2 passed; 1 failed; 0 ignored; 0 measured; 0
filtered out; finished in 0.00s


error: test failed, to rerun pass '--lib'
```

Change the function back to normal so we can answer the next question, who is faster? We will use the crate **criterion** to help us answer that.

Let us write our benchmark on **benches/fib_bench.rs**:

```
// import the necessary functions from criterion
use criterion::{criterion_group, criterion_main, Criterion,
BenchmarkId};
// import the fib functions
use test_and_bench::{fib_one, fib_two};


fn bench(c: &mutCriterion){
// Create a benchmark group
let mut group = c.benchmark_group("Fibonacci");
// For loop to put in inputs
```

```
For i in [0u32, 20u32].iter(){
// Add fib one
group.bench_with_input(
BenchmarkId::new("Fib One", i), i,
|b, i| b.iter(|| fib_one(*i))
);
// Add fib two
group.bench_with_input(
BenchmarkId::new("Fib Two", i), i,
            |b, i| b.iter(|| fib_two(*i)));
        }
// Group is finished
group.finish();
}


// Create criterion group
criterion_group!(fib_benches, bench);
// Add bench to criterion main
criterion_main!(fib_benches);
```

In our **bench** function, we create a benchmarking group aptly named Fibonacci. We create a for loop to iterate from 0 to 20, inputting those into our Fibonacci functions. Each is benched with the input with an ID. In the end, we put that the group is finished, and then create a group using the name **fib_benches** with our function **bench**.

Then, **fib_benches** is passed into the criterion main macro to run our group. For more information about the criterion, make sure to check out the documentation at **https://bheisler.github.io/criterion.rs/book/index.html**.

Run **cargo bench** and you can look at a detailed report placed inside **target/ criterion/report/index.html**. Refer to *Figure 1.1* where there is a graph for each function to see who won:

ibonacci/Fib One/0

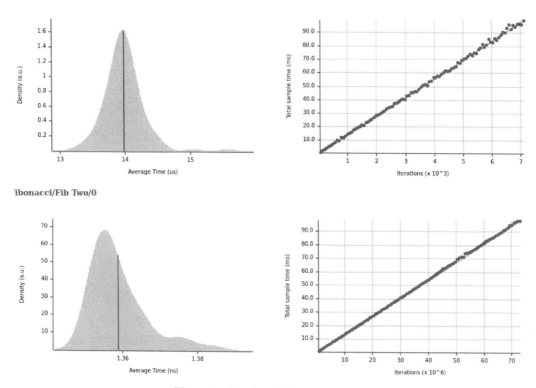

Figure 1.1: *Results of Fib One vs Fib Two*

To some readers' surprise, the concurrent model is slower than the recursive, and this makes sense since each time a function occurs, a thread needs to be made and joined. This adds up and creates additional latency.

Structs and Enums

Structures and enumerations provide users with the ability to create their own custom data type. Both of them use a form of property, while enums are a bit more abstract. In C/C++, they were commonly prefixed with the **typedef** keyword as follows:

```
typedef struct{
        double real;
        double imaginary;
}complex_t;
```

```
typedef enum {
        Red,
        Green,
Blue
}Colours;
```

In Rust, we have three variates of structures while enums also follow three different styles of configuring properties.

Structures

Structures are used to define custom data types using properties and defined data types for each. In Rust, we have the following three different types of struct:

1. Traditional C Struct

2. Tuple Structs

3. Empty Struct

We will visit each with an example and discuss how we may use each of them.

Traditional C Struct

As expected from the name, this type of struct follows a similar style to how C defines structs. Let us do a side-by-side comparison, or rather, in our case, an up-by-down comparison:

```
// C Struct
typedef struct {
int Foo;
uint8_t Bar;
char* Baz;
} MyStruct;


// Rust Struct
Struct MyStruct{
Foo: i32,
Bar: u8,
Baz: String
}
```

To access the property, we use the "." *(dot)* operator followed by the field's identifier as follows:

```
MyStruct.Foo = 32;
```

The properties and structure itself are private by default and will need to be made public by using the **pub** keyword as follows:

```
pub struct MyStruct{
pub Foo: i32,
pub Bar: u8,
pub Baz: String
}
```

Tuple Struct

A tuple struct has no field names, and instead, all data types are placed inside parentheses. Accessing properties work the same as tuples; this is done by having the index after the dot operator. This can be seen in the following:

```
struct TupStruct(String, u8, i32);


// To access properties
fn newTuple(s: String, u: u8, i: i32){
let mut tuple: TupStruct = TupStruct("".to_string(), 0, 0);
// we could just do
// let tuple: TupStruct = TupStruct(s, u, i);
// But I wanted to show how to access properties
tuple.0 = s;
tuple.1 = u;
tuple.2 = i;
}
```

Empty Struct

An empty struct has no fields or types; it is just empty inside. These structs can be used alongside traits to define some type of abstraction; we will not use empty structs much in this book, but like the loop statement, it is just good to know they exist. An empty struct can be seen like the following:

```
struct Empty;
```

Enumerations

Let us switch gears and look at enumerations. We have already seen enums before, when we were working on our guessing game. Enumerations provide a level of abstraction to the user. While the syntax of enums stays the same unlike structures, the way you can define the properties can vary.

We will go from a basic option to an advanced option for configuring a **Server** enum. Let us look at our first enum:

```
enum Server{
IPV4,
IPV6,
}
```

If we wanted our server to connect via IPV4, we can do **Server::IPV4**. As you can see to access properties in enums, we use the ":::" operator.

Let us say along with knowing it is the IP form. We want the actual address as well; we can define the enum like the following:

```
enum Server{
        IPV4([u8; 4], u8)
        IPV4([u8; 4], u8)
}
```

```
// Our server can be like the following
// let server = Server::IPV4([10, 30, 0, 1], 255);
```

That is pretty useful to know the protocol and address. As you can notice with declaring arrays, we can define the type and how many there should be with the syntax **[type; qty]**.

What if we needed even more information?

For example, to connect to a Samba server, we need a port, username, password, and a name. To deal with this, we add a struct inside the enum's field:

```
enum Server{
IPV4{
address: ([u8; 4], u8),
port: u32,
name: String,
username: String,
password: String
```

```
},
IPV6{
address: ([u8; 4], u8),
port: u32,
name: String,
username: String,
password: String
},
}

// To create a new Server instance we do:
/*
let server = Server::IPV4{
address: ([10, 20, 30, 40], 255),
port: 445,
name: "MyShare".to_string(),
username: "MyUserName".to_string(),
password: "Password123".to_string()
}
*/
```

Structures and Enumerations play a crucial role in Rust, and as such, in the next chapter, we will delve into them in greater detail, how to apply Object Oriented Programming techniques to them, and see how they compare to C++ classes.

Conclusion

This chapter helps us provide the basics of Rust to start writing basic programs. We used this as an opportunity to compare C++ side by side to flatten Rust's learning curve. While most of the syntax is fairly the same, we get to see many new keywords to simplify our workflows such as **match** statements or the in keyword. As we continue getting exposure to a lot of these concepts in the later chapters, a lot of the content in this chapter will become second nature.

Key facts

- For the best experience in Rust, it is recommended to use Cargo.
- To declare a binding, use the keyword **let**.
  - To explicitly state the data type, use **: <type>** after the identifier.

- Avoid if/else nests by using a **match** statement.
  - This can be suggested by using the **clippy** tool (run **cargo clippy**).
- A reference cannot outlive its owner
- If there's a mutable borrow to a value, no other references are allowed in the same scope.
- If there is no mutable borrow that exists, you may have any number of immutable borrows.
- To declare publicity, use the keyword **pub**.
- The three types of structs are:
  - Empty structs
  - Tuple structs
  - C-style structs

Exercises

1. Write a program that asks the user for a file path and content to write to it.

2. Write a program that asks the user for the number of students; for each student, enter the name and grade. At the end of the program, print each student collected with the format, **"name: grade"**.*(Recommended to use HashMap from std::collections)*.

Answers

1. This question can be done very simply; we first need to ask the user for a path using **std::io::stdin**. We use that path to create a file using **std::fs::File::create(&path)**. We then proceed to ask the user to enter the contents they want to write in the file, and we write it using **file.write_all()**.

    Create a file **ch1_ex1.rs** and add the following imports on the top of the file:

    ```
    use std::io::{stdin, Write};

    use std::fs::File;
    ```

    First, we need to ask the user the file's path, and with the path, we can create a new file:

    ```
    fn main(){
    let mut path=String::new();
        // ask for path
    ```

```
println!("Please enter file path: ");
    // read input
stdin().read_line(&mutpath).unwrap();
    // create new file from input
let mut file=File::create(&path.trim()).unwrap();
```

Secondly, ask for the content to write to the file, and write it to the file using **write_all** and turning the **String** into bytes(**&[u8]**) using the **.as_bytes()** method:

```
    // ask for content to write
let mut content=String::new();
println!("Please enter content for file: ");
stdin().read_line(&mutcontent).unwrap();
file.write_all(&content.trim().as_bytes()).unwrap();
}
```

If we compile the program using **rustc ch1_ex1.rs** and run it (**./ch1_ ex1**), we can see the result as follows:

```
$ rustc ch1_ex1.rs
$ ./ch1_ex1
Please enter file path:
test.txt
Please enter content for file:
I am a really happy jellybean
$ cat test.txt
I am a really happy jellybean
```

2. In this question, we get to use hashmaps, and this is found in **std::collections::HashMap**. The program can be split into three parts:

    1. Get the number of students to record.
    2. Record each student's name and grade.
    3. Print the record.

To begin this exercise, create a new file **ch1_ex2.rs** and add the following imports on the top of the file:

```
use std::collections::HashMap;
use std::io::stdin;
```

To get the number of students to record, we ask the user to input the number of students, and we trim and parse the input to a **u8**:

```
fn main() {
let mut input = String::new();
    // Ask and get number of students
println!("Please enter the number of students: ");
stdin().read_line(&mutinput).unwrap();
let num_of_stu: u8 = input.trim().parse().unwrap();
```

Our record of the students will be collected in a **HashMap<K, V>,** which has generics **K** for key and **V** for value. We can create an empty hashmap using the **new()** method:

```
// Key is student name
// Value is student's grade
Let mut students: HashMap<String, f32> = HashMap::new();
```

To enter each student's name and grade, we will use a helper function **enter_student** to get the user input for the name and grade, then insert it into the hashmap, **students**:

```
fn enter_student(students:&mutHashMap<String, f32>, num:u8) {
let mut input=String::new();
println!("Please enter student {}'s name: ", num);
stdin().read_line(&mutinput).unwrap();
let name = input.trim();
println!("Please enter student {}'s grade: ", num);
let mut input_two = String::new();
stdin().read_line(&mutinput_two).unwrap();
let grade: f32 = input_two.trim().parse().unwrap();
students.insert(name.to_owned(), grade);
}
```

We use a for loop to iterate from 1 to **num_stu** inclusively (using ..=) since we are not indexing an array, this is completely fine to do.

```
for i in 1..=num_of_stu{
enter_student(&mutstudents, i);
}
```

In the end, we can iterate through the name and grade values, and print each student in our hashmap:

```
println!("List of Students: ");
for (name, grade) in&students{
println!("{name}: {grade}")
}
```

When we compile the program using **rustc ch1_ex2.rs** and run it (**./ch1_ex2**), we can see the result as follows:

```
$ rustc ch1_ex2.rs
$ ./ch1_ex2
Please enter the number of students:
2
Please enter student 1's name:
john
Please enter student 1's grade:
87.4
Please enter student 2's name:
tom
Please enter student 2's grade:
67.8
List of Students:
tom: 67.8
john: 87.4
```

CHAPTER 2
OOP in Structs and Enums

Introduction

Rust's object-oriented programming is surrounded by using structures and enumerations. They provide a lot of versatility and create ease in a developer's workflow. You can create implementations (bounded methods), implement traits (inheritance), and reduce duplicates using generics. It is impossible to write a large project in Rust without structures; we will look through all the different ways you can expand its abilities.

Classes in C++ were one of the key differences between it and C; hence, the alternate name for C++ is C with Classes. Over the years, object-oriented programming has gotten a fair amount of heat, but it still stands as one of the major paradigms in programming. So how does Rust, a language that stands between functional and object-oriented programming, implement this aged paradigm?

Structure

In this chapter, we will discuss the following topics:

- From classes to structures
- Implementations
- Traits

- o   Deriving traits for structs / enums
- o   Type aliasing
- • From templates to generics
  - o   Generic structs
  - o   Generic traits

Objectives

By the end of this chapter, the reader will learn how to expand the use of their structures. This starts simply by using implementations to write bounded methods, using either **self** (to use) or **Self** (to create an instance). We dive deeper into traits that allow a form of inheritance, a topic that will be used very often throughout the book. Lastly, we will show how to compact a codebase by using generics that are tied down with traits and allow a developer full control of the generics able to be used.

From classes to structures

To better understand classes, let us take a look at a simple C++ class:

```cpp
#include<iostream>
class Foo{
private:
        // members
int bar;
int baz;
    // constructor
public:
Foo(){
        bar =45;
        baz =32;
}
    // bounded method
void do_something(){
        bar = baz + bar;
        baz--;
}
    // destructor
~Foo(){
```

```cpp
        // integers don't need to be freed
        std::cout <<"Bye "<< bar <<" and "<< baz << std::endl;
}


};

int main(){
Foo f =Foo();
    f.do_something();
}
```

```
// Output: Bye 77 and 31
```

We can notice a class having the following properties:

- Members
  - Used to act as fields for a class, similar to this in other OOP languages.
- Constructor
  - Used to create a new instance of a class.
- Bounded methods
  - Used as exclusive methods to a class.
- Destructor
  - Used when freeing a class instance.

How are these seen in Rust? Let us take a look at the class we made, except using Rust's structs and implementations. The Rust version can be seen as follows:

```rust
struct Foo{
    // members => fields
    bar: i32,
    baz: i32,
}
// bounded methods => implementations
// to declare use keyword impl
impl Foo{
    // to create instance return Self
    // to use instance use self, &self or &mut self in the parameters
    // constructor
pub fn new()->Self{
```

```
    Foo{
        bar:45,
        baz:32
    }
}
    // bounded method
pub fn do_something(&mut self){
self.bar =self.bar +self.baz;
self.baz -=1;
}
}
// structs will automatically be deallocated
impl Drop for Foo{
fn drop(&mut self){
println!("Bye {} and {}",self.bar,self.baz)
}
}
fn main(){
let mut foo = Foo::new();
    foo.do_something();
}
```

In our program, we showed how Rust translates the class properties for structs; we have fields performing the same role as members, the implementation block serving the role of the structs' bounded methods, and the new function being our constructor. We use the Drop trait to act as our destructor. All types implement Drop that handles deallocating memory when a value is out of scope, or its lifetime has ended. We did specify what should happen when **drop()** gets invoked When we compile our program (**rustc foo_class.rs**) and run the program (**./foo_class**),we should get the same result.

Implementations

Implementations provide users with a way to write exclusive functions for structs and enums. It can also be used to implement traits, but this will be discussed later in this chapter.

To create an implementation for a struct/enum, use the keyword **impl** followed by the name of the struct/enum. Inside the **impl** block, we can declare functions for our struct/enum, but how do we access or create an instance of it? That is where self and Self come in respectively. We can use them in the following ways:

- Accessing a struct/enum's value, which means to use the dot (".") operator, in a function we pass, self, &self, or&mut self-depending on our borrowing needs as the first parameter.

- To return a struct/enum, which means to use the path separator(::), we either return the struct/enum's name or Self.

To understand this concept in a better way, let us jump on to an example:

```
pub struct Foo{
    x: i32
}
impl Foo{
    // Constructor
pub fn new(x: i32)->Self{
        // if param matches field name,
        // we do not need to do Foo{x: x}
Self{x}
}
    // public function
    // can be accessed as Foo.update()
pub fn update(&mut self){
self.update_self()
}
    // private function
    // cannot be accessed outside of impl block
fn update_self(&mut self){
self.x =(self.x *2)+5;
}
}
fn main(){
let mut foo = Foo::new(11);
println!("Foo is {}",&foo.x);
    foo.update();
println!("Updated foo to: {}",&foo.x)
}
```

In our struct Foo, we have a private field x that has a 32-bit integer type. We create an implementation for Foo with three functions: **new, update**, and **update_self**.

Our new functions act as our constructors, and in Rust, this is a common practice. Do note that in our new function, instead of having the conventional Foo{x: bar}, since in our case, the parameter bar = x or the same identifier is the field, we can just put Foo{x}.

The update function is public and inside uses a helper function called **update_self**; we can only access this function inside the **impl** block because it is private. If we try to access private functions outside the impl block, we will be slapped with a compiler error. This visibility is on par with how C++ sees its bounded methods.

Traits

Traits provide users with a way of having a form of polymorphism. In C++, this was done using Inheritance, but in Rust, we use traits to extend a struct/enum's versatility in a more generic way. Before we continue with traits, let us remind ourselves how C++ does inheritance. We would have a class with public virtual functions, and then whatever class inherits it, would either use it, or they may override it. We can see this in the following code:

```cpp
#include<iostream>
using namespace std;
class Instructions{
public:
virtual void d_up(){cout<<"Moving up!"<<endl;}
virtual void d_down(){cout<<"Moving down!"<<endl;}
virtual void d_left(){cout<<"Moving left!"<<endl;}
virtual void d_right(){cout<<"Moving up!"<<endl;}
};
// Robot inherits Instructions
class Robot:public Instructions{
    // let's have our robot have inversed
    // left and right instructions
public:
void d_left() override{cout <<"Moving right!"<<endl;}
void d_right() override{cout <<"Moving left!"<<endl;}
};
int main(){
```

```
Instructions ins;
Robot robot;
Instructions* i = &ins;
    cout <<"Instructions: "<<endl;
    i->d_left();
    i->d_right();
    i =&robot;
    cout <<"Robot: "<<endl;
    i->d_left();
    i->d_right();
return 0;
}
/* Output:
Instructions:
Moving left!
Moving up!
Robot:
Moving right!
Moving left!
*/
```

Let us see how this would look like in Rust, and discuss each part of the code:

```
// Turned our Robot class to empty struct
struct Robot;
// To show default values
struct DefaultRobot;
// Instruction trait
// Either functions can be declared or
// set like fn foo(param)->return;
pub trait Instructions{
fn d_up(&self){println!("Moving up!")}
fn d_down(&self){println!("Moving down!")}
fn d_left(&self){println!("Moving left!")}
fn d_right(&self){println!("Moving right!")}
}
```

```
// Implemented Instructions to Robot using impl <trait> for <struct>
impl Instructions for Robot{
    // override the functions
fn d_left(&self){println!("Moving right!")}
fn d_right(&self){println!("Moving left!")}
}
impl Instructions for DefaultRobot{
    // keeping defaults
}
fn main(){
let robot: Robot = Robot;
let defrobot: DefaultRobot = DefaultRobot;
println!("Instructions: ");
    defrobot.d_left();
    defrobot.d_right();
println!("Robot: ");
    robot.d_left();
    robot.d_right();
}
/* Output:
Instructions:
Moving left!
Moving right!
Robot:
Moving right!
Moving left!
 */
```

Traits contain a list of methods that can be used by different structs/enums. In our case, since the **Robot** class had no members, we can choose to use an empty struct for Robot, along with DefaultRobot that will have no functions overridden.

There is an advantage of using Rust's traits compared to C++'s virtual functions; the first is achieving a data-oriented model, while Rust's traits are purely based on this model. The virtual functions of C++ have a hard time achieving this model. The other challenge of using the virtual functions of C++ is achieving a CPU-friendly cache design because traits are already based on a data-oriented model; it is able to achieve this easily.

The trait is simply declared using the keyword trait along with an identifier. Inside the trait block, we can either list or declare functions:

```
trait Foo{
    // list
    fn bar(&self, baz: i32) -> i32;
    // declare
    fn laz(&self) -> f32{
        // do something
    }

}
```

To allow our struct to inherit these functions, we implement the trait for our desired struct. We use the syntax impl <trait> for <struct> to do this. We see that for declared functions, we can either leave them alone or override them. However, if a function is listed, it must be declared when implemented.

Deriving traits

In Rust, we have derived macros which are macros that implement a trait onto a struct/enum in the form of **#[derive(<trait>)]** on top of the struct/enum. It is very common too, at the minimum, to derive the traits **Debug &Clone** onto a trait. This helps with cloning the struct and being able to print the struct in debug mode:

```
#[derive(Debug, Clone)]
struct Foo(String, u8);
```

We will make our own derive macros in the metaprogramming chapter. But it is good to know these macros exist since they provide a lot of usability to us and will be used very often throughout this book.

Type aliasing

If we had a node with the form:

```
pub struct Node{
    value: String,
    next: Option<Rc<RefCell<Node>>>,
    prev: Option<Rc<RefCell<Node>>>,
}
```

How would we make our life less of a pain, and less like using C/C++'s **typedef** mess? Well, we would use type aliasing and to do so, we use the keyword **type** followed by an identifier and assigned it to the desired type, this can be seen as follows:

```
type Link = Option<Rc<RefCell<Node>>>;


pub struct Node{
      value: String,
      next: Link,
      prev: Link,
}
```

Doesn't that look a lot cleaner? There are plenty of opportunities where **type** will be useful so having this in your back pocket will help you in the long term and avoid long type structures.

From templates to generics

Generics are used in a programming language to act as a data type to generalize a function, structure, and so on. This can help reduce repetitive code (like a sum function for every data type) and improve versatility. However, generics should be used wisely and not be put everywhere, as they can produce the exact opposite of their benefit since the compiler needs to accommodate the generic.

In C++, generics were implemented by the use of templates and are shown as follows:

```
#include<iostream>
template<class T>
// template<type identifier, ...>
T greater( T one, T two){
      if (one > two){
            return one;
      } else if (two > one){
            return two;
      } else {
            // they are equal, return any of them
            return one;
      }
}
```

If we need to rewrite this in Rust, it would look like this:

```rust
use std::cmp::{Ord, Ordering};

fn greater<T: Ord>(one: T, two: T) -> T{
    return match one.cmp(&two){
        Ordering::Less => two,
        Ordering::Greater => one,
        Ordering::Equal => one,
    }
}
```

To declare generics in a function, we use the <> operator that has the syntax **<identifier : trait>**. If we need to declare multiple traits for a generic, we need to use the + operator to concatenate the traits. However, having all those generic definitions at the beginning of your function can leave it looking messy. This is the point when the **where** keyword comes into the scene, via which we can leave it all in the end. Let us rewrite our previous function, but add some output to it:

```rust
use std::fmt::Display;
use std::cmp::{Ord, Ordering};
fngreater_alt<T>(one: T, two: T)
where T: Ord + Display{
match one.cmp(&two){
        Ordering::Less =>println!("{} is greater", two),
        Ordering::Greater =>println!("{} is greater", one),
        Ordering::Equal =>println!("They are equal"),
}
}
```

The **Display** trait allows us to print the value, while the rest of the code is almost the same. You can notice that we use **where** at the end of the function. This leaves the function looking a lot cleaner and pleasant to the user's eyes.

Generic structs

Creating generic structures follows a similar syntax to functions, where the generic is declared after the identifier:

```rust
struct Foo<T: Bar>{
    a: T,
```

```
        b: T
}
```

Implementations are a bit different per se; a generic definition must be made after the **impl** keyword and one after the struct's identifier:

```
impl <T: Bar> Foo <T>{
        pub fn new(a: T, b:T) -> Self{/*something*/}
}
```

If you notice, none of our functions inside the **impl** block has any generic definitions. This is because the definition after the **impl** keyword already handles it, and the generic definition after the struct's identifier shows that the struct contains generics.

Generic traits

Creating generic traits also follows the same syntax as a generic struct, as the generic definition follows after the identifier, (**trait Foo<T>{}**). We will look at creating our own generic trait, **Bar** as follows:

```
trait Bar<T: Clone, K: Copy + Clone, V: Clone + Debug>{
fn only_clone(&self)-> T;
fn copy_clone(&self)-> K;
fn debugged(&self)-> V;
}
```

What if we need to implement this? What would it look like? We will need to define the generics for the **impl,** trait, and also struct. This is shown in the following code:

```
use std::clone::Clone;
use std::fmt::Debug;

struct Baz<T, K, V>{
    t: T,
    k: K,
    v: V,
}

impl<T: Clone, K: Copy + Clone, V: Clone + Debug> Bar<T, K, V>for Baz<T, K, V>{
fn only_clone(&self)-> T{self.t.clone()}
```

```
fn copy_clone(&self)-> K{self.k}

fn debugged(&self)-> V{self.v.clone()}

}
```

If we create a main function and create a **Baz** struct that contains valid types for each generic, let us see how this plays out:

```
fn main(){

let baz = Baz{

        t:"hello".to_string(), // String implements Clone

        k:11, // Primitives implement Copy + Clone

        v:vec![1,2,4,9] // Vec implements Debug and Clone

};


println!("T: {}", baz.only_clone()); // T: hello

println!("K: {}", baz.copy_clone()); // K: 11

println!("V: {:?}", baz.debugged()); // V: [1,2,4,9]

}
```

Refer to the following for a better understanding of the preceding code:

- The generic type **T** expects a data type that implements the **Clone** trait, and the first thing that came into my mind was **String**. This owned type can only be cloned and not copied. As you can see, our **Baz.t** binding has been assigned to a **String**.

- The **K** type expects a data type that implements the **Clone & Copy** traits. Fortunately for us all, primitive data types implement both. So, in our example, we assigned the binding **Baz.k** to an u8.

- The **V** type expects a data type that implements the **Clone& Debug** traits. In Rust, all arrays implement **Debug & Clone**, so we can see all the elements inside the array. Thus, we can make multiple owners. In our case, we assigned **Baz.v** to a **Vec<u16>**.

Conclusion

In this chapter, we explored how to expand the capabilities of Rust's structs/enums with things like *implementations, generics, and traits*. We looked at how these are similar to bounded methods of C++ in classes, templates, and inheritance, respectively, and with that in mind, we see how crucial structs/enums are in Rust.

Key facts

- In an **impl** block:
    - To use a struct/enum in its parameter, use the keyword **self**.
    - To return the struct/enum, use the keyword **Self**.
- To implement a trait to a struct/enum, use the syntax **impl {trait} for {struct/enum}**.
- To define a generic:
    - Generally, use the syntax **< {name} : {traits} + ...>.**
    - For implementations: **impl <{name}> {struct/enum} <{name}>.**

Exercises

1. Create a library for Complex Numbers using generics and functions to add and subtract them, as well turning them into a tuple. *(Look at the traits Add, Sub, and From)*
2. Create an enum which has partial ordering and create a function to sort an array of it.
3. Create a struct that can become an iterator. *(Implement IntoIterator)*

Answers

For these answers, we will create a single library with each exercise in its own file with the *src/lib.rs* file acting as a central file for testing each solution.

To begin, create a new library, **cargo new —lib ch2_exerices** and create the following files that correspond to their respective exercise number in the **src** directory:

1. **complex.rs**
2. **part_ord.rs**
3. **iter_.rs**

1. In this question, we hope to make a simple complex number struct. Simple in our case means being able to add and subtract complex numbers. To refresh your memory, a complex number has two parts: a real and an imaginary number (ex. 2 + 5i where 2 is real, 5 is imaginary).

   To begin, import the following at the top of **src/complex.rs**:

   ```
   use std::fmt::{Display, Formatter};
   use std::ops::{Add, Sub};
   ```

We can now create our struct **Complex** with a generic of type **T**, and we derive the following traits onto it:

- **Debug**: Allows to print in debug mode.

- **Copy**: All numbers implement the Copy trait.

- **Clone**: Allows us to use the **clone()** method and is required by **Copy**.

- **ParitalOrd**: Allows us to partially compare values.

- **PartialEq**: Allows us to partially equal values and is required by **PartialOrd**.

```
#[derive(Debug, Copy, Clone, PartialOrd, PartialEq)]
pub struct Complex<T>{
// Real number
pub r: T,
// Imaginary number
pub i: T,
}
```

To allow our type to add/subtract, we need to implement the **Add/Sub** trait to our trait, so that we can add it to our **impl** block. We expect that when a new **Complex** is made, the type must implement **Copy**, **Clone**, **Add**, and **Sub**. When implementing **Add/Sub**, it expects a type for its type **Output**, so we assign it to **T**:

```
// Add/Sub expects a type for output, so we assign it to T
impl<T: Copy + Clone + Add<Output = T> + Sub<Output = T>>
Complex<T>{
pub fn new(r: T, i: T) ->Self{
Self{
            r, i
        }
    }
pub fn add(&mut self, other: &Self){
self.r = self.r + other.r;
        self.i = self.i + other.i;
}
pub fn sub(&mut self, other: &Self){
self.r = self.r - other.r;
```

```
        self.i = self.i - other.i;
    }
}
```

For some added functionality, it would be nice if we can print the complex number in its numeric form, as well as be able to make a tuple into a complex number.

We implement **Display** to allow custom formatting for our struct, **Complex**:

```
impl<T: Display> Display for Complex<T>{
fn fmt(&self, f: &mut Formatter<'_>) -> std::fmt::Result {
write!(f, "{} + {}i", &self.r, &self.i)
    }
}
```

To convert a tuple into a complex number, we implement **From<(T, T)>** for our struct **Complex**, as this allows us to have the function **Complex::from()**:

```
impl<T> From<(T, T)>for Complex<T>{
fn from(t: (T, T)) ->Self {
Self{
r: t.0,
i: t.1
}
    }
}
```

We can now create the following simple test in **src/lib.rs** to test if our adding and subtracting works:

```
mod complex;
use complex::Complex;

#[cfg(test)]
mod tests{
use super::*;
#[test]
fn test_complex(){
let mut complex = Complex::new(8, 7);
complex.add(&Complex::new(9,8));
```

```
complex.sub(&Complex::from((7,6)));

assert_eq!(complex, Complex::new(10, 9))
    }
}
```

When we run the **cargo test**, we should get the result shown as follows:

```
Finished test [unoptimized + debuginfo] target(s) in 0.82s
Running unittests src/lib.rs (target/debug/deps/ch2_exercises-
eca3ee4d1f38c108)


running 1 test
test tests::test_complex ... ok


test result: ok. 1 passed; 0 failed; 0 ignored; 0 measured; 0
filtered out; finished in 0.00s
```

2. Our next question is very simple; we need to write a struct or enum that implements **PartialOrd** and is able to sort an array of the struct or enum.

   For this question, I decided to simply make an enum, **Status,** that has these three variants:

   1. Done (1)
   2. In Progress (0)
   3. Planned (-1)

   To make our lives easier, we will make our enum representable as an 8-bit integer (**i8**), and we can then define each variant their respective value. Our goal for our sorting function is to sort by greatest to lowest, or from Done to Planned:

```
#[derive(Debug, Clone,PartialEq, PartialOrd )]

#[repr(i8)]

// Allows us to assign integer values to each variant

// This helps us with ordering

pub enum Status{

Done = 1,

InProgress = 0,

Planned = -1

}
```

Our function **sort_status** takes in a mutable borrow of an array of statuses and sorts it using the function **sort_by** and since we have **PartialOrd** implemented, we can use **partial_cmp** inside to sort from highest to lowest:

```rust
pub fn sort_status(statuses: &mut Vec<Status>){
// to sort we will use sort_by
    // to compare we will use partial_cmp
    // we will order from highest to lowest
statuses.sort_by(|low, high|
        high.partial_cmp(&low).unwrap());
}
```

We can now test this function in our file **src/lib.rs** as follows:

```rust
mod complex;
use complex::Complex;
mod part_ord;
use part_ord::{Status::*, *};


#[cfg(test)]
mod tests{
use super::*;
#[test]
fn test_complex(){...}
#[test]
fn test_part_ord(){
let mut statuses =
vec![Done,InProgress,Planned,Planned,Done,InProgress];
sort_status(&mut statuses);
assert_eq!(statuses, vec![Done,Done,InProgress,InProgress,
Planned, Planned])
    }
}
```

When we test the library using **cargo test**, we can see the success as follows:

```
Finished test [unoptimized + debuginfo] target(s) in 0.28s
Running unittests src/lib.rs (target/debug/deps/ch2_exercises-
eca3ee4d1f38c108)
```

```
running 2 tests
test tests::test_complex ... ok
test tests::test_part_ord ... ok


test result: ok. 2 passed; 0 failed; 0 ignored; 0 measured; 0
filtered out; finished in 0.00s
```

3. For our third question, I decided to make a knockoff Linked List where instead of having a head and tail being linked together, we have a value. With every new value-added, the old is pushed into an archive array.

The actual iterator will only iterate the archive since if we wanted to include the current value, we would have duplicate values when the iterator is used. Let us look at our struct, **Archiver** so we can get a better idea of what we are dealing with:

```
use std::iter::IntoIterator;


#[derive(Debug, Clone, PartialOrd, PartialEq)]
pub struct Archiver{
pub value: Option<i32>,
    pub archive: Vec<i32>
}
```

We will add simple **new**, **push**, and **pop** functions to ease testing. Let us discuss how each function will work:

- **Archiver::new()**
  - o Creates a new empty archiver; this means that the **value** will be **None** and the **archive** will be a new empty vector.

- **Archiver.push(i32)**
  - o Pushes a new value into the archiver, but we must solve two different cases of **value**.
    - If the value is **None**, that means the archiver is new, so we just make **Archiver.value = Some(value).**
    - If the value is **Some(v)**, we must push the current value, **v** into **Archiver.archive** and bind **value** to **Archiver. value**.

- **Archiver.pop() -> Option<i32>**

  o Returns the current value and makes **Archiver.value** the last element from **Archiver.archive**:

```
impl Archiver{
// Creates an empty archiver
pub fn new() ->Self{
Self{
value: None,
archive: Vec::new()
        }
    }
// Pushes an item to value and pushes old value to archive
pub fn push(&mut self, value: i32){
// if value is None, then this is a new archiver
match self.value{
None => {
self.value = Some(value)
        }
Some(v) => {
self.archive.push(v);
            self.value = Some(value)
        }
    }
}
// Pops value and makes value last item in archiver
pub fn pop(&mut self) -> Option<i32>{
let value = self.value;
    let new_value = self.archive.pop();
    self.value = new_value;
value
    }
}
```

We are now ready to implement **IntoIterator** for **Archiver**, but it has a few requirements:

- **Item**: What type each item in the iterator will be

    o   In our case, that will be an **i32.**

- **IntoIter**: What kind of iterator we will be turning this into

    o   In our case, we will be turning into **std::vec::IntoIter.**

- **fn into_iter(self) -> Self::IntoIter; :** The function that turns the struct into an iterator.

    o   We will simply return **self.archive.into_iter():**

```
impl IntoIterator for Archiver{
type Item = i32; // each item in the iterator will be i32
    // our into_iter type will use the Vec implementation
type IntoIter = std::vec::IntoIter<Self::Item>;

    fn into_iter(self) ->Self::IntoIter {
self.archive.into_iter()
    }
}
```

We can now create a test for our struct, **Archiver** and see if our iterator works as expected:

```
mod complex;
use complex::Complex;
mod part_ord;
use part_ord::{Status::*, *};
mod iter_;
use iter_::Archiver;
#[cfg(test)]
mod tests{
use super::*;
#[test]
fn test_complex(){...}
#[test]
fn test_part_ord(){...}
#[test]
```

```
fn test_iter(){
let mut archiver = Archiver::new();
archiver.push(90); // value = 90
archiver.push(67); // value = 67, archive = [90]
archiver.push(88); // value = 88, archive = [90, 67]
// double each value in the archive
archiver.archive = archiver
      .clone()
.into_iter()
.map(|x| x*2)
.collect(); // archive = [180, 134]
assert_eq!(archiver, Archiver{
value: Some(88),
archive: vec![180, 134]
      })
   }
}
```

When we run **cargo test**, we should get success as follows:

```
Finished test [unoptimized + debuginfo] target(s) in 0.25s
Running unittests src/lib.rs (target/debug/deps/ch2_exercises-
eca3ee4d1f38c108)


running 3 tests
test tests::test_complex ... ok
test tests::test_iter ... ok
test tests::test_part_ord ... ok


test result: ok. 3 passed; 0 failed; 0 ignored; 0 measured; 0
filtered out; finished in 0.00s
```

CHAPTER 3
Error Handling

Introduction

Error handling is a very important topic in any language, as it allows the developer to handle edge cases in a program or to prevent user errors. In any case, knowing how to handle errors is something you need to know in Rust.

Rust offers two different types to handle errors, the **Option<T>** and **Result<T, E>** types. These two types allow error handling for different cases, as well as provide users with an easier experience in error handling. We will explore how to handle errors and create our own error type.

Structure

In this chapter, we will discuss the following topics:

- The Option<T> Type
- The Result<T, E> Type
  - Converting a Result to an Option
- Creating a Custom Error Type

Objectives

In this chapter, we introduce you to Rust's elegant error handling types, Option and Result. While guessing if a file returns NULL or trying to catch and throw an error seemed fine, once you start seeing how Rust handles errors you will not want to go back to the old ways. You will see how to either panic or gracefully handle errors, as well as creating your own error type.

Error Handling in C, C++, and Rust

Before we get into greater detail, let us look at how C, C++, and Rust handle errors. The reason we added C is because **perror()** is still quite a neat error handler and also to showcase error handling without using a *try and catch* method:

Here is a C example code:

```
// C Example:
// Our program will attempt to open a file
#include<stdio.h>
#include<errno.h>

void attemptFile(FILE*file, char*path){
int errnum;
file=fopen(path, "rb");
// check if the file is NULL
if(file==NULL){
// we have an error
// Use perror()
perror("Error opening file");
    } else{
// no error so we can safely close the file
printf("File exists, closing...");
fclose(file);
    }
}

int main(){
FILE* file;
attemptFile(file, "foo.txt");
```

```
return 0;
}
```

```
// Output:
// Error opening file: No such file or directory
```

As you can see, in our C program, we check whether opening the file resulted in any error. If it results in an error, it returns **NULL**. When it does not result in an error, we proceed to print the file that exists and close it. When the error occurs, we get an **errno**, and **perror()** uses the **errno** with a given message to print the error.

Here is a C++ example code:

```
// C++ Example using try and catch
// In this program we will attempt to login
#include<iostream>
using namespace std;
void login(int password){
try
    {
        // our actual password
 int actual=97979;
        // does our guess equal the actual password
if(password==actual){
            // if so we are logged in
cout<<"Logged in successfully!"<<endl;
        } else {
            // if not, throw that password away
throw(password);
        }
    }
    // catch the password
catch(int password)
    {
        // you are denied logging in
cout<<"Login denied: "<<password<<" is wrong!"<<endl;
    }
}

int main(){
```

```
login(8888);
return 0;
}
```

```
// Output:
// Login denied: 8888 is wrong!
```

In our C++ program, we create a function that expects a guess of a password. If they are the same as the actual password, then you are logged in. But if you guessed wrong, and we throw the password away, the error handler catches it and returns an error message. This try-and-catch approach is generally very long and time-consuming.

Here is a Rust example code:

```
// Rust Example using the Result type
// Our program will attempt to login with a password
fn login(password:u32) ->Result<String, String>{
let actual:u32=97979;
if actual==password{return Ok(format!("Logged in successfully!"));}
        else { return Err(format!("Login denied: {} is wrong!",
password)); }
}
fn main(){
match login(8888){
Ok(o) =>println!("{}", o),
Err(e) =>println!("{}", e)
    }
}
```

```
// Output:
// Login denied: 8888 is wrong!
```

Our Rust program is to represent our C++ program. You can already notice how much shorter the Rust program is; using the Result type, we either have an Ok or Err value. We use a match statement to print either result in our main function. With our review of error handling done, we can get into greater detail with Rust's version of error handling.

The Option<T> type

The Option type provides users to pass an *"optional"* value and also gives us access to Rust's version of **NULL**, **None**! We can see how the **Option** enum looks like the following:

```
pub enum Option<T>{
        Some(T),
        None,
}
```

As you can see, a value is either something or nothing. Let us now look at an example to see how we may go about handling the error:

```
fn to_uint(i:i32) ->Option<u32>{
    // uint can only be positive integers
    if i>=0{
            return Some(iasu32)
    } else {
            return None
    }
}
```

In this function, we attempt to convert a signed 32-bit integer into an unsigned one. We make sure that the integer is positive, if not we return **None**. Follow the given steps to see the different ways we can handle this error:

1. Unwrap the error. If an error occurs, the program will simply panic:

   ```
   let uint = to_uint(2).unwrap();
   ```

2. Use a **match** statement to handle each case for **Some** and **None**:

   ```
   let uint = match to_uint(2){
       Some(u) => u,
       None => 0 as u32,
   };
   ```

The Result<T, E> type

While the **Option** type, with its variants **Some** and **None**, is perfect for optional values, while the **Result** type is used for better error handling and the results are straightforward. Either an Ok or Err value is returned. In most functions that require actual error handling, you should expect and use a **Result**, as shown in the following code:

```
pub enum Result<T, E>{
        Ok(T),
        Err(E),
}
```

In the code example stated as follows, you can see that we use a **Result** in the case of a divide-by-zero error. It is also common to use a **Result** in our main function using the **std::io::Error** type. The reason we usually use this is because most errors implement this or use it. This also makes our main function look a lot similar to C. Refer to the code as follows:

```
fn divide(first:f32, second:f32) ->Result<f32, String>{
match second{
        0.0=>Err("Cannot be divided by zero!".to_owned()),
        _=>Ok(first/second)
    }
}


use std::io::Write;
fn main() ->Result<(), std::io::Error>{
        let mut file=std::fs::File::open("foo.txt")?;
        file.write_all("hello".as_bytes())?;
        Ok(())
}
```

If we run this program, we get the following amazing error:

Error: Os { code: 2, kind: NotFound, message: "No such file or directory" }

We get the error code, what kind of error it is, and a message about what the error is. You may be confused by it. The operator sure is confused as well and that leads us to how we could handle errors with **Result**:

Consider the following example:

```
use std::io::Error;
use std::fs;


fn main() ->Result<(), Error>{
        let source=fs::read_to_string("foo.txt");
```

```
        Ok(())
}
```

Let us now consider our options to handle this so that we can use the **String** value inside:

1. Unwrap the error, and panic if the error occurs:

```
let source = fs::read_to_string("foo.txt").unwrap();
```

2. Expect the error and print a message if the function panics when an error occurs.

```
let source = fs::read_to_string("foo.txt").expect("Couldn't read
file");
```

3. Match the **Ok** and **Err** values:

```
let source = match fs::read_to_string("foo.txt"){
    Ok(s) => s,
    Err(e) => {
        return Err(Error::from(e))
    }
};
```

4. Use the ? operator since **read_to_string** returns the same **std::io::Error** as our **Result**:

```
let source = fs::read_to_string("foo.txt")?;
```

Converting a Result to an Option

You may need to convert a **Result<T, E>** into an **Option<T>**. A common use case for this is in a web application where you would rather not have the web server panic if an error occurs and instead, return a **None** value. To do this, we use the implementation method, **ok()** in **Result** to turn it into an **Option**:

```
fn source(path: &str) -> Option<String>{

    read_to_string(path).ok()

}
```

This example isn't practical, but it provides a conceptual example. As said before, this can be seen in web servers or other uses where you would rather not have the application stop if an error occurs.

Creating a custom error type

In this section, we will create a project called **our_error** for fun, and we will experiment by checking how communist a word/text is; if it is not, we will return an error. So, let us get started with our project:

```
$ cargo new our_error
$ cd our_error
$ cargo add rand
$ cargo add thiserror
```

To use **cargo add**, install **cargo-edit** via **cargo install cargo-edit**.

Let us start with writing our error type in **src/error.rs** and look at what we will handle:

Our application determines how communist or Marxist a text is, not by any actual linguistic means, but by the amount of "ours", and a randomly generated Marxism value. We will have the following errors:

- Too Capitalist
  - Marxism value is between 0-15
- Not Ours
  - There is no "our" in the text
- Not Marxist
  - Marxism value is between 16-75
- Nothing
  - Text is empty
- IO
  - An IO Error

Let us import **Error** from **thiserror** in **src/error.rs**:

```
// Import the Error derive macro

use thiserror::Error;
```

Next, we will create our enum **OurError** while deriving **Error** and **Debug** on the top:

```
// Derive Error and Debug for OurError
#[derive(Error, Debug)]
pub enum OurError{
```

To add our custom error text for each variant, we add the attribute **#[error("Foo")]** on the top. To add format, use **{index}** in the text:

```
// We can create an error message using #[error(message)]
#[error("The text `{0}` is too capitalist!")]
TooCapitalist(String), // if marxism is 0-15
#[error("The text contains no `ours`!")]
NotOurs, // contains no ours in text
#[error("The text is not Marxist enough!")]
NotMarxist, // if marxism is 16-75
#[error("THERE IS NO TEXT, TRECHARY!!!")]
Nothing, // text is empty
#[error("A problem with your manifesto")]
IO(#[from]std::io::Error), // an io error
}
```

The complete file should look like this:

```
// Import the Error derive macro
use thiserror::Error;


// Derive Error and Debug for OurError
#[derive(Error, Debug)]
pub enum OurError{
    // We can create an error message using #[error(message)]
    #[error("The text `{0}` is too capitalist!")]
    TooCapitalist(String), // if marxism is 0-15
    #[error("The text contains no `ours`!")]
    NotOurs, // contains no ours in text
    #[error("The text is not Marxist enough!")]
    NotMarxist, // if marxism is 16-75
    #[error("THERE IS NO TEXT, TRECHARY!!!")]
    Nothing, // text is empty
    #[error("A problem with your manifesto")]
    IO(#[from]std::io::Error), // an io error

}
```

We are now ready to start tackling our **src/main.rs**, and for the same, we will need to carry out the following steps:

1. Read text from the user.

2. Check whether the input is empty and if so, print the Nothing error.

3. Check whether the input has no "our", and if so, print the NotOurs error.

4. Create a randomly generated value.

5. Match the value to the different ranges; it can be either too capitalist, not Marxist enough or perfect.

Let us begin by adding the imports we will need:

```rust
// Import error.rs
mod error;
use std::io::stdin;
use error::*;
use rand::Rng;
```

To make our life a little easier, we will make a helper function to check whether a string contains any "ours". If it does not contain the word, we return a **NotOurs** error:

```rust
fn any_ours(source: &str) -> Result<(), OurError>{
if source.contains("our"){
Ok(())
    } else {
Err(OurError::NotOurs)
    }
}
```

Let us now finally start with the steps to tackle our **src/main.rs**:

1. We will get the user input using a string buffer and **std::io::stdin().read_line()**:

```rust
fn main(){
// get user input
println!("Please enter text from your manifesto: ");
    let mut input = String::new();
// read from stdin and match the Result
match stdin().read_line(&mut input){
Ok(_) => (),
Err(e) =>eprintln!("{}", e.to_string())
    };
```

2. We will check whether the input is empty. This can be done by using the implemented method **is_empty()** which returns **true** if it is empty, and **false** if not.

```
// check if empty, if so return error

if input.is_empty(){

eprintln!("{}", OurError::Nothing.to_string());

}
```

3. We will then utilize our helper function, **any_ours** and match it. If it is okay, we move along, and if not, we print the error:

```
// check if text contains any ours
match any_ours(&input){
Ok(_) => (),
Err(e) =>eprintln!("{}", e.to_string())
};
```

4. We will next create our random generator the same way we did in *Chapter 1, Introduction to Rust*:

```
// random generator

let mut rng = rand::thread_rng();

// This random generator will determine the marxism

let marxism = rng.gen_range(0..100);
```

5. Lastly, we match our Marxism value to a range. However, when matching for a range, you can only do inclusive ranges defined by **start ..= end** because the usual exclusive range **start .. end** is not stable:

```
// check the marxism level to see how marxist it is
    // ..= is inclusive range
match marxism{
0..=15 =>eprintln!("{}",
            OurError::TooCapitalist(input.clone()).to_string()),
16..=75 =>eprintln!("{}",
            OurError::NotMarxist.to_string()),
_ =>println!("Good my fellow communist")
    }
}
```

6. Our project is complete, and the main file should look the same as follows:

```rust
// Import error.rs
mod error;
use std::io::stdin;
use error::*;
use rand::Rng;
fn any_ours(source: &str) -> Result<(), OurError>{
if source.contains("our"){
Ok(())
    } else {
Err(OurError::NotOurs)
    }
}
fn main(){
// get user input
println!("Please enter text from your manifesto: ");
    let mut input = String::new();
// read from stdin and match the Result
match stdin().read_line(&mut input){
Ok(_) => (),
Err(e) =>eprintln!("{}", e.to_string())
    };
// check if empty, if so return error
if input.is_empty(){
eprintln!("{}", OurError::Nothing.to_string());
}
// check if text contains any ours
match any_ours(&input){
Ok(_) => (),
Err(e) =>eprintln!("{}", e.to_string())
    };
// random generator
let mut rng = rand::thread_rng();
// This random generator will determine the marxism
let marxism = rng.gen_range(0..100);
// check the marxism level to see how marxist it is
    // ..= is inclusive range
```

```
match marxism{
0..=15 =>eprintln!("{}",
OurError::TooCapitalist(input.clone()).to_string()),
16..=75 =>eprintln!("{}",
            OurError::NotMarxist.to_string()),
_ =>println!("Good my fellow communist")
    }
}
```

We can see some results of running our program as follows:

```
$ cargo run
Please enter text from manifesto:
our project is amazing
The text is not Marxist enough!


$ cargo run
Please enter text from manifesto:
We cannot be hindered by the bickered capitalists
The text contains no `ours`!
The text is not Marxist enough!
```

How could we improve?

An obvious first is not to write a program about communism, but except that we could've done some of the following to improve the project:

- Create a CLI parser like **clap** or **structopt**.

- Add colour to our printing to symbolize success and errors.
    - o This can be done using **termcolor**.

- Develop an actual algorithm that looks at certain keywords, and how much they occur. This can be done using filters, collecting the number of occurrences and providing some sort of amount to it.

Conclusion

This chapter provided a gateway into the simplicity of Rust's error handling types, **Option** and **Result**, which provided amazing versatility to different cases of problems. Throughout the rest of the book, we used error handling in one way or another, and with continuous exposure, you will become confident in dealing with errors.

We saw how to pass optional values using the **Option** type. This type is used very often for optional parameters, but it can also be used, for example, in Linked Lists where the next node could be **None**.

Secondly, we saw how to properly handle errors using the **Result** type, which either has an **Ok** value or **Err** value, which provides nice ways to handle either spectrum or is the better way to go than **Option** for errors.

Lastly, we saw how to create our own error type using the crate **thiserror**. Alternatively, we could use the standard library's **Error** macro to derive, but using a crate like **thiserror** not only provides simplicity but scalability. If you would like to look at how to do it the standard library way, it is best to follow the *Rust By Example* documentation (**https://doc.rust-lang.org/rust-by-example/error/multiple_error_types/define_error_type.html**)

Key facts

- It is best to avoid using **unwrap()** or **expect()** as much as possible. It is better to gracefully handle an error rather than panicking. There are times when it is your only option, and in those situations, it is not your fault.

- For proper error handling, use a **Result** type so that you can handle it if a value is okay or if there is an error.

- For optional values use **Option**; it is a perfect option *(pun intended)* since you may use **None** if no value needs to be passed.

- Avoid using **if/else** statements for error handling. Instead, use **match** whenever possible.

Exercises

1. Rewrite the program and instead of printing the errors, return the error. *This involves changing the return from () to Result<(), OurError>.*

2. Take in the first two improvements I've listed and try to convert **our_error** into a command line interface program which writes errors/successes in colors and operates using a command like **our_error manifesto —text <text>**.

3. Take in the last improvement listed and develop an algorithm to determine a Marxism value, given a string. A simple algorithm can be made by counting the amount of "our", keywords and matching "our <keyword>" and assigning an amount to add for each case.

Answers

1. When rewriting this program, we will need to change all our **match** statements to accommodate our new **Result** to return. For anything that returns **Result<T, OurError>** we use **?** while we change the rest of the error printing to **Err(OurError::<error>)**.

    The change to our main function can be seen as follows:

    ```
    fn main() -> Result<(), OurError>{
    println!("Please enter text from your manifesto: ");
        let mut input = String::new();
    // read from stdin and match the Result
    stdin().read_line(&mut input)?;
    // check if empty, if so return error
    if input.is_empty(){
    return Err(OurError::Nothing);
    }
    // check if text contains any ours
    any_ours(&input)?;
    // random generator
    let mut rng = rand::thread_rng();
    // This random generator will determine the marxism
    let marxism = rng.gen_range(0..100);
    // check the marxism level to see how marxist it is
        // ..= is inclusive range
    match marxism{
    0..=15 =>Err(OurError::TooCapitalist(input.clone())),
    16..=75 =>Err(OurError::NotMarxist),
    _ =>Ok(println!("Good my fellow communist"))
        }
    }
    ```

    An advantage is that the first error that is caught will stop the program, and we won't have to deal with a waterfall of errors printing, as follows:

    ```
    $ cargo run
    Please enter text from your manifesto
    Our hero
    Error: NotMarxist
    $ cargo run
    ```

```
Please enter text from your manifesto:
Hero
Error: NotOurs
```

2. The two improvements we will focus on relate to material that we will get hands-on in the next chapter, but doing this exercise will give you an easier time. To start let us begin with copying our project to **our_error_exercise_2**, and once that is done, delete everything in **src/main.rs** and add the following crates:

```
$ cargo add structopt
```

```
$ cargo add termcolor
```

Structopt will provide us with a way to create command line interfaces by deriving a struct/enum, while **termcolor** provides us with a way to write colours to stdout or stderr.

To begin with, we will first add in all of the necessary imports for our **src/main.rs** file:

```
// Imports

mod error;

use std::io::{self, Write};

use error::*;

use structopt::StructOpt;

use termcolor::{Color, ColorChoice, ColorSpec, StandardStream,
WriteColor};

use rand::Rng;
```

Next, we will write functions, **write_error** and **write_success** that writes message in red and green, respectively. **Write_error** will write to **stderr** while **write_success** will write to **stdout**. The code we will see is based on the code samples shown in the **termcolor** repository, and if you would like more information about the crate, I recommend going to **https://crates.io/crates/termcolor for more information**:

```
fn write_error(message: &str) -> io::Result<()> {

// Creates our standard stream to stderr

let mut stderr = StandardStream::stderr(ColorChoice::Always);

// Sets the standard stream to print red

stderr.set_color(ColorSpec::new().set_fg(Some(Color::Red)))?;

// Writes our message
```

```
writeln!(&mut stderr, "{}", message)

}

fn write_success(message: &str) -> io::Result<()>{

// Creates our standard stream to stdout

let mut stdout = StandardStream::stdout(ColorChoice::Always);

stdout.set_color(ColorSpec::new().set_fg(Some(Color::Green)))?;

// Write our message

writeln!(&mut stdout, "{}", message)

}
```

With printing colors out of the way, we need to write our enum to represent our command line interface. To do this, we derive **StructOpt** for the enum, as well as use the **#[structopt()]** attribute to customize the program and commands.

Our usage in our program is to pass text to a **manifesto** command; this means we would like the program to look like this:

```
// goal: our_error manifesto -t/-text <string>


#[derive(StructOpt, Debug)]
// use the #[structopt()] attribute for commands and the program
#[structopt(
    about = "Our Error determines how communist your words are",
    name = "Our Error"
)]
enum CLI{
#[structopt(about = "Determines how communist your manifesto is")]
Manifesto{
// our_error manifesto -t <string> [short]
        // our_error manifesto --text <string> [long]
#[structopt(short, long)]
text: String
    }
```

Our main function will return **io::Result<()>** to ease the usage of **write_error** and **write_success**. To collect the arguments for our enum **CLI**, we use the impl method **from_args()**:

```
fn main() -> io::Result<()>{

let cli: CLI = CLI::from_args();
```

After this, we need to use a **match** statement on our binding **cli** so we can handle each command. In our case, that's **CLI::Manifesto**. The actual handling is very similar to the original, as we are printing the errors and success, the difference is only that we are using our **write_*** functions. In the end, we return **Ok(())** since our main function is returning **io::Result<()>**:

```
match cli{
        CLI::Manifesto {text} => {
// Check if message is empty
if text.is_empty(){
write_error(&OurError::Nothing.to_string())?;
}
// Check if text doesn't contains "our"
else if !text.contains("our"){
write_error(&OurError::NotOurs.to_string())?;
}
// random generator
let mut rng = rand::thread_rng();
// This random generator will determine the marxism
let marxism = rng.gen_range(0..100);
        match marxism{
0..=15 => {
write_error(&OurError::TooCapitalist(text.clone()).to_string())?
},
16..=75 => {
write_error(&OurError::NotMarxist.to_string())?
},
_ =>write_success("You are a fellow communist!")?
}
        }
    }

Ok(())
}
```

After compiling, our program looks like this:

```
$ cargo run
Our Error 0.1.0
Our Error determines how communist your words are

USAGE:
    our_error <SUBCOMMAND>

FLAGS:
    -h, --help       Prints help information
    -V, --version    Prints version information

SUBCOMMANDS:
    help    Prints this message or the help of the given subcommand(s)
    manifesto    Determines how communist your manifesto is
```

We have the fun part of running our program multiple times and seeing if we get any results, but the added fun is seeing the text in colors:

```
$ ./target/debug/our_error manifesto -t "our hero is amazing"
The text `our hero is amazing` is too capitalist!
$ ./target/debug/our_error manifesto -t "America"
The text contains no `ours`!
The text is not Marxist enough!
$ ./target/debug/our_error manifesto -t "The manifesto is pure"
The text contains no `ours`!
You are a fellow communist!
```

3. Our algorithm is very simple, and as described stems from these three cases to which we will be giving an amount:

    1. Number of "our" [**5 for each "our"**]
    2. Number of keywords [**8 for each**]
    3. Matching "our <keyword>" in the string [**20**]

To start this exercise, we will copy the contents of **our_error_exercise2** and instead have it as **our_error_exercise3**. On the terminal, add/remove the following crates:

```
$ cargo rm rand # remove random numbers
$ cargo add lazy_static # adds in lazily evaluated static values
$ cargo add regex # adds in regular expressions
```

We will proceed to create a new file **src/algorithm.rs** and begin writing our algorithm, which begins with importing the necessary dependencies. We import the **lazy_static!** macro which allows us to define lazy static values inside its block, which is necessary for our **Regex** value:

```
use lazy_static::lazy_static;

use regex::Regex;
```

Let us define our global values inside a **lazy_static!{}** block. We will define two bindings, one being our keywords; this will be contained inside a Vector with **vec![]**. Since we want the keyword to last for the entire program, we will need to define a lifetime, **static** for our **Vec<&str>** so the values won't be outlived. The second binding will be our regex pattern for matching "our <keyword>" or in regex terms **"^our [a-zA-Z]$"**. The **Regex::new(&str)** function returns a **Result<Regex, Error>** since a user can put in an invalid expression:

```
lazy_static!{
static ref OUR_PAT: Regex = Regex::new("^our [a-zA-Z]$").unwrap();
    static ref KEYWORDS: Vec<&'static str> = vec![
"leader",
"great",
"people",
"goods",
"needs",
"nation"
];
}
```

To make the development of the algorithm easier, I decided to write a struct **Marxism**, which contains a source string, a count of the number of "our", and a vector of the words in the source string:

```
pub struct Marxism{
pub source: String,
our_count: u32,
words: Vec<String>
}
```

Our **Marxism::new()** function takes in a string, creates a vector of the words by collecting the words split by whitespace, counts the number of "our" by a filter, and returns a **Marxism** struct:

```
impl Marxism{
```

```
pub fn new(source: &str) ->Self{
let words: Vec<String> = source
            .split_whitespace() // type Iterator<Item=&str>
.map(|x|x.to_string())// every x turns into string
.collect(); // collects iterator into a vec
let our_count = words
            .iter() // makes words into an iterator
.filter(|x|x.as_str().eq("our")) // filters by looking if x ==
"our"our"
.count() as u32; // returns the count as u32
Self{
source: source.to_string(),
our_count,
words
        }
    }
```

Our next goal is to write an **evaluate()** function. We go by each case starting with the "our" count as we embedded it into our struct. Next, we count how many keywords are inside words by filtering as we did for **our_count**. Lastly, we check whether the string has a match with our pattern using the function **is_match** in our **OUR_PAT** static binding.

After we go through adding from each case, we can return the result which will then be used to determine how Marxist the text is:

```
pub fn evaluate(self) ->u32{
let mut result = 0;
/* Our criteria to evaluate:
        5 for each "our"
        8 for each keyword
        20 for our <keyword>
        */
        // The easiest to start with is our count
result += 5 * self.our_count;
        let keyword_count = self.words
.iter() // makes words into iterator
.filter(|x| KEYWORDS.contains(&x.as_str()))
// filters how much of these words are keywords
.count() ;// returns the count
```

```
result += 8 * keyword_count as u32;

// check is source matches regex pattern
if OUR_PAT.is_match(&self.source){
        result += 20
}
    result
}
}
```

We now need to change our **src/main.rs** so it now evaluates the algorithm. Thus, we first need to import it (make sure to remove **rand**):

```
mod algorithm;

use algorithm::Marxism;
```

Next, we replace our random number generation with our algorithm as follows:

```
let marxism = Marxism::new(&text);
match marxism.evaluate(){
0..=15 => {
write_error(&OurError::TooCapitalist(text.clone()).to_string())?
},
16..=75 => {
write_error(&OurError::NotMarxist.to_string())?
},
_ =>write_success("You are a fellow communist!")?
}
```

Compile the program and try it out a few times:

$ ./target/debug/our_error manifesto -t "our nation has a great leader"

```
The text is not Marxist enough!
```

$ ./target/debug/our_error manifesto -t "our nation has a greater leader with our nation that's our nation, what great leader does our nation have"

```
You are a fellow communist
```

CHAPTER 4
Project – Building a CLI App

Introduction

In this chapter, we will create a command-line interface application, which sends a list of names and accompanying markdown content. The markdown code will be converted into HTML code using the **markdown** crate and written into an HTML file. All the HTML files will be stored inside a zip file with a download button on the web server's homepage.

To understand this better, we expect prior knowledge of the following from the user:

- File's name
- MarkDown content

If we call this array **MarkdownContent**, then a sample JSON file could look like the following:

```
{
    "MarkdownContent": [
        {
            "name": "foo",
            "content": "# Header 1 *I am a really cool text*"
        },
```

```
        {
            "name": "bar",
            "content":"## Header 2 wow I am __suprised__!!!"
        }
    ]
}
```

We want our command-line application to have a **generate** command, so we can run **html_creator generate -p sample.json**. On running that, we will get the following files in the zip file:

foo.html:

```
<h1 id="header-1-n-i-am-a-really-cool-text-">Header 1 <em>I am a really
cool text</em></h1>
```

bar.html:

```
<h2    id="header-2-n-wow-i-am-__suprised__-">Header    2    wow    I    am
<strong>suprised</strong>!!!</h2>
```

This chapter will introduce you to using popular crates like **structopt,** for argument parsing, a **rocket** for web servers, **serde** for serializing and deserializing, and so on.

To begin this project, create a new library **cargo new —lib html_creator** and add the following dependencies in **html_creator/Cargo.toml**:

```
[dependencies]
# argument parsing
structopt = "0.3.26"
# custom error types
thiserror = "1.0.31"
# web servers
rocket = {version = "0.5.0-rc.2", features = ["json"]}
# sends web requests
reqwest = {version = "0.11.11", features = ["json"]}
# serializing & deserializing
serde = {version = "1", features = ["derive"]}
# serializing & deserializing for json
serde_json = "1"
# asynchronous executor
tokio = {version = "1", features = ["full"]}
# converts markdown to html
```

```
markdown = "0.3.0"
# for zipping files
zip = "0.6.2"
# for opening links from terminal
open = "3.0.2"
```

As you can see, we have a lot of crates in this project and they all help with different aspects of the project. Let's see which section they each help with:

- **html_creator** library
    - o **markdown**: Allows us to generate any kind of markdown to HTML.
    - o **serde**: Allows us to serialize and deserialize an enum or a struct.
    - o **serde_json**: Allows us to turn a struct into a JSON or vice versa.
    - o **thiserror**: Creates our own custom error types.
    - o **zip**: Creates zip files to compress our HTML files.
- **html_creator** command line app
    - o **structopt**: for command line argument parsing
    - o **reqwest**: for sending web requests
    - o **Tokio**: for the asynchronous executor
- **html_creator** web server
    - o **rocket**: for creating a web server

Structure

- Creating the base of the application
- A crash course in Async
- Creating the web server
- Creating the client
- Testing out the client
    - o How can we improve
- How to publish?

Objectives

By the end of this chapter, the reader will understand the process of creating a command line application in Rust. We will take a look at how a project can be separated, and in our case, we will develop a small web server and a client to interact with it. After we have created our project, the reader will learn how to publish the application we have developed on **https://crates.io**.

Creating the base of the application

To start building the project, make sure to create a *bin* directory inside the root of the project folder. Inside **bin,** create two files, **app.rs** and **server.rs**. These two files will be used to create our client application and web server, respectively.

To begin our work on the library, import the following on the top of **src/lib.rs**:

```
use markdown::to_html;
use serde::{Deserialize, Serialize};
use serde_json::from_str;
use std::fs::{read_to_string, File};
use std::io::Write;
use thiserror::Error;
use zip::result::ZipError;
use zip::write::FileOptions;
use zip::CompressionMethod::Stored;
use zip::ZipWriter;
```

A question we need to ask is, what are we sending to the server? Well simply put, we are sending in an array of the structure Markdown which has field name and content. We will use the name to create a file for the converted HTML to go into. Let us create our **Markdown** struct:

```
#[derive(Debug, Deserialize, Serialize, Clone)]
pub struct Markdown {
    pub name: String,
    pub content: String,
}
```

An order will be an array of our **Markdown** struct, as follows:

```
#[derive(Debug, Deserialize, Serialize, Clone)]
pub struct Order {
    pub MarkdownContent: Vec<Markdown>,
}
```

The errors we will be handling will be simple, and they are as follows:
- No name in the **Markdown** object
  - ○ Cannot write a name for the file if no name is present

- No content in the **Markdown** object
    - o No reason to create a whole file if no content exists
- Zip Error
    - o To avoid a lot of unwrapping for zip writing
- IO Error
    - o To avoid a lot of unwrapping for io-related errors

This can be seen in the **OrderError** enum as follows:

```
#[derive(Debug, Error)]

pub enum OrderError {

    #[error("Markdown Request {0} has an empty name, cannot process
order!")]

    NOName(usize),

    #[error("Markdown Request `{0}` has no content, cannot process
order!")]

    NOContent(String),

    #[error("Zip Error")]

    Zip(#[from] ZipError),

    #[error("IO Error")]

    IO(#[from] std::io::Error),

}
```

To make our life easier, we have also created a type alias **OrderResult<T>** to ease development:

```
pub type OrderResult<T> = Result<T, OrderError>;
```

The steps for the implementations we need to do for **Order** are as follows:

1. Create an **Order** from a JSON file (**from_file()**).
2. Check the **Order.MarkdownContent** for errors (**check_errors()**).
3. Generate the zip file and return the path to it (**generate()**).

The first function, **from_file()** simply needs a string path and returns **Self** using the function **serde_json::from_str()** along with **std::fs::read_to_string()** to deserialize the JSON into our struct, **Order**:

```
impl Order {
    // creates order struct from string
```

```
    pub fn from_file(path: &str) -> Self {
        from_str(read_to_string(path).unwrap().as_str()).unwrap()
    }
```

Our second function **check_errors()** checks the struct, **Order** for errors by iterating and checking whether the name is empty. If so, return an error, **OrderError::NOName** with the index. We also need to check whether the content is empty; if so, return an error, **OrderError::NOContent** with the name. If it doesn't match those two criteria, then skip it:

```
Pub fn check_errors(&self) -> OrderResult<()> {
    // iterates through the array and checks for errors
    for I in 0..self.MarkdownContent.len() {
        if self.MarkdownContent[i].name.is_empty() {
            return Err(OrderError::NOName(i));
        } else if self.MarkdownContent[i].content.is_empty() {
            return Err(OrderError::NOContent(self.MarkdownContent[i].name.
clone()));
        } else {
            continue;
        }
    }
    Ok(())
}
```

Our last function is the most important one, and it is **generate()**. This actually generates our zip file to download. We use **&self** and a path; we use the path for our zip file, as well as in the end to return. We first need to check for any errors, and if they exist, the server is informed. Please note that we will not stop the server when an error occurs; this is not ideal for web servers. Instead, we will print the error (logging would be recommended). We will create a zip file, and for each **Markdown** struct in **MarkdownContent**, we will use the name for our HTML file, and the content to be converted to HTML using **markdown::to_html()** before being written to the HTML file. After all of the files are completed, we finish the zip file and return the path:

```
pub fn generate(&self, path: &str) -> OrderResult<String> {
        let zip_path = format!(""{}.zi"", path);
        // check it for errors
        self.check_errors()?;
        let zip_file = File::create(&zip_path)?;
        let mut zip = ZipWriter::new(zip_file);
```

```
        // our file options for compression
        let options = FileOptions::default().compression_method(Stored);
        for i in &self.MarkdownContent {
            // starts on new file
            zip.start_file(format!""{}.htm"", &i.name), options)?;
            // writes the html content into the file
            zip.write_all(to_html(&i.content).as_bytes())?;
        }
        // finish the zip writer
        zip.finish()?;
        // return the zip path
        Ok(zip_path.clone())
    }
}
```

A crash course in Async

Asynchronous programming is a very important concept, and when we consider web servers, it is used all the time. An asynchronous function in Rust follows the syntax, **async fn** and is what we call a **Future**. The advantage of using an asynchronous function versus a synchronous function is that while the function waits for another **Future** to complete, it does not block the current thread. Instead, it waits for the other task to finish asynchronously. When an **async fn** is used, you need to follow the function with the **.await** to satisfy the **Future** trait implemented to it:

```
async fn foo(){
...
}

async fn bar(){
    let f = foo().await
}
```

The simple definition of a future is a task or process that is not done immediately. Instead, it will be done later. Since our initial read/write of the asynchronous is likely to fail (the task is not immediately to happen), *polling* exists to keep retrying at a later time. If we observe the **Future** trait, we can see the following:

```
pub trait Future {
    type Item;
    type Error;
```

```
    fn poll(&mut self) -> Result<Self::Item, Self::Error>;
}
```

A future has an item which would be whatever is going to be returned; this can be an error, or **Box<std::error::Error>**, or a polling function. To manage the asynchronous operations, we need a reactor, and that is where **tokio** comes in. The **tokio** crate is a reactor, event loop, runtime, and more wrapped all in one. Although we will use **tokio** in the simplest form in this project, we will see more use of it in the networking chapter. The **tokio** crate, as you can imagine, runs a task schedular to manage and run each asynchronous task so they can make use of lower APIs, which notifies event changes like **epoll** (for Linux), **kqueue** (for macOS), and **IOCP** (for Windows).

To understand asynchronous programming in Rust, it is highly recommended that the reader looks at the official Rust documentation, at **https://rust-lang.github.io/async-book/01_getting_started/01_chapter.html**.

Creating the web server

Our web server requires using the **rocket** crate, although some may judge not using the popular **actix** crate. However, in our case, **rocket** is used due to familiarity. If you are interested in the **actix** framework, take a look at **https://actix.rs/**, and if you want more information on **rocket**, take a look at **https://rocket.rs/**.

To begin, add the following imports on the top of **src/bin/server.rs**:

```
use html_creator::*;
use rocket::fs::NamedFile;
use rocket::serde::json::Json;
use rocket::{get, launch, post, routes};
use std::fs::File;
use std::io::Write;
```

To review in web development, we have an abbreviation called **CRUD**:

- **Create**: POST method
- **Read**: GET method
- **Update**: PUT method
- **Delete**: DELETE method

In **rocket**, we get each of these methods as macros, and if you look at our imports, we are using **get** and **post**. This makes sense since we need to generate our zip files from an order (post), and then download the file using the file name (get).

We will use the route "/gen" for generating our zip files. To do this, we wrap our struct, **Order** in **Json<T>** and using it, we generate a zip file with a generic path name, "order". If an error occurs, we just print the error to stderr using **eprintln!()**. After we generate the zip files, we use the zip path to update our homepage's download button:

```
// we need to be able to generate with path /gen
#[post("/gen", data = "<order>")]
async fn generate(order: Json<Order>) {
    // turns json into Order
    let order = order.into_inner();
    let path = match order.generate("order") {
        Ok(p) => p,
        Err(e) => {
            eprintln!("{}", e.to_string());
            return;
        }
    };
    generate_page(&path).await;
}
```

To generate our download page, we will not create a fancy frontend interface. Since we want the focus on the backend aspects, we will instead create a simple download link. We will make our hyperlink to have the correct path by formatting it into the tag:

```
// generate page will generate a download page to download our zip file
async fn generate_page(path: &str) {
    let html = format!("<a href=\"{}\" download=\"order\"> Download your order!</a>", path);
    let mut file = File::create("index.html").unwrap();
    file.write_all(html.as_bytes())
        .unwrap();
}
```

To open our index file in path "/", we need to create a get function to open our **index.html**. We will use **rocket::fs::NamedFile**, as this allows us to open a file on the web. We will also use **NamedFile** for allowing the user to download their zip file in the path "**/<path>**":

```
// to open our index.html
#[get("/")]
async fn index() -> Option<NamedFile>{
```

```
    NamedFile::open("index.html").await.ok()
}
// we need to be able to download the file given a path
// NamedFile allows the us to send the file if exists
#[get("/<path>")]
async fn download(path: String) -> Option<NamedFile> {
    NamedFile::open(&path).await.ok()
}
```

All the server's functions are done, and all that is left is to create our main function. There are two ways to do this. Firstly, we can launch a rocket application using the implemented **launch()** method in **rocket::build()**. Secondly, we can use the **launch** macro.

In **rocket::build()**, we can do a fair amount of customization to the server. However, in our case, we just need to mount our functions to the path "/". To mount these functions to a path, we will use the **routes!** macro, which contains a vector of the function's identifiers. We will use the latter as it is the more common approach. Moreover, it also allows us to not even declare an actual **main** function:

```
// this will act as our main function of the server
#[launch]
async fn rocket() -> _ {
    rocket::build()
        .mount("/", routes![generate, download, index])
}
```

To view our server, run the command **cargo run —bin server,** and you will be able to see our website at **http://127.0.0.1:8000/**. To be able to make full use of our server, we will need a client to send requests to our server, and be able to send our users to the homepage where they can download their zip files.

Creating the client

Our client application will be written in **src/bin/app.rs** and will showcase creating a command line application in Rust using a very popular crate, **structopt**. There is also **clap** (which **structopt** uses internally), which can be found at **https:// crates.io/crates/clap**. Structopt provides a "higher" abstraction to the **clap** crate, as in simplifying parsing a **struct/enum** for your commands. If you would like complete control over everything, then **clap** will give you everything at the expense of navigating through the various ways of creating a command line application with it.

Before we begin writing the client, we need to take a step back and think of the commands we need for this program. Our first objective is to allow the user to generate a zip file using a **generate** command. The **generate** command will need a path to the JSON file, so we will have the user add a path flag **(-p/–path <file>)**. Thus, our client will know where to find the JSON file.

Next, we will need a way for the user to access the download page. We will call this command **open**. We will use the **open** crate which contains the **that()** function. This will open a user's default browser from the terminal to our specified web path, which will be **http://127.0.0.1:8000/**.

To begin writing our client application, we will import the necessary dependencies at the top of the file along with convenient **const** bindings (global immutable values, the type must be declared):

```
use html_creator::*;
use reqwest::Client;
use structopt::StructOpt;


const INDEX_PATH: &str = "http://127.0.0.1:8000/";
const GEN_PATH: &str = "http://127.0.0.1:8000/gen";
```

To create our client application, we need a struct/enum to derive the **StructOpt** macro to, so that each variant can act as a different command. In our case, we will use an enum, **CLI**:

When we derive the **StructOpt** macro, we are able to use the attribute **#[structopt]** to specify the name of a command, and the short/long names of a flag:

```
#[derive(Debug, StructOpt)]
#[structopt(
    nam" = "html cre"tor",
    abou" = "Creates a compressed file of converted MD f"les"
)]
pub enum CLI {
    #[structopt(abou" = "Generates a zip file of html files from a json
file o"der")]
    Generate {
        #[structopt(short, long)]
        // short is -p
        // long-s --path
        path: String,
    },
```

```
    #[structopt(abou" = "Opens users to download "age")]
    Open,
}
```

We can now move onto the **main()** function that will be asynchronous because we will be using an asynchronous web server. It is reasonable to also have our client asynchronous, since it also required from **reqwest**. To actually run the asynchronous application, we will need to use an executor. We will use the popular **tokio** crate which has the macro **#[tokio::main]** which is placed on top of our main function and will manage our async runtime.

To handle the commands in our enum, **CLI**, you will need to use the implemented function, **from_args()** which returns our enum, **CLI**. We will then proceed to use a **match** statement on our **CLI** value and handle each variant in the enum.

Our generate command requires us to read a JSON file, and send that order to our server. To do this, we need to create an order using **Order::from_file()**. After that, we will need to create a new client using **reqwest::Client::new()**. With the client, we can send a post request using a chain of methods, along with sending it as JSON. Once we send the request, we tell the user to use the command **html_creator open**.

Our **open** command is very simple and uses the **open** crate to open a link from the terminal to the default web browser. In our case, for example, that's Mozilla Firefox. We use the function, **open::that()** using the **INDEX_PATH** to go to our homepage, which contains a button to download our zip file:

```
#[tokio::main]
async fn main() -> OrderResult<()> {
    let cli: CLI = CLI::from_args();
    match cli {
        CLI::Generate { path } => {
            // Get order from file
            let order = Order::from_file(&path);
            // create a new client to send requests
            let client = Client::new();
            // create a post request
            let _ = client
                .post(GEN_PATH) // post requires a url
                .json(&order) // posts the order as json
                .send() // sends the requests
                .await // await since send is an asynchronous function
                .unwrap(); // panic if it fails
            print"n!("Use html_creator open to access the download
```

```
p"ge!")
        }
        CLI::Open => open::that(INDEX_PATH)?,
    }
    Ok(())
}
```

We have completed writing our application, and now, we have the task to test our application. Thus, we will write a JSON order and send a request to see if it works.

Testing out the client

To test our client, let's begin with writing an order in the file, **orders.json** (in the root of the project). We will then proceed to add two simple orders. However, you can also add in your own content or even add an extension to write the order file for you:

```
{
  "MarkdownContent": [
    {
      "name": "Test1",
      "content": "# hello I am really c__ool__\n## Second header\n##
Third header"
    },
    {
      "name": "Test2",
      "content": "**This is cool** I am so _excited!_"
    }
  ]
}
```

To test our client, we first need to start our server, and open a terminal at the project directory with the following command:

$ cargo run —bin server

With the server running at **https://127.0.0.1:8000**, we can now use our client's generate command in a different terminal:

$ cargo run —bin app — generate -p orders.json

We can open our download page using **cargo run –bin app – open**, and download our file, **order.zip**, which should contain two files inside, **Test1.html** and **Test2. html**.

If we look at each file, we are pleasantly given the HTML converted code of our markdown content:

Test1.html:

```
<h1'id='hello_i_am_really_c'ool'>hello I am really c<strong>ool</
strong></h1>


<h2'id='second_he'der'>Second header</h2>


<h2'id='third_he'der'>Third header</h2>
```

Test2.html:

```
<p><strong>This is cool</strong> I am so <em>excited!</em></p>
```

How can we improve

To bring simplicity in building our first project, some compromises were made, that in a production sense, should be addressed. Here are some things that can be improved to add better usability to the user:

- Use unique file names when creating a zip file to avoid overwriting zip files.

- Create a command to read a directory of markdown files and create an order file from it (helps avoid manually adding a bunch of markdown content).

- In our example, we used **unwrap()**; however, in a production program, panicking in a backend application is not recommended. To improve our application, it is best to properly handle the errors instead of using **unwrap()**; this can be by returning an **Option**.

How to publish?

To publish a crate, we need to follow a few steps to make sure that cargo and **crates. io** have enough metadata and all changes are committed. First, we will start with the simplest step and that is adding the necessary metadata on **Cargo.toml**.

We will need to add a **description** and **license** to be able to publish. It is recommended to add *repository, homepage, documentation,* so that users can look into more information of your library or application:

```
[package]
```

```
...
description= "Create html files from a directory of markdown files"
license= "IT"

[dependencies]
...
```

Next, we need to make sure all changes are added and committed on git:

```
$ git init # reinitializes git repo in project
$ git add -A # adds all changes
$ git commit -m "First commit" # commits changes with message
```

Create an account on **https://crates.io**. Once you do, visit **https://crates.io/me** to create an API token, and make sure to copy it.

```
$ cargo login
please paste the API Token found on https://crates.io/me below
# paste the token that was copied
```

Now, you are able to publish the application using `cargo publish`. As you can see, it is fairly straightforward, and even if you forget any of these steps, `cargo publish` will let you know with the error.

Conclusion

In this chapter, we created our own web server, and command line application. We were introduced to asynchronous programming, which is commonly used in web applications. We also explored how to use the keywords **async** and **await**. In our web server, we were introduced to one of the popular Rust web frameworks, **Rocket**, and its useful macros to handle HTTP methods. In our command line application, we learned my favorite command line argument parser, **StructOpt**, and saw how it allows a struct/enum to organize the commands/flags.

In conclusion, this project allowed us to explore creating a Rust project from start to finish, and also, to publish our proud project. Rust allows developers to easily scale into large projects; for example, my project **texcreate** has a workspace of 6 libraries, and I wouldn't be able to do it as easily without Rust.

Key facts

- To create an asynchronous function, use the syntax **async fn**.
- Asynchronous functions implement the **Future** trait. To satisfy this trait, use the syntax **.await** after using the function.

- For the best help, when using new crates, refer to their documentation.
- Be careful when naming flags, since two flags cannot share the same short name.
  - o   **-p** can't be for flags pain and peace.
  - o   Instead use long names to make the user's life easier.

Exercises

1. Make **html_creator** create uniquely named zip files (Use the crate **uuid**)
2. Make a command **create** to read a directory of markdown files and create an order file from it. (**-d** for directory path, **-o** for output path)

Answers

1. To start this exercise, copy our original project to a new directory named **hc_ex1** and add the **uuid** crate:

    ```
    $ cargo add uuid –features v4
    ```

    The version 4 feature allows our user identity to be randomly generated. The change to add randomly generated file names only occur in two places in our project, the **generate()** function in **Order** and **generate()** in **src/bin/server.rs**.

    To fix the **generate()** function in **Order**, we need to remove our path parameter, and instead create a **Uuid** inside the function, and add it to **zip_path** using its **to_string()** function:

    ```
    pub fn generate(&self) -> OrderResult<String> {
        // creates a random identifier
        let path = uuid::Uuid::new_v4();
        let zip_path = format!("{}.zip", path.to_string());
        ...
    }
    ```

    The next fix goes to the post function, **generate()** in **src/bin/server.rs** and this just involves removing the parameter, "order":

    ```
    #[post("/gen", data = "<order>")]
    async fn generate(order: Json<Order>) {
        ...
        let path = match order.generate() {
        ...
    ```

```
}
```

Now, when you test the application, we create files like **6db8d04e-082c-4238-9a74-0367b0a2b885.zip** instead of **order.zip**. This should help us avoid overwriting someone else's file.

2. To start our exercise, copy our work in **hc_ex1** to a new project directory, **hc_ex2**. Now, we need to discuss our strategy on the new **create** command in the following steps:

    1. Read the directory of a given path.

    2. Extract the file name and content from each markdown file.

    3. Create a new JSON file from the order and a given path.

Let's start our work in **lib.rs**. We will start with the simple functions to help us in the future. To begin, replace your imports on the top of *lib.rs* with the following:

```
use markdown::to_html;

use serde::{Deserialize, Serialize};

use serde_json::{from_str, to_string_pretty};

use std::fs::{read_dir, read_to_string, File};

use std::io::Write;

use thiserror::Error;

use zip::result::ZipError;

use zip::write::FileOptions;

use zip::CompressionMethod::Stored;

use zip::ZipWriter;
```

Our first function is a **new** function to **Markdown**. Since we will be needing it when we need to collect our struct, **Markdown** for the order:

```
impl Markdown{
    pub fn new(name: String, content: String) -> Self{
        Self{
            name,
            content
        }
    }
}
```

Our next function will be used later, but it is good to write now. That is, **create_json_file()** in our struct, **Order**. We will simply create a new file and write the JSON content (using **serde_json::to_string_pretty()**) to the file:

```
Pub fn create_json_file(&self, path: &str) -> OrderResult<()>{
    let mut file = File::create(path)?; //creates files
    let json = to_string_pretty(&self).unwrap(); //creates json string
    file.write_all(json.as_bytes())?; // writes the file
    Ok(())
}
```

How exactly will we extract the necessary information for our **Markdown** vector required in the struct, **Order**? First, we will start off by reading the directory using **std::fs::read_dir()**. We will iterate through the directory entries, grabbing the filename, and reading the files. We will push each of these values and return an Order.

Here are some things to consider while we extract:

- Make sure the file is a markdown file.
  - o Check whether the extension is ".md".
  - o If the extension isn't, we skip the file.

- Make sure the file name doesn't contain ".md".
  - o You don't want foo.md.html, instead we want **foo.html**.

- Tell the user we are processing a file.
  - o An excellent debugging tool for us.
  - o We can make sure each file is being processed.

We will create our function under **generate()** in the **impl** block of **Order**. To start off, let's create a new markdown vector for us to push extracted values in:

```
pub fn extract(path: &str) -> OrderResult<Self> {
    // will collect all of our markdown values
    let mut md_content = Vec::new();
```

Next, we need to iterate through **std::fs::read_dir()** which returns **Result<ReadDir>**, which makes each entry have type **Result<DirEntry>**. Thus, to make our life easier, we create a new binding **entry** in the loop, which will handle the **Result** in **entry**. Thus, we are left with the **DirEntry**. To tell the user which file we are processing, we chain the **path()** function in entry which returns the path of the file, with the **display()** function that will allow us to print the path:

```
// iterate all of the entries in read_dir()
```

```
for entry in read_dir(path)?{
    // handle error so we entry is DirEntry
    let entry = entry?;
    // notify user we are processing it
    println!("Processing {}", entry.path().display());
```

We will create a binding **path** to contain **entry**'s path so we do not run into issues of freeing a temporary value. With the path, we can get the extension of the entry. Since the **extension()** function returns **Option<&OsStr>**, we need to unwrap it and turn it into a string using **to_str()**.

Note: OsStr is how the operating system represents a string.

```
// grab the path
let path = entry.path();
// get the extension of the path
let extension = path.extension()
    .unwrap()
    .to_str();
```

We can use a **match** statement to either handle markdown files or skip any other file. When we handle the markdown files, we extract the filename, and make sure to replace the ".md", and then get the content using **std::fs::read_to_string** using our binding, **path**. We push the markdown value to **md_content**. Once the **for** loop ends, we return the order using our vector, **md_content**:

```
        // make sure the extension is markdown
        match extension{
            Some("md") => {
                // extract filename from it
                let filename = path.file_name()
                    .unwrap()
                    .to_str()
                    .unwrap()
                    .replace(".md", "");
                // read the file using the path
                let content = read_to_string(&path)?;
                // push a new markdown value
                md_content.push(Markdown::new(filename, content))
            },
```

```
            _ => continue
        }


    }
    Ok(Self {
        MarkdownContent: md_content,
    })
}
```

With everything set internally in **Order**, we can now head over to *src/bin/app.rs* and add in our new command, **create**. To begin, we first need to add it as a new variant in our enum, **CLI**. As discussed earlier, we expect two arguments: a directory path to read from and an output path for the json order:

```
Pub enum CLI {

    ...

    #[structopt(about"= "Create an order from a directory of
markdown fi"es")]
    Create {
        #[structopt(short, long)]
        directory: String,
        #[structopt(short, long)]
        output: String,
    },
}
```

Since we added a new variant to **CLI**, we need to add a new case to the **match** statement in our main function. We will simply create a new order using **Order::extract()**, using the directory path, and create a new JSON file using **create_json_file()** using the output path:

```
match cli {

    ...

    CLI::Create { directory, output } => {
        // grab the order from the directory path
        let order = Order::extract(&directory)?;
        // create a new json file from the order
        order.create_json_file(&output)?;
    }

}
```

To test our new application, create a directory **markdown_test** inside the root of the project, and add the following files with their content:

```
markdown_test/01.md:
# This is the first file
> This is a quote with code
> ```
> let example = Example::new();
> ```
```

```
markdown_test/02.md:
## This is the second message
We are very **bold** or *italics*. This is a link to [google]
(https://google.com)

### This is the third message
We are very cool
```

```
markdown_test/03.md:
### This is the third message
We are very cool with `single line code` or multi line code

```rust
fn seventy() -> i32 {
    let x = 50;
    x += 20;
    return x;
}
```
```

Let's create **orders.json** using the **create** command and generate our zip file:

```
# in seperate tab
$ cargo run —bin server

# in seperate tab
$ cargo run —bin app — create -d markdown_test -o orders.json
$ cargo run —bin app — generate -p orders.json
$ cargo run —bin app — open
```

When we extract our zip file and open each file, we are greeted with their converted HTML code:

01.html:

```
<h1 id='this_is_the_first_file'>This is the first file</h1>


<blockquote>
<p>This is a quote with code</p>


<pre><code>let example = Example::new();</code></pre>
</blockquote>
```

02.html:

```
<h2 id='this_is_the_second_message'>This is the second message</
h2>


<p>We are very <strong>bold</strong> or <em>italics</em>. This is
a link to <a href='https://google.com'>google</a></p>
```

03.html:

```
<h3 id='this_is_the_third_message'>This is the third message</h3>


<p>We are very cool with <code>single line code</code> or multi
line code</p>


<pre><code class="language-rust">fn seventy() -&gt; i32 {
    let x = 50;
    x += 20;
    return x;
}</code></pre>
```

CHAPTER 5

Concurrency in Rust

Introduction

Rust not only guarantees memory safety in its programs but also does the difficult job of being thread safe as well. This safety allows developers to run code simultaneously and fearlessly, without having to deal with race conditions (accessing data inconsistently), deadlocks (threads waiting for each other, preventing them from continuing), and other bugs that are common in C/C++ concurrent programs.

In this chapter, we will explore using the standard library's threads, alongside the new scoped threads from Rust 1.63.0. Using threads is half the story of concurrency; we will need to use types to pass values inside threads so that we can modify their values.

Structure

- Smart pointers
- The importance of concurrency
- Implementing concurrency using threads
- Passing values using channels
- Using locking types to write/read bindings

o   Single-threaded access using Mutex

o   Multi-threaded reader using RwLock

Objectives

By the end of this chapter, the reader will be able to fearlessly create concurrent models in their programs, by safely sharing and syncing values between threads. This will introduce readers to smart pointers that provide heap allocation types, using them to pass values safely across threads with other synchronous types such as channels, Mutex, and RwLock.

Smart pointers

Smart pointers in Rust allow a developer an easy way to create heap-allocated bindings. We will explore the various smart pointers that we will see throughout this book. Something to keep in mind is that all of these smart pointers own the value inside.

Heap-allocated values using box

The easiest way to create a heap-allocated value is using the **Box** type. This allocates memory on the heap for the value inside. Some uses for this could be for linked lists, or for returning unknown-sized values.

If we tried creating our own linked list without Box, we will face issues of recursion as follows:

```
type Link = Option<Node>;
struct Node{
    value: u32,
    next: Link,
    prev: Link,
}


struct LinkedList{
    length: usize,
    head: Link,
    tail: Link
}


/* Compiler Error:
```

```
error[E0072]: recursive type `Node` has infinite size
  → test.rs:2:1
  |
2 |  struct Node{
  |  ^^^^^^^^^^^ recursive type has infinite size
3 |      value: u32,
4 |      next: Link,
  |            ---- recursive without indirection
5 |      prev: Link,
  |            ---- recursive without indirection
  |
help: insert some indirection (e.g., a `Box`, `Rc`, or `&`) to make
`Node` representable
  |
4 ~      next: Box<Link>,
5 ~      prev: Box<Link>,
  |
*/
```

Taking the recommendation from the compiler, let's fix our **Link** type and replace **Option<Node>** with **Option<Box<Node>>**. This will allow us to recursively access and use our node. If we try to compile our code, we would no longer face a compiler error for our node, so how do we use the **Box** type?

To create a new **Box** value, we use the **Box::new()** function, as shown in the following code. This allocates memory on the heap for the value inside, as well as owning the value. To access the value inside, we de-reference it using a raw pointer "*". The function **into_inner()** for **Box** is still currently experimental, but once stabilized, it would be the better choice.

```
fn main(){
    let boxed = Box::new(8);
    println!("{}", *boxed)
}


// Output:
// 8
```

Reference counting using Rc & Arc

If we want multiple owners of a value, we need to use reference counting to guarantee memory safety. We saw this being used to demonstrate scopes. To refresh our memory, reference counters increment when a new owner is created (using **clone()**), and decrement when is dropped (either using **drop()** or out of scope).

The difference between **Rc** and **Arc** is that **Arc** is an atomic reference counter, which implements the **Sync** trait, which further allows it to be used for multithreaded workloads. In this chapter, we will use **Arc** very often. Thus, to gain familiarity, let's take a look at some examples of using it:

```
use std::sync::Arc;

fn main(){
    let mut val = Arc::new(90);
    // make_mut returns &mut T
    // to access T, dereference using *
    *Arc::make_mut(&mut val) += 10;
    let mut other_val = val.clone();
    *Arc::make_mut(&mut other_val) += 100;
    // to access value inside, use *
    println!("Other val: {}", *other_val);
    println!("Val: {}", *val);
}
/* Output:
Other val: 200
Val: 100 */
```

In the preceding example, we showed some of the functions we will use for our purposes. However, if you need to create a weak reference, you can use the **Arc::downgrade()** function, or if you need a count of owners, you can use **strong_count()** for **Arc** and **weak_count()** for **Weak**.

Interior mutability using Cell and RefCell

One of the borrowing rules we discussed was only having one mutable borrow in scope at a time. If you wanted to get around this, you would need to use **Cell** or **RefCell**. You might wonder if it is possible.

This is what we call interior mutability. Essentially, we use the advantage of unlimited immutable borrows with the ability to mutably change the value inside.

To understand it better, consider the following **struct**:

```
use std::cell::Cell;


#[derive(Debug, Copy, Clone)]
struct Something{
    normal: i32,
    cool: Cell<i32>
}
```

If we create an immutable binding of the struct, **Something**, we should not be able to update the values inside, right? Well, yes and no. We cannot update values in the normal field, whereas the cool field will be able to, even though the binding is immutable. Let's see what this actually looks like:

```
fn main(){
    let smth = Something{
        normal: 32,
        cool: Cell::new(90)
    };
    // immutable error
    // smth.normal += 1;
    smth.cool.set(30); // this is fine though
    println!("{:?}", smth)
}
// Output: Something { normal: 32, cool: Cell { value: 30 } }
```

The difference between **Cell** and **RefCell** lies in if the value implements **Copy**. The cell requires the inner value to implement the **Copy** trait, while **RefCell** doesn't and uses runtime locking to guarantee memory safety. If we do need to use interior mutability, most of the cases will use **RefCell** since most types implement only **Clone,** excluding primitive types.

The importance of concurrency

In the modern age, we have computers with multiple cores, and the need for a multithreaded program to take advantage of it is becoming increasingly popular. Concurrency is the ability to run processes simultaneously on separate threads. This helps take advantage of a processor's multithreaded capabilities. How does Rust guarantee thread safety?

The answer to this question lies in two different traits, **Send** and **Sync**. The Rustnomicon (technical Rust documentation) explains that if a type implements **Send**, it is safe to send it to another thread. Similarly, if a type implements **Sync**, it is safe to share between threads (**T** is **Sync** iff **&T** is **Send**). It is recommended to take a look at the Rustnomicon for the official documentation in **Send** and **Sync**, **https:// doc.rust-lang.org/nomicon/send-and-sync.html**.

Concurrency for a simple program might be less effective. However, for a project that is large, like a **GTK** application, using separate threads to process users request, loading a page, and so on will make the application more responsive to the user. Using techniques like parallelism or concurrency comes to the question of what the project does, and how one of these techniques can be used effectively.

Implementing concurrency using threads

To start this section, make sure that your Rust compiler is at least on version 1.63.0. Check either using `rustc -V` or update with `rustc update stable`. We need our compiler to this version because 1.63.0 introduced scoped threads, which will be discussed later on. Rust's standard library threads use the native OS's threads; this is very useful when considering lower-level programming. To create a new thread, we use the function `std::thread::spawn()` which returns a **JoinHandle**. A **JoinHandle** allows a thread to join onto another thread, and this handle is owned and cannot be cloned.

Let's take a look at a simple example of using threads:

```rust
use std::thread;

fn main(){
    let mut handles = Vec::new();
    for i in 0..10{
        handles.push(
            thread::spawn(move ||{
                println!("{}", i)
            })
        );
    }
    for handle in handles{
        handle.join().unwrap();
    }
}
```

However, what if we instead wanted to print a vector's elements? In that case, let us look at the following example:

```
use std::thread;


fn main(){
    let elements = vec![1,2,3,4,5,6,7];
    let mut handles = Vec::new();
    for i in 0..elements.len(){
        handles.push(
            thread::spawn(move ||{
                println!("{}", elements[i]);
            })
        );
    }
    for handle in handles{
        handle.join().unwrap();
    }
}
```

If we try to compile this program, we are faced with the following error:

```
  |
4 |     let elements = vec![1,2,3,4,5,6,7];
  |         -------- move occurs because `elements` has type `Vec<i32>`,
which does not implement the `Copy` trait
...
8 |             thread::spawn(move ||{
  |                           ^^^^^^^ value moved into closure here, in
previous iteration of loop
9 |                 println!("{}", elements[i]);
  |                                -------- use occurs due to use in closure


error: aborting due to previous error


For more information about this error, try `rustc --explain E0382`.
```

We will be able to solve this issue when we discuss **Mutex,** but we can also use scoped threads as well. This is a new feature added in Rust 1.63.0, and it allows non-static values to be safely passed into threads, unlike the standard library's threads which require static values. Take a look at the following example:

```
use std::thread::scope;

fn main() {
    let elements = vec![1, 2, 3, 4, 5, 6, 7];
    for i in 0..elements.len() {
        // creates a scope for spawning threads
        scope(|s|
            s.spawn(|| println!("{}", elements[i])).join().unwrap()
        );
    }
}
```

When creating scoped threads, if a thread is not joined, the scope will automatically join it before the function is returned. In our case, since we only had one thread spawned in the scope, we needed to make sure that it was joined back to the main thread or it may have been outlived.

The advantage of using scoped threads is being able to spawn multiple threads that uses *non-'static* bindings; this reduces the need for smart pointers and thus leads to less use of the heap space. Having threads that automatically rejoin back to the main thread after dropping isn't a new idea. In C++, we have **jthread** which provides a type similar to **std::thread** but automatically rejoins on destruction. Although we won't be using this new type of thread much in the rest of this chapter, I do see this type being used more in the future.

Passing values using channels

Message passing provides developers with a multi-producer and single-subscriber queue, which allows values to be sent and received either synchronously (**sync_channel()**) or asynchronously (**channel()**). Both channel types are found in **std::sync::mpsc** and the difference between the two is the buffer. Since **channel()** is asynchronously, it doesn't block any threads; hence, having an "unlimited" buffer, while **sync_channel()** has a bounded buffer and blocks the thread until the message is received.

The **channel()** function returns a tuple, **(Sender<T>, Receiver<T>)**. The common binding naming convention when creating channels is (tx, rx), which stands for a transmitter and receiver, respectively.

What if we wanted to receive a message on a separate thread, while on the main thread we send a user inputted message? Let's go through how we would implement this:

To start, create a file called **channel_example.rs** and import the following on the top:

```
use std::thread;
use std::sync::mpsc::channel;
use std::io::{Result, stdin};
```

In our main function, we will return **Result<()>** using **std::io::Result**. Next, to set up, we will need to create a new channel using the common naming convention **(tx, rx)**. To later process our user input, we will create a string buffer, **input** which will be initiated using **String::new()**:

```
fn main() -> Result<()>{
    // create a new channel
    let (tx, rx) = channel();
    // create new string for input
    let mut input = String::new();
```

Now, when we create our separate thread to receive our message, we will not immediately join the thread, but instead create a join handle for it. Inside our thread, we will handle receiving a message (**rx.recv()**) using a **match** statement. Either we print the message, receive the message, or the error:

```
    // create new thread to handle receiving message
    let recv_handle = thread::spawn(move ||{
        // handle receive value using match
        match rx.recv(){
            // if we get the message, print a received message
            Ok(msg) => println!("Received message: {}", msg),
            // if we get an error, print error to stderr
            Err(e) => eprintln!("{}", e.to_string())
        }
    });
```

We can prompt the user to enter a message and read it using **stdin().read_line()**, using our string buffer **input**, and send the message using **tx.send()**:

```
    println!("Please enter a message to send: ");
    // get user input
```

```
stdin().read_line(&mut input)?;

tx.send(input.trim().to_owned()).unwrap();
```

Since we have sent our message, we can join our receiver thread to the main thread using the **join()** method. Since our main function returns a **Result**, we will need to end the function using **Ok(())**. You could also do this when you join **recv_handle**, but it is preferred to have an **Ok(())** at the end since it looks like a C program:

```
//join receive handle to main thread
recv_handle.join().unwrap();
Ok(())
}
```

When we compile and run our program, you should be able to nicely send and receive messages:

```
$ rustc channel_example.rs
$ ./channel_example


Please enter a message to send:
Hi how are you?
Received message: Hi how are you?
```

Channels are very useful, but what if you just wanted to write/read values across threads? In that case, we will need to use locking types, **Mutex** or **RwLock**, which will be discussed next.

Using locking types to Write/Read bindings

Channels are nice, but we do not always want to send and receive values across threads. Instead, it would be ideal to be able to safely write/read bindings across threads. This is when locking types come into play; in Rust, we have two different types:

1. Mutex (Single-threaded access)
2. RwLock (Multithreaded reader)

Before we discuss each of them, it is important to remember that while reading can become multithreaded, writing will always be a single-threaded task (only one thread can write at a time). The reason behind this is very simple: if multiple threads are writing to the same value, data can become overwritten or corrupted. Thus, a locking type when writing to a value will block the thread until it is finished.

Single-threaded access using Mutex

Mutex or mutual exclusion provides a way to write/read a binding by locking the value (using the **lock()** method). This returns a **MutexGuard** type, which guards the value, or blocks the thread until the task is finished (dropped out of scope). The value will automatically be unlocked when it is out of scope (no need for an **unlock()** method), and another thread can lock the value.

How would we safely share the **Mutex** across multiple threads? If such a case arises, we would use **Arc** or the Atomic Reference Number counter. Using the **Arc::clone()** function, a thread can gain ownership of the value safely (increases the reference counter) and when out of scope, the reference counter decreases.

To demonstrate using **Mutex**, we will create a program to ask for students' grades and enter them as well as print them in separate threads. To keep our program simpler, we will use a vector for the grades that will be wrapped in **Arc<Mutex<T>>**.

Create a file **mutex_example.rs** and add the following imports as well as a **Students** type alias for **Arc<Mutex<Vec<u32>>>**:

```rust
use std::io::{stdin, Result};
use std::sync::{Arc, Mutex};
use std::thread;
pub type Students = Arc<Mutex<Vec<u32>>>;
```

We will use some helper functions to help reduce clutter. First, let us create a function to create an empty **Students** type:

```rust
fn new_empty_students() -> Students {
    Arc::new(Mutex::new(Vec::new()))
}
```

Our last helper function will ask the user for the student's grade and return the grade by trimming and then parsing the string:

```rust
fn get_grade(student_num: u32) -> u32 {
    // get user input of grade
    println!("Please enter grade for student {}: ", student_num);
    // create empty string for input
    let mut input = String::new();
    // read stdin for input
    stdin().read_line(&mut input).unwrap();
    // trim then parse the string as u32
```

```
        input.trim().parse().unwrap()
}
```

We can now start working on our main function. We will return **Result<()>** and begin by initiating our students and a vector for our thread's join handles:

```
fn main() -> Result<()> {
    let students = new_empty_students();
    let mut join_handles = Vec::new();
```

Next, we will need to ask the user for the number of students that they will have and process the input:

```
    // get number of students
    println!("Please enter number of students: ");
    let mut num_input = String::new();
    stdin().read_line(&mut num_input)?;
    // parse input into u32
    let num_stu: u32 = num_input.trim().parse().unwrap();
```

Since we have the number of students, we can use a **for** loop to get each student's grade and create a thread to push each of their grades. Once we create the thread, we will push it to **join_handles**, so that we can join them in our main thread at the end.

We create a loop to count from 0 to the number of students with the task of entering the grades for each student. First, we need a mutable reference to **students**, so in our loop, we create a binding **s**, which is a clone of **students (students.clone())**. We get the grade using our helper function, **get_grade(i+1)** while making sure we put **i + 1** since our count starts at 0. Since we have a copy of **students** and their grades, we create a thread **t** to push our grades to. To write to **s**, we need to create a new binding, **s** and lock it. After we lock it, we push the grade into it and push the thread into our binding, **join_handles** (so we can join the threads later):

```
    // loop to get each student's grades
    for i in 0..num_stu {
        // get shared access to students
        let mut s = students.clone();
        // create a thread to enter student's grade
        let grade = get_grade(i + 1);
        let t = thread::spawn( move || {
            let mut s = s.lock().unwrap();
            s.push(grade)
```

```
    });
    join_handles.push(t);
}
```

Our next job is to print the student's grades. We want it to look like **Student {num}**
=> Grade {grade}. To accomplish this, we will create a thread that will lock
students, loop through the index, and print in the specified format. After we create
the thread, we will need to push it to **join_handles**:

```
let t = thread::spawn(move ||{
    let s = students.lock().unwrap();
    for i in 0..s.len(){
        println!("Student {} => Grade: {}", i+1, s[i])
    }
});
join_handles.push(t);
```

Now, all that is left is to iterate through all of our join handles and join them to the
main thread. Once that loop is complete, we return **Ok(())**, since our main function
returns **Result<()>**:

```
for jh in join_handles {
    jh.join().unwrap();
}
Ok(())
}
```

Now that our program is complete, let's compile and run our program:

```
$ rustc mutex_example.rs
$ ./mutex_example
Please enter number of students:
2
Please enter grade for student 1:
98
Please enter grade for student 2:
69
Student 1 => Grade: 98
Student 2 => Grade: 69
```

Multi-threaded reader using RwLock

RwLock provides users a way to read values in multiple threads, while writing values remains a single-threaded task. The advantage of using RwLock over Mutex is reading tasks; if a reader panics and its guard becomes poisoned, the lock of the value is not poisoned. It is only possible for the lock to be poisoned if the lock is exclusively written to a value.

To read a value, we use the **read()** method. Writing is very similar as well, and we use a **write()** method for it. These tasks, like any locking type, will block the thread until the process is finished. To demonstrate **RwLock**, we will write a program to read a directory. We will record it if something is a file or directory, further record its contents (file's content, if directory we say "Directory"), and its path.

To start our example, create a file **RwLock_example.rs** and add the following imports on the top:

```
use std::fs::{read_dir, FileType, read_to_string};
use std::path::PathBuf;
use std::sync::{Arc, RwLock};
use std::thread;
use std::io::Result;
```

We will create a struct named **Info** that will contain fields for the file type, content, and path:

```
// Represents all of our information needs
#[derive(Debug, Clone)]
struct Info{
    type_: FileType,
    content: String,
    path: PathBuf,
}
```

To make our life easier, we will create a **new()** function in an **impl** block for **Info**. For this, we will need parameters for the file type, content, and path:

```
impl Info{
    pub fn new(type_: FileType, content: String, path: PathBuf) -> Self{
        Self { type_, content, path }
    }
}
```

To help us, we will create a type alias for **Arc<RwLock<Vec<Info>>>** called **Infos**, and a function, **new_infos()** to create an empty **Infos**:

```
// create type alias for the shared state Info vector
type Infos = Arc<RwLock<Vec<Info>>>;
// creates a new empty Infos
fn new_infos() -> Infos{
    Arc::new(RwLock::new(Vec::new()))
}
```

We can now begin on our main function, which will also return **std::io::Result<()>**. Our first task is to read a directory. In our case, we will create a directory *important* and create a new **Infos**:

```
fn main() -> Result<()>{
    // we will read a directory called important
    let dir = read_dir("important")?;
    // create a new shared state vector for infos
    let infos = new_infos();
```

To write and read to our **infos** binding, we will create a thread **t**, which will iterate through **dir**. We will be able to check the file type, get the appropriate content, and the file's path. Once we are done writing in our loop, we will read it to a binding, **updated**. With our **updated** binding, we will then iterate through using the **iter()** method, chain it with **map()** to print each **&Info** value, and return the void binding, **u**:

```
    // create a thread to read the directory
    let t = thread::spawn(move ||{
        // clone infos into our thread
        let i = infos.clone();
        // iterate through dir for each DirEntry
        for d in dir{
            // unwrap the dir entry
            let d = d.unwrap();
            // lock to write
            let mut i = i.write().unwrap();
            // get the file type
            let type_ = d.file_type().unwrap();
```

```
            // initiate the content
            let mut content = String::new();
            // if content is directory, put "Directory"
            if type_.is_dir(){
                content.push_str("Directory")
            } else {
                // if file get the content from read_string()
                content = read_to_string(d.path()).unwrap()
            }
            // push the Info struct to i
            i.push(Info::new(type_, content, d.path()))
        }
        // update our vector using read()
        let updated = i.read().unwrap();
        // iterate through updated using map to print each &Info
        let u = updated.iter().map(|x|{
            let mut type_ = String::new();
            // if type is directory, print Directory
            if x.type_.is_dir(){·
                type_.push_str("Directory")
            } else {
                // if type is file, print File
                type_.push_str("File")
            }
            // get the path as &str
            let path = x.path.to_str().unwrap();
            println!("Path: {} | File type: {} \nContent: \n{}\n",
            path, type_, x.content)
        }).collect::<()>();
        // return this collection of prints
        u
    });
```

In the end, we will need to join the thread to our main thread and return **Ok(())**, since our main function returns **Result<()>**:

```
    // join the thread
    t.join().unwrap();
    // return Ok at the end
    Ok(())
}
```

Before we compile our program, create a directory **important** and fill it with random files and directories. For the sake of our example, we have some empty files with short text inside them:

```
$ rustc rwlock_example.rs
$ ./rwlock_example
Path: important/very_important | File type: Directory
Content:
Directory


Path: important/test.txt | File type: File
Content:
test test test


Path: important/lala.text | File type: File
Content:
lalalalalalaalalalalalala


Path: important/empty.txt | File type: File
Content:
```

Using locking types is useful to safely write/read bindings across threads. There are also asynchronous versions in the **tokio** crate, which allows them to act in an asynchronous matter. If your application requires a lot of reading, it would be recommended to use **RwLock** while generally, **Mutex** should be fine. Another way to increase performance is using parallelism. Along with concurrency in the **rayon** crate, it allows users to convert their code into parallel tasks, like iterators.

Conclusion

In this chapter, we took a look into Rust's fearless concurrency and discussed how we can use the standard library's thread module to spawn processes into a different thread and join them back into our main thread. We also looked at how to safely share values across threads using **Arc**, send/receive values using **channels**, or write/read values in threads using locking types.

Key facts

- Wrap a value inside an **Arc** to send it across multiple threads safely.
- To send/receive values, use **channels** or **sync_channels.**
- Have a separate thread for receiving values, while sending values in the main thread.
    - Join receiving thread after sending the value.
- Locking types block threads when writing. This is to safely write a value without overwriting/corrupting the value.

Exercises

1. Create a comment/messaging application that receives messages and displays them to the users (can be on the web using **rocket**). Make sure to ask for their name and message, while recording the name, message, and received time (using **chrono**).
2. Create a program that lists an RSS feed (use the **rss** crate) on the web. It would be good to use threads to process the HTML code and channels (using the **crossbeam** crate) to send/receive Feed values.

Answers

1. Our messaging application will be web-based and using forms, we will ask the user to submit a name and message. The messages will be shown as follows; this will be done by keeping the messages saved in a JSON file, **messages.json**. To begin, let's create our project:

    ```
    $ cargo new –lib messenger
    ```

    Add the following dependencies:

    ```
    [dependencies]
    chrono = "0.4.22"
    rocket = {version = "0.5.0-rc.2", features = ["json"]}
    serde = { version = "1.0.143", features = ["derive"] }
    serde_json = "1.0.83"
    ```

    - Chrono will allow us to record the current time.
    - Rocket will allow us to create a web server.

- Serde will allow us to serialize/deserialize a struct/enum.

- Serde_json will allow us to serialize/deserialize a value to JSON.

Before we continue, we need to create some files in the root of the project that will be used in our code:

1. Create a file **messages.json** and add an empty array to it.

2. Create a file **index.html** and leave it empty.

3. Create a file **base.html** and add the following to it:

```html
<!DOCTYPE html>
<html lang=»en»>
<head>
  <meta charset="UTF-8">
  <title>Home</title>
</head>
<body>
<form method="post" action="/">
  <h3>Send a Message!</h3><br>
  <label for="name">Name</label><br>
        <input    type="text"    name="name"    id="name"
placeholder="Name..."><br>
  <br>
  <label for="message">Message</label><br>
  <textarea name="message" id="message" cols="40" rows="5"
placeholder="Message..."></textarea> <br>
  <br>
  <input type="submit" value="Submit">
</form>

<div>
  <h2>MESSAGES</h2>
  {}
</div>
</body>
</html>
```

Now that we have a place to store our messages, a home page for our web application, and a base file we will use when generating our home page. We can start work on our library in **src/lib.rs**:

Add the following imports on the top of the file:

```
use std::fs::{File, read_to_string};
use rocket::form::FromForm;
use serde::{Deserialize, Serialize};
use chrono::Utc;
use serde_json::{from_str, to_string_pretty};
use std::io::{Result, Write};
```

Now, we can create our struct to represent our user's message, aptly named **Message**. We need to derive **Serialize**, **Deserialize** so we can turn it into JSON, while **FromForm** will allow **rocket** to process it as a HTML form. We will need to have the **received_at** field as an **Option<String>** since we will be automatically setting it and not the user in the form:

```
#[derive(Debug, Clone, Serialize, Deserialize, FromForm)]
pub struct Message{
    // name of individual
    pub name: String,
    // message of the user
    pub message: String,
    // when the message was received
    pub received_at: Option<String>
}
```

The functions we will need to implement for **Message** are a way to set the message's **received_at** field to the current time, and a way to turn our message into HTML code.

Before we show our functions, this is how we want our HTML code to look:

```
<div>
    <h4>Name [Received Time]</h4>
    <p>Message </p>
</div>
```

Now, let's take a look at our implemented functions:

```rust
impl Message{
    // updates a received message to current time
    pub fn received(&mut self){
        self.received_at = Some(Utc::now().to_string())
    }
    // turns our message into our needed html code
    pub fn to_html(&self) -> String{
        // will contain all of the html parts
        let mut html_parts = Vec::new();
        // a tuple of the beginning and ending div tags
        let div_header = ("<div>", "</div>");
        // push the beginning div
        html_parts.push(div_header.0.to_string());
        // html version for our name and received_at
        let name = format!("\t<h4>{} [{}]</h4>",
                    &self.name, self.received_at.clone().unwrap());
        // message will be placed as paragraph text
        let message = format!("\t<p>{}</p>", &self.message);
        // push the name first
        html_parts.push(name);
        // push the message
        html_parts.push(message);
        // push the endng div tag
        html_parts.push(div_header.1.to_string());
        // join all of the html code seperated by new line
        html_parts.join("\n")
    }
}
```

Our next need is a way to get a vector of messages, and a way to rewrite our **messages.json**:

```rust
// returns a vector of Message from messages.json
pub fn get_messages() -> Vec<Message>{
```

```
        from_str(&read_to_string("messages.json").unwrap()).unwrap()
}
// rewrites messages.json with a vector of Message
pub fn rewrite_messages(messages: Vec<Message>) -> Result<()>{
    // gets our messages into json code
    let string = to_string_pretty(&messages).unwrap();
    // create messages.json
    let mut file = File::create("messages.json")?;
    // write our json code into messages.json
    file.write_all(string.as_bytes())?;
    Ok(())
}
```

Lastly, we need a function to return the base HTML code from *base.html*. This will simply return the string from **std::fs::read_to_string()**:

```
// returns the base of the html file for index.html
pub fn get_base() -> Result<String>{
    // read base.html
    let s = read_to_string("base.html")?;
    // return the string
    Ok(s)
}
```

To start our work on the web server, we need to create a directory **src/bin** and create a file inside it, **src/bin/server.rs**. Add the following imports on the top:

```
use std::fs::File;
use rocket::{get, post, launch, routes, uri};
use rocket::form::Form;
use messenger::*;
use std::io::Write;
use rocket::fs::NamedFile;
use std::thread;
use std::sync::{Arc, Mutex, RwLock};
use rocket::response::Redirect;
```

In our server, we will use two functions to process requests for us. Firstly, we will need a function to handle when the user submits a form; this will be a POST request and will push a new message into our messages array from **messages.json** and rewrite **messages.json**.

Secondly, we will need a function to write and open our homepage, **index.html**. This will be a GET request. We will create a thread to process our HTML code for each message. If there are no messages, it will just return "No Messages". We will use **Mutex** to write to a vector for our HTML code, while **RwLock** will be used for reading our messages vector across threads.

Let's begin with writing the function, **post_message()**. We expect the data for it to be a form, so we will have the parameter be of type, **Form<Message>**. To get the message inside, we use the function, **into_inner()**. Our immediate action with this message is to update its time since it has been received. We will then proceed to get our messages using **get_messages()**. We push our message to our messages vector, and use this new vector to rewrite *messages.json* using **rewrite_messages()**. To avoid the user needing to go back, or reentering the URL after they submit, we redirect our user to our yet-to-be-made function, **index()** which will instantaneously update the message board:

```
#[post("/", data = "<message>")]
pub fn post_message(message: Form<Message>) -> Redirect{
    // get Message from Form
    let mut message = message.into_inner();
    // update message's received_at
    message.received();
    // get the list of messages
    let mut messages = get_messages();
    // push the latest message
    messages.push(message);
    // rewrite index.html
    rewrite_messages(messages).unwrap();
    // redirect to home page
    Redirect::to(uri![index])
}
```

To begin writing our **index()** function, we should create our file, *index.html*, initiate a vector for our HTML code wrapped in **Arc and Mutex**, and initiate our messages vector which will be wrapped in **Arc** and **RwLock**:

```
#[get("/")]
pub async fn index() -> Option<NamedFile>{
    // create new index file
    let mut index_file = File::create("index.html").unwrap();
    // collects all of the html message parts
    let html_parts = Arc::new(Mutex::new(Vec::new()));
    // contains all of the messages to be read across threads
    let messages = Arc::new(RwLock::new(get_messages()));
```

The next simplest thing we can do is get our baseHTMLl code using our function, **get_base()**:

```
// has the base for index.html
let mut base = get_base().unwrap();
```

Our thread will return a **String** so when we spawn the thread, we will need to clone **html_parts** and **messages** into our thread. We will have bindings that will lock **html_parts** so we can write/read, while we lock to reading for **messages**:

```
// create a thread to process and return the messages html code
let html = thread::spawn(move ||{
    // clone html_parts to this thread
    let h = html_parts.clone();
    // lock h so we can write to html_parts
    let mut html_parts = h.lock().unwrap();
    // clone messages to this thread
    let m = messages.clone();
    // lock m to read
    let m_read = m.read().unwrap();
```

It is completely useless to start processing our HTML code if there are no messages. Thus, to avoid wasted work, we will check whether **m_read** is empty, and if so, early return "No Messages" as an HTML paragraph text:

```
// if messages is empty return No Messages
if m_read.is_empty(){
    return "<p>No Messages</p>".to_string();
}
```

If we do have messages, we iterate through **m_read**, making sure to dereference and then borrow it to get type **&Message** for binding **i**, we push the HTML code from **i.to_html()**:

```
// iterate through the messages and push the html code
for i in &*m_read{
    html_parts.push(i.to_html());
}
```

Lastly, to return a **String**, we join combined the strings in **html_parts** using **join()** and use a newline as our separator. We then join the thread to the main thread, so that our binding **html** will be a **String** and not a **JoinHandle**:

```
    // return the combined html code seperated by new line
    html_parts.join("\n")
}).join().unwrap();
```

Our next step is to update our base HTML code by replacing "{}" with our combined HTML code. We then write it all to our binding, **index_file** and open **index.html** using **NamedFile::open()**:

```
    // replace {} in base with html code
    base = base.replace("{}", &html);
    // write base into index.html
    index_file.write_all(base.as_bytes()).unwrap();
    // open index.html
    NamedFile::open("index.html").await.ok()
}
```

Lastly, we need to write our main function, **rocket()** to launch our server:

```
#[launch]
async fn rocket() -> _ {
    rocket::build()
        .mount("/", routes![index, post_message])
}
```

We can run our program using **cargo run** and visit **http://127.0.0.1:8000/**. Since our **messages.json** is empty, we are greeted with having no messages as shown in *Figure 5.1:*

Figure 5.1: Initial launch of messenger

However, when we start submitting some messages, as shown in *Figure 5.2*, the messages are shown as MESSAGES as we had expected:

Figure 5.2: Messenger usages results

2.   This project is based on an actual service planned to be built on a website; our goal is to use an RSS feed to list its content. Here is what we will be collecting:

- Article's title
- Published date
- Article's link
- Categories
- Description

To begin, let's create a new project using **cargo new rss_feed** and add the following dependencies:

```
[dependencies]
rocket = "0.5.0-rc.2"
rss = "2.0.1"
crossbeam = "0.8.2"
```

We will use the crossbeam crate for channels instead of the standard library's version because crossbeam offers better performance, and their channel is multi-producer and multi-consumer, unlike the standard library's multi-producer, single-consumer model.

To begin, remove everything in **src/main.rs** and add the following imports:

```
use std::fs::{create_dir, read_to_string};
use crossbeam::channel::{Sender, Receiver, unbounded};
use rss::{Channel, Item};
use std::fs::File;
use std::io::Write;
use std::path::Path;
use std::thread;
use rocket::{launch, get, routes};
use rocket::fs::{FileServer, NamedFile};
```

Our next task is to create our struct, **Feed** with the fields reflecting on what we will be collecting:

```
// Struct to represent each Feed's article
#[derive(Debug, Clone)]
pub struct Feed{
    pub title: String,
    pub pub_date: String,
    pub link: String,
    pub categories: Vec<String>,
    pub description: String,
}
```

For our feed, we will need to create a **new()** function using an RSS channel's item, or **rss::Item**. Our first task when creating **Feed** is to have a vector of all of the category's names, so let's start with that:

```rust
impl Feed{
    // create a new feed by picking the necessary info from a
channel's item
    pub fn new(item: &Item) -> Self{
        // create a vector for all of the categories
        let mut categories =  Vec::new();
        for c in &item.categories{
            // push in the name of each category
            categories.push(c.name.clone())
        }
```

Our next task is to create **Feed** or **Self** and that requires cloning item fields and unwrapping them since they are all wrapped in **Option**. Since I have made sure that each file exists in the XML file we will use, we won't have to worry about panicking:

```rust
        Self{
            title: item.title.clone().unwrap(),
            pub_date: item.pub_date.clone().unwrap(),
            link: item.link.clone().unwrap(),
            categories ,
            description: item.description.clone().unwrap(),
        }
    }
}
```

The next function we will need to write is a **to_html()** function that builds how each article will be in our **index.html** file and their respective **Feed/ foo.html** file. To make sure our path doesn't cause us problems, we will need to remove question marks, single quotes, and whitespaces from the title:

```rust
pub fn to_html(&self) -> String{
    // for the file name we will need to manipulate the title
    let mut title = self.title.clone();
    // remove whitespace from the title
    title = title.replace(" ", "");
    // remove any ? to not mess with the path
```

```
    if title.contains("?"){
        title = title.replace("?", "");
    } else if title.contains("'"){
        title = title.replace("'", "");
    }
    // the path will be under the Feed directory
    let path = format!("Feed/{}.html", title);
```

For our feed's file, we will have it contain the article's description:

```
// create the file in path
let mut file = File::create(&path).unwrap();
// write the article's description inside of the file
file.write_all(self.description.as_bytes()).unwrap();
```

Now, we can work on how each feed will look in our **index.html** file; let's look at how it should be:

```
<a href='path'><h4>Title</h4></a>
<h5> Published at Pub_Date </h5>
<h5> Categories category 1, ...</h5>
<a href='link'><h5> View Online </h5>
```

For each line, we will use **format!()** so we can add our variables into it's respective place. For **self.categories**, we will be joining it together as one string, using the **join()** method, with a comma seperator. After each line is created, we put them in a vector using **vec![]** and return the string using **join()** with a newline seperator:

```
    // this content will be placed inside index.html
    let title = format!("<a href='{}'><h4>{}</h4></a>", &path,
&self.title);
    let pub_date = format!("<h5> Published at {} </h5>", &self.
pub_date);
    let categories = format!("<h5> Categories {} </h5>",
    &self.categories.join(","));
    let view = format!("<a href='{}'><h5> View Online </h5>",
&self.link);
    // create a vector with all of our html code
    let html_parts = vec![title, pub_date, categories, view];
```

```
        // join it all in one string seperated by newline
        html_parts.join("\n")
    }
}
```

Now, we can start the task of sending the feeds using channels. We will create a function, **send_feeds** that will require a vector of **Item** and a **Sender<Feed>**. To send each **Feed** value, we will iterate through the vector of items, create a new feed using the feed, and send the feed. How will we approach sending it? We will use **crossbeam::thread::scope()** to spawn a scoped thread to send each feed:

```
// sends feed in a scoped thread
pub fn send_feeds(items: &Vec<Item>, tx: Sender<Feed>){
    // iterate through each item
    for i in items{
        // create a new feed from the &Item
        let feed = Feed::new(i);
        // create a new scope
        crossbeam::thread::scope(|s| {
            // spawn a scoped thread
            s.spawn(|_| {
                // send feed
                tx.send(feed).unwrap()
            }).join().unwrap()
        }).unwrap(); // joins the thread
    }
}
```

Now that we have sent all of these **Feed** values, it would make sense to create a function to retrieve them. So, we will create a function called **retrieve_feeds()** which will require a **Receiver<Feed>** and the number of items as **usize**. This function will be used to also return the string for **index.html**, so our first need is to create a vector for each html code and for the join handles:

```
// retrieves feed and returns string for index file
pub fn retrieve_feeds(rx: Receiver<Feed>, items_num: usize) ->
String{
    // empty vector to place all of our html code for index.html
```

```
let mut html = Vec::new();
// empty vector for all of our threads used to turn feed into html
let mut handles = Vec::new();
```

To avoid problems with the directory **Feed** not existing, let's check whether the directory exists; if not, we will create it:

```
// check if Feed/ exists, if not create the directory
if !Path::new("Feed").exists(){
    create_dir("Feed").unwrap()
}
```

We can now use our items number to iterate from 0 to the number and receive each feed, create a new thread to turn it to a html string, and push the join handle to **handles**:

```
// iterate through the amount of items
for _ in 0..items_num{
    // receive feed
    let feed = rx.recv().unwrap();
    // spawn handle of turning feed to html string
    let t = thread::spawn(move || feed.to_html());
    // push handle to be joined later
    handles.push(t)
}
```

Lastly, we will need to iterate through **handles**, and since our **JoinHandle** returns a **String**, we will push the result to HTML and return HTML as one string using **join()** with a newline separator:

```
    // iterate through each handle, and push the string to html
    for h in handles{
        html.push(h.join().unwrap())
    }
    // return index.html string seperated by new line
    html.join("\n")
}
```

To use these functions, we will create our function, **index()** that will create and open **index.html**. This function will use **rocket::get** to specify that it is used when a GET request to path "/":

```
#[get("/")]
async fn index() -> Option<NamedFile>{
```

Before we continue, however, we need to download our feed's XML file. You can use any RSS XMLfile you'd like, we will be downloading the file from **https://dev.to/feed/mustafif** and saving it to the project as **feed. xml**. To create an **rss::Channel**, we will need to read **feed.xml** and use **Channel::read_from()** with the string as bytes (using the **as_bytes()** function):

```
// reads feed.xml
let feed_string = read_to_string("feed.xml").unwrap();
// create a channel by reading feed_string as bytes (&[u8])
let channel = Channel::read_from(feed_string.as_bytes()).unwrap();
```

To create a new channel, we will use **crossbeam::unbounded()** which will create a channel with no limit to the number of receivers or senders. With our sender, **tx** and receiver, **rx**, we can now start sending and retrieving feeds. Let's begin with sending feeds using **send_feeds()** after we declare our unbounded channel:

```
// create a new unbounded channel
let (tx, rx) = unbounded();
// send the feeds by placing the channel's items and cloning tx
send_feeds(&channel.items, tx.clone());
```

Since **retrieve_feeds()** is used to also get *index.html*'s content, it would be wise for us to create **index.html** and then proceed to get the content:

```
// create index.html
let mut file = File::create("index.html").unwrap();
// get content by retrieving the feed with cloning rx and item's length
let index_content = retrieve_feeds(rx.clone(), channel.items.len());
```

With the content for *index.html* in our hands, we can write it to **index.html** as bytes and then open the file using **NamedFile::open()**:

```
    // write the content to index.html as bytes
    file.write_all(index_content.as_bytes()).unwrap();
    // open index.html
    NamedFile::open("index.html").await.ok()
}
```

Now, we can create our main function, **rocket()** that will be mounted with two different paths:

- "/" for opening *index.html*
- "/Feed" for opening the files in the *Feed* directory

```
#[launch]
fn rocket() -> _{
    rocket::build()
        // mount index() in "/"
        .mount("/", routes![index])
        // mount the feed files in path "/Feed"
        .mount("/Feed", FileServer::from("Feed"))
}
```

When we run our project using **cargo run** and open **http://127.0.0.1:8000**, we will see a list of articles as shown in *Figure 5.3*:

TexCreate v2.2 Released!

Published at Tue, 19 Apr 2022 21:28:39 +0000

Categories programming,tex,opensource,news

View Online

TexCreate v2.1 Released!

Published at Mon, 18 Apr 2022 18:04:19 +0000

Categories programming,tex,news

View Online

Any Golang?

Published at Thu, 14 Apr 2022 01:32:07 +0000

Categories go,programming

View Online

Why no Python in MKProj?

Published at Mon, 11 Apr 2022 14:06:22 +0000

Categories python,programming

View Online

TexCreate Version 2 Released!!!

Published at Mon, 04 Apr 2022 16:05:24 +0000

Categories rust,tex,mkprojects,programming

View Online

Mufi Concept Toy-Lang

Published at Wed, 30 Mar 2022 19:29:14 +0000

Categories programming,computerscience

View Online

***Figure 5.3**: List of articles from dev.to/mustafif*

If we open one of the articles, we will see its description, as shown in *Figure 5.4*:

I've been considering implementing my own toy language (which I hope I can expand to a more production) once I finish reading reading Robert Nystorms Crafting Interpreters. This language similar to clox in the book will be written with a byte-code compiler in either C or Rust. My current idea is to go C, and down the line start porting it to Rust if I'd like, so how does the language look like?

Well it will be an OOP Language, so it will feature things like classes, and follow a C-style syntax. Let's look at a sample program to get a better idea:

```
class Foo{
    var member1;
    var member2;
    func new(val1, val2){
        member1 = val1;
        member2 = val2;
    }
}

func main(){
    var foo = new Foo(5, 4);
}
```

This is a rough idea, but again this is all concept and can easily change. I will probably start off as a dynamic typing, but as a preference I'd like to make the language statically typed, and have separate mutable and immutable bindings like var/const. This language will have a garbage compiler (a mediocre one), and will start with a builtin standard library.

I already made a little logo for the language, comment your thoughts about this project, and contributors are welcomed to join this interesting, and pain with the fun project.

Figure 5.4: *Description of article "Mufi Concept Toy-Lang"*

CHAPTER 6
Networking in Rust

Introduction

As a systems programming language, Rust is a perfect choice to do networking-related tasks, whether it is transmitting data through TCP or UDP protocols. In this chapter, we will explore how you can create different networking models in Rust, whether it is a synchronous IO model (blocking) or an asynchronous IO model (non-blocking). We will gain better experience in crates such as **tokio**, and also take some time to use the Rust standard library's **net** module which provides the basics of networking.

Structure

In this chapter, we will cover the following topics:

- The protocol stack
- Exploring the Net module
- Creating a synchronous IO model
- Creating an asynchronous IO model

Objectives

By the end of this chapter, the reader will understand the basics of networking in Rust, using either an asynchronous model or a synchronous one. This will be done using the Rust standard library's net module and for asynchronous models using the popular **tokio** crate.

The protocol stack

Before we take a look at how Rust handles basic networking and how we could utilize it, we first need to understand one major thing: the protocol stack.

The protocol stack is a stack of protocol layers that handles different aspects of how a device will send a process from it to a network. To explain the protocol or network stack, let us observe protocols from the lowest to the highest abstraction layers in *Table 6.1*:

Protocol	Layer
IEEE 802.11ax	Physical
Wifi 6E	Data Link
IP	Network
TCP/UDP	Transport
FTP (File Transfer Protocol)	Application

Table 6.1: *Protocols from abstraction layers*

Physical layer

The physical layer represents the physical medium a device will use to connect to a network. In our example, we will use a Wi-Fi card, which could be a USB adapter or a PCI Express card. However, what is important is that its protocol is IEEE 802.11ax, which defines the Wi-Fi standard.

For those wondering about the difference between Wi-Fi 6 and 6E, it all boils down to the radio frequencies. While we have been used to the two frequency bands (2.4/5 GHz) for a long time, 6E introduces three bands (2.4/5/6 GHz) which can be taken full advantage of, by newer devices/routers.

Data link layer

After the physical layer, comes the data link layer, which represents how data is transferred between nodes across the physical layer. With Wi-Fi cards, this can mean data from the radio frequencies becomes data packets a computer can use.

Network layer

The network layer is responsible for uniquely identifying a network, using a mechanism called IP addresses. The two types of **Internet Protocol (IP)** addresses are IPV4 and IPV6, in which version 4 contains 4 octets of 8-bit unsigned integers. IPV4 was good until the Internet became huge with billions of IP addresses; so IPV6 was created with 8 octets of 16-bit unsigned hexadecimal numbers.

Transport layer

The transport layer is responsible for how network packets are transported across networks. The two popular protocols for this are the **Transmission Control Protocol (TCP)** and **User Datagram Protocol (UDP)**, and the difference between them is the guarantee that a connection is established.

TCP does a three-way handshake: firstly, a situation arises when a client wants to establish a connection with some type of server. The server sends a segment called **Synchronize Sequence Number (SYN)** to attempt communication with the server.

Secondly, the server sends a response to the client's request with an **acknowledgement (ACK)** and sends a segment, **SYN-ACK,** that tells the client that their request has been acknowledged.

Lastly, the client acknowledges the server's response and both the client and server have now successfully established a connection with each other.

If anyone has done a ping test, they might know that this test uses TCP to check whether the connection can be established (useful to see if a network exists), and measures the speed and loss of data packets being transferred (useful for latency and speed tests).

UDP establishes a connection to a server with no acknowledgement and is more efficient than TCP with the cost of reliability. An example of an application using UDP would be video streaming, which requires very fast connection speed and does not mind having the user lose some frames or resolution to watch their video.

Application Layer

The application layer contains protocols that give applications an abstract way to communicate with a network. One example may be HTTP, which is used internally by the **world wide web** and low-level libraries (**hyper**) which communicate how a request/response is sent.

Another example is the **File Transfer Protocol (FTP)**, which is commonly used by people when writing websites. This protocol can be used with applications like FileZilla or a Samba server to access files from a remote server.

Exploring the Net module

For basic networking in Rust, you can use the standard library's **net** module which can provide you with some of the following:

- TCP communication
  - o **TcpListener** for listening for incoming connections over a socket
  - o **TcpStream** for writing/reading data in a TCP connection
- UDP communication using the **UDPSocket** type
- IP addresses of either IPv4 or IPv6
  - o This is **IPv4Addr** and **IPv6Addr**, respectively
- Socket addresses of either IPv4 or IPv6
  - o This is **SocketAddrV4** and **SocketAddrV6**, respectively

For further information, it is recommended to look into the official Rust documentation of the **net** module, **https://doc.rust-lang.org/std/net/index.html**.

The main use of the **net** module is needing a simple interface for IP or Socket addresses and TCP communication. With that in mind, let's write two small programs to listen to a socket address via TCP and another to connect to our listener.

The first program we will write is to listen to a socket address via TCP, create a file, **listen.rs**, and add the following imports:

```
use std::io::Result;

use std::net::TcpListener;
```

To handle the errors from **TcpListener**, we will have our **main()** function return **Result<()>** from the **io** module:

```
fn main() -> Result<()>{
```

To create a TCP listener that binds to an address, we can use the **bind()** method from **TcpListener** which requires an address, we will use **127.0.0.1:8080**. Since the **bind()** method returns **Result<TcpListener, Error>**, we will handle the error using the **?** operator:

```
let listener = TcpListener::bind("127.0.0.1:8080")?;
```

Our program will be very simple; we will either report to the user if we have a connection from some address or if it was refused from some type of error. To do this, we will use the **accept()** method which returns **Result<(TcpStream,**

SocketAddr), Error> in a **match** statement so we can handle the case we have an **Ok** value and an **Err** value:

```
match listener.accept(){
```

If the connection is accepted, we will print out that we have a connection from some address. Since our **Ok()** value is a tuple of a TCP stream and socket address, we will choose to ignore the stream, and only use the address with the identifier, **addr**. To display **addr**, we can either use the syntax, **(":?", addr)** or **("addr:?")**, we will choose the latter:

```
Ok((_, addr)) => println!("Connection from {addr:?}"),
```

If the connection is refused or an error occurs, we will handle this under the **Err()** value and will tell the user the connection has been refused alongside the cause of the error. We will choose to display our error the same way as we did with the socket address:

```
        Err(e) => println!("Connection refused: {e:?}")

    }
```

Since our **main()** function returns **Result<()>**, we will return **Ok(())** at the end, if everything succeeds, then our program will exit successfully:

```
    Ok(())

}
```

If we compile and run our program, it doesn't do anything. This is because we have yet to write a program that connects to our listener. To begin, create a file **connection.rs** and add the following import on the top of the file:

```
use std::net::TcpStream;
```

In our **main()** function, we want to be able to connect to our listener's address at **127.0.0.1:8080**. We want to handle the **Result<TcpStream>** with an **if let** statement where if we have an **Ok()** value, we tell the user we have connected to the listener, and if not we failed to connect:

```
fn main(){
    if let Ok(_stream) = TcpStream::connect("127.0.0.1:8080"){
        println!("Connected to listener!")
    } else {
        println!("Failed to connect to listener...")
    }
}
```

With our listener and connector created, we can compile both programs and run them in separate terminals:

```
# terminal 1
$ rustc listen.rs
$ ./listen


# terminal 2
$ rustc connection.rs
$ ./connection
Connected to listener!


# terminal 1
New connection from 127.0.0.1:44718
```

Creating a synchronous IO model

To explore creating synchronous IO models, we will create an ordering system using Redis to send commands to our server's socket and reply back. The example in this section is based on *Mastering Rust – Second Edition's* "Synchronous network IO project"[1]. However, instead of sending messages, we will be doing processor orders.

Before we begin our project, you may be wondering what the difference between a synchronous and asynchronous IO model is. The simplest difference is how a socket (a file descriptor that allows APIs to communicate to two processes in a network) is read/written to: a synchronous model blocks the thread, while an asynchronous model does not block the thread.

To begin with our project, download **redis-cli** by following the instructions for your system at **https://redis.io/docs/getting-started/installation/**.

Next, we will create our project and add the dependencies:

```
$ cargo new orders_sync
$ cd orders_sync
$ cargo add chrono lazy_static
$ cargo add resp --git https://github.com/creativcoder/resp
```

---

1   Sharma, R., & Kaihlavirta, V. (2019, January). *Mastering Rust Second Edition*. Packt subscription. Retrieved September 9, 2022, from https://subscription.packtpub.com/book/application-development/9781789346572/12/ch12lvl1sec08/synchronous-network-io

The **resp** crate will help us encode and decode our strings into valid **redis** commands so that we can properly send and receive orders.

Let us begin our work in **src/order.rs** with the following imports at the top of the file:

```
use std::collections::HashMap;
use lazy_static::lazy_static;
use std::sync::Mutex;
use chrono::{Utc, DateTime};
use resp::Value;
```

To make our life easier, we will create our own "database" inside a lazy static block; this is to help keep this project simple. Our database, **ORDERS** is a hashmap with string keys, and **Order** values wrapped in **Mutex**, so that we can safely write/read it lazily. Another item we will need to keep lazily is the current time (**Utc::now()**), which will be used to keep track of when orders are created:

```
lazy_static!{
    static ref TIME_NOW: DateTime<Utc> = Utc::now();
        pub   static   ref   ORDERS:   Mutex<HashMap<String,Order>>   =
Mutex::new(HashMap::new());
}
```

Our **Order** struct will be easy; its only fields are for the item and for when the order was created. Our item will expect an enum, **Item** which for fun, will be Intel processors i5-12600, i7-12700, and i9-12900 or variants **I5**, **I7**, and **I9**, respectively:

```
// Represents an order from a user
#[derive(Debug, Clone)]
pub struct Order{
    item: Item,
    created_at: String,
}
// Represents a store's or manufacturer's items
// We will do intel processors using msrp USD
#[derive(Debug, Copy, Clone)]
pub enum Item{
    I5, // I5-12600
    I7, // I7-12700
```

```
    I9, // I9-12900
    Nil // if product doesn't exist
}
```

In terms of implemented functions, we will need a **new()** (expecting the item's name) and the **to_string()** function for **Orders** with **to_string()** being implemented from the **ToString** trait:

```
impl ToString for Order{
    fn to_string(&self) -> String {
        format!("Item: {} [${}] -- Created at: {}",
                &self.item.to_string(), &self.item.get_price(), &self.
created_at)
    }
}


impl Order{
    pub fn new(item: &str) -> Self{
        Self{
            item: Item::new(item),
            created_at: TIME_NOW.to_string(),
        }
    }
}
```

For **Item**, we will need the implemented functions, **new()** (expecting the item's name), **get_price()** to return the processors' MSRP USD prices, and a **to_string()** function, which is implemented from the **ToString** trait:

```
impl ToString for Item{
    fn to_string(&self) -> String {
        match &self{
            Item::I5 => "i5-12600".to_string(),
            Item::I7 => "i7-12700".to_string(),
            Item::I9 => "i9-12900".to_string(),
            Item::Nil => "Item doesn't exist".to_string()
        }
    }
```

```
}

impl Item{
    pub fn new(item: &str) -> Self{
        match item{
            "i5" => Self::I5,
            "i7" => Self::I7,
            "i9" => Self::I9,
            _ => Self::Nil
        }
    }
    pub fn get_price(&self) -> u32{
        match &self{
            Item::I5 => 240,
            Item::I7 => 350,
            Item::I9 => 590,
            Item::Nil => 0
        }
    }
}
```

Before we continue writing in **src/order.rs**, we should start our main function in **src/main.rs**. In our main file, add the following imports on the top:

```
mod order;
use order::*;


use resp::Decoder;
use std::io::{BufReader, Write};
use std::net::{TcpListener, TcpStream};
use std::env;
```

Our first job in our **main()** function is to define an address for our TCP listener to bind to. We will allow our user to define one if they would like. If not, we will have a default at localhost with port 6378. To just get the address, we will have **env::args()** skip the first value and go to the next, which will be whichever address the user would like:

```
fn main() {
    // by default redis reads from port 6378
    let address = env::args()
        .skip(1)
        .next()
        .unwrap_or("127.0.0.1:6378".to_owned());
```

With our address, we can now bind it to a TCP listener via **TcpListener::bind()**. When we do this, we will also allow the user to know we are listening at this address:

```
// create tcp listener
let listener = TcpListener::bind(&address).unwrap();
// let user know where orders_sync is listening from
println!("orders_sync listening on: {}", &address);
```

To handle each stream from the TCP listener, we use a **for** loop in each stream from **listener.incoming()**. The stream will have type **Result<TcpStream>**, so our job is to unwrap it inside the loop, let the user know about this incoming connection, and handle it:

```
    // handle each incoming stream
    for tcp_stream in listener.incoming(){
        let tcp_stream = tcp_stream.unwrap();
        println!("New incoming connection from: {:?}", tcp_stream);
        handle_incoming(tcp_stream);
    }
}
```

Below our **main()** function, we can write our function, **handle_incoming()** which expects a **TcpStream**:

```
fn handle_incoming(stream: TcpStream){
```

Before we can decode our stream for our redis program, the decoder needs a reader. We will hence create a new buffer reader using **BufReader::new()**. With the stream wrapped in a reader, we can create a new decoder using **Decoder::new()** and decode it with the **decode()** function:

```
let mut tcp_stream = BufReader::new(stream);

let decoder = Decoder::new(&mut tcp_stream).decode();
```

The **decode()** function returns a **Result<Value>**, and so we will handle the **Result** using a **match** statement where if the command is valid, we process it and write the reply to the stream. If the command is not valid, we write the error to stderr with **eprintln!()**. To know which commands are valid in redis, it is recommended to take a look at the official site, **https://redis.io/commands/**:

```
match decoder{
    Ok(value) => {
        let reply = process_order(value);
        match tcp_stream.get_mut().write_all(&reply){
            Ok(()) => (),
            Err(e) => eprintln!("Error: {:?}", e)
        }
    }
    Err(e) => {
        eprintln!("Invalid command: {:?}", e);
    }
};
}
```

In our program, we expect the following commands for the orders:

- **GET**: With the name for the order, we will print the order.
- **SET**: With a name and item, we will create a new order.
- **DEL**: With a name, we will delete the order.

In our file, **src/order.rs**, we will create the function **process_order()**, which will expect a **Value** and return **Vec<u8>** or bytes:

```
pub fn process_order(msg: Value) -> Vec<u8> {
```

Our task is to encode a reply for the redis client, our reply will have the type **Result<Value, Value>**, and either variant, **Ok** or **Err** will be encoded and returned:

```
let reply: Result<Value, Value> = ...

    match reply{
        Ok(r) | Err(r) => r.encode()
    }
}
```

What will go into our binding, **reply**? We will use an **if let** statement to see if our parameter **msg** is a **Value::Array(v)**, where **v** is **Vec<Value>**. Within the **if** block, we will match the first element of **v** (**&v[0]**) to see if it matches the commands we had listed above. For each case, we will use **Value::Bulk(s)** and check whether the inner **&String** is "get", "set" and "del" (making **s** lowercase using **.to_ lowercase()**). For each command, we will have a function to handle it, and we will have a default case which will return **Err(Value::Err())** with a string, "Invalid command" inside. To complete the **if let** statement, we need an **else** statement which will copy our default value in the **match** statement:

```
let reply: Result<Value, Value> = if let Value::Array(v) = msg {
    match &v[0] {
        Value::Bulk(ref s) if &s.to_lowercase() == "get" => handle_get(v),
        Value::Bulk(ref s) if &s.to_lowercase() == "set" => handle_set(v),
        Value::Bulk(ref s) if &s.to_lowercase() == "del" => handle_del(v),
        _ => Err(Value::Error("Invalid command".to_string())),
    }
} else {
    Err(Value::Error("Invalid Command".to_string()))
};
```

After **process_order()**, we will write the function **handle_get()** which will expect a **Vec<Value>** and since we need the binding, **reply** to be **Result<Value, Value>**, we will return a **Result<Value, Value>**. The **get** command for us expects a name, and in return will reply with the details of the order using the **to_string()** method. Our first job inside the function is to iterate through the array and skip the first element since that is the command, and collect the rest:

```
pub fn handle_get(values: Vec<Value>) -> Result<Value, Value> {
    let v = values.iter().skip(1).collect::<Vec<_>>();
```

Before we even decide to look into the values, what if the array is empty? We will need to return an error because we need a name for the **get** command:

```
// we expect the name of the individual
if v.is_empty() {
    return Err(Value::Error("Expected Name for GET command".to_string()));
}
```

To read into our orders, we need to lock **ORDERS**:

```
// lock orders so we can read it
```

```
let orders = ORDERS.lock().unwrap();
```

To create our reply, we will use an **if** **let** statement to check whether **Value::Bulk(ref s)** = **&v[0]**; if so, we will try getting the order in **orders** using the **get()** method and chaining it to **map()** to turn the **Order** into a **Value::Bulk** with the order's string wrapped inside. Since this will return an **Option<Value>**, we will chain **map** with **unwrap_or** with the default value **Value::Null**. If the value is not equal to **&v[0]**, then in our **else** statement, we will return **Value::Null** to **reply**:

```
// create a reply, by trying to get the order using the name
// if an order can't be found we will return Value::Null
let reply = if let Value::Bulk(ref s) = &v[0] {
    orders
        .get(s)
        .map(|o| Value::Bulk(o.to_string()))
        .unwrap_or(Value::Null)
} else {
    Value::Null
};
```

Now, we can return the reply wrapped with **Ok()**:

```
    // return the reply
    Ok(reply)
}
```

The next command we need to handle is the **set** command. For this command, we expect a name and an item for the order. Just like the previous function, we will skip the first **Value** in our array, and check whether the array is empty or if the length is not exactly 2:

```
pub fn handle_set(values: Vec<Value>) -> Result<Value, Value> {
    let v = values.iter().skip(1).collect::<Vec<_>>();
    // we expect the name of the individual
    if v.is_empty() || v.len() != 2 {
        return Err(Value::Error(
            "Expected Name and Item for SET command".to_string(),
        ));
    }
```

Since the **set** will create a new order, we will lock **ORDERS** but have the binding mutable so we can insert a new name and order:

```
let mut orders = ORDERS.lock().unwrap();
```

We will use a **match** statement for the first and second elements in **v** and handle two different cases. The first case is they are **Value::Bulk** with strings inside, which we can insert into **orders**, with the **key** as the name and **value** as the item which we can use with **Order::new()**. The second case will be our default, and we will use the macro, **unimplemented!()** to inform the user that our command is not implemented for these values:

```
match (&v[0], &v[1]) {
    (Value::Bulk(key), Value::Bulk(value)) => {
        let _ = orders.insert(key.to_string(), Order::new(value));
    }
    _ => unimplemented!("SET not implemented for {:?}", v),
}
```

If everything goes well, we will return a **Value::String()** wrapped in **Ok()** with a string to tell the user the order has been created:

```
    Ok(Value::String("Order Created!".to_string()))
}
```

Before we continue to handle the **del** command, let us see how we can edit or update an order. This is also done by the **set** command. The neat quality with hashmaps is that if the key exists inside, then the value associated with it will be removed and updated with the new value. The **insert()** function we use, returns **Option<V>** where V is the value. However, since we do not care about the old value, we ignore it.

We can now begin our last command to handle, which will be the **del** command, which expects a name. The first few lines in this functions is copied from **handle_get()** where we skip the first value in the array and check whether the array is empty. If it is empty, we return an error telling the user we expect a name:

```
pub fn handle_del(values: Vec<Value>) -> Result<Value, Value> {
    let v = values.iter().skip(1).collect::<Vec<_>>();
    // we expect the name of the individual
    if v.is_empty() {
        return Err(Value::Error("Expected Name for DEL command".to_
string()));
    }
```

In this function, we will write to our orders, so we will lock **ORDERS** with the binding being mutable:

```
let mut orders = ORDERS.lock().unwrap();
```

We will then use a **match** statement on the first element in **v**, similar to **handle_set()**. We will have two cases: the first checks whether the value is **Value::Bulk(key)** and using the key, we will remove the order using the **remove()** function. The **remove()** function does return an **Option** but we will proceed to ignore it. The other case is the default, and like **handle_set()**, we will use the macro, **unimplemented!()** to tell the user that the value is not implemented:

```
match &v[0] {
    Value::Bulk(key) => {
        let _ = orders.remove(key);
    }
    _ => unimplemented!("DEL not implemented for {:?}", v),
}
```

In the end, we can return a **Value::String** wrapped in **Ok()** telling the user that the order has been deleted:

```
    Ok(Value::String("Order Deleted!".to_string()))
}
```

Testing using Redis

Make sure you have **redis-cli** installed, and open two terminal tabs:

```
# Terminal tab 1
# We will compile and run orders_sync
$ cargo run


orders_sync listening on: 127.0.0.1:6378


# Terminal tab 2
$ redis-cli -p 6378
127.0.0.1:6378> set bob i7
Order Created!


$ redis-cli -p 6378
```

```
127.0.0.1:6378> set tim i9
Order Created!

$ redis-cli -p 6378
127.0.0.1:6378> get bob
"Item: i7-12700 [$350] -- Created at: 2022-09-04 00:04:03.260111010 UTC"


$ redis-cli -p 6378
127.0.0.1:6378> del tim
Order Deleted!


$ redis-cli -p 6378
127.0.0.1:6378> get tim
(nil)
```

If we hop back onto terminal tab 1, we can see the following incoming connections:

```
orders_sync listening on: 127.0.0.1:6378
New incoming connection from: TcpStream { addr: 127.0.0.1:6378, peer:
127.0.0.1:49240, fd: 4 }

New incoming connection from: TcpStream { addr: 127.0.0.1:6378, peer:
127.0.0.1:33990, fd: 4 }

New incoming connection from: TcpStream { addr: 127.0.0.1:6378, peer:
127.0.0.1:39752, fd: 4 }

New incoming connection from: TcpStream { addr: 127.0.0.1:6378, peer:
127.0.0.1:49696, fd: 4 }

New incoming connection from: TcpStream { addr: 127.0.0.1:6378, peer:
127.0.0.1:34414, fd: 4 }

New incoming connection from: TcpStream { addr: 127.0.0.1:6378, peer:
127.0.0.1:34420, fd: 4 }

New incoming connection from: TcpStream { addr: 127.0.0.1:6378, peer:
127.0.0.1:35464, fd: 4 }

New incoming connection from: TcpStream { addr: 127.0.0.1:6378, peer:
127.0.0.1:35472, fd: 4 }

New incoming connection from: TcpStream { addr: 127.0.0.1:6378, peer:
127.0.0.1:56962, fd: 4 }

New incoming connection from: TcpStream { addr: 127.0.0.1:6378, peer:
127.0.0.1:48820, fd: 4 }
```

Creating an asynchronous IO model

Asynchronous according to the Cambridge Dictionary is defined as *something not happening or done at the same time or speed*. The advantage of an asynchronous model compared to a synchronous one is the idea of concurrently running a process with non-blocking threads. But how is this possible? The technique or mechanic that operating systems use is called *polling*. Polling is a continuous check of processes and their state. The loop to check each process and its state already sounds very inefficient. Thus, kernels like Linux use *epoll*, which notifies when a process's state has changed (watching the file descriptors). So now the question arises, how does Rust interact with polling and create asynchronous tasks?

The Future trait

A future in Rust represents a value that will not be completed immediately but will be done later. This is all done using the **Future** trait, as follows:

```
pub trait Future {
    type Output;
  fn poll(self: Pin<&mut Self>, cx: &mut Context<'_>) -> Poll<Self::Output>;
}
```

The poll function according to the **futures** crate documentation found at **https://docs.rs/futures/0.3.24/futures/future/trait.Future.html** is used to attempt to resolve the future to a final value. It registers the current task to wake up if the value is not yet available. The function returns the following:

- **Poll::Pending** : If the future is not ready yet.

- **Poll::Read(val)**: Returns with the result **val** if the future is finished successfully.

The **Future** trait is commonly used from the **futures** crate, and whenever we need to use it and other traits relating to futures like **Stream** and **Sink**, we will utilize this crate.

From Mio to Tokio

As a developer, it is hard to manage the low-level cases of polling and reading events from the operating system, and thankfully we do not need to. The **mio** crate is a low-level IO library that focuses on non-blocking APIS as well as event notifications for building high performance IO apps. We do not need to do projects on creating an asynchronous task scheduler; someone already did it for us.

The **tokio** crate which combines the **future** and **mio** crate is an asynchronous library that provides everything you will need. For example, it provides a work-stealing task schedular, non-blocking APIS, TCP/UDP sockets, and more. If you are doing asynchronous tasks, you will most likely use **tokio**.

Another notable mention is the crate **async-std** which is a project to provide asynchronous versions of the standard library.

In this chapter, we will take advantage of **tokio**'s TCP/UDP sockets to create a program that will echo back whatever the user enters to a socket. This program is an example in the **tokio** repo, found at **https://github.com/tokio-rs/tokio/blob/master/examples/echo.rs**. It is a perfect choice to show how to run two programs concurrently.

To begin, let us create the project and add the necessary dependencies:

```
$ cargo new echo
$ cd echo
$ cargo add tokio —features full
$ cargo add tokio-util --features tokio-util/codec
$ cargo add futures bytes
```

Our project will be separated into two applications: the first being the TCP listener who will read a byte stream and write back to the socket with the same text. The second application will connect to the listener and allow the user to write messages to the socket.

We will begin with writing the TCP listener in **src/main.rs**, and add the following imports on the top:

```
use tokio::io::{AsyncReadExt, AsyncWriteExt};
use tokio::net::TcpListener;


use std::env::args;
use std::error::Error;
```

To have our main function run in **tokio**'s runtime, we will use the macro **#[tokio::main]** on the top of our **main()** function and have it return **Result<(), Box<dyn Error>>**, so we can handle most errors:

```
#[tokio::main]
async fn main() -> Result<(), Box<dyn Error>>{
```

Our next task is to either allow the user to enter an address for the TCP listener to bind to, or we will define the default at localhost with port 6378. To directly get the address, we will skip the first element of **std::env::args()**, since that contains the name of the program:

```
// allows the user to pass in an address,
// if they don't the default is 127.0.0.1:6378 to listen on
let address = args()
    .nth(1)
    .unwrap_or("127.0.0.1:6378".to_string());
```

Our next obvious task is to bind our address to our TCP listener, and let the user know that we are now listening on this address:

```
// Create a Tcp listener to listen on
let listener = TcpListener::bind(&address).await?;
// let the user know which address we are listening on
println!("Listening on {}", &address);
```

Next, we will create a loop and will asynchronously wait for an inbound socket using **listener.accept()**, which accepts incoming connections to the listener:

```
// We will create a loop for which whatever
// the user enters will be echoed right back to them
loop{
    // we will asynchronously wait for an inbound socket
    let (mut socket, _) = listener.accept().await?;
```

When we read and write back from our socket, we want these tasks to run in the background and when ready to be ran concurrently. To allow this to happen, we will use **tokio::spawn()** which spawns a new asynchronous task that can be executed concurrently to other tasks. This follows similar to **std::thread::spawn()**, where we have a block inside the function, which will be executed. Instead of using the keyword **move**, we will instead use **async move**:

```
// to concurrently read from the user then write back to them
// we will use tokio::spawn to asynchronously run this in the background
// this allows for the tasks to not block threads
tokio::spawn(async move {
```

Next, we will define a buffer from which we will read into and to write from. Our buffer will be a **Vec<u8>** defined as **vec![0;1024]** which represents a buffer of 1KB:

```
// create a buffer to read from
let mut buf = vec![0;1024];
```

We will read and write to the socket in another loop. To read from the socket, we use the **read()** function, passing in a mutable reference to our buffer. This returns an index to how many bytes were read. Before we write to the stream, if the data is nothing or zero, we will just return, as writing nothing is a waste. If we do have data, we will write to the socket using the **write_all()** function using a slice of our buffer from the first element to **data**, the value read by our socket:

```
        // in an infinite loop we will read from and write back to the user
        loop {
            let data = socket
                .read(&mut buf)
                .await
                .expect("Couldn't read from socket");
            // if the data is empty, there is no reason to write back
            if data == 0{
                return ;
            }
            socket.write_all(&buf[0..data])
                .await
                .expect("Couldn't write to socket");
        }
    });
}
}
```

If we run this program, nothing happens because nothing has been connected to our socket. Thus, we have no input to read from. That changes when we write our program to connect to our TCP listener. To get started, create a directory **bin** in our **src** directory and create a file **src/bin/connect.rs** with the following imports on the top:

```
use bytes::Bytes;
use futures::{future, Sink, SinkExt, StreamExt, Stream};
use tokio::io;
use tokio::net::TcpStream;
use tokio_util::codec::{BytesCodec, FramedRead, FramedWrite};

use std::env::args;
```

```
use std::error::Error;
use std::net::SocketAddr;
```

Next, we will write the magic to help us connect to our TCP listener and be able to stream and sink the bytes being written. But what does stream and sink even mean? **Stream** is a sequence of values (in our case, bytes) produced asynchronously, while **Sink** is a value to which other values can be sent to asynchronously. To help generalize this, we have our **stdin** being a value that implements the **Stream** trait since we will be "streaming" input from the user in the form of bytes, while our **stdout** will be a value that implements the **Sink** trait. In our case, the **stdout** will be written to and other values produced asynchronously, will be sent to it.

In our **connect()** function, we require three parameters: firstly, an address to connect to, secondly, a mutable **stdin** which implements the **Stream** trait, and thirdly, a mutable **stdout** which implements the **Sink** trait. The function will then return **Result<(), Box<dyn Error>>** to help handle a majority of the error handling:

```
async fn connect(
    address: &SocketAddr,
    mut stdin: impl Stream<Item = Result<Bytes, io::Error>> + Unpin,
    mut stdout: impl Sink<Bytes, Error = io::Error> + Unpin,
) -> Result<(), Box<dyn Error>>{
```

Our first step is to obviously connect to the socket. This is done using **TcpStream::connect()** and we will assign this to a binding, **stream**. With the stream, we can split it into a tuple with a read half and write half using **stream. split()**:

```
// create a stream to connect to an address
let mut stream = TcpStream::connect(address).await?;
// split the stream into a readhalf and writehalf
let (read, write) = stream.split();
```

To create a new sink, we will use **FramedWrite::new()**, which will create a sink of frames that is encoded with the **AsyncWrite** trait. The **new()** function requires two parameters, an inner value that implements **AsyncWrite**, which will be our binding **write** and an encoder. In our case, that will be using **BytesCodec::new()**, which is a simple decoder and encoder for bytes:

```
// create a new sink that's writable using FramedWrite
let mut sink = FramedWrite::new(write, BytesCodec::new());
```

To create our new stream, we will use **FramedRead::new()**, which will create a stream of values decoded by a value with the **AsyncRead** trait. The **new()** function requires an inner read value which implements **AsyncRead**, which will be our binding, **read** and a decoder, which like before, is **BytesCodec::new()**. We will use the **filter_map()** function to match each **Result<BytesMut, Error>**. If we have an **Ok(byte)**, we will ready the future using **future::ready()**, with an option of bytes. To turn the **BytesMut** into **Bytes**, we use **bytes.freeze()** wrapped in **Some()**. If we have an error, we print the error with **eprintln!()** and return **future::ready(None)** so we can know that it did not complete successfully and stop the stream. We then chain **filter_map()** with **map()** with **Ok** inside:

```
// to convert our stream into bytes, we will filter_map the Result<BytesMut,
Error>

let mut stream = FramedRead::new(read, BytesCodec::new())
    .filter_map(|byte|match byte{ // match the Result<BytesMut, Error>
  // turns BytesMut into Bytes
        Ok(bytes) => future::ready(Some(bytes.freeze()))),
        Err(e) => {
          // if there is an error, we print to stderr, and stop the stream
            eprintln!("Error in reading from socket: {}", e.to_string());
             future::ready(None)
        }
    }).map(Ok);
```

We have two futures we want to join: the first is to have the **sink** complete, after a stream has been fully processed into it using the **send_all()** function with **stdin**. Our other future is to send the stream all, to **stdout** for it to be able to write to **io::stdout()**. To join these two futures, we will use the **future::try_join()** function which joins the result of both futures, and waits for both to complete or one to have an error:

```
// try to join our sink sending to stdin
// and the stdout sending to stream
match future::try_join(sink.send_all(&mut stdin), stdout.send_all(&mut
stream)).await{
   Err(e) => Err(e.into()),
    _ => Ok(())
 }
}
```

With the **connect()** function finished, we can start working on our **main()** function, which will be fairly short since a lot of the work is already taken care of. To begin, just like for our TCP listener, we will declare our main function to run on **tokio**'s runtime with the **#[tokio::main]** macro. We will also be returning **Result<(), Box<dyn Error>>** like last time to handle much of the error handling:

```
#[tokio::main]

async fn main() -> Result<(), Box<dyn Error>>{
```

Next, we will need an address to connect to; our default address will be localhost at port 6378. So, by default, our program is guaranteed to connect with our TCP listener. To make the string into type **SocketAddr**, we will use the **parse()** function:

```
// get the address from the user
    let address = args()
        .nth(1)
        .unwrap_or("127.0.0.1:6378".to_owned());
    let address: SocketAddr = address.parse()?;
```

For our **connect()** function, we have got the address to connect to; our next task is to get **stdin**, which will be a **Stream** created by **FramedRead::new()** with the inner reader being **io::stdin()** and the encoder being **BytesCodec::new()**. To get a stream of bytes, we will map **stdin** using the **map()** function and for each frame, we will map its bytes (type **BytesMut**) and to turn it into **Bytes**, we will use the **freeze()** function:

```
// create a new stdin using FramedRead
    let stdin = FramedRead::new(io::stdin(), BytesCodec::new());
// turn the BytesMut from standard input into a stream of bytes
    let stdin = stdin.map(|i|i.map(|bytes|bytes.freeze()));
```

The last parameter that we need to get is **stdout**, which is a **Sink**, which will be created using **FramedWrite::new()** with **io::stdout()** being the inner writer and **BytesCodec::new()** being the decoder:

```
    let stdout = FramedWrite::new(io::stdout(), BytesCodec::new());
```

Now, we can use our **connect()** function passing in a reference of **address** and using our **stdin** and **stdout** bindings. In the end, if everything runs successfully, then we return **Ok(())**:

```
    connect(&address, stdin, stdout).await?;

    Ok(())

}
```

To run our application, we will need to open two terminal tabs:

```
# Terminal 1: Run our TCP listener
$ cargo run --bin echo
Listening on 127.0.0.1:6378


# Terminal 2: Run our connector and enter text
$ cargo run --bin connect
hello
hello
echo
echo
this is coming twice
this is coming twice
```

How can we improve?

This is a neat program, but what are some simple ways using which we improve it such that it becomes user friendly?

- The first improvement is just letting the user know we have connected to the address x.x.x.x:port.

- The second improvement we can make is letting the user know to enter text. As a developer, we know that if we enter the text, **io::stdin()** will read the bytes and **io::stdout()** will write the message back to us. However, does the user know this?

- Lastly, in terms of the TCP listener, it would be nice to know that we have got a connection. This can make debugging easier if this were to be scaled into a larger project.

With these improvements said, why don't we go back into our project and add these to make our program a bit more user friendly.

The first improvement is to let the user know we have connected to an address. This will be placed in our **connect()** function in **src/bin/connect.rs** and under the binding **stream**, which we connect to an address using **TcpStream::connect()**:

```
...
let mut stream = TcpStream::connect(address).await?;
// tell the user we have connected
println!("Connected to {}", address.to_string());
```

. . .

The second improvement is letting the user know how to enter text, as well as trying to find where it was a tricky. We want it to be outputted after the user knows what address we have connected to, but we want it before they enter text. Therefore, we place it right before we join our futures:

```
// Let the user know to enter text
println!("Enter text: ");
match future::try_join(. . .
```

To notify the user from the TCP listener that we have an incoming connection, we need to refactor our tuple, which is returned from **listener.accept()**. The function returns a tuple of **TcpStream** and **SocketAddr**, and so, instead of ignoring the socket's address, we can print it out:

```
let (mut socket, addr) = listener.accept().await?;
    // print that we have a new incoming connection
    println!("Incoming connection from {}", addr.to_string());
```

Let us now rerun our program with these small improvements added. As before, we will use two terminal tabs:

```
# Terminal 1: Run the tcp listener
$ cargo run --bin echo
Listening on 127.0.0.1:6378
# Terminal 2: Run our connector
Connected to 127.0.0.1:6378
Enter text:
# head back to terminal 1 to see a connection notification
Listening on 127.0.0.1:6378
Incoming connection from 127.0.0.1:5947
```

Conclusion

In conclusion, this chapter has explored mainly the aspects of creating IO models with TCP/UDP listeners and streams. We looked at creating a redis server to process orders with a synchronous IO model, utilizing the standard library's **net** module. We furthered explored the basics of asynchronous programming, with the idea of polling values, to run tasks concurrently with non-blocking threads. In the end, we explored the grand **tokio** crate, which provides different IO primitives in an asynchronous manner, as well as providing task schedular which uses work-stealing.

Key facts

- When reading/writing to a socket, values must be decoded or encoded into bytes respectively.

- A simple bytes decoder/encoder is **BytesCodec** found in **tokio-util** or **tokio-codec**.

- A future in Rust represents a value that is not executed immediately, but will be later.

- To check whether a future is pending or ready, the **Future** trait uses the **poll()** function.

- The **Stream** trait represents a sequence of values produced asynchronously.

    o To create frames of stream values, you can use **FramedRead** which requires an inner reader (implements **AsyncRead**) and a decoder.

- The **Sink** trait represents a value which other values can be sent asynchronously.

    o To create frames of sink values, you can use **FramedWrite** which requires an inner writer (implements **AsyncWrite**) and an encoder.

Exercises

1. Create a UDP ping test that binds an address to two different UDP sockets and have the first client to send "PING" to the second client with a reply of "PING". (This exercise can be found at **https://github.com/tokio-rs/tokio/blob/master/examples/udp-codec.rs**).

Answers

1. To get started with this exercise, let us create a new project and add the necessary dependencies:

```
$ cargo new udp_ping_async
$ cd udp_ping_async
$ cargo add tokio-stream bytes futures
$ cargo add tokio —features full
$ cargo add tokio-util —features tokio-util/codec
```

The goal of this project is for two clients, which we will simply name *a* and *b* to connect to the same UDP socket and send/receive messages to each other a finite number of times. To start, let us begin writing in *src/main.rs* with the following imports on the top of the file:

```
use tokio::net::UdpSocket;
use tokio::{io, time};
use tokio_stream::StreamExt;
use tokio_util::codec::BytesCodec;
use tokio_util::udp::UdpFramed;

use bytes::Bytes;
use futures::{FutureExt, SinkExt};
use std::env;
use std::error::Error;
use std::net::SocketAddr;
use std::time::Duration;
```

Just like before in our **echo** project, we will have our **main()** function asynchronous, and to have it run on **tokio**'s runtime, we will use the macro, **#[tokio::main]** on top of the **main()** function. It will also return **Result<(), Box<dyn Error>>** so we can handle most of the errors in our program:

```
#[tokio::main]
async fn main() -> Result<(), Box<dyn Error>>{
```

We will allow the user to define their own address; in the case that they don't, we will default to the address **127.0.0.1:0**. To get the address directly, we will chain **env::args()** with the **nth()** function which will return the nth element of an array. Since we expect the address to be the second or element 1, we put **nth(1)** which returns **Option<String>**. To handle the **Option**, we will use chain the **nth()** function with the **unwrap_or()** function with the previously mentioned default address:

```
// create an address
let address = env::args()
    .nth(1)
    .unwrap_or("127.0.0.1:0".to_owned());
```

We will create two clients **a** and **b** which will both bind to our UDP socket's address using **UdpSocket::bind()**:

```
// Bind both clients to our socket
```

```
let a = UdpSocket::bind(&address).await?;
let b = UdpSocket::bind(&address).await?;
```

To start the ping later down, we will need to keep client **b**'s local address, this is done using the **local_addr()** function which returns a **SocketAddr**:

```
// get b local address
let b_addr = b.local_addr()?;
```

When we worked with TCP, we used **FramedRead** and **FramedWrite** to act as a getting framed **Stream** and **Sink** values, respectively. With UDP, we will use **UdpFramed** which acts as a unified **Stream** and **Sink** interface, we will create a new **UdpFramed** for each client using the **UdpFramed::new()** function that requires a socket and codec. The codec we will use is our best friend **BytesCodec** which can be placed using **BytesCodec::new()** and act as our decoder or encoder. The **UdpFramed::new()** function in our case will return **UdpFramed<BytesCodec>**, which we be a parameter in our **ping()** and **pong()** functions:

```
// create a udp frame for both clients
let mut a = UdpFramed::new(a, BytesCodec::new());
let mut b = UdpFramed::new(b, BytesCodec::new());
```

Before we continue our **main()** function, it would be best to start writing our functions, **ping()** and **pong()**. Let's start with **ping()** which will allow client **a** to start the conversation with **b**. To do this, we will require a socket and an address, essentially using socket **a**'s udp frame to send messages to client **b**'s local address. This function will return **Result<(), io::Error>**; we will use **io::Error** since any error being handled in this function will be I/O related:

```
async  fn  ping(socket:  &mut  UdpFramed<BytesCodec>,  b_addr:
SocketAddr) -> Result<(), io::Error> {
```

To begin our message, let us have our socket send an initial "PING" message to **b_addr**. To send the message, however, we can't just send a string, instead we will send **Bytes** using **Bytes::from("PING".as_bytes())** along with **b_addr**:

```
// send message PING in bytes to b
socket.send((Bytes::from("PING".as_bytes()), b_addr)).await?;
```

Now, we can create a **for** loop (from 0..6) to send and receive messages from **socket**. In the beginning of our loop, we will get the next value of our socket's stream which returns **([u8], SocketAddr)**, with the bytes we will tell the user we have received a message using **String::from_utf8_lossy()** which turns bytes into a string. With the address, we will send a message back, just like our initial message with the difference of using **addr** instead of **b_addr**:

```
// from 0 to 6, we will receive and send messages to b
    for i in 0..6usize {
        // returns the next value of our stream ([u8], SocketAddr)
        let (bytes, addr) = socket.next().map(|e|e.unwrap()).await?;
        // we will print the index of the iterator
        println!("({}) ----------------------------", i);
        // print that we have received b's message,converting the
bytes to string
        println!("[a] recv: {}",String::from_utf8_lossy(&bytes));
        // send ping back to b
        socket.send((Bytes::from(&b"PING"[..]), addr)).await?;
    }
```

If everything goes well inside the loop, then we can return **Ok(())** in the end of our function:

```
    Ok(())
}
```

The next function we need to create is **pong()**; this function only requires a socket's udp frame and will return **Result<(), io::Error>** for the same reasons of **ping()**:

```
async fn pong(socket: &mut UdpFramed<BytesCodec>) -> Result<(),
io::Error> {
```

Since this function's job is to receive and send a message back to **a**, we will define a timeout for our function. We will have a timeout of 200 milliseconds or 2 seconds using **Duration::from_millis(200)**:

```
// create a timeout of 2 seconds
    let timeout = Duration::from_millis(200);
```

We need to be able to send and receive messages once a future is completed within our timeout to create a loop upon this requirement, we will use a **while let** statement to check whether a tuple of **(BytesMut, SocketAddr)** is equal to our timeout. The bytes represent the message received from b, and the address will be used to send a message back with the message "PONG".

To make this possible, our **let** statement looks a bit of a disaster with being wrapped in **Ok(Some(Ok(bytes, addr)))**, but this is done to handle all of the errors from **time::timeout(timeout, socket.next())**:

```
while let Ok(Some(Ok((bytes, addr)))) = time::timeout(timeout,
socket.next()).await {
```

Inside our while loop, we will first tell the user that **b** has received a message using **bytes**; like before, we will use **String::from_utf8_lossy()** to convert the **BytesMut** into a **String**:

```
// print we have received a's message
        println!("[b] recv: {}", String::from_utf8_lossy(&bytes));
```

Next, we will send a message back to **addr** which will be our client **a**; we will send the message in the same manner, instead of "PING", we will send "PONG":

```
        // send the message PONG in bytes back to a
        socket.send((Bytes::from("PONG".as_bytes()), addr)).await?;
    }
```

If everything works well in our while loop, we can then return **Ok(())** so we know everything executed successfully.

With these functions written, we can continue working on the **main()** function; our next task in it is to create two futures, **a** will be created using **ping()** and the binding **b** will be created using **pong()**. We will need to mutably borrow the udp frames for each respective client, with **ping()** also requiring the binding, **b_addr**:

```
  // begin by having a send a ping to b
    let a = ping(&mut a, b_addr);
    // then b will receive a's ping and send back pong
    let b = pong(&mut b);
```

Now, we can try to join these futures to run concurrently; we will need to match the macro **tokio::try_join!()**. If we get an **Err** value, we will print out the error using **eprinln!()**, and if we get any other value we will print that we are done.

```
  // run both futures at the same time of a and b sending messages back and
forth
        match tokio::try_join!(a,b){
            Err(e) => eprintln!("An error has occurred: {:?}", e),
```

```
        _ => println!("done")
    }
```

If everything works properly in our function, then we can return **Ok(())** at the end:

```
    Ok(())
}
```

We can now run our UDP Ping program with **cargo run** and you should see the following result:

```
$ cargo run
[b] recv: PING
(0) ---------------------------
[a] recv: PONG
[b] recv: PING
(1) ---------------------------
[a] recv: PONG
[b] recv: PING
(2) ---------------------------
[a] recv: PONG
[b] recv: PING
(3) ---------------------------
[a] recv: PONG
[b] recv: PING
(4) ---------------------------
[a] recv: PONG
[b] recv: PING
(5) ---------------------------
[a] recv: PONG
[b] recv: PING
done
```

CHAPTER 7
Project – GTK App

Introduction

For those who are not aware, GTK is a set of libraries and APIS to help create native Linux desktop applications for the GNOME desktop environment. Usually, GTK applications are written in C or Vala, while there are also bindings for other languages such as in Rust (using C/C++ raw bindings).

The first question we need to answer is should you use GTK? The answer depends on your use case, but its main advantage is building an application that inherits the theme of the GNOME desktop environment. However, if you are not using one, and are neither a KDE user nor anything else, it is not a strong argument. There are other frameworks for desktop applications such as Tauri, which we will explore later in this book, that provides a Rust alternative to Electron. The GTK crate is still a very much difficult crate to work with; the complexity of turning structures into GObjects, and the overall need to use smart pointers do not sound like a nice experience to most. For a cross-platform application, GTK is not your best bet; it is primarily used in Linux environments and compared to the actual cross-platform crates, it is not a viable option. To learn other emerging GUI frameworks, it is best to explore **https://www.areweguiyet.com/#ecosystem** for different crates to build desktop apps in. To get the best experience in this chapter, it is highly recommended to use some type of Debian Linux environment, such as Ubuntu (WSL on Windows) to work on this project.

What app will we build? We will use one of the examples in the GTK-rs's repository, a grocery list app. This app will allow you to add, edit, and delete items. Each row will have the item's name along with a counter that can be increased or decreased, as shown in *Figure 7.1*:

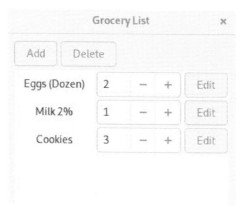

Figure 7.1: Preview of Grocery List application

Our application can be split into three parts. Firstly, we need to create our row data that contains the items and a counter. The next part will use the row data and create a model using it, and lastly, with the model and row data, we will be able to build our UI and run our application.

We will learn how to turn Rust structures into GTK's GObjects and use them to create a fully functional desktop application. In this chapter, we will use GTK-3 bindings due to having issues with GTK-4.

Structure

In this chapter, we will cover the following topics:

- Setting up our GTK application
- Row data for our grocery list
- Storing rows into a model
- Assembling the final application

Objectives

By the end of this chapter, the reader will be able to understand how to write a native Linux desktop application using the GTK framework or family of crates in Rust. We will see the advantages and disadvantages of the GTK framework and get our first hands to experience developing a GUI with Rust and using methods to process different events.

Setting up our GTK application

Before we even start creating a new cargo application, we need to install the GTK library on a Debian Linux system. It can be installed in the command line:

```
# update and upgrade your packages
$ sudo apt-get update && sudo apt-get upgrade
# install the gtk-3 dev library
$ sudo apt-get install libgtk-3-dev
```

On other systems, it is recommended to follow the installation instructions from the GTK website, **https://www.gtk.org/docs/installations/**. With GTK installed, we can start creating our application using **cargo** and add the dependencies using **cargo add**:

```
$ cargo new grocery_list
$ cargo add gtk glib once_cell gio
```

For this project, it is best to understand what each of these crates will do for us, so we can use them effectively:

- **gtk**: The gtk crate provides us with all the different bindings to create a desktop application. This library uses bindings of gtk-3.

- **glib**: The glib crate provides a library that contains bindings to GLib and GObjects.

- **once_cell**: This library provides a way to create single assignment lazy types; we will need this for our row data.

- **gio**: The gio crate provides bindings for general-purpose IO, networking, and so on. for GTK.

With a couple of our projects, we have usually used a **mod.rs** file when trying to import files in a separate directory. Another way to import other files from a directory is to create a file of the name of the directory in the same directory level as **main.rs** or **lib.rs**.

In our project, we will need to create directories **row_data** and **models** to manage our row data and models, respectively. Each of these directories will contain an **imp. rs** file to contain all the value's implementation. In our main **src** directory, we will have **main.rs**, **row_data.rs**, and **model.rs**. The files **row_data.rs** and **model.rs** will be used to turn our Rust structure into a **GObject** for GTK.

The project structure should look like the following:

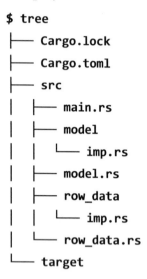

```
$ tree
├── Cargo.lock
├── Cargo.toml
├── src
│   ├── main.rs
│   ├── model
│   │   └── imp.rs
│   ├── model.rs
│   ├── row_data
│   │   └── imp.rs
│   └── row_data.rs
└── target
```

Row data for our grocery list

To begin our work on the rowdata, we will edit **src/row_data/imp.rs** and import the following on the top of the file:

```
use glib::subclass::prelude::*;
```

```
use gtk::{glib, prelude::*};
```

```
use std::cell::RefCell;
```

```
use glib::{ParamSpec, ParamSpecString, ParamSpecUInt, Value};
```

Our row data needs the following: an item and a count. To avoid the need to always mutably borrow our row data, we will use **RefCell** to take advantage of interior mutability. The item's name will be wrapped in an **Option**, and if the user decides to not enter a name, the row will not be created. We will also derive the **Default** trait to our struct to provide us with a convenient **default()** function, which will create a default row data. In our case, since both fields are wrapped in **RefCell** will be **RefCell::default()**:

```
#[derive(Default)]
pub struct RowData{
    item: RefCell<Option<String>>,
    count: RefCell<u32>
}
```

The next thing we need to do for our struct **RowData** is let it be a GObject. In our case, that would be a subclass. To do this, we need to use the attribute macro **#[glib::object_subclass]** to implement the **type_data()** and **type_()** functions in our implementation of the **ObjectSubclass** for **RowData**. In the trait, we will only need to define three values, a constant **NAME** which we will name RowData, a type, which will be the struct, **RowData** and the parent type which is **glib::Object** since we are making our struct a subclass to **Object**:

```
// declaring row data for GObject type system
#[glib::object_subclass]
impl ObjectSubclass for RowData{
    const NAME: &'static str = "RowData";
    type Type = super::RowData;
    type ParentType = glib::Object;
}
```

To be able to set, get, and define the properties for our Object is to implement the **ObjectImpl** trait for **RowData**. The first function we will define is the **properties()** function, which will return a **&'static [ParamSpec]**. The **ParamSpec** type is the metadata for a parameter. To be able to create a static array of **ParamSpec**, we will use the **once_cell** crate. This allows us to create a **Lazy** value while being able to assign it. After we create our static binding **PROPERTIES**, we will return it as a reference using the **as_ref()** function.

In our **ParamSpec** vector, we will need to define two elements; the first is a **ParamSpecString** for our item field, which will need a name, obviously "item", a nickname which we will be as "Item", a blurb "Item". The next parameter is a default value, since our item is an **Option**, we will have the default as **None**, and the flag for the parameter will be **READWRITE** since we want to be able to read and edit the item's name.

The second element will use the **ParamSpecUInt** type for our count field. Just like with the item field, we will have a name of "count", the nickname of "Count" and a blurb of "Count". The minimum and the default value will be 0, and the maximum is 100 (for no particular reason). The flag for this parameter will also be **READWRITE** since we want to be able to read and edit the count of an item:

```
fn properties() -> &'static [ParamSpec] {
    use once_cell::sync::Lazy;
    static PROPERTIES: Lazy<Vec<ParamSpec>> = Lazy::new(|| {
        vec![
            ParamSpecString::new(
```

```
                    "item",
                    "Item",
                    "Item",
                    None,
                    glib::ParamFlags::READWRITE
                ),
                ParamSpecUInt::new(
                    "count",
                    "Count",
                    "Count",
                    0,
                    100,
                    0,
                    glib::ParamFlags::READWRITE
                )
            ]
    });
    PROPERTIES.as_ref()
}
```

The next function we will implement is **set_property()**. This function uses a parameter spec and a value. We will match the name of the parameter spec and replace the value of the respective parameter, whether an item or a count and if it is not one of them, we will say that it is unimplemented using the **unimplemented!()** macro.

To replace the value, we first need to turn the **Value** struct into the type our field needs, which would be either an **Option<String>** or **u8**. We can then replace the value inside our field using the **replace()** method from **RefCell** which replaces the current wrapped value with a new one:

```
fn set_property(&self, _obj: &Self::Type, _id: usize, value: &Value,
pspec: &ParamSpec) {
    match pspec.name(){
        "item" => {
            let item = value.get().unwrap();
            self.item.replace(item);
        }
```

```
        "count" => {
            let count = value.get().unwrap();
            self.count.replace(count);
        }
        _ => unimplemented!()
    }
}
```

We have so far defined our default properties; a setter for our property. The only thing we have left is to define a getter. To do this, we will define the function **property()** and use the parameter spec so we can match its name and return a **glib::Value**. Depending on if it is an item or count, we will borrow the value and turn it into a **glib::Value** with **to_value()**. Just like in **set_property()**, our default case in the **match** statement will be unimplemented:

```
    fn property(&self, _obj: &Self::Type, _id: usize, pspec: &ParamSpec)
-> Value {
        match pspec.name(){
            "item" => self.item.borrow().to_value(),
            "count" => self.count.borrow().to_value(),
            _ => unimplemented!()
        }
    }
}
```

The last work we need to do for our row data is wrap it so it can act just like a GObject binding to GTK. We will work on **src/row_data.rs** and import the following on the top of the file:

```
mod imp;
```

```
use gtk::glib;
```

To wrap it as a GObject, we will use the **glib::wrapper!** macro and inside its block, we will define a new tuple struct **RowData** with **ObjectSubclass<imp::RowData>** inside. We want our application to access this **RowData** as it will act like a GObject binding to GTK:

```
// public part of the RowData type, this behaves like a gtk-rs style GObj
binding
```

```
glib::wrapper! {
    pub struct RowData(ObjectSubclass<imp::RowData>);
}
```

For our new **RowData** struct, we will create an implementation for it, so that we can create a **new()** function. We will require an item and a count so that we can create a new row with values. Since our **RowData** is a **glib::Object** now, we will use the **glib::Object::new()** function that needs a borrowed array as the property. The array will contain a tuple of the property's name and value (both being borrowed). Since the **glib::Object::new()** function returns a **Result**, we will simply **unwrap()** it:

```rust
impl RowData{
    pub fn new(item: &str, count: u32) -> Self{
        glib::Object::new(&[("item", &item), ("count", &count)]).unwrap()
    }
}
```

Storing rows into a model

Our first part of our application has been completed, and so now we can use the **RowData** we created to store in a model. To begin our work, we will edit **src/model/imp.rs** with the following imports on the top of the file:

```rust
use gio::subclass::prelude::*;
use gtk::{gio, glib, prelude::*};
use std::cell::RefCell;
use glib::{Object, Type};
use crate::row_data::RowData;
```

Since our model's job is to store a list of **RowData**, we will wrap it in a vector so that we can dynamically store them. We will also use interior mutability using **RefCell** so that we can dynamically use our list mutably while having the functions only using it as an immutable binding.

We will also derive the **Debug** and the **Default** trait to our struct **Model**, so that we can have a convenient **default()** function while the **Debug** trait is required.

To make our life a little easier, we will have the struct **Model** be a tuple struct since we only have one field inside the struct, and it requires less typing to do **Model.0** than **Model.list**:

```rust
#[derive(Debug, Default)]

pub struct Model(pub RefCell<Vec<RowData>>);
```

To have our **Model** act like a **GObject**, we will need to have it be an **ObjectSubclass** like **RowData**, and this is done by implementing the **ObjectSubclass** trait to **Model**.

We will also need to have the attribute **#[glib::object_subclass]** on top of our implementation.

Inside the implementation, we will need to define some constants and type aliases. For the constant **NAME**, we will simply call it Model, while the **Type** will be our struct **Model**. Since we are having the model as an object subclass, the **ParentType** will be **Object**. The last type alias to add is **Interfaces** which will be a tuple of interfaces implemented by our type, and for our case, we will have one element being the interface trait, **gio::ListModel**:

```
#[glib::object_subclass]
impl ObjectSubclass for Model{
    const NAME: &'static str = "Model";
    type Type = super::Model;
    type ParentType = Object;
    type Interfaces = (gio::ListModel,);
}
```

We will next implement the **ObjectImpl** trait to **Model**, and we will not need to change any of the properties for **Model**:

```
impl ObjectImpl for Model{}
```

The actual work will go to the **ListModelImpl** trait which we will implement to **Model**. This trait does three things for us, return the type of the item (**item_type()**), return the number of items (**n_items()**), and return an item using a position (**item()**):

```
impl ListModelImpl for Model{
```

The first function we will work on is **item_type()** which will return the types of our items. Luckily for us, we will simply return the type of the **RowData** using the function, **static_type()**:

```
fn item_type(&self, _list_model: &Self::Type) -> Type {
    RowData::static_type()
}
```

The next function we will work on is **n_items()**, which will return the number of items in the list. Well, that just sounds like returning the length of the vector, and to do this, we will borrow our vector using the **borrow()** function and return the length using **len()**. Since the length function returns a **usize** and we need to return a **u32**, we will simply use **as u32** when returning the length:

```
fn n_items(&self, _list_model: &Self::Type) -> u32 {
```

```
self.0.borrow().len() as u32
}
```

The last function we will need is **item()** which will return an **Object<Object>** given a position. The easiest step is to borrow the vector using **borrow()**. Now that we have immutably access to the inner vector, we can use the **get()** function along with the position as a **usize** which will return an **Option<&RowData>**. We can chain the **get()** with the **map()** function using a parameter **o** which will be type **&RowData**. With the parameter **o**, we will turn it into a **RowData** using **clone()** and then upcasting it to an **Object** using the **upcast::<Object>()** function in a turbofish manner:

```
fn item(&self, _list_model: &Self::Type, position: u32) -> Option<Object>
{
    self.0
      .borrow()
      .get(position as usize)
      .map(|o|o.clone().upcast::<Object>())
  }
}
```

With the implementations of **Model** completed, we can work on the main model file in **src/model.rs** and add the following imports on the top:

```
mod imp;
```

```
use crate::row_data::RowData;
use glib::subclass::prelude::*;
use gtk::{gio, glib, prelude::*};
```

Just like for **RowData**, we will create a new public struct **Model**, which will be wrapped as a GObject using the **glib::wrapper!** macro. Inside the block, we will create a new struct **Model**, which will be a tuple struct with an **ObjectSubclass<imp::Model>** inside. To tell the wrapper that our struct **imp::Model** implements the **gio::ListModel** interface, we will write **@implements gio::ListModel** after the tuple:

```
glib::wrapper! {
    pub struct Model(ObjectSubclass<imp::Model>) @implements gio::ListModel;
}
```

With our new **Model** struct created, it would be useful to create some functions for it, namely, a way to create a new **Model (new())**, a way to add more items to the model (**append()**) and a way to remove items (**remove()**).

The first function we will need to create is a **new()** function, which will utilize **glib::Object::new()** and we will leave an empty array for the properties. Since the function does return a **Result**, we will simply use **unwrap()**:

```
impl Model{
  pub fn new() -> Model{
    glib::Object::new(&[]).unwrap()
  }
```

The next function we need to work on is a way to append new items to our model. In this function, we will need to use a model (**&self**) and an object, and in our case, we want **&RowData**.

The first task is to get the inner struct, **Model** so we can push items into it, so how do we access it? We use the **imp()** function which will return the inner private struct inside an object, we will name this binding **imp**.

The next task is to get the index of the item when we push it to the vector; to do this, we will have a binding **index** be the result of the closure. Inside the closure, we will borrow **imp.0** mutably using **borrow_mut()** and assign it to binding **data**. We will push the row into **data**, but since the object is type **&RowData**, we will use the **clone()** function to get an owned version of the value. At the end of the closure, we will return the length of **data** – 1, since array indexes start at 0.

The last thing we need to do when we append to the model is note that its items have been changed. We use the **items_changed()** function which requires a position, removed number and added number, so for our case, we will put:

```
self.items_changed(index as u32, 0, 1)

  }
```

The last function we will need is a way to remove items; in this function, we will need an index, so we can use it to remove an item and tell the model it has changed:

```
pub fn remove(&self, index: u32){
```

To get the inner struct, **Model**, we use the **imp()** function again to retrieve the inner instance of **Model** and assign it to the binding, **imp**. Using the binding, imp, we will mutably borrow our list using **borrow_mut()**, and remove the element using the **index as usize**. In the end, we will tell the object that items have changed using the **index** as the position and putting 1 for removed, and 0 for added:

```
        let imp = self.imp();
        imp.0.borrow_mut().remove(index as usize);
        self.items_changed(index, 1, 0)
    }
}
```

Assembling the final application

We have completed two-thirds of the project; we have a way to create rows and a model to store them in, but now we need to create the actual UI for the application. To begin, let us add the following imports on top of **src/main.rs**:

```
mod model;

pub mod row_data;


use gtk::{
    glib::{self, clone},
    prelude::*,
    ResponseType,
};

use row_data::RowData;
```

Before we create a function to build the application's UI, we may as well create our **main()** function. In our **main()** function, we will first need to define our GTK application using **gtk::Application::new()**, and inside the **new()** function, we will add an application ID which is of type **Option<String>** and flags for the application. The application ID will simply be **com.grocery_list**. Typically, you would put some type of organization ID, but we do not have one. Since the parameter is an **Option**, we will put the string in **Some()**. The applications flags will be the default; we have no particular reason to choose a specific flag, so we will leave it as **Default::default()**:

```
fn main() {
    let application = gtk::Application::new(
        Some("com.grocery_list"),
        Default::default(),
    );
```

Next, we will need a way to add our UI builder to our application, and that is done using the **connect_activate()** function in **Application**. The function **connect_**

activate() requires a function as a parameter, and so we will put the function **build_ui()**, which we will write after. Now that we have a way to connect the application to build the UI; we can run the application using the **run()** function:

```
application.connect_activate(build_ui);

application.run();
```
}

Building the user interface

With the **main()** function completed, we can now start writing the function to build our application's UI. Let us first define the function **build_ui()** with the parameter of an application with type, **&gtk::Application**:

```
fn build_ui(application: &gtk::Application) {
```

The first step when creating an application is the application's window. We will create a new window using **gtk::ApplicationWindow::new()** with our parameter **application**:

```
let window = gtk::ApplicationWindow::new(application);
```

With our binding **window**, we can start defining the properties for our Windows, such as title, border width, position, and default size. To define the title, we will use the **set_title()** function with the title of "Grocery List". We then want our border width to be 10 pixels, so we will use the **set_border_width(10)**, where 10 will be in pixels. The position of our window should be centered, so using the function **set_position()** we will put in **gtk::WindowPosition::Center** to define the window's position. Lastly, the window's default size will be 320 x 480 pixels; this is done using the **set_default_size()** with the first parameter being the width, and the second being the height:

```
window.set_title("Grocery List");

window.set_border_width(10);

window.set_position(gtk::WindowPosition::Center);

window.set_default_size(320, 480);
```

The items will be stored in vertical boxes; we will create a binding **vbox** to be a new **gtk::Box** with a vertical orientation using **gtk::Orientation::Vertical** with a spacing of 5 pixels:

```
let vbox = gtk::Box::new(gtk::Orientation::Vertical, 5);
```

Next, we can define our **Model** as a binding **model**, which will later be used alongside a **ListBox** which we can also define as a binding, **listbox**:

```
let model = model::Model::new();

let listbox = gtk::ListBox::new();
```

We next need to bind our model to the list box using **bind_model()**. This function requires a model (wrapped in **Option**), and a function to create a widget. Before we look into creating the widget function, let us define the first half of **bind_model()**:

```
listbox.bind_model(Some(&model),
```

Our whole function will be inside the **clone!()** macro which is from the **gtk** crate, which is used to pass strong or weak references of values inside a closure. The reference we will be using is **window** and to define a weak reference, we will put **@ weak** before it, and define it as using the default panic (using **@default-panic**):

```
clone!(@weak window => @default-panic,
```

We will then define a parameter **item** in our closure and to make sure values are moved in the closure, we will put the keyword **move** before defining our parameter:

```
 move |item| {
```

We will create a new **ListBoxRow** to a binding **box_** and create a binding **item**, which will use the parameter we have, that is, **item**, and downcast it to a **RowData** using **downcast_ref::<RowData>()**. We will also need to use a horizontal box, which will be created using **gtk::Box::new()**, but the orientation will be horizontal (**gtk::Orientation::Horizontal**), with a spacing of 5 pixels:

```
let box_ = gtk::ListBoxRow::new();
let item = item.downcast_ref::<RowData>().expect("Row data is of wrong
type");
let hbox = gtk::Box::new(gtk::Orientation::Horizontal, 5);
```

The items in our rows will be using labels, so we can start by creating a binding **label**, which will be created using **gtk::Label::new()**. We can then bind the property of "item" with our label, and the name "label" using **bind_property()**. We will chain this method with **flags()** with the binding flags DEFAULT and SYNC_CREATE which from common our understanding, will create the label synchronously. Lastly, to build this, we will chain the **build()** method:

```
let label = gtk::Label::new(None);
item.bind_property("item", &label, "label")
    .flags(glib::BindingFlags::DEFAULT | glib::BindingFlags::SYNC_CREATE)
    .build();
```

We can then pack the label into our horizontal box, **hbox** using the **pack_start()** function:

```
hbox.pack_start(&label, true, true, 0);
```

For our counter, we will use a spin button and create it with a range of 0 to 100, with a step of 1. To do this, we will use the function, **gtk::SpinButton::with_range()** to create a new **SpinButton** to a new binding **spin_button**:

```
let spin_button = gtk::SpinButton::with_range(0.0, 100.0, 1.0);
```

Just like how the label was binded to the item, we will bind **spin_button** to the item using "count", borrowing **spin_button**, and the name "value". The flags will be DEFAULT, SYNC_CREATE, and BIDIRECTIONAL. After chaining **bind_property()** and **flags()**, we will build it by chaining **build()** at the end. After that, we can pack the spin button to **hbox** by using the **pack_start()** function:

```
item.bind_property("count", &spin_button, "value")
            .flags(glib::BindingFlags::DEFAULT | glib::BindingFlags::SYNC_
CREATE | glib::BindingFlags::BIDIRECTIONAL)
        .build();
hbox.pack_start(&spin_button, false, false, 0);
```

The next button we need to create is an edit button. We will create a new button using **gtk::Button::with_label()** with a label of "Edit". We will use the method **connect_clicked()** to add a function when the button is clicked. Inside **connect_clicked()**, we will use the **clone!()** macro again with a weak reference to **window**, and a strong reference to **item**:

```
let edit_button = gtk::Button::with_label("Edit");
```

```
edit_button.connect_clicked(clone!(@weak window, @strong item => move |_|
{
```

The first thing we need to do when a user edits an item is for a dialog to open up. So our first task is to create a dialog. We will create a new dialog using **gtk::Dialog::with_buttons()** which asks for a title, parent, flags, and buttons. Our title will be "Edit Item", the parent is a reference to the window, our flag will be **MODAL**, and the button will be a close button with the title "Close", and a close response type:

```
let dialog = gtk::Dialog::with_buttons(Some("Edit Item"), Some(&window),
gtk::DialogFlags::MODAL,&[("Close", ResponseType::Close)]);
```

We will set the default response as **ResponseType::Close** using the **set_default_response()** function while we will also put the connected response to close the dialog with **connect_response()**:

```
dialog.set_default_response(ResponseType::Close);
```

```
dialog.connect_response(|dialog, _| dialog.close());
```

In the dialog window, we need to be able to add different buttons for entering a new label or incrementing/decrementing an item's count. To declare a content area, we will create a new binding, **content_area** which will be assigned to **dialog. content_area()**:

```
let content_area = dialog.content_area();
```

Now, we can create an entry using **gtk::Entry::new()**; this will be used to rename our item's label. With the entry, we will bind its property to **item** with the source as "item", the target being **&entry** and the target property being "text". Just like our spin button, the flags will be DEFAULT, SYNC_CREATE, and BIDIRECTIONAL. At the end of the chain of **bind_property()** and **flags()**, we will build the property using **build()**:

```
item.bind_property("item", &entry, "text")
    .flags(glib::BindingFlags::DEFAULT | glib::BindingFlags::SYNC_CREATE |
glib::BindingFlags::BIDIRECTIONAL)
    .build();
```

We want our entry to be able to close when activating it (enter), and to be able to do this, we use the **connect_activate()** function. Inside the function, we will use the **clone!()** macro with a weak reference to dialog; with dialog, we will send a response to close using the **response()** function with **ResponseType::Close**:

```
entry.connect_activate(clone!(@weak dialog => move |_| {
    dialog.response(ResponseType::Close);
}));
```

With all the work done for **entry**, we can add it to **content_area** using the **add()** function:

```
content_area.add(&entry);
```

For our counter, we will need to create a spin button; like before, we will use **gtk::SpinButton::with_range()** with a minimum of 0, a maximum of 100, and a step of 1:

```
let spin_button = gtk::SpinButton::with_range(0.0, 100.0, 1.0);
```

With the **spin_button**, we will need to bind its properties to **item** like before, and after building it, we can add **spin_button** to **content_area**:

```
item.bind_property("count", &spin_button, "value")
    .flags(glib::BindingFlags::DEFAULT | glib::BindingFlags::SYNC_CREATE |
glib::BindingFlags::BIDIRECTIONAL)
```

```
    .build();
content_area.add(&spin_button);
```

At the end of the edit button's **connect_clicked()** function, we will make the dialog show everything using **show_all()**:

```
    dialog.show_all();
}));
```

Since the **edit_button** is finished, we can pack it in our horizontal box, **hbox** using **pack_start()**:

```
hbox.pack_start(&edit_button, false, false, 0);
```

With the horizontal box having all the pieces it needs, a label, a spin button, and an edit button, we can add it to our main vertical box using the **add()** function:

```
box_.add(&hbox);
```

When the user presses the edit button, we want the button to emit a click; to do this, we will use the **connect_activate()** function to our vertical box, **box_**. Inside the function and inside **connect_activate()**, we will use the **clone!()** macro with a weak reference to **edit_button**; with the **edit_button**, we will emit a click using the **emit_clicked()** function:

```
box_.connect_activate(clone!(@weak edit_button => move |_| {
    edit_button.emit_clicked();
}));
```

Now, we can have the vertical box show everything using the **show_all()** function, and after this, we can upcast **box_** to a widget using the **upcast::<gtk::Widget>()** function as a turbofish of type **gtk::Widget**:

```
    box_.show_all();


    box_.upcast::<gtk::Widget>()
}));
```

If we have all these widgets of grocery items, we need a way to scroll through them; this is fairly simple by creating a new scrolled window and adding the **listbox** to it. When creating a new scrolled window using **gtk::ScrolledWindow::new()**, we will set both horizontal and vertical adjustment as **gtk::Adjustment::None**. To add **listbox** to the scrolled window, we will again use the **add()** function:

```
let scrolled_window = gtk::ScrolledWindow::new(gtk::Adjustment::NONE,
gtk::Adjustment::NONE);
scrolled_window.add(&listbox);
```

What's left you may ask? Well, we still don't have a functionality to add/delete items, and without those, our program is completely useless. Let's first start working on the add button, by creating a horizontal box and a button.

The horizontal box will be assigned to the binding, **hbox** and created using **gtk::Box::new()** with the orientation as **gtk::Orientation::Horizontal** with a spacing of 5 pixels. This box will be used for our add and delete buttons.

The add button will be assigned to the binding, **add_button** and will be created with the label, "Add" using the **gtk::Button::with_label()** function. This function will create a new **Button** for us along with an assigned label to it:

```
let hbox = gtk::Box::new(gtk::Orientation::Horizontal, 5);


let add_button = gtk::Button::with_label("Add");
```

When the user presses the add button, we need a dialog to open up where a user can enter a name for the item and set the count for it. To do this, we will use the **connect_clicked()** function with the **clone!()** macro inside so we can have weak references to **window** and **model**:

```
add_button.connect_clicked(clone!(@weak window, @weak model => move |_| {
```

The first thing we need to create is a dialog using **gtk::Dialog::with_buttons()**. In the function, we will define a title as "Add Item", the parent will be a **window**, the flags will be **MODAL** and we will have a borrowed array of two buttons. The first button will be an "Ok" button with a response type, **ResponseType::Ok** and the other button will be "Cancel" with a response type, **ResponseType::Cancel**:

```
let dialog = gtk::Dialog::with_buttons(Some("Add Item"), Some(&window),
gtk::DialogFlags::MODAL, &[("Ok", ResponseType::Ok),

("Cancel", ResponseType::Cancel)]);
```

We will then make the dialog have a default response type as **ResponseType::Ok**, so if a user for example presses *enter*, the dialog will treat that signal as Ok:

```
dialog.set_default_response(ResponseType::Ok);
```

To be able to add our entry and spin button to create items, we will need to add them to the dialog's content area. To help with this, we will declare the binding, **content_**

area which will be assigned to the dialog's content area using the **content_area()** method from **dialog**:

```
let content_area = dialog.content_area();
```

With the content area set, the first thing to add to it is an entry for the item's name, we will declare a new entry with **gtk::Entry::new()**. Then, with our entry, we will add a response to it when activated to send a response to the dialog with **ResponseType::Ok**. To do this, we will need to use the **connect_activate()** function again and inside it, use the **clone!()** macro and have a weak reference to **dialog**. Using **dialog**, we can send a response using the **response()** function, and after this, we can add the entry to **content_area**:

```
let entry = gtk::Entry::new();
entry.connect_activate(clone!(@weak dialog => move |_| {
    dialog.response(ResponseType::Ok);
}));
content_area.add(&entry);
```

Now that we have added our entry, we can add the spin button next so we can increment or decrement an item's count. We will create a spin button using **gtk::SpinButton::with_range()** with a minimum of 0, a maximum of 100, and a step of 1. After we create our spin button, we will add it to **content_area** using the **add()** function:

```
let spin_button = gtk::SpinButton::with_range(0.0, 100.0, 1.0);

content_area.add(&spin_button);
```

We need to create a response to append our dialog's content to a **RowData**, we will use the function, **connect_response()** to create a function along with using the **clone!()** macro. We will use a weak reference to **model**, **entry**, and **spin_button** while also having parameters of **dialog** and a response, **resp**:

```
dialog.connect_response(clone!(@weak  model,  @weak  entry,  @weak  spin_
button => move |dialog, resp| {
```

We will grab the text from our entry using the **text()** function from **entry** and assign it to the binding, **text**. We will only append the data to **model** only if the text isn't empty and the response is **ResponseType::Ok**. If the user doesn't enter an entry, we will close the dialog, or cancel the dialog, we will close it:

```
    let text = entry.text();
                if !text.is_empty() && resp == ResponseType::Ok {
                    model.append(&RowData::new(&text, spin_button.value()
```

```
as u32));
                }
            dialog.close();
        }));
```

In the end of our add button's **conncect_clicked()** function, we will show all of our **dialog** using the **show_all()** function:

```
dialog.show_all();

    }));
```

Our add button is completed; now, we can add it to our horizontal box, **hbox** and we can start creating our delete button, and that is done like how we created **add_button** using **gtk::Button::with_label()**:

```
hbox.add(&add_button);

let delete_button = gtk::Button::with_label("Delete");
```

To delete an item, a user needs to select a specific row and press the delete button. How would we do this in Rust? Well, first we will need to use the **connect_clicked()** function for **delete_button** so we can configure what happens when the user clicks the button. We will use the **clone!()** macro inside with a weak reference to **model** and **listbox**:

```
delete_button.connect_clicked(clone!(@weak model, @weak listbox => move
|_| {
```

The first thing we need is obvious, the selected row, but how do we get it? Well, their reason we referenced **listbox** is that it has the function, **selected_row()** which will return an **Option<ListBoxRow>**:

```
let selected = listbox.selected_row();
```

To get the inner **ListBoxRow**, we will use an **if let** statement assigning a binding **selected** if there is something. Within our **if** block, we will get the index using the **index()** function from **ListBoxRow** and use that index to remove the row using our model's **remove()** function (making sure to turn the **usize** to **u32** with **as**):

```
if let Some(selected) = selected {
            let idx = selected.index();
            model.remove(idx as u32);
        }
    }));
```

That is all that we need to do for our delete button, so now we can add it to our horizontal box, **hbox** which also contains our add button:

```
hbox.add(&delete_button);
```

Now, we can add the horizontal box, **hbox** to our main vertical box, **vbox** using the **pack_start()** function, and after it, we want to add our scrolled window, **scrolled_window** so it can be below our add and delete buttons:

```
vbox.pack_start(&hbox, false, false, 0);

vbox.pack_start(&scrolled_window, true, true, 0);
```

Now, we can finally add our vertical box, **vbox**, to our main window, using the **add()** function, then at the end of our program, we can show everything in our window using the **show_all()** function:

```
    window.add(&vbox);

    window.show_all();

}
```

Testing our GTK application

To run the application, we simply need to run **cargo run**. However, to add some extra optimizations to our program, we will run the program in release mode using **cargo run –release**. When you compile the program, you should be presented with a similar window as shown in *Figure 7.2:*

Figure 7.2: *Start up window of Grocery List App*

If we add an item for example 2 eggs, we are shown the Add Item dialog, as shown in *Figure 7.3*:

Figure 7.3: *Adding Items Dialog in Grocery List App*

What if we change our mind on the eggs, and instead only need 1? Then, we can press the edit button and are greeted with an **Edit Item** dialog as shown in *Figure 7.4*:

Figure 7.4: *Edit Item Dialog in Grocery List*

To delete the item, we will just need to select the item and press the **Delete** button.

Conclusion

In this chapter, we explored the **gtk** crate by creating a native Linux grocery list desktop application. With the overall difficulty of this chapter with trying to find out how things work in **gtk**, the lack of documentation in **https://docs.rs/crates/gtk** and the absurd need to turn Rust types in GObjects, we find the overall experience to be distasteful.

However, the chapter aimed at showing how creating a desktop app fully in Rust can be and as other crates emerge, maybe the experience will be a lot better.

We explored turning Rust types into GObjects by implementing them as a subclass, and later wrapping them as an Object using the **glib::wrapper!()** macro. Using these GObjects, we were able to write a function to build the application's user interface and configure the different actions for each button.

Key facts

- GTK is recommended to use when developing a fully native Linux application in Rust.

- To turn a Rust struct into a GObject, you will need to implement the **ObjectSubclass** trait along with the **#[glib::object_subclass]** attribute.

- The **once_cell** crate is useful for initializing and assigning a **Lazy** value.

Exercises

1. Create an application that can create multiple windows when pressing a button. (This example can be found at **https://github.com/gtk-rs/gtk3-rs/tree/master/examples/multi_window**).

2. Create an application that has a progress bar and will start once the user presses a **start** button. (This example can be found at **https://github.com/gtk-rs/gtk3-rs/tree/master/examples/progress_tracker**).

Answers

1. This exercise is from the **gtk3-rs** repository, and we will go through its example of creating multiple sub windows using a button and notifying the user events happening on the main window. To begin, we will create a new project and add the **gtk** crate:

```
$ cargo new multi_windows
$ cd multi_windows
```

```
$ cargo add gtk
```

To begin, we will work on *src/main.rs* and add the following imports on the top of the file:

```
use gtk::glib;
use gtk::prelude::*;


use std::cell::RefCell;
use std::collections::HashMap;
use std::rc::Rc;
```

Like our project, **grocery_list**, we will have a function to build our main user interface while the main function will create an application, connect the UI, and run the application. In the **main()** function, we will create a new application using **gtk::Application::new()** with an application id of "**com.multi_window**" wrapped in **Some()** since the function expects an **Option<&str>**, and we will set the flags for the function as default using **Default::default()**:

```
fn main(){
    // create a new application
    // id will be com.multi_window
    // flags will be set as default
    let application = gtk::Application::new(
        Some("com.multi_window"),
        Default::default()
    );
```

To connect the function, **build_ui()** which will be responsible for generating our user interface, we will use the function **connect_activate** and pass in **build_ui** so when the program starts the function will be called:

```
    // connect the ui to the application
    application.connect_activate(build_ui);
```

After we connect the user interface of the application, we can finally run the application and that is simply done using the **run()** function:

```
    // run the application
    application.run();
}
```

Before we start creating our user interface with the function, **build_ui()**, we have some helper functions to create to make our life easier. The first function we will write is to create the application's main window, **create_main_window()**. We expect an application (type **&gtk::Application**) and we will return the main window or a **gtk::ApplicationWindow**:

```
fn create_main_window(application: &gtk::Application) ->
gtk::ApplicationWindow{
```

The first step is easy; we will create a new application window using **gtk::ApplicationWindow::new()** which will expect an application. After we have created a new application window, we need to set a title, "Multi Window" using the **set_title()** function, after that we will need to set the default size of the application using **set_default_size()**, we will settle with 400 x 320 pixels or a height of 400 pixels, and a width of 320 pixels. The window should be centered and to do this, we will set the position as center with **gtk::WindowPosition::Center** in the **set_position()** function. After we have set these configurations, we can show everything and return the application window:

```
let window = gtk::ApplicationWindow::new(application);
// set the title
window.set_title("Multi Window");
// set default size
window.set_default_size(400, 320);
// make the window centered
window.set_position(gtk::WindowPosition::Center);
// show everything
window.show_all();
window
}
```

The next helper function we will create is for generating ID numbers, **generate_new_id()**, we will simply assign ID's starting from 0 and incrementing 1 from there. Since we will be using hashmaps for storing our windows with their respective ID, we can simply use a **while** loop checking if a value exists for our ID; if so, we will keep incrementing until we get a **None** value, this is by chaining the **get()** function with the ID which will return an **Option<Value>**, and using the **is_some()** which will return **true** if the value isn't **None** and **false** if it is:

```
fn generate_new_id(windows: &HashMap<usize,
glib::WeakRef<gtk::Window>>) -> usize{
    let mut id = 0;
    while windows.get(&id).is_some(){
        id += 1
    }
    id
}
```

The last helper function is to help create new sub windows, **create_sub_window()**, we will need a reference to the application, a title for the sub window, an entry from the main window, an ID, and a reference to the windows. A little note on the windows because we will need to clone, and borrow the windows quite often, the inner **HashMap** is wrapped in **a** reference counter, and reference cell (**Rc<RefCell<>>**):

```
fn   create_sub_window(application:   &gtk::Application,   title:
&str,   main_window_entry:   &gtk::Entry,   id:   usize,   windows:
&Rc<RefCell<HashMap<usize, glib::WeakRef<gtk::Window>>>>){
```

We want these new subwindows to be top level windows, so we will create a new binding, **window** which will be a **gtk::Window** and created using it's **new()** method which requires a type, which we will pass in **gtk::WindowType::Toplevel** as we would like it to be:

```
let window = gtk::Window::new(gtk::WindowType::Toplevel);
```

With our new sub window, we can add it to our main application using the **add_window()** function by borrowing **window**:

```
application.add_window(&window);
```

Just like how we have been creating windows this chapter, we will need to set a title (using **set_title()**) and set a default size for the window (using **set_default_size()**), for the title, we will use our parameter **title**, while the default size will be the same as the main window, 400 x 320 pixels:

```
window.set_title(title);

window.set_default_size(400, 320);
```

When the user closes our sub window, we want the entry of the window to be removed, so we will use the **connect_delete_event()** function with the **glib::clone!()** macro inside. We will use a weak reference to windows and have the default return be **Inhibit(false)**, which means we will not inhibit the default signal handlers:

```
window.connect_delete_event(
```

```
        glib::clone!(@weak windows => @default-return Inhibit(false),
move |_, _| {
```

Inside this block, we will need to mutually borrow **windows** so we can remove the entry using our parameter **id** and the **remove()** method. After we have removed the entry, we will return **Inhibit(false)**:

```
windows.borrow_mut().remove(&id);
```

```
        Inhibit(false)
```

```
    }),
```

```
  );
```

Inside the sub window, we want a button that when clicked will notify the main window which sub window has been clicked. Let's first create the button with a label using the function, **gtk::Button::with_label()**, the label will be named "Notify main window with ID *foo*" where *foo* will be the ID number:

```
    let button = gtk::Button::with_label(
```

```
&format!("Notify main window with id {}", id));
```

Our next task is to make our button useful; to do this, we will use the **connect_ clicked()** function. Inside the function, we will need a weak reference to our parameter, **main_window_entry** so we can set our notification inside its buffer. To set our notification inside of **main_window_entry**'s buffer, we will need to use the **buffer()** method to have access to its buffer, and chain the method with **set_text()** to place our notification, all of this being inside of **glib::clone!()**'s block:

```
button.connect_clicked(glib::clone!(@weak   main_window_entry   =>
move |_| {
```

```
        // When the button is clicked, let's write it on the main
window's entry!
```

```
        main_window_entry.buffer().set_text(&format!("sub window
{} clicked", id));
```

```
    }));
```

With the functionality of our button completed, we can add it to our **window** using the **add()** function. After this, we can show everything on our window and we will need to add the sub window into our hashmap, **windows**. To add a new sub window into **windows**, we will first need to mutably borrow it using the **borrow_mut()** function and chain the method with the **insert()** function, where **id** will be the key, and we will create a weak reference to **gtk::Window** using the **downgrade()** method:

```
window.add(&button);


window.show_all();
// Once the new window has been created,
// we put it into our hashmap so we can update its
// title when needed.
windows.borrow_mut().insert(id, window.downgrade());
}
```

With everything we have written so far, they are all completely useless if we don't have a way to use them, and that's where the function, **build_ui()** comes in which will generate the application's user interface. The function will only require one parameter which will be a reference to our main application, which is already done when we pass it through **connect_activate()** in our **main()** function:

```
fn build_ui(application: &gtk::Application){
```

The first thing we must do is initialize our collection of sub windows which will all be kept inside a hashmap with an ID as a key (type **usize**) and a weak reference to a **gtk::Window** (type **glib::WeakRef<gtk::Window>**. Since we will need to share this hashmap, and borrow it often we will wrap the hashmap inside a reference counter and reference cell:

```
// our windows will be stored in a hashmap
 let windows: Rc<RefCell<HashMap<usize, glib::WeakRef<gtk::Window>>>>
= Rc::new(RefCell::new(HashMap::new()));
```

Our main window is created using our helper function, **create_main_window()** which will require our parameter, and **application** and assigned to the binding, **window**:

```
// we will assign our main window using the function create_main_
window()
    let window = create_main_window(application);
```

Changing each sub window's title is too much of a chore, so why don't we make an entry and allow it to update all of the sub window's titles at once. First, we will create a new entry using **gtk::Entry::new()** and after assign it a placeholder text telling the user that it can update all of the titles; this is done using the **set_placeholder_text()** function:

```
// allow all sub window's title to change at once
let windows_title_entry = gtk::Entry::new();
// set placeholder for the entry
 windows_title_entry.set_placeholder_text(Some("Update  all  sub-
window's titles"));
```

When the entry has noticed a change, we will update all the sub window's titles; to start this, we will use the function, **connect_changed()** which will allow us to configure an event when the entry has been changed and we will use the **glib::clone!()** macro to have a weak reference to our windows (since we need to update all of their titles) and a parameter, **windows_title_entry** which will be the entry from the user:

```
 windows_title_entry.connect_changed(glib::clone!( @weak windows
=> move |windows_title_entry|{
```

To get the text from the entry, we will need to grab it from the entry's buffer using the **buffer()** method and receive the inner text using the **text()** method:

```
// get the entry's text from the buffer
let text = windows_title_entry.buffer().text();
```

To change the titles for our sub windows, we will need to iterate through each of the sub window by borrowing **windows** using the **borrow()** method and chaining it with the **values()** method to get each of the **WeakRef<gtk::Window>**. Each **window** we will be getting in our iterator will be an **Option**, so we will use an **if let** statement to only handle values that have **Some(w)** where **w** is a **WeakRef<gtk::Window>**, and we will upgrade it to a **gtk::Window** using the **upgrade()** method. With each window, we can then set the title by borrowing **text** and using the **set_title()** method:

```
 for window in windows.borrow().values(){
            if let Some(w) = window.upgrade(){
                w.set_title(&text)
            }
        }
    }));
```

When a user clicks on a sub window, we want an entry to notify the user in our main window that sub window *foo* has been clicked, where *foo* is the ID.

To get started, we will create a new entry using **gtk::Entry::new()** and assign it to a binding, **entry**. With **entry**, we will make it unable to be edited using the **set_editable()** method and putting in false, and we will put a placeholder on it using the **set_placeholder_text()** method:

```
// create a new entry for notifications
let entry = gtk::Entry::new();
// make it unable to be edited
entry.set_editable(false);
   entry.set_placeholder_text(Some("Event notifications will be
sent here"));
```

We keep talking about creating sub windows, but we still don't have a way to create any, well that's because we need a button! The button in question will be created using **gtk::Button::with_label()** with a label telling the user to create a new window:

```
// create a button to create subwindows
let button = gtk::Button::with_label("Create a new window");
```

To create a new sub window, we will need to create an event when the button is clicked, so we will utilize the **connect_clicked()** function, and we will use the **glib::clone!()** macro to have weak references to the **windows_title_entry**, **entry** and **application**:

```
button.connect_clicked(
        glib::clone!(@weak windows_title_entry, @weak entry, @weak
application => move |_| {
```

Inside we will first need to generate a new ID for our sub window, this is done using our helper function, **generate_new_id()** by borrowing **windows** and using the **borrow()** function to access the inner **HashMap**. Next, we will need to create a new sub window; this is done by using the helper function, **create_sub_window()**. This function will require a reference to our application, a title which is retrieved from the **windows_title_entry**'s buffer and chained with the **text()** method, a reference to the entry (so we can set a notification for), an ID to assign to the sub-window and a reference to **windows** so we can add it to the **HashMap**:

```
        let id = generate_new_id(&windows.borrow());
            create_sub_window(&application,
                &windows_title_entry.buffer().text(),
                &entry,
```

```
                id,
                &windows
            );
        })
    );
```

We will create a **Box** to store all of our buttons/entries, the orientation will be vertical using **gtk::Orientation::Vertical** with a spacing of 5 pixels:

```
// create a layout to add all of the widgets to
let layout = gtk::Box::new(gtk::Orientation::Vertical, 5);
```

If we observe a preview our application in *Figure 7.5*, we can see how we want the order of our widgets:

1. The windows title entry.

2. The button to create a new sub window.

3. The notification entry.

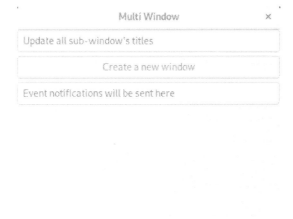

Figure 7.5: *Preview of Multi Window Application*

As we have listed, we will add each of these widgets by using the **add()** method from the binding, **layout**. After we are done adding our pieces to **layout**, we can add **layout** to our main window with the **add()** method as well, after this we can show everything using the **show_all()** method:

```
// add window's title entry
layout.add(&windows_title_entry);
```

```
// add our subwindow create button
layout.add(&button);
// add the notification entries
layout.add(&entry);
// add the layout to main window
window.add(&layout);
// show everything
window.show_all()
}
```

With the **build_ui()** function completed, we can compile and run our program. As we have done before, for some extra optimizations to our program, we will run the program in **release** mode using **cargo run --release**.

If we create a sub window and click it, we will see our notification on the main window as shown in *Figure 7.6*:

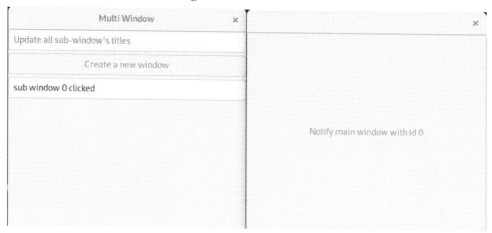

Figure 7.6: Multi Window Notification View

If you wanted this program to be even crazier, you could make the sub windows also have buttons to create a sub window and have some type of manager to deal with the different layers.

Another way to improve this program is to make your main window a sort of window manager, what I propose is every time a sub window is created, a new button would be created, which you could edit their name, ID, and close it (send a shutdown signal to window *foo*).

2. This exercise like our project and previous exercise is from the examples directory from the **gtk3-rs** repository. The goal of the application is for the user to be able to press a start button and for a progress bar to run and report that a task has been completed. If this makes absolutely no sense, don't worry we will be able to see it in action once we write our program, and unlike the other ones this follows a different strategy for writing our application.

Before we even consider something complicated, let's start with the basics of creating our application and adding **gtk** as a dependency:

```
$ cargo new progress_tracker
$ cd progress_tracker
$ cargo add gtk
```

To begin, let's head over to our main file in *src/main.rs* and add the following imports on the top of the file:

```
use gtk::prelude::*;
use gtk::{gio, glib};


use std::cell::{RefCell, Cell};
use std::rc::Rc;
use std::thread;
use std::time::Duration;
```

Before we even work on any functions (which there will be quite a bit of), let's create some structs that will help us create the application's UI and progress mechanism. We will go from highest abstraction down to lowest.

The first struct will be **Application**, which will contain one public field which is **widgets** and will have a reference counter to widgets since we will need multiple owners:

```
pub struct Application{
    pub widgets: Rc<Widgets>

}
```

The next struct is obvious and that would be **Widgets** which will contain all of the different widgets for our application. All of the fields will be public; the first being a main window which if you haven't caught on yet is **gtk::ApplicationWindow**. The next field is a header; we will define our own struct, **Header** which is a wrapper of **gtk::HeaderBar**. Since we will have two different views, to manage them we will have a view stack of type

gtk::Stack, and as discussed the last two fields will be the main view of struct, **MainView** and a completed view of struct, **CompleteView**:

```rust
pub struct Widgets{
    pub window: gtk::ApplicationWindow,
    pub header: Header,
    pub view_stack: gtk::Stack,
    pub main_view: MainView,
    pub complete_view: CompleteView,
}
```

The headerbar is used to define the top portion of a window, such as the title and buttons like close, minimize/maximize. In the struct, **Header**, we will have a private field, **container** which will be **gtk::HeaderBar**, our purpose for this wrapper is to easily be able to work on the header:

```rust
pub struct Header {
    container: gtk::HeaderBar,
}
```

The main view of the application contains a grid to customize the application's layout, a progress bar, and a button to start the progress bar. The button and the progress bar will be contained inside of the grid; hence, why the field name is **container**:

```rust
pub struct MainView {
    pub container: gtk::Grid,
    pub progress: gtk::ProgressBar,
    pub button: gtk::Button,
}
```

The complete view may make the main view sound incomplete, but in reality, this view will be used when the progress bar is finished and we display that the task is completed. We will only have one field inside of the struct and that would be **container** with type, **gtk::Grid**:

```rust
pub struct CompleteView {
    pub container: gtk::Grid,
}
```

With all of our different structures out of the way, we can start working on them so they can be useful to us. WE will work from lowest to highest abstraction.

Let us begin with working on our **CompleteView**. The goal of this view is to look like *Figure 7. 7*:

Figure 7.7: Preview of Completed View

We want the label, *Task complete* to be centered and be able to expand horizontally and vertically. To begin, we will create a **new()** function for **CompleteView** and create a new label using **gtk::Label::new()**:

```
impl CompleteView {
    pub fn new() -> Self {
        let label = gtk::Label::new(None);
```

Where's the string "Task complete"? Well that will be added using the function **set_markup()**, along with that we will set our label's horizontal alignment (**set_halign()**) and vertical alignment (**set_valign()**) to be centered using **gtk::Align::Center**. Since we want this label to be able to vertically and horizontally expand, we will use the functions **set_vexpand()** and **set_hexpand()** and set them to true:

```
label.set_markup("Task complete");
label.set_halign(gtk::Align::Center);
label.set_valign(gtk::Align::Center);
label.set_vexpand(true);
label.set_hexpand(true);
```

We can now create our container using **gtk::Grid::new()** and have it to also be able to expand vertically/horizontally using the methods **set_hexpand()** and **set_vexpand()** and setting them to true. After this, we can add the label to our container using the **add()** method and return an instance of **CompleteView** with the container inside:

```
        let container = gtk::Grid::new();

        container.set_vexpand(true);

        container.set_hexpand(true);

        container.add(&label);


        Self { container }
    }
}
```

Now, we can work on the struct, **MainView**, which we need to look like *Figure 7.8*:

Figure 7.8: Preview of the Main View

The main view has three parts: a container, a progress bar, and a button. We will create a **new()** function for **MainView**, and begin with creating a progress bar using **gtk::ProgressBar::new()**:

```
impl MainView {
    pub fn new() -> Self {
        let progress = gtk::ProgressBar::new();
```

As you can see in *Figure 7.8*, we want the progress bar to have a label on top of it; we can easily do this with the **set_text()** method and passing in "Progress Bar" wrapped in **Some()**. To have that text shown, however, we need to use the function, **set_show_text()** to true. The last thing that the progress bar will need is the ability to be horizontally expandable, and we will do this using the **set_halign()** function to true:

```
        progress.set_text(Some("Progress Bar"));

        progress.set_show_text(true);

        progress.set_hexpand(true);
```

The next thing we need to create is a start button. To create a new button, we will use the **gtk::Button::new()** function and set the label as "start" using the **set_label()** method and we only want this button to be always be centered horizontally; this can be done using **set_halign()** and passing in **gtk::Align::Center**:

```
let button = gtk::Button::new();

button.set_label("start");

button.set_halign(gtk::Align::Center);
```

With the start button and progress created, we can now create a new grid so we can attach these widgets together. We will assign our new grid to the binding, **container** and to create a new **gtk::Grid**, we will use its **new()** method:

```
let container = gtk::Grid::new();
```

To attach our widgets to the container, we will use the **attach()** method which expects a widget, and values for left, top borders as well as a width and a height. For our progress bar, we want it to be above our button, so it will have top 0, width and height 1, the button will have the same expect its top will be 1 so it can be below (both will have left as 0):

```
container.attach(&progress, 0, 0, 1, 1);

container.attach(&button, 0, 1, 1, 1);
```

We will set the **container**'s row spacing as 12 with the **set_row_spacing()** function and we will set the border width as 6 using the **set_border_ width()** function. We want the **container** to be vertically and horizontally expandable, this requires passing in true in the **set_vexpand()** and **set_ hexpand()** methods:

```
container.set_row_spacing(12);

container.set_border_width(6);

container.set_vexpand(true);

container.set_hexpand(true);
```

With our container finished, we can create a new **MainView** using the bindings, **container**, **progress**, and **button**:

```
Self {
    container,

    progress,

    button,
```

```
            }
        }
    }
```

With **MainView** completed, we can start working on our header which inside contains a headerbar which is used to customize an application's header. In our **new()** function, we will assign the binding, **container** to a new headerbar using **gtk::HeaderBar::new()**. In our header, we want the title of the window to be "Progress Tracker", since the function, **set_title()** requires an **Option<&str>**, our string will be wrapped in **Some()**. The last thing we will need in our header is to have it show a close button; this is done by passing true in the function, **set_show_close_button()**. After this, we can return a new **Header** using the binding, **container**:

```
impl Header {

    pub fn new() -> Self {

        let container = gtk::HeaderBar::new();

        container.set_title(Some("Progress Tracker"));

        container.set_show_close_button(true);


        Self { container }

    }

}
```

We have so far worked on our main view, completed view, and the header for our application. How do we put these different pieces together? Well, they all fit inside our struct, **Widgets** which will hold all of the different widgets for our main application. We will write a **new()** function which will require borrowing the application (**&gtk::Application**):

```
impl Widgets {

    pub fn new(application: &gtk::Application) -> Self {
```

The first thing we need to do is create a completed and the main view; these will be created using **CompletedView::new()** and **MainView::new()**, respectively.

```
        let complete_view = CompleteView::new();

            let main_view = MainView::new();
```

We will create a new view stack using **gtk::Stack::new()**; the purpose of the view stack is that we can switch between our main and completed views.

First, we need to add some customizations, so we will set the border width to 6 and have it vertically/horizontally expandable:

```
let view_stack = gtk::Stack::new();
    view_stack.set_border_width(6);
    view_stack.set_vexpand(true);
    view_stack.set_hexpand(true);
```

We can now add our main and completed view to the view stack; this is done using the **add()** function. We want the main view added first, so we will borrow the inner container (**&main_view.container**), and then we will add the completed view in the same manner:

```
    view_stack.add(&main_view.container);

    view_stack.add(&complete_view.container);
```

Before we can start working on the main application window, we need to create a new header using **Header::new()**. After our header is created, we can create a new application window using **gtk::ApplicationWindow::new()** and passing in our parameter **application**:

```
let header = Header::new();

    let window = gtk::ApplicationWindow::new(application);
```

We want the window to be centered, so this is done by setting the window position to **gtk::WindowPosition::Center** using the **set_window_position()** function. To utilize our binding, **header**, we will use the function, **set_titlebar** which requires a borrowed widget wrapped in an **Option**. We want the application window's default size to be 500 x 250 pixels, we will set this using **set_default_size()** where 500 is the width and 250 is the height. We can add our **view_stack** to **window** using the **add()** function; once we do this, we can show everything using the **show_all()** function. The last task needed for our window is to handle when the window should close using the **connect_delete_event()**, and we will use **window** and have it close using the **cloe()** function. Since we do not want to inhibit the default handlers, we will make sure to return **Inhibit(false)** in **connect_delete_event()**:

```
        window.set_window_position(gtk::WindowPosition::Center);
        window.set_titlebar(Some(&header.container));
        window.set_default_size(300, 100);
        window.add(&view_stack);
        window.show_all();
```

```
window.connect_delete_event(move |window, _| {
    window.close();
    Inhibit(false)
});
```

With our application window finished, we can return a new **Widgets** using our bindings, **window**, **header**, **view_stack**, **main_view**, and **complete_ view**:

```
Self {
    window,
    header,
    view_stack,
    main_view,
    complete_view,
    }
}
}
```

The last struct we need to work on is **Application**. We will need to write two functions for it; the first being a **new()** function which will require a reference to the application so we can create the widgets. The other function will be **connect_progress()** which we will use to run our progress bar in the application.

The first function we will create will be the **new()** function which requires a borrowed **gtk::Application** for a parameter and will return **Self**:

```
impl Application{
    // creates a new app
    pub fn new(app: &gtk::Application) -> Self{
```

We will create a new binding, **app** which will be a new **Application** by assigning the field, **widgets** to a new **Widgets** using the **new()** method with our parameter, **app**. Since the **widgets** field has type, **Rc<Widgets>**, we will need to wrap our **Widgets::new()** in **Rc::new()**:

```
    // create a new application
        let app = Application{
            // widgets will be created by wrapping Rc with a new
Widgets using app
```

```
widgets: Rc::new(Widgets::new(app))
};
```

With our binding, **app**, we want to start the progress mechanism using the function so we will work on next, **connect_progress()**, after that we can return **app**:

```
// does the progress bar for our application
app.connect_progress();
// return the application
app
}
```

The last function we need to work on for the struct, **Application** is the **connect_progress()** function. The function will only use **&self** and return nothing. The first thing we will do is set up a binding, **active** that we will use to determine if the progress bar is active or not. Since we will need to pass it through **glib::clone!()**, we will have it wrapped in the reference counter, **Rc** and since we will need to either **get()** or **set()** the inner bool, we will wrap our **bool** in **Cell** as well (since **bool** implements **Copy** and **Clone**). By default, the **active** binding should be false since when the user opens our application, we want to press the *start* button for it to be active:

```
fn connect_progress(&self){
    let active = Rc::new(Cell::new(false));
```

With the binding, **active** set to false, we are ready to handle the event when the user presses the *start* button which is done using the function **connect_clicked()**, and we will use **glib::clone!()** to have a weak reference to **self.widgets**:

```
self.widgets.main_view.button.connect_clicked(
        glib::clone!(@weak self.widgets as widgets => move |_|{
```

First, if **active** is already true, then we have nothing to do for our *start* button. To check this, we will use **active.get()** which will return our bool, using an **if** statement; if it is true, we will simply return, after the **if** statement, we will set **active** to true using the **set()** method:

```
if active.get(){
        return;
}
active.set(true);
```

To create the actual progression in our progress bar, we will utilize channels from **glib** which require a priority, we will set default priority, and as per naming convention, our channel will be a tuple of bindings **tx** (transmitter) and **rx** (receiver):

```
let (tx, rx) = glib::MainContext::channel(glib::PRIORITY_DEFAULT);
```

We will spawn a thread that will use a **for** loop to iterate from 0 till 10 and send the number wrapped in **Some()** using the **send()** function in **tx**. After we send the value, we will have the thread sleep for 0.5 seconds or 500 milliseconds. After the **for** loop is completed, we will send **None**:

```
thread::spawn(move || {
        for v in 1..=10 {
                let _ = tx.send(Some(v));
                thread::sleep(Duration::from_millis(500));
        }
        let _ = tx.send(None);
});
```

To receive the values we have sent, we will use the **attach()** function which expects a context and a function; we have no context so it will be set as **None** and we will create the function using **glib::clone!()** with a weak reference of **active**, and **widgets** using the default return of **glib::Continue(false)** and have a parameter **value** which is an **Option<i32>**. We will use a **match** statement on **value**:

```
rx.attach(None, glib::clone!(@weak active, @weak widgets => @
default-return glib::Continue(false), move |value| match value {
```

Let's first work on the **Some(value)** case, with the value, we will set a fraction to our progress bar using the **set_fraction()** function, where we will divide the value by 10.0, to turn the integer into a float we will use **f64::from()**:

```
Some(value) => {
    widgets
        .main_view
        .progress
        .set_fraction(f64::from(value) / 10.0);
```

Once the **value** reaches 10, our **for** loop is completed, so panic mode right? No, instead that means the task is completed and we can use our **view_**

stack in **widgets** and set the visible view to the completed view using the function, **set_visible_child()**:

```
if value == 10 {
    widgets
        .view_stack
        .set_visible_child(&widgets.complete_view.container);
```

We want the completed view to stay on for 1.5 seconds or 1500 milliseconds, so we can do this using the function, **glib::timeout_add_local()**. Along with the interval time, we also need to pass in a function, we will use **glib::clone!()** to have a weak reference to **widgets** and have the same default return as our current function. Inside the **clone!()**, we will set the progress bar back to 0 using **set_fraction()** and reset the view to the main view using **set_visible_child()** and return **glib::Continue(false)** at the end:

```
glib::timeout_add_local(Duration::from_millis(1500),
glib::clone!(@weak widgets => @default-return glib::Continue(false),
move || {

    widgets.main_view.progress.set_fraction(0.0);
    widgets
            .view_stack
            .set_visible_child(&widgets.main_view.container);
        glib::Continue(false)
    }));
}
```

At the end of the case for **Some(value)**, we will return **glib::Continue(true)**; lastly, in the **None** case we will set **active** to **false** and return **glib::Continue(false)** since the loop is completed (since we send **None** at the end):

```
glib::Continue(true)
            }
            None => {
                active.set(false);
                glib::Continue(false)
            }
```

```
        })));
      }),
    );
  }
}
```

With the **Application** struct all completed, we can finally work on the **main()** function, and that all starts with setting our program name and creating a new application. To set the program name, we will use the function **glib::set_program_name()**, since the function expects an **Option<&str>**, we will need to pass in "Progress Tracker" wrapped in **Some()**.

We will then create a new binding, **application** and create a new **gtk::Application** using the **new()** method, it expects an application ID, we will use **Some("com.progress_tracker")**, and our flags will be empty using **gio::ApplicationFlags::empty()**:

```
fn main() {
    glib::set_program_name(Some("Progress Tracker"));

    let application = gtk::Application::new(
        Some("com.progress_tracker"),
        gio::ApplicationFlags::empty(),
    );
```

We want everything we create to happen when the application starts up. To handle this, we will use the **connect_startup()** function passing in a parameter, **app** which will have a type, **&gtk::Application**. With an **app**, we can create a new **Application**, and assign it to a binding, **application**. When we create the new **Application**, we have everything in terms of the user interface ready, the next task is to contain the application inside a **RefCell** and an **Option**, we will call this binding, **application_container**. The application container will be used when we need to handle shutting down our application:

```
    application.connect_startup(|app| {
        let application = Application::new(app);
        let application_container = RefCell::new(Some(application));
```

To handle the shutdown, we will use the **connect_shutdown()** function. Inside the function, we will create a new binding, **application** that will mutably borrow **application_container**, take its value out of the **Option**, and we will simply drop it, but you can do whatever you might find necessary when shutting down:

```
app.connect_shutdown(move |_| {
    let application = application_container
        .borrow_mut()
        .take()
        .expect("Shutdown called multiple times");
    // Here we could do whatever we need to do for shutdown now
        drop(application);
    });
});
```

Since we have everything already built and ready during start-up, we can use the function, **connect_activate()** and leave the parameters and function inside it empty. After this, we can run our application using the **run()** function and that completes the project:

```
application.connect_activate(|_| {});
application.run();
}
```

We are now ready to run and test our application. To do so, we will run the program in release mode using **cargo run –release** and you'll see the different phases of our application. In *Figure 7.9*, we see the Progress Tracker Start-up Window:

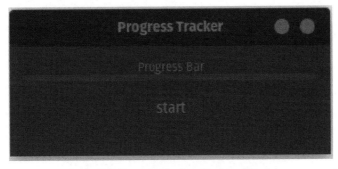

Figure 7.9: *Progress Tracker Start-up Window*

In *Figure 7.10*, we can see the Progress Bar Running Task:

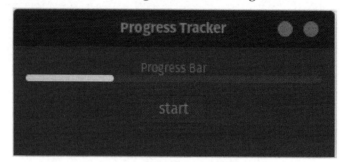

Figure 7.10: *Progress Bar Running Task*

In *Figure 7.11*, we see the Progress Tracker Task Completed:

Figure 7.11: *Progress Tracker Task Completed*

## CHAPTER 8

Unsafe Rust and FFI

Introduction

Rust itself is a memory-safe language that helps you avoid problems such as data races and segmentation faults by using Rust's ownership models. As good as this is, if someone is working on an embedded project, or using C bindings, they may need to have some type of access to the binding's memory and may want to ignore its lifetime/ownership. When a developer does this, however, they must know what they are doing or some type of data corruption could happen, or some type of unusual behavior could occur.

Being able to use unsafe code in Rust essentially allows users to tell the compiler, *"Hey you might think this code is a bit…not your style but trust me I know what I'm doing."* If you are working on a low-level program, hardware will always be unsafe, and not letting users be able to handle it themselves, removes versatility in Rust as a systems programming language. In fact, the Rust standard library contains a lot of unsafe code, but there is nothing to worry babout because they are professionals in this case.

Anything done in C is considered unsafe in Rust, for example, the use of **unions**, or mutably updating a constant value (***const foo**) you may ask what is considered *unsafe?* The following are considered unsafe by nature:

- Dereferencing a raw pointer (Raw pointers are ***const/*mut foo**)

- Calling an unsafe function (**unsafe fn bar()**)
- Accessing or updating a mutable static binding (**static mut baz**)
- Implementing an unsafe trait (**unsafe impl Send for Foo**)
- Accessing fields of unions

Structure

In this chapter, we will cover the following topics:

- Using the Unsafe keyword
- Using C in Rust
- Using Rust in C

Objectives

By the end of this chapter, readers will be able to understand what unsafe Rust is and how to wisely use it and learn how to integrate different languages into Rust and vice versa, using **Foreign Function Interface** (**FFI**). While Rust is safe, as a systems programming language, it also needs to allow developers low-level access, similar to what can be done in C, which is where unsafe Rust comes in, and we will look at how to use it wisely. Lastly, to learn how to integrate C code into a Rust project or vice versa, we will need to look at Rust FFI, which provides a way to link these programs.

Using the unsafe keyword

To declare code as **unsafe**, you can either use an unsafe block or prefix a statement with the **unsafe** keyword. Let us consider the following unsafe operation. Dereferencing a raw pointer, how would we let a binding point to another binding's memory address? We could use a raw pointer which is either ***const foo** or ***mut foo** (immutable and mutable raw pointer, respectively). But you may ask, what is a raw pointer? Raw pointers are like C pointers; they are allowed to ignore a binding's ownership/lifetime by being able to have multiple mutable/immutable pointers point to the same location. They have no guarantee of valid memory, are allowed to be null pointers, and do not automatically implement **Drop**.

If we have a mutable binding **x** and assign it with the value of 32, how would we create a raw pointer, y that points to **x**? We can use the keyword, **as** and use **x** as shown here:

```
// raw_pointer.rs
```

```
fn main(){
    let x: i32 = 32;
    let y = &x as *const i32;
}
```

However, what if we want to print **y**? The type ***const i32** does not have any default formatter, and so we will need to dereference it. But what if the memory is null? In that case, this operation would be unsafe! Well, we know that **x** exists and has not been dropped out of scope yet, so using this pre-existing knowledge we should be fine to use an **unsafe** block to print y by dereferencing it:

```
// raw_pointer.rs
fn main(){
    let x: i32 = 32;
    let y = &x as *const i32;
    unsafe{
    println!("This is y: {}", *y);
    }
}
```

If we compile this code using **rustc raw_pointer.rs**, we will get an output of "This is y: 32". For those curious, how would we have this code result in a segmentation fault? It's scarily easy because if we do not borrow **x**, the code will result in a segmentation fault and the compiler does not tell us this is wrong. There are two different ways to think of this: one reason this results in a segmentation fault is because you are taking ownership of a binding you want a reference to, and the second way to think of this is if you want the location of a binding, you want its pointer.

Unsafe functions

The difference between a safe and unsafe function is that an unsafe function can only be called within an unsafe block (even inside a safe function). Since a safe function can contain unsafe code internally, why would someone even prefix their function as unsafe? The answer to this is stability. Imagine you create a library, and a function internally has a lot of unsafe code, and because of that undefined behavior starts occurring, thus leaving the user utterly confused.

However, if the user does know the function is unstable and unsafe, they may use it to their discretion, leaving you not liable for complaints. Let us look at an example of creating an unsafe function and using it inside a safe function.

Our example will use the unsafe nature of updating a mutable static binding; one reason we may do this instead of using **const ACTIVE: Mutex<bool> = Mutex::new(false)** is because some programs may want to sacrifice some safety for more performance.

We will begin with creating a mutable static binding using **static mut**. We will have the default value as false since whatever is active should be inactive in the beginning:

```
// unsafe_function.rs
static mut ACTIVE: bool = false;
```

To change the task's activity from false to true, we will create an unsafe function, **change_active()** which will ask for a bool, and change our static binding **ACTIVE** to whatever we want it to be. To create an unsafe function, we simply need to prefix the **fn** keyword with **unsafe**:

```
// the user should know this operation is unsafe
unsafe fn change_active(active: bool){
    ACTIVE = active
}
```

If we want to use the function **change_active()** inside our **main()** function, we will need to use an **unsafe** block inside the function, since **main()** cannot be unsafe. Inside the block, we will print the current activity of our task, then proceed to change it to true using **change_active(true)**. It would be nice to tell the user this before we reset it back to **false** and report that it has been reset:

```
fn main(){
    unsafe{
    // do something
    println!("Currently task is {}", ACTIVE);
    // now we need ACTIVE to be true
    change_active(true);
    println!("Activity of task is now {}", ACTIVE);
    // do something more
    // reset ACTIVE to false
    change_active(false);
    println!("Task is reset to {}", ACTIVE);
    }
}
```

What if we wanted to turn a smart pointer into a raw pointer? Consider a heap-allocated value **box_** (we cannot use the identifier **box** because it is a reserved keyword) which is created using the **Box** smart pointer. If we want a mutable raw pointer from a **Box** value, we would need to use the **into_raw()** function; however, since the raw pointer will not be deallocated, we will need to drop it when we no longer need it.

First, we will need to create a function to turn a **Box** pointer into a mutable raw pointer, ***mut i32**. To do this, we will have a parameter, **box_** which will be of the type **Box<i32>**. Since the function **Box::into_raw()** consumes the pointer, it is wise for the parameter to take ownership. We will let the user know that our pointer is turning raw and to tell them the inner value, we will simply need to dereference the parameter, **box_**. After this, we will use the turbofish syntax to tell the **into_raw()** function that our inner value is **i32**:

```
// box_to_raw.rs
fn to_raw(box_: Box<i32>) -> *mut i32{
    println!("Turning box of value {} into raw", *box_);
    Box::<i32>::into_raw(box_)
}
```

The next function we will write appears almost like a C program, and that is to write a function to free our mutable raw pointer. We can simply drop the value, but we want to tell the user we are freeing the value, and to do that, we need to dereference a raw pointer and that is unsafe! Thus, we will write an unsafe function **free_raw()** that will require a parameter, **raw** of type ***mut i32** and inside the function, we will let the user know we are freeing a raw pointer with some value before we proceed to drop it using the **drop()** function:

```
unsafe fn free_raw(raw: *mut i32){
    println!("Dropping raw pointer of value: {}", *raw);
    drop(raw)
}
```

Now, we can write our **main()** function. We will first create a binding, **box_** which will be our heap-allocated binding using the **Box** type. Since we want the type of our binding to be **Box<i32>**, we will use the **Box::new()** function and pass a random integer like 32 into it:

```
fn main(){
    let box_: Box<i32> = Box::new(32);
```

We can create our raw pointer using the function **to_raw()**, and the binding **box_**, and assign it to a new binding, **raw**. The function will consume our binding, **box_** so that after this function we can no longer use it:

```
// consumes box and returns a mutable raw pointer to it
let raw: *mut i32 = to_raw(box_);
```

Since we have our binding **raw** which is a mutable raw pointer means that we can change its value and to do that, we will need to dereference it so we can assign an **i32** to it. Since dereferencing a raw pointer is unsafe, and our function, **free_raw()** is also unsafe, we may as well have both updating the binding, **raw** and freeing it in the same unsafe block:

```
unsafe{
    // change the value of the raw pointer
    *raw = 87;
    free_raw(raw)
}
}
```

If we compile our program using **rustc box_to_raw.rs** and run it, we will get the following output:

```
$ rustc box_to_raw.rs
$ ./box_to_raw
Turning box of value 32 into raw
Dropping raw pointer of value: 87
```

We have looked at how to use the unsafe keyword and use them for functions. What if want a struct/enum to implement a trait which contains unsafe functions? We will cover this aspect in the following section.

Unsafe traits

You might be wondering what type of unsafe traits even exist and the only things that come to mind are the traits **Send** and **Sync**. Why are they unsafe? If you recall, the **Send** trait is used to allow a value to be sent across threads safely, thus implementing this trait to a value means you must know it is safe to do. The **Sync** trait is more cautious because it is used to guarantee that a value's references can safely be shared across threads. For the most part, we do not implement this trait because if we create a new struct/enum, depending on the values inside, the **Send** and **Sync** traits are automatically implemented. So how about an empty struct?

Before we start implementing **Send** and **Sync**, let us create a program which uses an unsafe trait we will define, called **TrustMe**. This trait will have two functions: one to turn a struct into a boxed struct, and the other will use a struct to create a mutable raw pointer and an ID. To begin, we will create a file **unsafe_trait.rs** and import the standard library's reference counter:

```
// unsafe_trait.rs

use std::rc::Rc;
```

To keep track of assigning IDs for our struct's pointers, we will use a mutable static binding, **COUNTER** which will be of type **u32** with a default value of 0. After our static binding, we can define our empty struct **Empty** and derive the **Copy** and **Clone** traits to it:

```
static mut COUNTER: u32 = 0;

#[derive(Copy, Clone)]

struct Empty;
```

Now, we define our unsafe trait **TrustMe**. One thing to keep in mind is that even though the trait may be defined as unsafe, this does not mean that all the functions are implicitly unsafe, unlike publicity. The reason to prefix a trait as unsafe is the same reason as functions and that is to inform the users that there are unsafe operations happening and to use them at their discretion.

The other fact we must keep in mind with traits is when we return an instance **Self**, we need to make sure that in the declaration **Self** has a known size during compilation. This is done using **Sized**. If not appropriate and you need to remove this bound, you can use the syntax **?Sized**.

The first function will take ownership of **self** and return a boxed version of our object; we will define it as **return_box()** and it will contain **Box::new()**:

```
unsafe trait TrustMe{
    fn return_box(self) -> Box<Self> where Self: Sized{
        Box::new(self)
    }
}
```

The last function will be unsafe and return a tuple containing a mutable raw pointer of an instance and an ID of type **u32**. We will require the ownership of **self** and we will name the function **return_ptr()**. Our first step is to create a boxed pointer using our handy function, **return_box()**:

```
unsafe fn return_ptr(self) -> (*mut Self, u32) where Self: Sized
{
    let b = self.return_box();
```

To create a pointer, we will use the function **Box::into_raw()** using our binding **b**. After we have our raw pointer, we need to get an ID, and that is why our function is unsafe. To get the ID, we will update our counter by 1 (modifying mutable static is unsafe) and return our pointer and counter in the form of a tuple:

```
    let ptr: *mut Self = Box::into_raw(b);
        COUNTER += 1;
        (ptr, COUNTER)
}
```

Outside our trait, we have a function to write to free our mutable raw pointer of **Empty**, the function **free_empty()** will require the raw pointer and ID. Thus, we can let the user know we are freeing the empty struct with some ID. After we let the user know, we can free the mutable raw pointer using the **drop()** function:

```
fn free_empty(ptr: *mut Empty, id: u32){
    println!("Freeing empty struct with id: {}", id);
    drop(ptr)
}
```

All what we have written will be completely useless if we do not implement the **TrustMe** trait for the **Empty** struct. Since our trait is unsafe, we will need to prefix our implementation statement with the **unsafe** keyword and because our trait has all the functions defined, we can leave it empty:

```
unsafe impl TrustMe for Empty{}
```

Now, we can begin working on our **main()** function, and we can start off with creating a binding **empty**, which will be a reference counted instance of the struct **Empty**. We will use the smart pointer **Rc** since we will need multiple owners of the struct, **Empty**. We can also initialize a vector that will store all the mutable raw pointers and IDs:

```
 fn main(){
    let empty  = Rc::new(Empty);
    let mut ptr_id = Vec::new();
```

Our main function so far has been safe, but now we need to start storing some raw pointers and IDs. To do so, we will need to place it inside an **unsafe** block. We will use a **for** loop to create 3 raw pointers and IDs, we will store each one inside of **ptr_id**:

```
    unsafe{
        for _ in 0..3{
```

```
        let empty = empty.clone();
        let (ptr, id) = empty.return_ptr();
        ptr_id.push((ptr, id));
    }
```

Now that we have a vector filled with tuples of mutable raw pointers and IDs, we can iterate through each of them and free them. Each time we free them the user will be notified that the empty struct of some ID is being freed:

```
    for (ptr, id) in ptr_id{
        free_empty(ptr, id)
    }
  }
}
```

If we compile and run our program as follows, you can see that we get the results we expected:

```
$ rustc unsafe_trait.rs
$ ./unsafe_trait
Freeing empty struct with id: 1
Freeing empty struct with id: 2
Freeing empty struct with id: 3
```

You might be wondering where are **Send** and **Sync**? The purpose of this program is to be a base for what we will need to do next. We have a way to create **Empty** structs and have a vector with multiple mutable raw pointers to it, but what if we wanted to create **Empty** structs inside multiple threads?

Let us create a new file **send_sync.rs** and copy everything from **unsafe_trait.rs** to it; we will go through all the necessary changes.

The first thing we will do is replace our imports, and remove the import for **Rc** with the following on the top of the file:

```
// send_sync.rs
use std::sync::Arc;
use std::thread;
```

Under our implementation of the **TrustMe** trait, we will also implement the **Send** and **Sync** traits for the struct, **Empty**. With these traits, we will be able to send and share our struct across multiple threads:

```
// implement send + sync for Empty
// we want to send & share these across threads
unsafe impl Send for Empty{}
unsafe impl Sync for Empty{}
```

We will need to replace the **Rc::new()** used in the binding **empty** in the **main()** function with **Arc::new()**. We can share our value across threads safely. We can also add a new vector that will hold all our thread's join handles, and we will name this binding **threads**, and add it after the binding, **ptr_id**:

```
let empty  = Arc::new(Empty);

...

let mut threads = Vec::new();
```

Inside our **unsafe** block, we will see most of the changes; the only thing to keep is the **for** loop at the end which iterates through **ptr_id** to free our raw pointers.

First, we will need to write a **for** loop; instead of going to 3, we will have it up to 10. Inside this loop, we will create a new owner of **empty** using the **Arc::clone()** function with a reference to **empty**:

```
for _ in 0..10{

    let empty = Arc::clone(&empty);
```

Now, we can spawn a thread and we will return an instance of **Empty** by dereferencing the binding **empty** inside. After we create this thread, we can push it to our vector, **threads**:

```
let t = thread::spawn(move ||{
    *empty
});
threads.push(t);
}
```

With a bunch of thread handles that contain an instance of the Empty struct, we will iterate through the threads vector and join its thread and assign it to a binding, empty. After this, we can use the **return_ptr()** method to get a tuple (**ptr, id**) which is a mutable raw pointer of Empty and an u32. With the tuple, we can push it to the vector, **ptr_id** which we will free in the loop we had kept:

```
for handle in threads{
        let empty = handle.join().unwrap();
        let (ptr, id) = empty.return_ptr();
```

```
        ptr_id.push((ptr, id));
    }
```

If we run our program, we should expect to see the same results as before but it will go until ten:

```
$ rustc send_sync.rs
$ ./send_sync
Freeing empty struct with id: 1
Freeing empty struct with id: 2
Freeing empty struct with id: 3
Freeing empty struct with id: 4
Freeing empty struct with id: 5
Freeing empty struct with id: 6
Freeing empty struct with id: 7
Freeing empty struct with id: 8
Freeing empty struct with id: 9
Freeing empty struct with id: 10
```

In this program, we have successfully created a program that shares a struct across threads (cannot guarantee safety) by implementing the traits, **Send** and **Sync**. With the experience we have with unsafe Rust, we can start adding C abstractions using **Foreign Function Interface (FFI)** in our programs.

Using C in Rust

Why would someone use C in Rust? Isn't the whole point of using the Rust programming language with its memory/thread safety supposed to remove the need to use C? Well, the answer depends on you, but the ability to interpolate C into your Rust programs and vice versa is really convenient to many developers. At the time of writing, the Rust kernel support is expected to be merged into the Linux 6.1 kernel (thus becoming the second official language) and is going to help many different projects (like Linux on native Apple silicon).

In this section, it is recommended that for the best experience, we use some type of Linux system; whether it is native, virtual, or windows Linux subsystem. We will need a C compiler. While **gcc** is a nice compiler, it is preferable to use **clang** because of its use of LLVM and better error reporting. The other tool we will use is **make** because **Makefiles** are really useful in these types of projects where multiple things need to happen.

You can install **clang** and **make** on the terminal using the following code:

```
# update and upgrade your packages
$ sudo apt-get update && sudo apt-get upgrade
# install clang 14
$ sudo apt-get install clang-14 --install-suggests
# install make
$ sudo apt-get install make
```

How do we bind a C program into Rust? We will make use of the **bindgen** crate, which when used in a **build.rs** file (a build script) allows us to generate bindings from C headers to our Rust program. We will also use the **cc** crate to compile our C source programs and headers into a shared object file (.so in Unix, .dll in Windows) for Rust to use.

Before we try working on a complicated Rust/C program, let us write a simple program that asks a user for two numbers to add, where the **add()** function will be written in C.

Where do we begin? Well, let us first create a new project **add_ffi** using the command **cargo new add_ffi**. Unlike other projects, we will have no dependencies. You might wonder about how then do we use **cc** and **bindgen**. Since these crates will be used for our build script, they will go under build dependencies as follows:

```
[dependencies]
[build-dependencies]
bindgen = "0.60.1"
cc = "1.0.73"
```

Before we write **build.rs**, it will be easier to visualize if we have our C program written. First, we will come to the header which will be created under a new directory **includes** and will be named **add.h**. In the root directory of our program, we will create a new file **add.c**.

Inside **includes/add.h**, we will need to import the library **stdint.h** so that we can use the 32-bit unsigned integer, **uint32_t**. We will define our **add()** function within an **ifndef** block. Although it is essentially unnecessary, yu might as well as be as safe as you can:

```
#ifndef ADD_H
#define ADD_H
#include «stdint.h»
uint32_t add(uint32_t a, uint32_t b);
#endif
```

We can write our **add()** function inside **add.c** by importing it from **includes/add.h** while the function returns **a** plus **b**:

```
#include "includes/add.h"


uint32_t add(uint32_t a, uint32_t b){
    return a + b;
}
```

To generate a shared library object and bindings for our Rust program, so that it can properly utilize our C program, we will need to write a build script. The build script will be compiled and run before our program is compiled so that our bindings and shared library can be created before the program is compiled or executed.

In the root directory of our project, create a file **build.rs** and add the following imports on the top of the file:

```
use bindgen::Builder;

use cc::Build;

use std::path::PathBuf;
```

We will now create a **main()** function and the first thing we want to do inside it is generate our shared library object. To do this, we will use the **Build** struct from the **cc** crate. We will create a new **Build** type using the **new()** method. After the **new()** method which creates an empty **Build** type, we will chain it with the **file()** method, which is used to define different *.c files (the **files()** method can be used to define multiple C files). In our case, it is the **add.c**. After the **file()** method, we will chain it with the **include()** method to define a directory of our headers, which will be the **includes** directory. Lastly, we chain these methods to the **compile()** method which expects a path for our shared library. We will leave it in the root of our directory with the name **add.so**.

> Note: The cc crate uses the default compiler in your system; if you want to use a specific compiler, you may use the compiler() method in your chain. In our case, we have opted not to use this because of issues found between testing in a native Linux system and Windows Subsystem for Linux (WSL).

```
fn main() {
    Build::new()
        .file("add.c")
        .include("includes")
        .compile("add.so");
```

With our shared library created, we can work on generating bindings for our program. We will use the **Builder** type from the **bindgen** crate. To create a new **Builder** type, we will use the **default()** method; since we are only interested in generating bindings from our header, the **header()** method will be chained where we can define the path to our header **includes/add.h**.

After the **header()** method, we can chain it to the **generate()** method which will return a **Result<Bindings, BindgenError>**. To handle the **Result**, we will unwrap it since in this case if our bindings fail, the program should not run and panic:

```
let bindings = Builder::default()
        .header("includes/add.h")
        .generate()
        .unwrap();
```

The bindings will create a Rust file. We will create an output path as **src/bindings. rs** using the **PathBuf::from()** function. With our output path, we will use the **write_to_file()** method from our binding **bindings** and like before, we will handle the **Result** using **unwrap()**:

```
    let out_path = PathBuf::from("src/bindings.rs");
    bindings.write_to_file(out_path).unwrap();
}
```

To get everything accessible to us, we should compile our program (**cargo build**) so that we can have all the shared library/bindings generated for us. After you compile your program, you will notice a new file **src/bindings.rs** which we will use in **src/main.rs**:

```
mod bindings;
use bindings::add;

use std::io::{stdin, Result];
```

We will ask the user to input two numbers separated by a comma for us to add and print the result. In our **main()** function, we will return **Result<()>** from **std::io** so that we can handle the error from **stdin()**. To get user input, we will initialize an empty string (using **String::new()**) to binding, **input** which will be made mutable:

```
fn main() -> Result<()> {
    let mut input = String::new();
```

Now, we want to inform our user about entering two numbers separated by a comma. After we inform them, we will use **stdin().read_line()** to read from standard input and mutably borrow our binding, **input**:

```
println!("Please put in two numbers to add (a,b): ");

stdin().read_line(&mut input)?;
```

To get the two numbers that are separated by a comma, we will create a binding **s** that will collect the strings split by a comma using the **split()** method from **input** and chaining it with **collect()**. Since the **collect()** method requires a data type, we will explicitly declare the binding **s** to have type **Vec<&str>**:

```
let s: Vec<&str> = input.split(",").collect();
```

We will assume the first element will be **a** and the second will be **b**. Both will be turned into a **u32** by chaining the **trim()** method (removes whitespace) and the **parse()** method (parses the string to other primitive types) and we will unwrap the error from **parse()**:

```
let a: u32 = s[0].trim().parse().unwrap();

let b: u32 = s[1].trim().parse().unwrap();
```

All our bindings from *bindings.rs* are considered unsafe. This is because according to Rust, everything in C is unsafe. So if we want to use our **add()** function, we will need to use it within an unsafe block, and we will do it with **println!()** to tell the user their result. Since our function returns **Result<()>**, we will add **Ok(())** at the end:

```
unsafe { println!("The result is {}", add(a, b)); }

Ok(())
```

```
}
```

Let us run our program and see if our program works as we expect it to:

```
$ cargo run
Please put in two numbers to add (a,b):
9,8
The result is 17
```

When we compile our program, you will notice a lot of warnings from **src/bindings.rs**; if we want to ignore all these, we can use the attribute macro **#[allow()]**.

Here are the three different warnings we will see:

- Never used values

- Not using upper camel case names

- Globals not being capitalized

Although it is recommended to fix these warnings, since **src/bindings.rs** is automatically generated, we cannot constantly change it. So in **src/main.rs**, we will use the **#[allow()]** on the top of our file to allow our different warnings:

```
#[allow(non_camel_case_types, non_upper_case_globals, unused)]
```

If you rerun the program, you will see no warnings, but make sure to use this macro for good reasons and not laziness. The compiler's warnings are there to help you.

We have looked at how we can use the **cc** crate alongside the **bindgen** crate to generate bindings from a C program into Rust. As nice as this is, what if we wrote a program in C and wanted to write the future parts in Rust? Most people who have written a large project in C/C++ would rather not rewrite the whole project in Rust. In the next section, we will look at how one may go about adding Rust features to their pre-existing C project.

Using Rust in C

The author's personal experience in using Rust for a C project was from their toy language project, Mufi-Lang. The entire bytecode compiler was written in C, but the author wanted to see how it would be to write a small standard library in Rust. The advantage of using Rust in C is that it is a lot easier than using C in Rust, such as requiring no additional crates or build scripts. All we need to do is use **extern** blocks, change our library type, and set our library path.

To better explain how we will use Rust in a C project, or in our case, one C source file **main.c**. To begin, open up the terminal and do the following:

```
$ cargo new rust_in_c --lib
$ cd rust_in_c
# create file main.c
$ touch main.c
# create file Makefile
$ touch Makefile
```

To understand what we will need to write in Rust, let us begin with writing our C program in **main.c**. Our goal for this project is to be able to find the difference of characters between two files, so we will need one function to find the difference between two strings and return an integer while the other will read from a file's path and return its string.

The functions will need to be forward-declared at the top of the file. We will also need the libraries **stdlib.h** so we can free our strings, and **stdio.h** so we can print our result:

```c
#include <stdlib.h>
#include <stdio.h>


int diff_strings(char* s1, char* s2);
char* read_file(char* path);
```

The two files we will compare will be **Cargo.toml** and **src/lib.rs**. These files were chosen for no particular reasons except that they are both files. We will use the function **read_file()** to assign the variables **cargoToml** and **libRs** their respective file's strings:

```c
int main() {
    char* cargoToml = read_file("Cargo.toml");
    char* libRs = read_file("src/lib.rs");
```

Now, we can print the result to the user using **printf()** and make sure to use the function, **diff_strings()** to get the difference between our two strings **cargoToml** and **libRs**. After we are done using our strings, we will proceed to free them using the **free()** function and make sure to cast them with **(void*)** inside them. Since **main()** returns an integer, it is always good practice to return 0 at the end:

```c
    printf("Result = %d characters", diff_strings(cargoToml, libRs));
    free((void*)cargoToml);
    free((void*)libRs);
    return 0;
}
```

Before we can start working on our library, we will need to change its properties a bit in **Cargo.toml**. Using the **lib** section, we need to declare our crate's type, which will be **cdylib** or a C dynamic library and we will make sure its name is **rust_in_c**:

```toml
[lib]
crate-type = ["cdylib"]
name = "rust_in_c"
```

With these changes added, if we compile our project using **cargo build**, we will see a dynamic library file in **target/debug**. In our case, that would be **target/debug/librust_in_c.so**.

To make our life easier by building our dynamic library and then linking it to **main.c**, we will edit our **Makefile**. We will have one directive named **build**. What we will need to do is first compile our library using **cargo build**. After we have our dynamic library, we can compile **main.c** using **clang**, but we will need some flags to link our library; first to add a directory to the library search path (**-L <path>**) where our path is **./target/debug**. Secondly, we will need to add the library's name (**-l<name>**) which is **rust_in_c** and lastly, we will output the binary as **main** (using flag –o):

```
build:
    cargo build
    clang main.c -L ./target/debug -lrust_in_c -o main
```

We cannot use our **Makefile** until we have written our library, so let us head over to **src/lib.rs** and add the necessary imports. We will need to make use of the standard library's **ffi** module which provides types related to handling data in non-Rust interfaces; for us we are interested in using **c_char** (represents **char** in C), **c_int** (represents **int** in C), **CStr** (represents a borrowed C string), and **CString** (represents an owned C string) as follows:

```
use std::ffi::{c_char, c_int, CStr, CString};
use std::fs::read_to_string;
```

To make sure that the names we use in Rust are the same in C, we will use the macro **#[no_mangle]** on top of our function. Another difference is that we must prefix our function declaration with the syntax **extern "C"** so that our program knows to have this function be represented in a way C recognizes it.

The first function we will write is **diff_strings()** which we have seen to require two dynamic character arrays or in Rust terms two mutable raw pointers of **c_char** named **s1** and **s2** and we will return a **c_int**:

```
#[no_mangle]
pub extern "C" fn diff_strings(s1: *mut c_char, s2: *mut c_char) -> c_
int{
```

How do we convert ***mut c_char** into a Rust **&str**?

First, we will create a **&CStr** with its method **from_ptr()** which turns a C raw string into a safe C string wrapper, which will be assigned to a bindng **s1_cstr**. Using **s1_cstr**, we can use the method **to_str** which returns **Result<&str, str::Utf8Error>** to get the inner string, we will use **unwrap()** and assign it to the binding **s1_str**. Lastly, we can use the binding **s1_str** and the method **len()** to store its length to the binding **s1_len**. These steps are also applied to the parameter **s2**, and since these operations are unsafe, this will all be inside an **unsafe** block:

```
unsafe {
    let s1_cstr = CStr::from_ptr(s1);
    let s1_str = s1_cstr.to_str().unwrap();
```

```
let s1_len = s1_str.len();


let s2_cstr = CStr::from_ptr(s2);
let s2_str = s2_cstr.to_str().unwrap();
let s2_len = s2_str.len();
```

Since **s1_len** and **s2_len** are type **usize**, do we need to be careful of finding the difference between the two lengths, or do we? The unsigned integers in Rust provide a useful method called **abs_diff()** which will return the absolute difference between two unsigned integers, which in our case is **usize**. Once we get the absolute difference, we can convert it to a **c_int** using the **as** keyword:

```
        s2_len.abs_diff(s1_len) as c_int

    }

}
```

We have completed our first function **diff_strings()**, and now we are ready to work on the second one which is **read_file()**. We will require a path in the form of a mutable raw pointer of **c_char** and we will return a mutable raw pointer of **c_char**:

```
#[no_mangle]
pub extern "C" fn read_file(path: *mut c_char)->*mut c_char{
```

To turn the **path** into a Rust string, we will use the same strategy as we have done before, which is creating a new **&CStr** using the **from_ptr()** method with the **path**. After we have created the **&CStr**, we can use the **to_str()** method and handle the **Result** using **unwrap()**, since these operations are unsafe we will need to place our case inside an unsafe block:

```
unsafe {
    let path_cstr = CStr::from_ptr(path);
    let path_str = path_cstr.to_str().unwrap();
```

Now that we have changed our path to a string, we can use the binding, **path_str** in the function **read_to_string()** to read the contents of a file. Since the function does return a **Result**, we will use **unwrap()** to handle its error:

```
let content = read_to_string(path_str).unwrap();
```

Now that we have the content of a file, we need to be able to turn it back into something C can use. So, our first step is to create an owned C string using the type **CString** and its method **new()**, which we will handle its **Result** using **unwrap()**:

```
let content_cstr = CString::new(content).unwrap();
```

Being able to return a mutable raw pointer back into C can result in undefined behavior. While going back and forth between different ways of returning ***mut c_ char**, we need some way to make sure it will not result in a segmentation fault. Some solutions used static bindings and transmuting the data in a **Box**. However, the most convenient method is using **into_raw()** from **CString**. This function will return ***mut c_char** but also will make sure to transfer the C string's ownership back to the C caller, exactly what is needed for us:

```
        content_cstr.into_raw()
    }
}
```

With our functions completed, we are ready to build our project and try running our program:

```
$ make build
```

```
cargo build
    Finished dev [unoptimized + debuginfo] target(s) in 0.00s
clang main.c -L ./target/debug -lrust_in_c -o main
```

However, if we try to run our program, we are given the following error:

```
$ ./main
./main: error while loading shared libraries: librust_in_c.so: cannot
open shared object file: No such file or directory
```

We may have linked our library to our program, but the system does not know where this mysterious library is from. So, before we run our program, we must export our library's path:

```
$ export LD_LIBRARY_PATH=./target/debug/
$ ./main
Result = 592 characters
```

Conclusion

In this chapter, we explored how to extend Rust's versatility using unsafe operations which need to be used with caution. Along with unsafe Rust, we explored how we can use C inside a Rust project using the crates, **cc** and **bindgen**, and vice versa using the **crate-type** field in the **lib** section in **Cargo.toml** and using the **extern "C"** syntax.

Key facts

- The following are considered unsafe in nature in Rust:
  - Dereferencing a raw pointer (Raw pointers are ***const/*mut foo**)
  - Calling an unsafe function (**unsafe fn bar()**)
  - Accessing or updating a mutable static binding (**static mut baz**)
  - Implementing an unsafe trait (**unsafe impl Send for Foo**)
  - Accessing fields of unions
- To access C types in Rust, you may use:
  - The **ffi** and **os** modules in the standard library
  - The **libc** crate

Exercises

The first two exercises are to help you see a practical use case for unsafe Rust, and also allow you to have an in-depth look into how some of the Rust types we use often are implemented. It is highly recommended to try out all of these exercises, and for more information on unsafe Rust, it is always recommended to read the Rustonomicon found at **https://doc.rust-lang.org/nomicon/intro.html**.

These exercise are built to better understand how to write and read to non-null pointers, as well as understanding how a type maintains ownership using markers. We will be seeing how to properly drop pointers in Rust by implementing the Drop trait, as well as getting to better understand how types like Vec and Arc are implemented in the Standard Library (do note these are simplifed).

1. Create a simplified version of **Atomic Reference Counter (Arc)** and have it be able to clone, count the number of references, and return the inner value with dereferencing. (This exercise is based upon the Rustonomicon guide found at **https://doc.rust-lang.org/nomicon/arc-mutex/arc.html**).

2. Create a simplified version of **Vec** and have it be able to push, pop, insert, and remove items along with the ability to iterate forward and back. (This exercise is based upon the Rustonomicon guide found at **https://doc.rust-lang.org/nomicon/vec/vec.html**).

3. Create a dynamic array in C that can contain different values (int, double, bool) and write a Rust program which is able to write/print the array in a repl (read-eval-print loop) environment. (Use **cc** and **bindgen** to link the C program, use the **rustyline** crate for a repl environment)

Answers

1. An atomic reference counter is used to safely share references of a value across multiple threads; this means the type **Arc** implements the traits, **Send** and **Sync** while expecting its inner type, **T** to implement both traits as well. Whenever a new owner is created, the atomic reference counter will increment its count, when an owner is dropped its count is decremented, and once it reaches 0, the pointer is dropped.

    To begin our exercise, create a new file **arc.rs**, since the **Arc** type is created using the Rust standard library; all our imports are from **std**. To give a briefing of what we will need, first we will need a way for the Rust drop checker to know we have some type of ownership of a value; this requires using the **marker** module, and within the module, we need the **PhantomData** type. **PhantoData** is a **zero-sized type** (ZST) that is used to mark things that act like they own a type; for our example, we will use a generic type **T**.

    The next thing we will need is a pointer to our generic **T**, while in most cases, ***mut T** does the job; we will make use of the **NonNull** type from the **ptr** module. The **NonNull** type is a wrapper over ***mut T**, but with the following differences:

    o   It is covarient to **T**.

    o   The pointer is never null.

    To do atomic operations, we will need to take advantage of the **atomic** module inside the **sync** module. We will need the module itself, the type **AtomicUsize** to keep count of our references, and the **Ordering** type. The **Ordering** type is used for how atomic memory is ordered and synchronized; the memory orderings Rust uses are the same used in C++20.

    Lastly, we will need a way to get our inner value, while **Arc** has methods like **get_mut()** which returns **Option<&mut T>**; the easiest way to get the inner value is to dereference it. So, for our **Arc** type, we will need to implement the trait, **Deref** to get the same effect.

    Now with our imports explained, you can add them on the top of the file:

    ```
    use std::marker::PhantomData;
    use std::ptr::NonNull;
    use std::sync::atomic::{self, AtomicUsize, Ordering};
    use std::ops::Deref;
    ```

    Our **Arc** type will be separated into two different structs. The first will be **Arc** that will contain a pointer to our second struct, **ArcInner** that includes the actual inner data and reference counting, and a marker to **ArcInner**, so we have some ownership of the inner values.

Both structs will be generic using a generic type **T**. For our struct, **Arc** we will have the first field be named, **ptr** with type **NonNull<ArcInner<T>>**, and our second field will be named, **phantom** with type, **PhantomData<ArcInner<T>>**:

```
// Atomic reference counter
pub struct Arc<T> {
    // pointer of inner reference counting
    ptr: NonNull<ArcInner<T>>,
    // marker to tell drop checker we have ownership over ArcInner
    phantom: PhantomData<ArcInner<T>>,
}
```

The struct **ArcInner** will have a field **rc** used for referencing counting and will make use of the type **AtomicUsize** for ordered and synchronized atomic counting. The second field will be called **data** and will be type **T**; this is the inner value that we are making multiple references of:

```
pub struct ArcInner<T> {
    // reference counting
    rc: AtomicUsize,
    // inner data
    data: T,
}
```

The first function we will need to write is a way to create a new instance of **Arc** and a way to get its reference count. We will first write the **new()** function which expects a value **T** and we will return the wrapper **Arc<T>**:

```
impl<T> Arc<T> {
    pub fn new(data: T) -> Arc<T> {
```

The first step is to create a new **ArcInner**; we will do this wrapped in **Box** (so we can turn it into a raw pointer) using its **new()** method. Our reference count **rc** should start at 1, and we do this using **AtomicUsize::new()**, and the **data** field will be use our parameter:

```
        // start reference counting at 1
        // create a new boxed value which we can use for NonNull
        let boxed = Box::new(ArcInner {
            rc: AtomicUsize::new(1), data,
        });
```

Now, we can create a new instance of **Arc** for the **ptr** field. We will create a new **NonNull** using its **new()** method. Inside **NonNull::new()**, we will need to turn the binding **boxed** into a mutable raw pointer which can be done using the method **Box::into_raw()**. Since **NonNull::new()** returns a **Result**, we will use **unwrap()** to handle the error. In terms of the field, **phantom** we just need to put in the zero-type struct, **PhantomData**:

```
Arc {
    ptr: NonNull::new(Box::into_raw(boxed)).unwrap(),
    phantom: PhantomData,
}
}
```

The next function we need to write is **count()** which will immutably use **Arc** and return **usize**:

```
pub fn count(&self) -> usize {
```

The reference count is kept inside **ArcInner**, so to get the inner value we need to get a reference of our pointer using the **as_ref()** method. Since this function is unsafe, we will do so inside an **unsafe** block:

```
// get inner value
let inner = unsafe { self.ptr.as_ref() };
```

To get the reference count, we need to use the **load()** method from our field **rc**. We will use the order **Ordering::Acquire**, and since the **load()** method returns **usize**, we can just return its result:

```
    inner.rc.load(Ordering::Acquire)
}
}
```

Since we want **Arc** to be able to share and send references safely across multiple threads, we will implement the **Send** and **Sync** traits. The requirement, however, is that our generic, **T** must implement both of these traits:

```
// implement send and sync for Arc, making sure T has sync and send
unsafe impl<T: Sync + Send> Send for Arc<T> {}
unsafe impl<T: Sync + Send> Sync for Arc<T> {}
```

To get the inner value of **Arc**, we need to be able to dereference it; this means if we have value **T** wrapped inside, we expect to get **&T** when we use the * (dereference) operator.

When we implement the **Deref** trait, it expects us to define a type for it to target; in our case, it will be our generic, **T**, the function, **deref()** will use our struct immutably and return **&Self::Target** or **&T**:

```
// dereferencing Arc<T> to get inner value
impl<T> Deref for Arc<T> {
    type Target = T;
    fn deref(&self) -> &Self::Target {
```

To get our inner **data**, we first need to get **ArcInner** from our field **ptr** and we will use the same strategy we used for the **count()** function and that is using the **as_ref()** method from **NonNull**. Since this function is unsafe, we will use this method inside an **unsafe** block and assign it to the binding **inner**. With the binding **inner**, we can return a reference to **inner.data**:

```
        // get inner by using NonNull::as_ref
        let inner = unsafe { self.ptr.as_ref() };
        &inner.data
    }
}
```

The next task we must do for an atomic reference counter is to be able to create multiple owners using **clone()**; however, when we create a new owner we must consider the following:

1. When a new owner is created, our reference count should be incremented by 1.

    a. We will use relaxed ordering when updating our count.

2. The old reference count must be less than the max value of **isize.**

    a. If it is, we must abort the process or we get an overflow.

We can now implement the **Clone** trait to **Arc** which only contains one function which is **clone()** that uses our value immutably and returns **Arc<T>**:

```
impl<T> Clone for Arc<T> {
    fn clone(&self) -> Arc<T> {
```

The first thing we need to do is update our reference count, so we first need to get our inner value using the unsafe method, **as_ref()** from the **NonNull** type:

```
        // get inner arc
```

```
let inner = unsafe { self.ptr.as_ref() };
```

To increment the value of our reference count, we will use the method **fetch_add()** which expects a value to add the current value with, and an atomic ordering. The value that will be added to our reference counter is 1, and the ordering is **Ordering::Relaxed**, the **fetch_add()** function also returns the previous value which we will assign as **old_rc**:

```
//using relaxed ordering to update reference count
let old_rc = inner.rc.fetch_add(1, Ordering::Relaxed);
```

As we had already stated earlier, we need to check whether our old reference count is greater than or equal to the max value of **isize**; if it is, we are going to overflow, so we must abort this process:

```
// if reference count is overflowing abort process
        if old_rc >= isize::MAX as usize {
            std::process::abort();
        }
```

With all our safety checks done, we can return a new instance of **Arc** using **self.ptr** for the **ptr** field and **PhantomData** for the **phantom** field. You might be wondering why we do not need to clone or borrow **self.ptr**, and this is because **NonNull** is still a raw pointer, and raw pointers do not follow Rust's lifetime and ownership values. We do clean this up when the value is dropped (this is shown when we implement the **Drop** trait):

```
        Self {
            ptr: self.ptr,
            phantom: PhantomData,
        }
    }
}
```

Whenever a reference of an atomic reference counter is dropped, we must be able to decrease the reference count by 1, and when the reference count is 0, we free the pointer. Specifically, we must do the following:

1. Decrease the reference count by 1 using ordering release.

    a. If the previous value isn't 1, we do not need to do anything else.

    b. If the previous value is 1, that means the current value is 0.

        i. We must then free the pointer.

2. Before freeing the pointer, we must atomically fence the data to prevent reordering of the use or deletion of the inner data.

3. We free the pointer by turning it into a **Box** using the pointer as a raw pointer.

    a. **Box** will call a destructor and deallocate the memory for us.

We can now implement the **Drop** trait for **Arc** which only contains one function **drop()** that mutably uses our value:

```
impl<T> Drop for Arc<T> {
    fn drop(&mut self) {
```

The first step as we had mentioned earlier is to decrement the reference count by 1. To do this, we will need to get the **ArcInner** value using the **as_ref()** method from the **NonNull** type which is unsafe:

```
// get inner value
        let inner = unsafe { self.ptr.as_ref() };
```

To decrease the reference count, we will make use of the **fetch_sub()** method from **AtomicUsize**; it expects a value to decrease its current value which will be 1, and an ordering to follow, we will use **Ordering::Release**. We need to check whether the previous value is 1 or not, so we will use an **if** statement to check whether the previous value isn't 1; if it isn't 1, we exit out of the function using **return**:

```
if inner.rc.fetch_sub(1, Ordering::Release) != 1 {
            return;
}
```

If the previous value is 1, this means our current reference count is 0, which means that we need to free our pointer, but as mentioned earlier in step 2, we need to atomically fence our data. What this means is that it prevents our compiler and CPU to reorder memory around our data; we will fence **Ordering::Acquire** so we can prevent storing/releasing our data. To fence **Ordering::Acquire**, we will use the **atomic::fence()** function:

```
// fence the data to prevent reordering of the use and
        // deletion of the inner data
        atomic::fence(Ordering::Acquire);
```

To be able to deallocate our pointer, we will make use of the **Box** smart pointer, and more specifically using its method **from_raw()**. The **from_raw()** function is unsafe and requires a mutable raw pointer, so we will pass in our pointer **self.ptr** as a mutable raw pointer using the **as_ptr()** method:

```
        unsafe { Box::from_raw(self.ptr.as_ptr()) };
    }
}
```

We can now play around with our **Arc** type in the **main()** function; this is the most simplified version we can create. The standard library contains ways to downgrade to a weak reference and upgrade back to **Arc**. These functions along with the plenty of optimizations from the standard library team will go beyond the scope of this book, but we built our own atomic reference counter, let us use it!

We will play around with creating multiple owners in different scopes and threads. Here is an example of using our **Arc** type:

```
fn main() {
    let arc: Arc<i32> = Arc::new(32);
    let mut threads = Vec::new();
    println!("Owners before first closure: {} with value of
{}",arc.count(), *arc);
    {
        let arc2 = arc.clone();
        println!("Owners in first closure: {} with value of {}",
arc.count(), *arc2 *2);
    }
    for i in 0..10{
        let new_arc = arc.clone();
        let t = std::thread::spawn(move ||{
            println!("Number of owners: {} with value of {}",
new_arc.count(), *new_arc * i)
        });
        threads.push(t);
    }
    for child in threads{
        child.join().unwrap();
    }
    println!("Owners in the end: {} with value of {}", arc.
count(), *arc)
}
```

If we compile our program using **rustc arc.rs**, and run it using **./arc**, we will see the following output:

```
$ rustc arc.rs
$ ./arc
Owners before first closure: 1 with value of 32
Owners in first closure: 2 with value of 64
Number of owners: 5 with value of 0
Number of owners: 7 with value of 64
Number of owners: 10 with value of 160
Number of owners: 9 with value of 224
Number of owners: 10 with value of 128
Number of owners: 9 with value of 192
Number of owners: 10 with value of 96
Number of owners: 8 with value of 256
Number of owners: 8 with value of 288
Number of owners: 8 with value of 32
Owners in the end: 1 with value of 32
```

2. A dynamic array is something that has existed in programming languages for a long time, whether it is **std::vector** from C++, **ArrayList** in Java, or **list** in Python. But how do we write one in Rust? Well, thanks to the wonderful guide from the Rustonomicon, we will be able to go through the steps of being able to write our own version of **Vec**; granted it will be simpler and less optimized.

To explain a dynamic array in a better way, let us consider a simple one written in C; this will give us a good idea of what to expect in Rust:

```
typedef struct
{
    char* chars;
    int length;
    int capacity;
}charArray;
```

In our characters array, we have three parts:

- A pointer array to a **char.**

- The length of the array, which keeps count of how many characters or values are in the array.

- The capacity of the array, which is the maximum number of characters our array can hold.

244 ▧ *Rust for C++ Programmers*

In a dynamic array, when the capacity is reached, which means that the length is equal to the capacity, we will need to grow or allocate more memory for our array. While some languages will grow by a scale of 1.5, Rust follows the same growth factor that C++ uses which is 2, or another way of thinking about it is once a vector is full, its capacity is doubled.

To begin our exercise, let us create a new file, **vec.rs**; before we simply put our imports on the top of the file, let us go through why we need and how we will use them.

The first module we will need to use from the standard library is the **ptr** module. Like our last exercise with creating an atomic reference counter, we will make use of the **NonNull** type. The **NonNull** type is a wrapper over a mutable raw pointer ***mut T** except that the type cannot be null, and the type is covariant. We will also need a way to write to and read from a pointer, we will use the **write()** function to overwrite a pointer's content without reading or dropping the old value, as it expects a destination and source. The **read()** function reads a value from a particular source without moving its value, which is very useful to us.

The second module we will be using is the **mem** module. This module will give us functions for dealing with memory in Rust. This could be returning the size of a type in bytes using the function **mem::size_of::<T>()** or taking ownership of value and forgetting it using **mem::forget()**.

The third module we will be using is to be expected and that is the **alloc** module. Since we will be allocating and deallocating memory for our vector, we will make use of the **alloc** module, and the **Layout** type found within the module. The **Layout** type provides a layout of a block of memory that our global allocator can use to either allocate, reallocate, or deallocate a value.

Lastly, if we want to be able to slice our vector, we will need to dereference our vector. To dereference our vector immutably, we implement the trait **Deref**; if we want to dereference mutably, we need to implement the trait **DerefMut**. Since we will implement both of these traits, we will need to import them from the **ops** module in the standard library.

With all our imports explained, we can import them on the top of **vec.rs**:

```rust
use std::ptr::{NonNull, write, read, self};
use std::marker::PhantomData;
use std::mem;
use std::alloc::{self, Layout};
use std::ops::{Deref, DerefMut};
```

In our last exercise, we had our type **Arc** split into the main struct and an inner pointer called **ArcInner**. We will use the same approach and split our vector into 2. The inner buffer will be called **RawVec** which will contain a pointer to a value, **T**, a capacity, and a marker to show we have some ownership over **T**.

The pointer will be **NonNull** since it is excellent to use for arrays and so we can guarantee that the raw pointer we have is not null. The capacity will be **usize**, which must be an unsigned integer since we cannot have the negative capacity, and **usize** is determined by the systems architecture size which is important to avoid overflow in various systems:

```
struct RawVec<T>{
  ptr: NonNull<T>,
  cap: usize,
    _marker: PhantomData<T>
}
```

We want **Vec** to implement **Send** if the generic **T** also implements it and the same for the trait **Sync**:

```
unsafe impl<T: Send> Send for RawVec<T> {}
unsafe impl<T: Sync> Sync for RawVec<T> {}
```

For **RawVec**, we need to create a **new()** method which will create an empty **RawVec**. In our exercise, we will not support ZSTs or zero-sized types so we can keep the program as focused as we can. We will use the macro **assert!()** along with the function **size_of()** from the **mem** module to make sure that the size of **T** is not 0:

```
impl<T> RawVec<T>{
  fn new() -> Self{
    assert!(mem::size_of::<T>() != 0, "TODO: implement ZST
support");
```

To initialize our pointer, we will make use of the method **dangling()** from the **NonNull** type. This will create a new **NonNull** that is dangling but well aligned; this is useful for **Vec** which lazily allocates memory. Since the vector is to be empty, our capacity will be 0 and our marker will simply have the type, **PhantomData**:

```
        RawVec { ptr: NonNull::dangling(), cap: 0, _marker:
PhantomData }
    }
```

The next thing we need **RawVec** to do is be able to grow. This will be used when a vector is full or its length is equal to its capacity. As discussed earlier, we will double the capacity of the vector; however, if the vector is new, or in other words, the capacity is 0, we will make its new capacity 1. We will not support any shrinking, either our vector can grow or be deallocated (from the **Drop** trait).

To begin, we will create the function **grow()** that uses **RawVec** mutably:

```
fn grow(&mut self) {
```

We will need to create a tuple with the first element being our new capacity, **new_cap** and our new layout (used by the allocator), **new_layout**. We will need to use an if statement to either handle if the capacity is 0 or not; if our capacity is 0, we will return a tuple with the capacity as 1, and create an array layout with size 1:

```
let (new_cap, new_layout) = if self.cap == 0 {
        (1, Layout::array::<T>(1).unwrap())
            }
```

If the capacity isn't 0, then we need to double its capacity. We will assign this to a binding **new_cap**. After we have our new capacity, we need to define an array layout with it. We will do this using **Layout::array::<T>()** where **T** is our genric; this will be assigned to the binding, **new_layout**. We can then return a tuple of **new_cap** and **new_layout**, respectively:

```
else {
        // This can't overflow because we ensure self.cap <=
isize::MAX.
        let new_cap = 2 * self.cap;


        // Layout::array checks that the number of bytes is
<= usize::MAX,
        // but this is redundant since old_layout.size() <=
isize::MAX,
        // so the `unwrap` should never fail.
        let new_layout = Layout::array::<T>(new_cap).
unwrap();
        (new_cap, new_layout)
        };
```

We need to make sure that our binding **new_layout**'s size isn't larger than the max value of **isize**; if it is, then our allocation is too large. We will use **assert!()** to check this for us:

```
// Ensure that the new allocation does not exceed `isize::MAX`
bytes.
```

```
assert!(new_layout.size() <= isize::MAX as usize, "Allocation too
large");
```

Now, we need to create a new pointer of **RawVec**; just like our new capacity and layout, we will have to handle two different cases. If the capacity is 0, then we are just allocating memory using **new_layout**. If not, we are reallocating memory using our old pointer, old layout, and new layout's size.

Let us create a binding **new_ptr** that will be assigned using an **if/else** statement. The first case we want to handle is if the capacity is 0. If it is, we will use the function **alloc::alloc()** to allocate memory for us using **new_layout**. This function is unsafe so we will have this inside an **unsafe** block:

```
let new_ptr = if self.cap == 0 {
        unsafe { alloc::alloc(new_layout) }
    }
```

If the capacity isn't 0, we will need to reallocate memory. In order to do so, we will need our old layout and old pointer. To get our old layout, we will use the function **Layout::array<T>()** with our current capacity, **self.cap** and assign it to the binding **old_layout**. The old pointer will be obtained using the method **as_ptr()** from **self.ptr**, then casting it to ***mut u8** using the **as** keyword, and assigning it to the binding, **old_ptr**.

To reallocate memory, we will use the function **alloc::realloc()** which requires the vector's old pointer, old layout, and the new layout's size. Since **realloc()** is unsafe, all of this will be done inside an **unsafe** block:

```
else {
        let old_layout = Layout::array::<T>(self.cap).
unwrap();
        let old_ptr = self.ptr.as_ptr() as *mut u8;
        unsafe { alloc::realloc(old_ptr, old_layout, new_
layout.size()) }
    };
```

We need to change our current pointer to **new_ptr**, but **new_ptr** is a mutable raw pointer and not a **NonNull**, so we will use the **new()** method from **NonNull** and use a **match** statement on it. Either the allocation succeeds where get some pointer, or it fails, **new_ptr** becomes null and we abort by handling the allocation error using the function **alloc::handle_alloc_error()** using **new_layout**:

```
// If allocation fails, `new_ptr` will be null, in which case we
abort.
        self.ptr = match NonNull::new(new_ptr as *mut T) {
```

```
            Some(p) => p,
            None => alloc::handle_alloc_error(new_layout),
        };
    }
}
```

We have managed to write a way to create the inner structure of a **Vec** called **RawVec** with a **new()** method that creates an empty **RawVec** and the **grow()** method which allocates/rellocates our vector. But what if the vector goes out of scope? We need to deallocate that memory since raw pointers do not abide to Rust's amazing ownership and lifetime rules. To be able to handle this case, we will need to implement the **Drop** trait for **RawVec** so we can properly deallocate our pointer:

```
impl<T> Drop for RawVec<T> {
    fn drop(&mut self) {
```

We are only deallocating memory if the vector has allocated memory or in other words, its capacity isn't 0, since you cannot deallocate something that does not exist.

Before we can deallocate memory, we will need our raw vector's layout and like before this is done using the function **Layout::array::<T>()** using **self.cap** as the size. We can now use the function **alloc::dealloc()** which requires our pointer as a mutable raw pointer and our layout. To turn our pointer into a mutable raw pointer, we will use the method, **as_ptr()** from **self.ptr**, then cast it as ***mut u8** using the as keyword. Like our other allocation functions, **dealloc()** is unsafe so we will use it under an unsafe block:

```
        if self.cap != 0 {
            let layout = Layout::array::<T>(self.cap).unwrap();
            unsafe {
                alloc::dealloc(self.ptr.as_ptr() as *mut u8,
layout);
            }
        }
    }
}
```

We have completed all the necessary work on **RawVec**, which means we can get into the main star of our exercise **Vec**. Inside the **Vec** struct, we will have two fields, **buf** and **len** where they mean buffer and length, respectively. The buffer will be a raw vector, **RawVec** with generic type, **T** and the length will have a type **usize**:

```
pub struct Vec<T> {
    // raw vector
    buf: RawVec<T>,
    // length of vector
    len: usize
}
```

The simplest things we can implement on **Vec** is **Send** and **Sync** as long as their generic, **T** also implements the respective trait:

```
// impl send and sync for vector
unsafe impl<T: Send> Send for Vec<T> {}
unsafe impl<T: Sync> Sync for Vec<T> {}
```

We can now start working on the methods for **Vec** and that starts with two helper functions, **ptr()** which returns a mutable raw pointer of **T** and **cap()** which returns **usize**.

The first helper function **ptr()** will immutably use **Vec** and return ***mut T**. This is all done by using the **as_ptr()** method from our buffer's pointer or **self.buf.ptr**:

```
impl<T> Vec<T> {
    fn ptr(&self) -> *mut T{
        self.buf.ptr.as_ptr()
    }
```

The last helper function, **cap()** will immutably use **Vec** and return the capacity of the buffer:

```
    fn cap(&self) -> usize{
        self.buf.cap
    }
```

We can now start working on some functions the users can use, and the most obvious method to create is **new()**. When we create a new vector, it is empty so that means our buffer will be empty using **RawVec::new()** and the length of the vector is 0:

```
pub fn new() -> Self {
    Vec { buf: RawVec::new(), len: 0 }
}
```

The next function that a lot of people use is **len()** which will immutably use **Vec** and return its length which is an **usize**:

```
pub fn len(&self) -> usize{
    self.len
}
```

When you create a vector, the next operation you are most likely to use is to push an element into it. When an element is pushed, it is placed at the end of the vector. The **push()** function will mutably use **Vec** and require an element of type **T**:

```
pub fn push(&mut self, elem: T){
```

We cannot push elements into a vector if it's full, so we will have an **if** statement to check whether the vector is full (the capacity is equal to the length); if it is, then we will grow it using **grow()** from **RawVec**:

```
    // if length is same as capacity, we will grow vector's
capacity
    if self.len == self.cap() {self.buf.grow()}
```

To add the element to our vector, we will need to overwrite our pointer's memory but we will do so at the place of **self.len** which is the ending element of the vector. To do so, we will need an **unsafe** block where will use the **write()** function using our pointer (using the **ptr()** helper function) and offset the pointer's location with the **add()** method, and use our element, **elem**:

```
unsafe {
    write(self.ptr().add(self.len), elem);
}
```

After we have overwritten our pointer, we are safe to increase the vector's length by 1 since a new element has been pushed:

```
    // increase length by 1
    self.len += 1;
}
```

The next function we will write is **pop()**, this function will mutably use **Vec** and return **Option<T>** because we have two cases to handle: if the vector's length is 0 no element exists in the vector, and if not we will return some value.

```
pub fn pop(&mut self) -> Option<T>{
```

As we have said the first case to handle is if the vectors length is 0, if it is we will return **None** since the vector is empty:

```
if self.len == 0{
        None
}
```

If the length isn't 0, we first will decrease the length by 1, and then use the **read()** function to read our pointer using the helper function, **ptr()** and the **add()** method to offset us to the last element in the array which is at **self.len**. Since **read()** is unsafe, we will use it within an **unsafe** block, and because we return **Option<T>**, we will wrap **read()** in **Some()**:

```
      else {
            self.len -= 1;
            unsafe{
                Some(read(self.ptr().add(self.len)))
            }
        }
    }
```

The next function we will work on is **insert()** which will mutably use **Vec** requires an index where to insert our element of type, **usize**, and an element of type, **T**.

```
pub fn insert(&mut self, index: usize, elem: T){
```

First thing we need to check is our **index**. If a user enters an index of 30 in a vector that has length 4, we are going to either have to tell them they're wrong or overwrite some memory that does not exist. We will use the **assert!()** macro to check whether the index is less than or equal to our index since an element can be added after all the elements; if the assertion fails, we say the index is out of bounds:

```
// <= is valid because elements can be inserted after everything
assert!(index <= self.len, "index is out of bounds");
```

The next check we need to do is if our vector is full, we cannot insert an element if our vector is full. So, we will check whether the capacity is equal to the vector's length; if it is, we will grow our vector:

```
if self.cap() == self.len {self.buf.grow()}
```

When we are inserting an element, we are placing an element at a certain place and moving all the other elements after the index one place over. Consider the following:

```
Vector A: [6, 7, 8, 9]
Length: 4
Elements:
6 => index 0
7 => index 1
8 => index 2
9 => index 3


Insert 5 at index 1


Vector A: [6,5,7,8,9]
Length: 5
Elements:
6 => index 0
5 => index 1 // 5 is at index 1
// all other elements are shifted by 1
7 => index 2
8 => index 3
9 => index 4
```

Before we can write our element into the vector, we need to shift all of the elements after the index by 1. To do this, we will use the function **ptr::copy()** which requires a source location, destination, and the length between them. Since all the rest of our function will use unsafe functions, we will do all of this inside an **unsafe** block. The source location is the offset of our pointer at **index** using the **add()** method, the destination is **index + 1**, and the length is the difference between our vector's length and **index**:

```
    unsafe{
            // ptr::copy(src, dest, len) "copy from src to dest
len elems"
            ptr::copy(self.ptr().add(index),
                self.ptr().add(index + 1),
                self.len - index
            );
```

After we have shifted each element at 1, we are good to overwrite our pointer at **index** using our element with the **write()** function. After we have written to our pointer, we can increase the vector's length by 1:

```
        write(self.ptr().add(index), elem);
        self.len += 1;
    }
}
```

The last function for **Vec** is **remove().** Since we are able to insert an element at some index, we should be able to remove an element using an index as well. As you may guess, the function mutably uses **Vec**, which requires an **index** of type, **usize**, and will return the element of type, **T**:

```
pub fn remove(&mut self, index: usize) -> T{
```

The first thing we need to do is check whether the index is less than our vector's length using the **assert!()** macro; if it isn't, then the index is out of bounds:

```
assert!(index < self.len, "index is out of bounds");
```

All the next operations will deal with some sort of unsafeness, so we will be creating an **unsafe** block where we will begin with decreasing the vector's length by 1:

```
unsafe{
        self.len -= 1;
```

We want to return the old value in the vector. To do so without moving the value is to use the **read()** function which expects a pointer, which will offset to **index** with the **add()** method:

```
let result = read(self.ptr().add(index));
```

After we have read our removed value, we will shift each element by 1 using **ptr::copy()**, where our source is the pointer at **index**, the destination is the pointer at **index + 1**, and the count is the difference between our vector's length and **index**. After we have shifted our elements, we can return the removed value, **result**:

```
        ptr::copy(self.ptr().add(index),
            self.ptr().add(index + 1),
            self.len - index
        );
        result
    }
```

```
        }
}
```

While most of the actual deallocation of our pointer is done when **RawVec** is dropped, we still need to deallocate our elements in the vector. To do this, all we will do is use a **while let** statement that will pop elements in our vector while there is **Some** value:

```
impl<T> Drop for Vec<T> {
    fn drop(&mut self) {
        while let Some(_) = self.pop() {}
        // deallocation is handled by RawVec
    }
}
```

If we want our vector as a slice, **&[T]** or **&mut [T]**, we will need to implement the **Deref** and **DerefMut** traits, respectively. When we implement these traits, we will be easily be able to slice our vector like the following:

```
fn main(){
    let mut vec = Vec::new();
    for i in 1..20{
        vec.push(i)
    }
    let slice = &mut *vec;
    slice[8] = 78;
    println!("{:?}", slice)
}
// Output: [1, 2, 3, 4, 5, 6, 7, 8, 78, 10, 11, 12, 13, 14, 15,
16, 17, 18, 19]
```

To make this example a reality, we first need to implement the **Deref** trait which requires a **Target** which for us is **[T]**. The **deref()** function will immutably use **Vec** and return a reference to **Target** or **[T]**:

```
impl<T> Deref for Vec<T>{
    type Target = [T];
    fn deref(&self) -> &[T] {
```

To easily return our vector as a slice, we will use the function **std::slice::from_raw_parts()** which will use our pointer and vector's length. Since this function is **unsafe,** we will do this under an **unsafe** block:

```
        unsafe{
```

```
            std::slice::from_raw_parts(self.ptr(), self.len)
        }
    }
}
```

Now, we can implement the **DerefMut** trait which has the function, **deref_ mut()** which will mutably use **Vec** and return **&mut [T]**:

```
impl <T> DerefMut for Vec<T>{
    fn deref_mut(&mut self) -> &mut [T] {
```

To create a mutable slice, we will use the function **std::slice::from_raw_ parts_mut()** which will also use our vector's pointer and length. Since this function is **unsafe**, we will do this under an **unsafe** block:

```
        unsafe{
            std::slice::from_raw_parts_mut(self.ptr(), self.len)
        }
    }
}
```

We are able to turn our vector into a slice using the dereference operator, but what if we just wanted to iterate it as follows:

```
fn main(){
    let mut vec = Vec::new();
    for i in 1..=5{
        vec.push(i)
    }
    for j in vec.into_iter(){
        println!("{}", j * 2)
    }
}
// Output:
2
4
6
8
10
```

To turn our vector into an iterator, we will need to create a new struct, **IntoIter** which will act as how our struct **Vec** will be when iterated. We will have three fields: a buffer that will be type, **RawVec<T>**, the starting element, and the ending element of the vector with type, ***const T**:

```
pub struct IntoIter<T>{
    _buf: RawVec<T>,
    start: *const T,
    end: *const T
}
```

To allow our struct **Vec** to become our iterator struct, **IntoIter**, we will need to implement the trait, **IntoIterator** for **Vec**. We will need to define two different type aliases, **Item** which will be what type each item will be when iterated. We need this to be the generic type, **T**. The second type alias is **IntoIter**, which is the type that our iterator will become; we need this to be the struct, **IntoIter**:

```
impl<T> IntoIterator for Vec<T> {
    type Item = T;
    type IntoIter = IntoIter<T>;
```

The function, **into_iter()** takes ownership over **Vec** and will return a new instance of **IntoIter**:

```
fn into_iter(self) -> IntoIter<T> {
```

Since many of the operations we are doing will be unsafe, we will define an **unsafe** block at the beginning of our function. Now that we are free to do unsafe operations, we need the buffer from our vector and its length, which will be assigned to the bindings **buf** and **len**, respectively. To get our buffer, we need to unsafely move it since it's a non-**Copy** type and our struct **Vec** implements **Drop** (so we cannot de-structure it). We will read the pointer using **ptr::read()** which reads a value from a source without moving it; our source is a borrowed **self.buf**:

```
let buf = ptr::read(&self.buf);
```

To get the length of the vector, we will simply assign **len** to **self.len**:

```
let len = self.len;
```

Since we do not want our vector to drop and run its destructor, we will use the function **mem::forget()** which will take ownership of **self** and "forget" about it. We aren't worried about a memory leak from this since when **IntoIter** is dropped, our pointer will run its destructor:

```
mem::forget(self);
```

We can now start constructing **IntoIter**, the first field being **start** which will be assigned the beginning value of our pointer using **buf.ptr.as_ptr()**. The **end** field will be assigned under an **if/else** statement. If the capacity is 0, the ending will also be **buf.ptr.as_ptr()** since we cannot offset a pointer unless it's been part of an allocation. If the capacity of the buffer isn't 0, we will offset the pointer by our vector's length using the method, **add()** with the binding, **len**. After this, we can assign the last field _**buf** the buffer, **buf**:

```
IntoIter {
    start: buf.ptr.as_ptr(),
    end: if buf.cap == 0 {
    // can't offset off of a pointer unless it's part
of an allocation
        buf.ptr.as_ptr()
    } else {
        buf.ptr.as_ptr().add(len)
    },
    _buf: buf,
    }
    }
    }
}
```

To be able to iterate forward using the struct, **IntoIter**, we need to implement the trait, **Iterator**. This trait requires a type alias, **Item** that represents what each item will need to be for our iterator; in our case, that's the generic, **T**:

```
impl<T> Iterator for IntoIter<T>{
    type Item = T;
```

Although the trait, **Iterator** has 74 methods that can be implemented for an iterator, we will only focus on two, **next()** and **size_hint()**. We will first work on the function, **next()** which will mutably use **IntoIter** and return an **Option<Self::Item>**.

```
fn next(&mut self) -> Option<Self::Item> {
```

The **next()** method is used to get the next item of an iterator but we have a problem, what if the starting element is the ending element? In that case, we will return **None** since there is no item next:

```
if self.start == self.end{
        None
}
```

But if there is another element, we will first need to read our pointer, **start** without moving it which requires the need of the unsafe function, **ptr::read()**:

```
else {
        unsafe{
            let result = ptr::read(self.start);
```

To move the starting element to the next element, we will assign **self.start** to itself offsetting the pointer by 1 using the **offset()** method. Now that we have our value, and we have moved the starting element to the next element, we can return the binding, **result** wrapped in **Some**:

```
self.start = self.start.offset(1);
            Some(result)
        }
    }
}
```

The next function **size_hint()** uses our struct, **IntoIter** immutably and is used to return the bounds of the remaining length of the iterator. Where we return a tuple of **(usize, Option<usize)** that represents the lower bound and upper bound, respectively:

```
fn size_hint(&self) -> (usize, Option<usize>) {
```

To get the length that's left in our iterator, we will need to get the difference of our starting and ending pointers as a **usize**, divided by the size of our generic type, **T**. We will assign this to a binding, **len**, and return a tuple of **len** and **Some(len)**:

```
    let len = (self.end as usize - self.start as usize) /
mem::size_of::<T>();
    (len, Some(len))
    }
}
```

We can have our iterator iterate forward, but what about backwards? Let us say I wanted to get every item from the last to the front, we can implement the trait, **DoubleEndedIterator**:

```
impl<T> DoubleEndedIterator for IntoIter<T>{
```

To be able to iterate backwards, we will implement the function **next_back()** which will mutably use **IntoIter** and return **Option<Self::Item>** just like **next()**:

```
fn next_back(&mut self) -> Option<Self::Item> {
```

Just like in **next()**, we will need to handle two different cases. If there is no element to go to next, we will return **None** (when the starting and ending pointers are the same). If we have an element to get next to, we will offset our **end** pointer back by 1 and then return the read value using **ptr::read()** with our new **self.end**:

```
        if self.start == self.end{
            None
        } else {
            unsafe{
                self.end = self.end.offset(-1);
                Some(ptr::read(self.end))
            }
        }
    }
}
```

The last step we need to do is to handle when **IntoIter** is dropped, while **RawVec** will handle its own deallocation, we want to ensure that each element is read:

```
// since IntoIter takes ownership, we want to be able to drop it
impl<T> Drop for IntoIter<T> {
    fn drop(&mut self) {
        // only need to ensure all our elements are read;
        // buffer will clean itself up afterwards.
        for _ in &mut *self {}
    }
}
```

With **IntoIter** completed, we are able to iterate our vector using the **into_iter()** method, while we can also iterate through our vector by dereferencing it as a slice. In this exercise, we looked at how to create a good enough vector that is similar to the one written in the standard library. Some things we did not go through that are discussed in the Rustonomicon are the following:

- Implementing **Drain** for the vector
  - Similar to **IntoIter** but borrows **Vec**
- Handling Zero-Sized Types

You may expand our current exercise by following the official guide at **https://doc.rust-lang.org/nomicon/vec/vec.html**.

3. Our last exercise involves FFI with the involvement of using a C dynamic array to handle an array of different values (**int, double, bool**). We will use the C bindings of our value array to write a repl in Rust where we can write to it and print our array.

To begin this exercise, we will create a new project and create the necessary structure for our C source code:

```
$ cargo new value_array
$ cd value_array
# add necessary dependencies
$ cargo add rustyline
$ cargo add bindgen cc --build
# create directory for C code
$ mkdir C
$ cd C
# create includes directory
$ mkdir includes
# create value and memory c files and header
$ touch value.c memory.c includes/value.h includes/memory.h
```

Before we start, let's look into the Rust side of this project. We need to create our dynamic array inside **C/includes/value.h**. The first thing we need to do inside our header is create a header guard and import the necessary headers:

```
#ifndef VALUE_ARRAY_VALUE_H
#define VALUE_ARRAY_VALUE_H

#include "stdbool.h"
#include <stddef.h>

// code will go under here

#endif //VALUE_ARRAY_VALUE_H
```

The first thing we need to create is an enum, **ValueType** which will be used to determine what type a value is inside our array. The four types we will have are boolean, int, double, and nil where nil will be used when some operation result in null:

```
typedef enum{
    VAL_BOOL,
    VAL_NIL,
    VAL_INT,
    VAL_DOUBLE
}ValueType;
```

The next struct we need to create is **Value**; inside **Value**, we will have the type of the value using **ValueType**, and to have different types, we will have a **union** inside as the field, **as**. Inside the **union**, we will have fields, **boolean**, **num_double**, and **num_int** with types **bool**, **double** and **int**, respectively:

```
typedef struct {
    ValueType type;
    union {
      bool boolean;
      double num_double;
      int num_int;
    }as;
}Value;
```

To ease our lives, we should create some macros to turn a **Value** into either a **bool**, **int**, and **double**. We will need to use a **Value** and return the needed type from **as**:

```
// some macros to turn value into int, double, bool
#define AS_BOOL(value) ((value).as.boolean)
#define AS_INT(value) ((value).as.num_int)
#define AS_DOUBLE(value)  ((value).as.num_double)
```

These macros are great but what if we needed to do the opposite? When we need to create a new **Value** from a **bool** value, we need to make sure it's type is **VAL_BOOL** and set inside a block **.boolean** to be our value, this and our other types are shown as follows:

```
// some macros to turn an int, double, bool into Value
#define BOOL_VAL(value) ((Value){VAL_BOOL, {.boolean=value}})
#define NIL_VAl         ((Value){VAL_NIL, {.num_int = 0}})
```

```
#define INT_VAL(value) ((Value){VAL_INT, {.num_int = value}})
#define DOUBLE_VAL(value) ((Value){VAL_DOUBLE, {.num_double =
value}})
```

We are now ready to define our value dynamic array which will have three fields:

- **capacity**: The capacity of our array.

- **count**: The count of values inside our array.

- **values**: An array of **Value** using a pointer.

With this in mind, we can see our **struct** defined as follows:

```
// a dynamic array for Value
typedef struct {
    int capacity;
    int count;
    Value* values;
}ValueArray;
```

The last task we need to do is forward declare some of the functions we will need as bindings, which includes the following:

- **initArray()**: Creates a new **ValueArray**

- **writeArray()**: Pushes a **Value** at the end of **ValueArray**

- **printValue()**: Prints a **Value** depending on its type

- **printValues()**: Prints the values inside **ValueArray**

- **intToVal()**: Turns an integer into a **Value**

- **doubleToVal()**: Turns a double into a **Value**

- **boolToVal()**: Turns a boolean into a **Value**

- **nilVal()**: Returns a nil **Value**

All of these can be seen as follows:

```
// creates a new empty array
ValueArray initArray();
// appends to the end of a value array
void writeArray(ValueArray* array, Value value);
// prints a value
void printValue(Value value);
```

```
// void prints all values
void printValues(ValueArray* array);
// turns int to Value
Value intToVal(int i);
// turns double into Value
Value doubleToVal(double d);
// turns bool into Value
Value boolToVal(bool b);
// returns NIL Value
Value nilVal();
```

We cannot do much work on our dynamic array if we cannot allocate memory. To do this, we need to work on **C/includes/memory.h** first and its source file after. Inside the header, we will again define its header guards and necessary imports:

```
#ifndef VALUE_ARRAY_MEMORY_H
#define VALUE_ARRAY_MEMORY_H

#include <stdlib.h>

// code goes under here


#endif //VALUE_ARRAY_MEMORY_H
```

We will define some macros to help to grow our capacity, and array. First for growing capacities, we will use a ternary operator to check whether the capacity is less than 8. If it is, we will make its capacity 8, and if not, we will grow it by 2:

```
// Grows the capacity of dynamic arrays
#define GROW_CAPACITY(capacity) \
    ((capacity) < 8 ? 8: (capacity) * 2)
```

When we grow the capacity of an array, we will then use that new capacity to grow the array. Our macro, **GROW_ARRAY()** will require a type to return from our reallocation, the pointer of our array, and a new count for the capacity:

```
// Grows the array with a desired capacity
#define GROW_ARRAY(type, pointer, newCount) \
        (type*)reallocate(pointer, \
        sizeof(type) * (newCount))
```

To reallocate our array's memory, we will forward declare the function **reallocate()** which needs a pointer and a new size:

```
// Used to reallocate memory for arrays
void* reallocate(void* pointer, size_t newSize);
```

Now, we can work on the file, **C/memory.c** with the following imports on the top of the file:

```
#include "includes/memory.h"
#include <stdlib.h>
```

The function we need to work on is **reallocate()** which is declared in our respective header returns **void*** or a general purpose pointer. This is used in our macro to return a pointer of a specified type, so let us declare our function:

```
void* reallocate(void* pointer, size_t newSize){
```

We will use **realloc()** with our parameters, **pointer**, and **newSize** and store the result to the variable **result**. The advantage of using **realloc()** is we can handle cases of growing or shrinking an array. In my toy language, Mufi-Lang, this function also handles freeing an array but we will handle that in Rust using **drop()**:

```
// use realloc to handle any grow, shrink, etc.
void* result = realloc(pointer, newSize);
```

If the allocation fails, then **result** will be **NULL** and if it is, then we need to abort the program with exit code 1:

```
// if allocation fails exit program
if (result == NULL) exit(1);
```

If the allocation did succeed, then we can return the result:

```
// return the result of the reallocation
return result;
}
```

We are now ready to write the source for our **Value** and **ValueArray** inside the file **C/value.c**, and the first step is to import the following on the top:

```
#include "includes/value.h"
#include "includes/memory.h"
#include <stdio.h>
```

The first function we need to create is **initArray()**, which will create an empty for us and return it. To do this, we will have to create an initialized variable **array** of type **ValueArray**. After this, we can start assigning its fields, for **values** we will declare the pointer as **NULL**, capacity and count as 0 (since the array is empty). After we have assigned the fields, we can return **array**:

```
ValueArray initArray(){
    ValueArray array;
    array.values = NULL;
    array.capacity = 0;
    array.count = 0;
    return array;
}
```

The next function we need to work is pushing a **Value** to our array. The function will return **void** but will use a pointer to the array and need a **Value**:

```
void writeArray(ValueArray* array, Value value){
```

Before we add an element, we need to check whether the array is full, and just like in our last exercise, this occurs when the capacity is equal to our count or length:

```
// Checks if array is full
if (array->capacity == array->count){
```

We will grow the capacity using our macro, **GROW_CAPACITY()** by assigning the array's capacity to the result using the array's current capacity:

```
array->capacity = GROW_CAPACITY(array->capacity);
```

We can then grow the array's pointer array of **Value** using the macro, **GROW_ARRAY()** by using **Value** as the type, **array->values** as the pointer and **array->capacity** as the new capacity:

```
array->values = GROW_ARRAY(Value, array->values, array->capacity);
}
```

To push the value at the end of the array, we will place it at the index of the array's count, and after we have done so, we can increment the count by 1:

```
// Append to the array
array->values[array->count] = value;
```

```
        array->count++;
}
```

The next function we need to create is **printValue()** which uses a **Value** and will print it depending on its type. To do so, we will make use of a **switch** statement where each case will be a **ValueType**. To get the inner value, we will use the **AS_*** macros depending on which type we are handling:

```
void printValue(Value value) {
    switch (value.type) {
        case VAL_BOOL:
            printf(AS_BOOL(value) ? "true\n" : "false\n");
            break;
        case VAL_NIL:
            printf("nil\n");
            break;
        case VAL_DOUBLE:
            printf("%g\n", AS_DOUBLE(value));
            break;
        case VAL_INT:
            printf("%d\n", AS_INT(value));
            break;
    }
}
```

To make our life easier for printing every value in a given array, we will write the function, **printValues()**. This function will use a pointer of a **ValueArray** and use a **for** loop to print every value in the array using **printValue()**:

```
void printValues(ValueArray* array){
    for(int i=0; i < array->count; i++){
        printValue(array->values[i]);
    }
}
```

Since **bindgen** won't create bindings to our C macros, we will disguise our macros to turn a type into a **Value** with the functions, **intToVal()**, **doubleToVal()**, **boolToVal()**, and **nilVal()**:

```
Value intToVal(int i){
```

```
    return INT_VAL(i);
}
Value doubleToVal(double d){
    return DOUBLE_VAL(d);
}
Value boolToVal(bool b){
    return BOOL_VAL(b);
}


Value nilVal(){
    return NIL_VAl;
}
```

With the C side of the project finished, we need to start looking at the Rust side of our project, and that starts with generating our C bindings using a build script. In the root of our project, create a file, **build.rs** and add the following imports on the top of the file:

```
use cc::Build;
use bindgen::Builder;
use std::path::PathBuf;
```

In our build script, we need to first compile a shared library using the **Build** type from the **cc** crate. We will create a new **Build** type using the **new()** method. To add our C source files, we will chain the **files()** method defining an array of our two paths, **C/value.c** and **C/memory.c**. Next, we need to define the directory of our headers, and we will chain the **include()** method with the path, **C/includes**, after which we can compile to **value_array.so** by ending the chain with the **compile()** method:

```
fn main() {
    Build::new()
        .files(["C/value.c", "C/memory.c"])
        .include("C/includes")
        .compile("value_array.so");
```

Now that we have our shared library, we are free to start generating bindings. The only header we care about using is **C/includes/value.h**. To create a new **Bindings** type from **bindgen**, we will use **Builder::default()** to create a default **Builder** type, after which we will chain the **header()** method using the path previously mentioned. After we have our header, we can generate the bindings by chaining the **generate()** method, since it returns a **Result**, we will end the chain with the **unwrap()** function:

```
let bindings = Builder::default()
    .header("C/includes/value.h")
    .generate()
    .unwrap();
```

We can now define an output path for our bindings file; we will simply have it in **src/bindings.rs**. After we have defined our output path, we will use the **write_to_file()** method from **bindings** to create our C bindings:

```
let out_path = PathBuf::from("src/bindings.rs");
bindings.write_to_file(out_path).unwrap()
}
```

Before we continue, its best to generate our bindings and to do so, we will run **cargo build**. After we build our project, we can head over to **src/main.rs** and add the following imports and macros:

```
#[allow(non_upper_case_globals, non_camel_case_types)]
#[allow(unused)]
mod bindings;

use std::ffi::c_int;
use bindings::{ValueArray, Value, initArray, writeArray,
printValues};
use bindings::{intToVal, doubleToVal, boolToVal, nilVal};
use rustyline::Editor;
```

How do we want our repl system to work? We need these three commands:

- **{type} : {value}**: Inserts a new value into our array with specified type.

- **print**: Prints all of the values in our array.

- **exit:** Exits the repl environment.

If the user does not enter any of these commands, we will say that the command is invalid.

When a user does our first command to insert a new value into our array, we need to create a way we can parse our string and return a **Value**. To do this, we will create the unsafe function, **get_value()**. As mentioned, this function will take a **String** and return a **Value**:

```
unsafe fn get_value(string: String) -> Value{
```

The first thing we need to do is split our string into 2 from the colon, and we will make sure that when we split the string and collect it; the length should be 2. If a user tries to do something like "int:76 int:89", we will return **nil**:

```
let s: Vec<&str> = string.split(":").collect();
if s.len() != 2{
    return nilVal();
}
```

Now, we can store our first element in **s** as **type_** and the second element as **value**, making sure that we use the **trim()** method on them to clear any extra whitespace:

```
let type_ = s[0].trim();
let value = s[1].trim();
```

To handle the different type cases, we will use a **match** statement on the binding, **type_** where we will handle the cases of "int", "double", "bool", and a default that returns **nil**. For each type, we will create a new binding, **value**, and use the **parse()** method and **unwrap()** on the string **value**. After we can use ***ToVal()** depending on the type to return a **Value** type, while for most we can directly pass in **value**, **intToVal()** required **value** to be casted as a **c_int**:

```
match type_{
    "int" => {
        let value: i32 = value.parse().unwrap();
        intToVal(value as c_int)
    }
    "double" => {
        let value: f64 = value.parse().unwrap();
        doubleToVal(value)
    }
    "bool" => {
        let value: bool = value.parse().unwrap();
        boolToVal(value)
    }
    _=> nilVal()
}
}
```

We can start working on our **main()** function where we will return **rustyline::Result<()>**. The use of this **Result** is so we can properly handle any error when we create a new **Editor**, which is the first thing we will create using its **new()** method:

```
fn main() -> rustyline::Result<()>{
    let mut rl = Editor::<()>::new()?;
```

After this, a lot of what we will do is unsafe so we will create an **unsafe** block. Inside the block, we will first need to create a mutable binding **va** which will be a new **ValueArray** using the **initArray()** function. But our functions require ***mut ValueArray** so we will create a new binding, **value_array** which will mutably borrow **va** as a ***mut ValueArray**:

```
unsafe {
    let mut va = initArray();
    let value_array = &mut va as *mut ValueArray;
```

To get our repl environment to run until we get the **exit** command is to use a **loop** statement. This will have our **loop** run indefinitely until the user exits the program. We will read the line using the **readline()** method with the prompt as >>:

```
loop {
    let readline = rl.readline(">> ");
```

The **readline()** method returns a **Result** which we will handle using a **match** statement; either we have an **Ok(line)** where will handle after or an **Err** which we will say there is no input:

```
match readline {
    Ok(line) => {
        // TODO Next
    }
    Err(_) => println!("No input")
    }
}
```

To handle our **line**, we will use an **if/else** statement to handle our 3 different commands. The first command we need to handle is a user inputting a new **Value** into our array. To check whether a user is trying to do this, we will use the **contain()** method to check whether the string contains a colon, if it does, we can write to our array. When we use the **writeArray()** function, we need to use the binding **value_array** and the function **get_value()** by cloning **line**, and after we have done this, we can tell the user the entry has been added:

```
if line.contains(":") {
    writeArray(value_array, get_value(line.clone()));
    println!("Entry added!");
}
```

The next command we need to handle is **print**. This is easy and we will use an **else if** statement to check whether **line** equals the string, and "print", if it does we will use the **printValues()** function with **value_array**:

```
else if &line == "print" {
  printValues(value_array);
}
```

If the user wants to exit the program, they need to use the **exit** command. This is simply breaking out of our loop, so we will print bye to the user and exit the loop. If the user hasn't entered any of our commands, we will tell them that the command is invalid:

```
else if &line == "exit" {
    println!("Bye!!!");
    break;
} else {
    println!("Command invalid");
}
```

After our loop, we can free our **value_array** using the **drop()** function, and after our **unsafe** block, we can return **Ok(())** since our **main()** function returns a **Result**:

```
        drop(value_array);
    }
    Ok(())
}
```

With our program completed, we can run the program and try out our repl environment:

```
$ cargo run
>> int:87
Entry added!
```

```
>> double:65.9
Entry added!
>> bool:true
Entry added!
>> int:76
Entry added!
>> print
87
65.9
true
76
>> exit
Bye!!!
```

CHAPTER 9
Metaprogramming

Introduction

Metaprogramming is the act of reading a program, manipulating it, and returning a modified version of the program. Another way of thinking about this is writing a program that generates code, in compiled languages such as C or Rust, and this is done during compile time, while dynamic languages may do this in runtime.

In C/C++, metaprogramming is found by using macros with **#define** or using the safer compile-time function, **constexpr**; while in Rust, it is a bit of a different story. In Rust, metaprogramming is a critical feature that we have been using since the beginning of the book, whether it is as simple as printing, using **println!()** or storing elements in a vector with **vec![]**. But we have also seen other types of macros such as **#[derive(Clone)]** or attributes such as **#[structopt(short, long)]**. What are all these different kinds macros?

In Rust, we can categorize macros as follows:

- Declarative macros
    - o Used for general metaprogramming
    - o Created using **macro_rules!**
- Procedural macros

- ○ *"Allows creating syntax extensions as execution from a function"* [1]
- ○ Can come in the following three forms:
  - ▪ Function-like macro: **foo!()**
  - ▪ Derive macro: **#[derive(Bar)]**
  - ▪ Attribute macro: **#[Baz]**

Structure

In this chapter, we will cover the following topics:

- When to create macros?
- Declarative macros
- Procedural macros

Objectives

By the end of the chapter, the reader will be able to start using techniques of metaprogramming to help simplify projects. After exploring metaprogramming with declarative or procedural macros, we will be able to determine when and which form is the best to tackle our problems.

When to create macros?

Macros are an amazing way to move computation to compilation time and reduce repetition, but they should not be used carelessly. In general, use macros when functions cannot do the task, or tasks where you will need to use the Rust syntax.

Consider the following:

```
let vec = {
    let mut vec = Vec::new();
    vec.push(76);
    vec.push(8);
    vec.push(9);
    vec.push(8);
    vec
};
```

---

1 *The rust reference*. Procedural Macros - The Rust Reference. (n.d.). Retrieved October 13, 2022, from https://doc.rust-lang.org/reference/procedural-macros.html

How can we create a macro so we do not need to keep having to write **vec.push()?**. In this problem, we can create a new declarative macro using **macro_rules!** Although we will look into this in detail in the next section, let us try to write a macro **vector![]** that will take an array of elements and return a vector.

To begin this example, create the file **vector.rs** and we will begin by declaring our macro **vector!** using **macro_rules!** The way we declare variables in Rust macros is by using the $ operator. Since we need our vector to handle repetition, we will wrap our parameter **$element** with **$()**, * which allows us to have any number of arguments. Macros have different types, to say that our elements are going to be Rust expressions, we give it the type, expr:

```
macro_rules! vector{
    ($($element: expr), *) => [
        // code goes in here
    ];
}
```

When the code expands, we want it to resemble the preceding example, so we will define our vector within a block. Inside the block, we will create a new mutable vector, **vec** using **Vec::new()**. After that, we will use the syntax, **$()*** to allow us to do something repeatedly; inside, we will push our parameter, **$element**. When we push everything to the vector, we can return it at the end of the block:

```
        {
            let mut vec = Vec::new();
            $(
                vec.push($element);
            )*
            vec
        }
```

We can now use our macro in the **main()** function. In our case here, we have conveniently added a comment to show how the macro expands during compilation:

```
fn main(){
    let vec = vector![98, 87, 30, 60];
    /* Expands to
    let vec = {
        let mut vec = Vec::new();
        vec.push(98);
        vec.push(87);
        vec.push(30);
```

```
        vec.push(60);
        vec
    }*/
    println!("{:?}", vec)
}
```

We can compile and run the program to see that our vector works:

```
$ rustc vector.rs
$ ./vector
[98, 87, 30, 60]
```

We created a macro that handles the repetition of a task easily in a single line. We have had to use the Rust syntax to do so, which leaves functions out of the question. However, carelessly using macros can lead to longer compilations and unnecessary code complexity if the same task can be done in a function.

Imagine we need to switch the values of two bindings, **a** and **b**. The solution is easy: we mutably use **a** and **b**, use a temporary binding **temp** to store **a**'s value, assign **a** to **b**, and **b** to **temp**. This can be seen in the following macro:

```
macro_rules! switch {
    ($a: expr, $b: expr) => ({
        let temp = $a;
        $a = $b;
        $b = temp;
    });
}
```

But this problem can also be easily solved in a generic function, thus removing the need for a declarative macro's complexity:

```
fn switch<T>(a: &mut T, b: &mut T){
    let temp = a;
    a = b;
    b = temp;
}
```

Now that we understand when and when not to use macros, we can start learning declarative macros for general metaprogramming in Rust.

Declarative macros

Declarative macros or macros for example are used for general metaprogramming. A declarative macro can be described as having a syntax that is function-like and uses Rust token types as parameters. This may sound familiar to **constexpr** functions from C++, although they may look like a function during compile-time the code inside of the function is expanded. Consider the following C++ program to convert degrees to radians:

```cpp
#include <iostream>
using namespace std;
constexpr double PI = 3.14159;
constexpr double ConvertDegreeToRadian(const double &dDegree)
{
    return (dDegree * (PI / 180));
}


int main()
{
    double dAngleInRadian = ConvertDegreeToRadian(90.0);
    cout << "Angle in radian: " << dAngleInRadian;
    return 0;
}
```

During compile time, there is no function called **ConvertDegreeToRadian()**; instead, the expression is expanded and can be thought to look something like the following:

```cpp
int main()
{
    double dAngleInRadian = {(90.0) * (3.14159/180)};
    cout << "Angle in radian: " << dAngleInRadian;
    return 0;
}
```

The advantage with using **constexpr** is the fact that it helps your program run faster and overall uses less memory. The use of **constexpr** is a safer method of metaprogramming compared to using the preprocessor **#define**, but both help reduce the need for function calls and can help keep code **Do not Repeat Yourself (DRY)**. The idea of how **constexpr** acts like a function and expands during compile time is exactly how Rust's declarative macros work. However, instead of using `const` expressions, we will use Rust token types as parameters that help take better advantage of Rust's syntax.

Before we go into making declarative macros, we should look at the different token types:

- **block**: This is a sequence of statements wrapped inside a closure.
  - For example: `{ let foo = 5; println!("{foo}"); }`

- **expr**: This matches any Rust expression.
  - For example: `if foo == bar { println!("Cool") } else { println!("Not cool") }`

- **ident**: This matches any identifier, which can be any name that is not a Rust keyword.
  - For example: `foo`, `long_identifier`

- **item**: This matches any module-level things, such as imports, type declarations, functions, and so on.
  - For example: `use std::sync::Arc; fn something() { println!("something") }`

- **meta**: This matches the parameters inside an attribute.
  - For example: meta: `foo = Rust: #[foo]`

- **pat**: This matches any pattern in Rust.
  - For example: `Some(a), _`

- **path**: This matches any path in Rust, which means any name that contains a namespace.
  - For example: `std::fs::File`

- **stmt**: This matches a statement in Rust.
  - For example: `let x = 1; if x == 1 { println!("yay") }`

- **tt**: This stands for Token Tree and will match a sequence of tokens in Rust.
  - For example: `{ if x == 1 { // do something } else { // something else } }`

Creating a declarative macro

When we start creating a declarative macro, we start with using `macro_rules!` followed by an identifier for the macro. After we create a block which we will use to match a pattern using integral variables (variables prefixed with a delimiter, $) and token types. This is done by having the parameters insida parentheses, ( ) after it is followed by a matching arm, => and one of the three delimiters:

- Brackets: { }

- Parentheses: ( )

- Square Brackets: [ ]

By default, declarative macros are private; to make a macro public, you will need to place the attribute, **#[macro_export]** on the top of the macro.

Repetition

In our macro **vector!**, you will notice that we used the syntax **($($element: expr), *),.** If we generalize the syntax to **$()***, we can discuss the different ways in which we can add repetition in a macro:

- To repeat zero or more times, use the token: *

- To repeat one or more times, use the token: +

- To repeat once at most, use the token: ?

Now that we understand for the most part how to create a macro, let us use this knowledge to write a macro to execute multiple functions. We will just need to use the function's identifier, so we will have our parameter have a type, **ident** and we will need our repetition to happen at least once. So, we will use the token, + for repetition:

```
macro_rules! multi{
    ($($f: ident), +) => ({
        // code goes in here
  });
}
```

To repeatedly execute our functions, we will use **$f()**; to execute the function inside of **$()+** so it can repeat at least once.

```
        $(
            $f();
        )+
```

To test our macro, we can define a few simple functions and use their identifiers in the macro, **multi!** in our **main()** function:

```
fn hello(){
    println!("Hello")
}
```

```
fn bye(){
    println!("Bye")
}

fn hello_bye(){
    hello();
    bye();
}

fn main(){
    multi![hello, bye, hello_bye]
}
```

If we compile and run the program, we should get the following output:

```
Hello
Bye
Hello
Bye
```

When we repeat variables, we can also use other delimiters to separate two of them, such as using a comma, semicolon, matching arm (=>), and period. Let us say we wanted to create a macro that automatically creates a **HashMap** and inserts a value to a key using matching arms, like the following:

```
let student_grades = map!{
    "alice" => 87,
    "john" => 67,
    "kyle" => 56
};

// expands to
let student_grades = {
    let mut map = std::collections::HashMap::new();
    map.insert(key, value)
    //...
    map
};
```

How can we create a macro **map!** to create the same behavior? Let us go step by step and start with creating the shell of a declarative macro with the parameter being repetitive with zero or more times separated by a comma:

```
macro_rules! map{
    ($(), *) => ({


});
}
```

Inside of **$()**, we will have two integral variables **$key** and **$value** that will be separated by a matching arm (**=>**). Since we want the key and value to be values, we can insert them into our hashmap; we will have their type be **expr**:

```
($($key: expr => $value: expr), *)
```

Inside the body of our macro, we need to replicate the expanded form of our preceding example. First, we will need to create a new mutable **Hashmap** and assign it to the binding **map**. After that, we will repeatedly insert our variables, **$key** and **$value** to **map** using the **insert()** method inside the repeater, **$()***. After we have inserted our data to **map**, we can return it at the end, as shown:

```
let mut map = std::collections::HashMap::new();
$(
        map.insert($key, $value);
)*
map
```

We can write a **main()** function to test out our macro and see if it works as we expected:

```
fn main() {
    let student_grades = map! {
        "alice" => 87,
        "john" => 67,
        "kyle" => 56
    };
    println!("{:?}", student_grades)
}
```

We can run and compile our program where we will see that we are returned with a **HashMap**, and it does contain all keys and values we inserted using matching arms:

```
{"john": 67, "kyle": 56, "alice": 87}
```

With the ability to create declarative macros for general metaprogramming, we can now move on to procedural macros. Unlike declarative macros, there are a few different kinds of procedural macros.

Procedural macros

A procedural macro, unlike a declarative macro, is used to manipulate and use Rust's syntax to generate new Rust code from a macro. When creating a procedural macro, the requirements are the same no matter which kind of macro you are trying to develop. This involves changing the **proc-macro** field under **[lib]** in **Cargo. toml** and using the two following crates:

- **syn**
- **quote**

The **syn** crate is a library used to parse a stream of Rust tokens in a syntax tree of Rust source code. What this allows us to do is; for example, when we create a derive macro, we will need to parse a **struct** or **enum**. We may extract and collect the **struct**/**enum**'s identifier, the fields' identifiers, and their types. With the ability to extract and collect the different Rust syntaxes and tokens, we can effectively create what we deem necessary to happen.

With the different tokens we have, how do we use the Rust code to generate? Well, that is where the **quote** crate comes in. The **quote** crate comes with the handy macro, **quote!** which helps us use our different parsed tokens from **syn** and interpolate them into the Rust code inside a block.

What are the three different kinds of procedural macros? You may have seen them without noticing throughout this book, but here they are:

- Derive macros
  - ○ Implements a trait onto a **struct** or **enum** below
  - ○ For example: #**[derive(Debug)]**

- Attribute macros
  - ○ Defines outer attributes that can be applied to **items**
  - ○ For example: #**[get("/")]**

- Function-like macros
  - ○ Acts like functions, however, the input is a **TokenStream** and is invoked using the macro invocation operator (!).
  - ○ For example: **sql!(SELECT * FROM table);**

Throughout our examples we will be using the tool, **cargo-expand** to see how our macro looks once it has been expanded. To use this tool, we will need to use the nightly toolchain of the Rust compiler:

```
$ rustup override set nightly
# to go back to stable, replace nightly with stable
$ cargo install cargo-expand
```

To examine each type of macro in its expanded form in the subsections that will follow, we will create a simple library so we may use the tool, **cargo-expand**:

```
$ cargo new --lib macros_expanded
```

Derive macros

The most used form of procedural macros is Derive macros. We use it in every project to implement necessary traits to **structs** or **enums** we define. Before we start creating our own macro, let us look at an example of how they work in an expanded form. Inside **macros_expanded/src/lib.rs**, add the following **struct** that derives the **Debug** trait:

```
#[derive(Debug)]
struct Foo{
    bar: String,
    baz: u8,
    laz: Vec<i8>
}
```

If we go into our project and run **cargo expand**, we will see the following output:

```
$ cd macros_expanded
$ cargo expand

#![feature(prelude_import)]
#[prelude_import]
use std::prelude::rust_2021::*;
#[macro_use]
extern crate std;
struct Foo {
    bar: String,
    baz: u8,
    laz: Vec<i8>,
```

```
}
#[automatically_derived]
#[allow(unused_qualifications)]
impl ::core::fmt::Debug for Foo {
    fn fmt(&self, f: &mut ::core::fmt::Formatter) -> ::core::fmt::Result
{
        match *self {
            Foo { bar: ref __self_0_0, baz: ref __self_0_1, laz: ref
__self_0_2 } => {
            let debug_trait_builder = &mut ::core::fmt::Formatter::debug_
struct(
                    f,
                    "Foo",
                );
                let _ = ::core::fmt::DebugStruct::field(
                    debug_trait_builder,
                    "bar",
                    &&(*__self_0_0),
                );
                let _ = ::core::fmt::DebugStruct::field(
                    debug_trait_builder,
                    "baz",
                    &&(*__self_0_1),
                );
                let _ = ::core::fmt::DebugStruct::field(
                    debug_trait_builder,
                    "laz",
                    &&(*__self_0_2),
                );
                ::core::fmt::DebugStruct::finish(debug_trait_builder)
            }
        }
    }
}
```

You might not completely understand what is going on in the expanded form, but here is the main idea of what is happening: When we derive a trait onto a **struct** or

enum, during compile time, the macro is expanded where the trait is automatically implemented to the data as defined in the procedural macro.

To get a better understanding of how the trait is automatically implemented onto the data, we will create our own derive macro, **Info**. The **Info** trait will be used to implement the method, **info()** that returns a **String** of a struct's name, fields name, and their types.

Consider the following **struct**, **Person**:

```
#[derive(Info)]
struct Person{
    name: String,
    age: u32,
    alive: bool
}
```

We expect the **String** of **Person::info()** to be the following:

```
Name: Person
            - alive: bool
            - name: String
            - age: u32
```

To begin with, we will create a project with two libraries inside it, the first containing the trait, **Info** and the other will contain the procedural macro for **Info**:

```
$ cargo new info_demo
$ cd info_demo
# contains the trait
$ cargo new --lib info
# contains the proc macro
$ cargo new --lib info_derive
```

We will then need to add the following changes to **Cargo.toml** for each of the following packages:

```
# info_demo/Cargo.toml
[dependencies]
info = {path = "info"}
info_derive = {path = "info_derive"}


# info_demo/info_derive/Cargo.toml
```

```
[lib]
proc-macro = true
[dependencies]
syn = { version = "1.0.102", features = ["extra-traits"] }
quote = "1.0.21"
info = {path = "../info"}
```

The easiest step is to create the trait, **Info** in **info/src/lib.rs**, we will have one method inside the trait, **info()** that will immutably use the **self**, and return a **String**:

```
pub trait Info{
    fn info(&self) -> String;
}
```

Since our library, **info_derive** has the **proc-macro** field set to **true**, we can use the library, **proc_macro** to create procedural macros. Inside **info_derive/src/lib.rs**, we will add the following dependencies:

```
extern crate proc_macro;
use proc_macro::TokenStream;
use quote::quote;
use syn::{parse_macro_input, Data, DeriveInput, Fields};
```

To create a function that will be invoked when the trait, **Info** is derived, we will need to use the attribute macro, **#[proc_macro_derive(Info)]** to define the function below that will be invoked. The function we will write is **info_derive()** which accepts a **TokenStream** as an input and returns **TokenStream**:

```
#[proc_macro_derive(Info)]
pub fn info_derive(input: TokenStream) -> TokenStream{
```

The first thing we will do is create a vector that will contain all our tokens that will be used to enter the struct's identifier, field and their types. After we create our vector, we can parse our **TokenStream** into a **DeriveInput** by using the macro, **parse_macro_input!()**:

```
    let mut insert_tokens= Vec::new();
    let parsed_input: DeriveInput = parse_macro_input!(input);
```

With our binding, **parsed_input** we can extract the identifier of the struct by assigning the binding, **indentifier** to **parsed_input.ident**, which will have a type, **Ident**:

```
let identifier = parsed_input.ident;
```

With the identifier available to us, this is the perfect time to push a new token into **insert_tokens**. We want the identifier to be the value under the key, **struct**; we will need to use the **quote!** macro to turn the statement of inserting our key and values into a binding **map**. To turn the identifier into a string, we will use the **stringify!()** macro to put the **identifier** in the **quote!** block, we will interpolate it by prefixing it with **#**:

```
insert_tokens.push(
    quote!{
        map.insert(
            "struct".to_string(),
            stringify!(#identifier).to_string()
        );
    }
);
```

Our trait, **Info** for simplicity will only support **struct**, while **enum** and **union** will not be implemented and will panic. To check which kind of data we are implementing for, we will use a **match** statement on **parsed_input.data** where we will handle the case of **Data::Struct(s)** and **other**:

```
match parsed_input.data{
    Data::Struct(s) => {}
    other => panic!("Info is not yet implemented for {:?}", other)
}
```

Inside our case where we have a **DataStruct** that we have assigned to the binding **s**, we will use an **if let** statement to assign the binding, **named_fields** as long as it's wrapped with **Fields::Named()** is **s.fields**:

```
if let Fields::Named(named_fields) = s.fields{
```

To get the fields from **named_fields**, we will assign the binding, **punc** to **named_fields.named**, after which, we will use a **for** loop to iterate through each **field** in **punc**:

```
let punc = named_fields.named;
for field in punc{
```

For each field, we will need its identifier, and data type and create a token that inserts this information into the **map**. To get the identifier, we will assign **ident** to the **ident** field from the binding **field** and since it returns an **Option**, we will use

unwrap(). To get the data type, we will assign **field_type** to the **ty** field from the binding **field**.

After we have the identifier and the field's data type, we will create a binding **insert_token** that will use the **quote!** macro. Inside the **quote!** macro's block, we will use **map.insert()** to insert the identifier as the key and the data type as the value (turned to string using **stringify!()** with the **to_string()** method. With the binding **insert_token**, we can push it to our vector **insert_tokens**:

```
let ident = field.ident.unwrap();
let field_type = field.ty;
let insert_token = quote!{
map.insert(
    stringify!(#ident).to_string(),
    stringify!(#field_type).to_string()
    );
    };
    insert_tokens.push(insert_token)
    }
}
```

Now that we have all the information we need, we can start working on the final form that implements the **Info** trait to a **struct**. We will create binding **tokens** and we will use the **quote!** macro to create our desired **TokenStream**. This starts with importing **HashMap** from **std::collections**, and the **Info** trait from **info**. When we are importing, since we want to ensure that our macro works in many contexts, we will use the absolute path which is prefixing the **use** path with the separator operator **(::)**:

```
let tokens = quote!{
  use ::std::collections::HashMap;
  use ::info::Info;
```

To implement the trait **Info** to our derived struct, we will need to interpolate the binding, **identifier** into our **quote!** Block. This is again used by prefixing it with the # operator:

```
impl Info for #identifier{
        fn info(&self) -> String{
```

We will need to create a binding **map** that will contain all the **String** versions of our tokens, and we will create a binding **info_parts** that will contain all the different formatted strings that will join and return at the end:

```
    let mut map = HashMap::new();
    let mut info_parts = Vec::new();
```

To repeatedly insert our tokens into the **map**, we will use the syntax **#()*** with our binding, **insert_tokens**. This will access each of the inner elements and run their token, where the first one enters our identifier under the key, **struct** and the other fields identifier with their type:

```
#(#insert_tokens)*
```

Now that our keys and values are inserted into the **map**, we can get the name of the struct using the **remove()** method using the key, **struct**. After this, we will insert the name into **info_parts** by formatting it in the form, **Name: foo**:

```
    let name = map.remove("struct").unwrap();
    info_parts.push(format!("Name: {}", name));
```

Now that we know the **map** only contains the field's identifiers and their types, we can iterate through the map in a for loop using a tuple, **(k, v)** where they are the key and values, respectively:

```
    for (k, v) in &map{
        let s = format!("\t - {}: {}", k, v);
        info_parts.push(s);
    }
```

We can use the **join()** method in **info_parts** with a newline, as the spacing to return the final **String** for the **info()** method. After this, we can return our **TokenStream** using the function, **TokenStream::from()** using the binding **tokens**:

```
            info_parts.join("\n")
        }
    }
    };
    TokenStream::from(tokens)
}
```

To test our macro, we will head over to **src/main.rs** and create a struct, **Person** deriving the **Info** trait onto it (importing **Info** from **info_derive**) and printing it with the **info()** method:

```
use info_derive::Info;


#[derive(Info)]
```

```rust
struct Person{
    name: String,
    age: u32,
    alive: bool
}

fn main() {
    let person = Person{
        name: "Mustafif".to_string(),
        age: 19,
        alive: true
    };
    println!("{}", person.info())
}
```

We can now try running our program to see the result, and we can see how it looks expanded (we will only show how the **Info** trait is expanded for **Person**):

```
$ cargo run
Name: Person
            - name: String
            - age: u32
            - alive: bool
$ cargo expand
#![feature(prelude_import)]
#[prelude_import]
use std::prelude::rust_2021::*;
#[macro_use]
extern crate std;
use info_derive::Info;
struct Person {
    name: String,
    age: u32,
    alive: bool,
}
```

```
use ::std::collections::HashMap;
use ::info::Info;
impl Info for Person {
    fn info(&self) -> String {
        let mut map = HashMap::new();
        let mut info_parts = Vec::new();
        map.insert("struct".to_string(), "Person".to_string());
        map.insert("name".to_string(), "String".to_string());
        map.insert("age".to_string(), "u32".to_string());
        map.insert("alive".to_string(), "bool".to_string());
        let name = map.remove("struct").unwrap();
        info_parts
            .push({
                let res = ::alloc::fmt::format(
                    ::core::fmt::Arguments::new_v1(
                        &["Name: "],
                        &[::core::fmt::ArgumentV1::new_display(&name)],
                    ),
                );
                res
            });
        for (k, v) in &map {
            let s = {
                let res = ::alloc::fmt::format(
                    ::core::fmt::Arguments::new_v1(
                        &["\t - ", ": "],
                        &[
                            ::core::fmt::ArgumentV1::new_display(&k),
                            ::core::fmt::ArgumentV1::new_display(&v),
                        ],
                    ),
                );
                res
            };
```

```
        info_parts.push(s);
    }
    info_parts.join("\n")
  }
}
```

Attribute macros

The second most common form of procedural macros we have seen is attribute macros. These are used on many occasions and even when we create procedural macros. In an attribute macro, there are two parameters: the meta information inside the attribute, and the item that it will be used on.

If the attribute has the parameters **attr** and **item** which are both **TokenStream**, we can describe each of these parameters as the following:

```
#[repr(u8)]
// attr: repr(u8)
// item: enum Status{}
enum Status{
    Active = 0,
    Inactive = 1
}
use rocket::get;
#[get("/")]
// attr: "/"
// item: fn index(){}
fn index(){}
```

In Rust, we have the following two kinds of attribute macros:

- **Inner Attribute**: #![attribute]
    - ○ Applies to the item that the attribute is declared within.
- **Outer Attribute**: #[attribute]
    - ○ Applies to the item that follows the attribute.

Now that we know about inner and outer attribute macros, we can discuss the different classifications of attributes:

- Built-in attributes
    - ○ These can go from conditional compilation, testing, deriving

- o   For example, `#[test]`, `#[derive()]`, `#[cfg()]`
- o   https://doc.rust-lang.org/reference/attributes.html#built-in-attributes-index

- Macro attributes
  - o   The standard kind of attribute macros
  - o   For example, `#[get("/")]`

- Derive macro helper attributes
  - o   Attributes attached to a derive macro
  - o   For example, `#[structopt()]`

- Tool attributes
  - o   Attributes used for external tools such as `rustfmt`
  - o   For example, `#[rustfmt::skip]`

While many Rust types accept attribute macros, we must make sure that we know what kind they accept. Some may only accept outer attribute macros, while others could accept both. All of these rules are declared in the Rust Reference and can be found here, **https://doc.rust-lang.org/reference/attributes.html**.

- All `item` types accept outer attribute macros.
  - o   `extern` blocks, functions, implementations, and modules accept inner attribute macros.

- Most statements in Rust accept outer attribute macros.

- Block expressions accept outer and inner attribute macros under the following conditions:
  - o   They are the outer expressions of an expression statement.
  - o   The final expression of another block expression.

- `enum` variants and `struct` and `union` fields accept outer attribute macros.

- `match` expression arms (foo => bar) accept outer attribute macros.

- Generic lifetime or type parameter (<'a, T>) accepts outer attribute macros.

- Function, closure, and function pointer parameters accept outer attribute macros.

Now that we understand the different kinds, classifications, and rules of attribute macros, let us try to create some of our own attribute macros. The goal of our project is to create the **item_info** attribute that will tell us the following information when placed under a function:

- The attribute in **item_info**
- The item that follows **item_info**
- The function's signature (**fn foo -> bar**)
- The function's block (**{ bar }**)

We will create a new project **attr_demos** and inside this binary project, we will create a library for our procedural macros:

```
$ cargo new attr_demos
$ cd attr_demos
$ cargo new --lib attr_macros
```

We will need to make the following changes in each of the package's **Cargo.toml**:

```
# attr_demos/Cargo.toml
[dependencies]
attr_macros = {path = "attr_macros"}


# attr_demos/attr_macros/Cargo.toml
[lib]
proc-macro = true

[dependencies]
quote = "1.0.21"
syn = {version = "1.0.103", features = ["full"]}
```

We will first write our attribute **item_info** in **attr_macros/src/lib.rs**, and to begin, we will add the following imports on the top of the file:

```
extern crate proc_macro;
use proc_macro::TokenStream;
use quote::{quote, ToTokens};
use syn::{ItemFn, parse_macro_input};
```

To create an attribute, we will need to put the attribute **#[proc_macro_attribute]** on top of our function, **item_info**. We will require two parameters **attr** and **item** that will both be **TokenStream** and we will return **TokenStream**:

```
#[proc_macro_attribute]
pub fn item_info(attr: TokenStream, item: TokenStream) -> TokenStream{
```

The easiest thing we can do is print out our attribute and item, and this is done by using the **to_string()** method for **attr** and **item**:

```
// print the attribute and item
println!("attribute: {}", attr.to_string());
println!("item: {}", item.to_string());
```

Our attribute will only be for functions, so to get the inner signature and block for our function, we will need to parse the **item** as an **ItemFn** using the **parse_macro_ input!** macro:

```
let item = parse_macro_input!(item as ItemFn);
```

To get our function's signature, we will need to access the binding, item's **sig** field; since the method **into_token_stream()** takes ownership of a value, we will clone **sig**. After using the **into_token_stream()** method, we will chain it with the **to_ string()** method, so that we can print the signature. To get our function's block, we will use the same strategy used for the signature. However, we will need to access the **block** field instead of **sig**:

```
let sign = item.sig.clone().into_token_stream().to_string();

let block = item.block.clone().into_token_stream().to_string();
```

We can now print our function's signature and block. However, after all this, we still want the function to happen. Thus, we will return a **TokenStream** that contains a **quote!()** with the **item** inside using the function **TokenStream::from()**:

```
// we will print the different information
println!("Signature: {}", sign);
println!("Block: {}", block);
TokenStream::from(quote!{
    #item
})
}
```

With the attribute created, we can use it in **src/main.rs** as follows:

```
use attr_macros::{item_info};

#[item_info("This is an attribute", foo = bar)]
fn hello(){
    println!("Hello")
}

fn main() {
    hello();
}
```

If we compile and run our code, we get the following result:

```
$ cargo run
attribute: "This is an attribute", foo = bar
item: fn hello() { println! ("Hello") }
Signature: fn hello()
Block: { println! ("Hello") }
    Finished dev [unoptimized + debuginfo] target(s) in 0.35s
     Running `target/debug/attr_demos`
Hello
```

What happens if we want an attribute to be included in a derive macro? Think about the derive macro **StructOpt** and its attribute **structopt**. To do this, we can include the attributes in the macro, **proc_macro_derive** by following the name of the macro with **attributes()** separated by a comma. Inside **attributes()**, you would list the different attributes as follows:

```
#[proc_macro_derive(Foo, attributes(bar))]
fn foo_derive(input: TokenStream) -> TokenStream
{
    // ...
}
```

```
#[proc_macro_attribute]
fn bar(attr: TokenStream, item: TokenStream) -> TokenStream{
    // ...
}
```

Then, you may derive the macro, **Foo** on a **struct**, **enum** or **union** and you will be able to use the attribute **bar** as well, like the following:

```
#[derive(Foo)]
struct Something{
    #[bar]
    field: {}
}
```

Useful attributes

Attributes play such a big role in Rust that we should be accustomed to the different kinds of built-in attributes that can make our life easier. We will look into macros that help with documentation, diagnostics, testing, and conditional compilation.

When we create a library, we may use different functions depending on the operating system that the program is being used on. If we want to control conditional compilation, we will need to use the configuration attribute (#**[cfg]**). Consider the following example:

```rust
#[cfg(target_os = "macos")]
fn macos(){
    // only compiles on MacOS
    println!("I am Mac")
}
#[cfg(target_os = "linux")]
fn linux(){
    // only compiles on linux distros
    println!("I am linux")
}
#[cfg(target_os = "windows")]
fn windows(){
    // only compiles on windows
    println!(" I am windows")
}


fn main(){
    #[cfg(target_os = "macos")]{
        macos()
    }
    #[cfg(target_os= "linux")]{
        linux()
    }
    #[cfg(target_os= "windows")]{
        windows()
    }
}
```

The reason we use the **cfg** essentially twice is because we only want the function to compile if it is our target OS. Although our example is quite simple, in complex programs, this could involve using raw bindings that are only supported in a particular operating system. This isn't the only use of the **cfg** attribute; all uses can be found at **https://doc.rust-lang.org/reference/conditional-compilation.html**.

If you are using q native Linux operating system (POP_OS!), you will get the result!

```
I am Linux
```

The next attribute we will talk about is testing the **test** attribute is something we have used before inside a tests module. A simple test can look like the following:

```
#[test]
fn is_it_two() {
    assert_eq!(1+1, 2)
}
```

However, what if you have a test that is not ready yet; let us say you are still developing the modules that are required for it to work. We wouldn't want to delete everything and end up having to rewrite everything once things are ready, or commenting would be too ugly, so we can instead use the **ignore** attribute:

```
#[test]
#[ignore = "this test isn't implemented yet"]
fn not_ready(){
    // ...
}
```

> **Note: The rustc test harness supports the --include-ignored flag to run ignored tests as well. Sometimes, we want to see if a test panics, and to do this, we can use the should_panic attribute and may optionally take a string that must appear within the panic message. If the string is not found, the test will fail, and we can create a test that should panic below:**

```
#[test]
#[should_panic = "19 and 21 are not the same"]
fn they_arent_equal(){
    assert_eq!(19, 21, "19 and 21 are not the same")
}
```

If we did not have the message inside **assert_eq!()**, then the test will fail. We have only seen a little bit in terms of Rust diagnostic attributes; this would be using the **allow** attribute when we used C bindings. The following attributes alter the default lint level, **allow**, **warn**, **deny**, and **forbid**.

For any lint check **lc**, we can describe each level as the following:

- **allow(lc)**: Overrides the check for **lc** so its violations will go unreported.

- **warn(lc)**: Warns about the violations of **lc** but the program will still compile.

- **deny(lc)**: Returns an error after it finds a violation from **lc**.

- **forbid(lc)**: Does the same as **deny** but the lint level cannot be changed afterwards

In a C/C++ program, you may use the warning flags -**Wall, -Wextra, -Werror, -Wno-unused-parameters**; if a program has unused parameters, the compilation will fail. The ability to add extra errors or adjust the linters in a compiler for your specific project needs is what we plan to do.

If we want to not allow unused variables in our program, we can either deny or forbid **unused_variables**, by default, this is at the warning level. Consider the following example:

```
fn two(a: u32) -> u32 {
    2
}


fn main(){
    let two = two(3);
    println!("{two}")
}
```

If we compile the program, we will get the following result:

```
warning: unused variable: `a`
 --> diagnostic.rs:2:8
  |
2 | fn two(a: u32) -> u32 {
  |        ^ help: if this is intentional, prefix it with an underscore:
`_a`
  |
  = note: `#[warn(unused_variables)]` on by default


warning: 1 warning emitted
```

However, let us say we want our project to not allow this and instead we want to change the warning to **deny**, then we can add the attribute **#[deny(unused_variables)]** at the top of the program:

```
#[deny(unused_variables)]
fn two(a: u32) -> u32 {
    2
```

```
}

fn main(){
    let two = two(3);
    println!("{two}")
}
```

Now, if we try to compile our program, it instead fails with the following error:

```
error: unused variable: `a:

  --> diagnostic.rs:2:8
   |
 2 | fn two(a: u32) -> u32 {
   |        ^ help: if this is intentional, prefix it with an underscore:
`_a`
   |
note: the lint level is defined here
  --> diagnostic.rs:1:8
   |
 1 | #[deny(unused_variables)]
   |        ^^^^^^^^^^^^^^^^^


error: aborting due to previous error
```

If you would like to check all the different link checks supported in **rustc**, this can be found using the command **rustc -W help**.

If you would like to nest lint check attributes, you may "turn on and off" lint checks for specific items as shown:

```
// by default non-snake-case is warn
// functions should be snaked case
#[deny(non_snake_case)]
pub mod foo{
    // allows non snake case
    #[allow(non_snake_case)]
    fn functionOne() {}
    // warns of non snake case
    #[warn(non_snake_case)]
```

```
    fn functionTwo(){}
    // must be snaked cased
    fn function_three(){}
}
```

The next diagnostic attribute that can be used when developing a library is the **deprecated** attribute. If you are planning to deprecate an item, you may add the **deprecated** attribute so that it will be flagged as deprecated in documentation. We will create a library which will be used in the next topic of documentation attributes. To do this run the command, **cargo new --lib doc_testing** on your terminal.

Inside **doc_testing/src/lib.rs**, we will create a struct **System**, and create two different methods to create a new instance of **System**. The first will be deprecated called **init()** and the other will be a more commonly named, **new()**. In the **deprecated** attribute, we can either have it by itself for a generic message or add a value to **note** for a custom message:

```rust
//! A random System structure
#[derive(Debug, Clone)]
pub struct System{
    /// start message for the system
    start_message: String,
    /// bytes for the system
    bytes: Vec<u8>
}
impl System{
    /// Initializes a new System
    #[deprecated(note = "init replaced with System::new()")]
    pub fn init(start_message: String, bytes: Vec<u8>) -> Self{
        Self { start_message, bytes}
    }
    /// Creates a new System
    pub fn new(sm: &str, bytes: &[u8]) -> Self{
        Self { start_message: sm.to_string(), bytes: bytes.to_vec() }
    }
}
```

If we run **cargo doc --no-deps --open**, we can see the two different methods of the **System** with our deprecated flag on the **init()** method as shown in *Figure 9.1*:

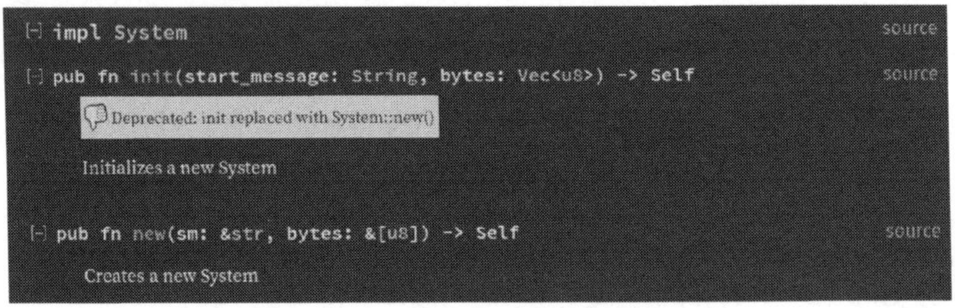

Figure 9.1: *Documentation of impl System*

If you noticed in our library, our struct, System's fields are never read or used. What if we wanted the fields to be used? The last diagnostic macro we will talk about is the **must_use attribue** which issues a warning if a struct's fields are to be used, or for functions if their parameters aren't used. The attribute can also include a message that will be printed alongside the warning when compiled.

When writing documentation for a library, it can be annoying using the documentation syntax, or you would rather have a separate directory with markdown files. Another way to write documentation for a library can be by using the **doc** attribute, we will replace the documentation comments we have with this:

```rust
#[doc = "A random System structure"]
#[derive(Debug, Clone)]
pub struct System{
    #[doc = "start message for the system"]
    start_message: String,
    #[doc = "bytes for the system"]
    bytes: Vec<u8>
}
impl System{
    #[doc = "Initializes a new System "]
    #[deprecated(note = "init replaced with System::new()")]
    pub fn init(start_message: String, bytes: Vec<u8>) -> Self{
        Self { start_message, bytes}
    }
    #[doc = "Creates a new System"]
    pub fn new(sm: &str, bytes: &[u8]) -> Self{
        Self { start_message: sm.to_string(), bytes: bytes.to_vec() }
```

```
        }
}
```

If we run **cargo expand**, we can see that the **doc** attribute is replaced with documentation comments, along with the implementations of the **Debug** and **Clone** traits:

```rust
#![feature(prelude_import)]
#[prelude_import]
use std::prelude::rust_2021::*;
#[macro_use]
extern crate std;
///A random System structure
pub struct System {
    ///start message for the system
    start_message: String,
    ///bytes for the system
    bytes: Vec<u8>,
}
#[automatically_derived]
impl ::core::fmt::Debug for System {
    fn fmt(&self, f: &mut ::core::fmt::Formatter) -> ::core::fmt::Result
{
        ::core::fmt::Formatter::debug_struct_field2_finish(
            f,
            "System",
            "start_message",
            &&self.start_message,
            "bytes",
            &&self.bytes,
        )
    }
}
#[automatically_derived]
impl ::core::clone::Clone for System {
    #[inline]
    fn clone(&self) -> System {
        System {
```

```
                start_message: ::core::clone::Clone::clone(&self.start_
message),
                bytes: ::core::clone::Clone::clone(&self.bytes),
            }
        }
    }
impl System {
    ///Initializes a new System
    #[deprecated(note = "init replaced with System::new()")]
    pub fn init(start_message: String, bytes: Vec<u8>) -> Self {
        Self { start_message, bytes }
    }
    ///Creates a new System
    pub fn new(sm: &str, bytes: &[u8]) -> Self {
        Self {
            start_message: sm.to_string(),
            bytes: bytes.to_vec(),
        }
    }
}
```

But what if we wanted to write about the struct **System** inside a separate markdown file, along with its usages? We can use the macro **include_str!()** with a path to the markdown file to include as documentation.

We will write a separate markdown file **system.md** in the root of the project with the following content:

```
# System

This is a random system structure.

- The `init()` method is deprecated instead use the `new()` method


## Usage

```rust

let system = System::new("Hello", &[9, 8, 7]);

```
```

If we go back to **src/lib.rs** and replace the documentation for System with **include_str!()** with the path of **../system.md**, we get the following expanded documentation:

```
#[doc = include_str!("../system.md")]

#[derive(Debug, Clone)]

pub struct System

...
```

```
$ cargo expand
/**# System

This is a random system structure.

- The `init()` method is deprecated instead use the `new()` method


## Usage
```rust
let system = System::new("Hello", &[9, 8, 7]);
```*/
pub struct System {
    ///start message for the system
    start_message: String,
    ///bytes for the system
    bytes: Vec<u8>,
}
```

Function-like macros

The last kind of procedural macro is a function-like macro. The difference between these and declarative macros is the ability to extensively use the Rust syntax. The ability to define your own custom syntax is very powerful; one usage I've seen for these is entering raw code of a different language like SQL.

We will try and create a few function-like macros. To begin, let's create a new cargo project to run and create our macros:

```
# Create the binary project to run the macros
$ cargo new fnmacros_demos
# enter the project
$ cd fnmacros_demos
# create the macros library
$ cargo new --lib fnmacros
```

We will now add the following changes to each of the packages **Cargo.toml**:

```
# fnmacros_demos/Cargo.toml
[dependencies]
fnmacros = {path = "fnmacros"}


# fnmacros_demos/fnmacros/Cargo.toml
[lib]
proc-macro = true


[dependencies]
quote = "1.0.21"
syn = {version = "1.0.103", features = ["full", "extra-traits"] }
```

The first macro we will write is called **three!()**, which will invoke a function three times given a call expression. If we have the following example:

```
fn hello(){
    println!("Hello")
}


fn main() {
    three!(hello());
}
```

Then, we expect the macro three to expand inside the **main()** function like the following:

```
fn main() {
    hello();
    hello();
```

```
    hello();
}
```

To begin writing our macro, we will head over to **fnmacros/src/lib.rs** and add the following imports on the top of the file:

```
extern crate proc_macro;
use proc_macro::TokenStream;
use quote::quote;
use syn::{parse_macro_input, Expr};
```

To create a function-like procedural macro, we will need to use the attribute, **proc_macro** on top of a function; one will be **three** which accepts a parameter **call** with type **TokenStream** and returns **TokenStream**:

```
#[proc_macro]
pub fn three(call: TokenStream) -> TokenStream{
```

The call expression is under the enum **Expr**. We will parse the **call** parameter as **Expr** using the macro, **parse_macro_input!()**. We will assign this value to the binding **parsed_call**, so we can assign the binding **call** to a **match** statement to **parsed_call**. We want to handle the case where we have **Expr::Call**, if we have any other type we will panic:

```
    let call = match parsed_call{
        Expr::Call(c) => c,
        other => panic!("Expression type {:?} is not allowed", other)
    };
```

We will need a vector to contain all the different calls of the function, so we will create a binding **invokes** that is mutable and assigned as an empty vector using **Vec::new()**:

```
let mut invokes = Vec::new();
```

We will create a simple for loop to iterate from 0 to 3 and we will push **invoke** with the macro, **quote!** that contains the binding, **call** interpolated with **#**:

```
    for _ in 0..3{
        invokes.push(
            quote!{
                #call;
            }
        )
    }
```

Now that we have our three function calls, we can create the binding **tokens** that repeatedly run our call inside **invokes** using the syntax **#()*** within a **quote!** block:

```
let tokens = quote!(
    #(#invokes)*
);
```

Now, we can return **tokens** using the function **TokenStream::from()**:

```
TokenStream::from(tokens)
}
```

We can now test out our previous example in **src/main.rs** and see if it works as expected:

```
use fnmacros::three;


fn hello(){
    println!("Hello")
}


fn main() {
    three!(hello());
}


$ cargo run
Hello
Hello
Hello
```

The next example we will write will be from the **syn** repository's example directory. The macro we will be writing is **lazy_static!** I think writing this macro is an excellent way to see how we can parse tokens, emit custom warnings, and see a complex example of a function-like procedural macro.

We will write it above our current macro **three!();** the ability to write warnings and errors will make use of an unstable feature, **proc_macro_diagnostic**. We will add the feature on the top of the file as well as replace our current imports with the following:

```
#![feature(proc_macro_diagnostic)]
extern crate proc_macro;
```

```
use proc_macro::TokenStream;
use syn::spanned::Spanned;
use quote::{quote, quote_spanned};
use syn::parse::{Parse, ParseStream, Result};
use syn::{parse_macro_input,Expr, Ident, Token, Type, Visibility};
```

To understand the different parts of the **LazyStatic** struct, we will create next, consider the following lazy static binding:

```
lazy_static!{
        pub static ref NAME: Mutex<Vec<i32>> = Mutex::new(Vec::new());
}
```

We can rewrite this statement in a more general sense which we will make use of in **LazyStatic**:

```
lazy_static!{
#visibility static ref #name: #type = #expr;
}
```

The visibility will determine whether a static binding will be public or private (pub or not), and after that it will be followed with the keywords **static** and then **ref**. The name refers to the identifier of the binding, and after that, it will be followed by a colon to declare our data type. The data type should be sized (size known during compile time) and can be safely sent across threads (implement the **Sync** trait). After the data type, we are followed by the assignment operator and then an expression to initialize our value. This will end with a semicolon.

The tokens that we care about are as follows:

- Visibility
- Name or identifier
- Type
- init expression

All these tokens will be kept in the **struct LazyStatic**, as shown:

```
struct LazyStatic{
    // the visibility of the static binding
    visibility: Visibility,
    // identifier of the binding
    name: Ident,
    // data type of the binding
```

```
        ty: Type,
        // the initializing expression of the binding
        init: Expr
}
```

The reason we went through the trouble of going through each token is because we will need to implement the trait, **Parse** to **LazyStatic** so that we can turn a **TokenStream** to **LazyStatic** using the macro, **parse_macro_input!()**:

```
// allows us to parse a TokenStream to LazyStatic
impl Parse for LazyStatic{
    fn parse(input: ParseStream) -> Result<Self> {
```

We will need to use the method **parse()** to get each **Token** value. For the ones we care about, we will assign them to a binding, the same as its respective field. For each token, we do not need to assign to like **static**, **ref**, colon (:), assignment operator (=), and semicolon (;), and we will use the **turbofish** operator to check whether the token is there (**parse::<Token![token]>**).

After we have parsed the whole statement, we can return a new **LazyStatic** wrapped in **Ok()** since the function returns a **Result**:

```
        // parse the visibility of the input
        let visibility = input.parse()?;
        // parse the static token
        input.parse::<Token![static]>()?;
        // parse the ref token
        input.parse::<Token![ref]>()?;
        // parse the identifier
        let name: Ident = input.parse()?;
        // parse the : operator
        input.parse::<Token![:]>()?;
        // parse the data type
        let ty: Type = input.parse()?;
        // parse the assignment operator (=)
        input.parse::<Token![=]>()?;
        // parse the init expression
        let init: Expr = input.parse()?;
        // parse the semi colon
        input.parse::<Token![;]>()?;
        Ok(
```

```
            Self {visibility, name, ty, init }
        )
    }
}
```

Now with the **Parse** trait implemented for **LazyStatic**, we can start working on the procedural macro, **lazy_static** with a parameter **input**, that has a type, **TokenStream** and will return **TokenStream**:

```
#[proc_macro]
pub fn lazy_static(input: TokenStream) -> TokenStream{
```

We will parse the parameter, **input** as a **LazyStatic**, where we will assign each of the fields as a binding, as shown:

```
let LazyStatic{
    visibility,
    name,
    ty,
    init
} = parse_macro_input!(input as LazyStatic);
```

The first thing we want to do is handle any kind of warning and error. In terms of warnings, we will warn the user to pick better names if they use generic names such as **FOO**, **BAR**, and **BAZ**. We will create an array that contains these names, after which we will iterate through each name to check whether our **name** is equal to one of them:

```
// create a warning if the name of the binding is too generic
// we will emit a warning for the following names
let generic_names = [«FOO», «BAR», «BAZ»];
for n in generic_names{
    if name == n{
```

With the identifier, we will first need to get it spanned using the **span()** method, which will be followed by an **unwrap()**. Then, to choose to emit a warning we will chain it to the **warning()** method along with a message inside. We will say the name is too generic, and then we can finally emit the warning using the **emit()** method:

```
            name.span()
            .unwrap()
            .warning("Name too generic")
            .emit();
    }
```

```
}
```

The next case we need to handle is if a user tries to initialize a binding with a void type, **()** with an empty tuple **()**. There is no reason someone should create a lazy binding and initialize it with **()**. Thus, if they do so, we will emit an error.

To do this, we will use an **if let** statement checking whether a tuple (**Expr::Tuple()**) is equal to our expression **init**. If so, we will check whether the field **elems** is empty (using the **is_empty()** method), and if it is, we will use the same strategy with our identifier, by spanning. However, to emit an error, we will instead use the **error()** method. After we have emitted the error, we do not want the macro to keep going. Instead, we will early return by returning an empty **TokenStream** with the **new()** method:

```
// create an error if the user tries to initialize using ()
// static ref UNIT: () = ();
if let Expr::Tuple(ref init) = init{
    if init.elems.is_empty(){
        init.span()
        .unwrap()
        .error("Cannot initialize static values using ()")
        .emit();
        return TokenStream::new();
    }
}
```

The two conditions we have for our static binding's data type are that it must implement the traits, **Sync** and **Sized** so that it can be shared across threads safely and its size is known during compile time. To assert that the type implements **Sync** and **Sized**, we will use the macro, **quote_spanned!()** so that we can span our type, **ty** (using the **span()** method) and create an empty struct where its type, **ty** implements **Sync** and **Sized**, respectively:

```
// check if the type implements the Sync trait
let assert_sync = quote_spanned!{ty.span() =>
    struct _AssertSync where #ty: ::std::marker::Sync;
};

// check if the type is Sized
let assert_sized = quote_spanned!{ty.span() =>
    struct _AssertSized where #ty: ::std::marker::Sized;
};
```

We will need to write a **TokenStream** for turning our initialization expression into a raw pointer. To do so, we will use **Box::into_raw()** with **Box::new()** inside, along with our initialization expression inside the **new()** method. We will store this inside the binding, **init_ptr** and this will be used when we do initialization using **std::sync::Once**:

```
let init_ptr = quote_spanned!{ init.span() =>
    Box::into_raw(Box::new(#init))
};
```

With all the prerequisite **TokenStream** bindings created, we can start working on the expanded form of our macro, **lazy_static!()**. What gets created is an empty struct, using our visibility and identifier of the binding, after which we will implement the **Deref** trait to our struct:

```
let expanded = quote!{
    #visibility struct #name;
    impl ::std::ops::Deref for #name{
```

In the **Deref** trait, we will need to define a type alias, **Target** which will be our data type, and the function, **deref()** will return a reference to our type:

```
        type Target = #ty;
        fn deref(&self) -> &#ty{
```

The first thing we must make sure of the inside **deref()** is if our data type implements **Sync** and **Sized**. Thus, we will include our bindings, **assert_sync** and **assert_sized**:

```
            #assert_sync
            #assert_sized
```

To run an initialization of a global binding once and only once, we will use the **Once** type from **std::sync**. First, we will define a static binding **ONCE** and create a new **Once** value using the **new()** method. We will then need to create a mutable static binding **VALUE**, that is a mutable raw pointer to our type, and we will assign it an initial value of 0 as a mutable raw pointer to our type:

```
            static ONCE: ::std::sync::Once = ::std::sync::Once::new();
            static mut VALUE: *mut #ty = 0 as *mut #ty;
```

The next operation we will do is unsafe. First, we need to use the **call_once()** method from our binding **ONCE**, which will initialize **VALUE** to our binding, **init_ptr**. The reason this is done inside an unsafe block is because modifying a mutable static binding is considered unsafe. We then need to dereference **VALUE** (dereferencing a raw pointer is also unsafe) and return a reference to it:

```
        unsafe{
            ONCE.call_once(|| VALUE = #init_ptr);
            &*VALUE
        }
    }
}
};
```

With our macro created, we can start using it and this will be done in **src/main.rs** where we will try to define three static bindings. The first static binding will contain a type that does not implement **Sync**, the second will contain a generic name, and the third will try to initialize with an empty tuple. Since our **lazy_static!** macro does not support recursion, each of the static bindings will be created in a separate **lazy_static!** block.

We will keep our previous example inside **src/main.rs** so that with our changes, it will look like the following:

```rust
use fnmacros::{three, lazy_static};
lazy_static!{
    static ref FOO: String = String::new();
}
lazy_static!{
    static ref NO: *mut u8 = 0 as *mut u8;
}
lazy_static!{
    static ref VOID: () = ();
}
fn hello(){
    println!("Hello")
}
fn main() {
    three!(hello());
}
```

If we try to compile our program, we are given the following errors and warnings:

```
$ cargo build
warning: Name too generic
 --> src\main.rs:4:16
  |
```

```
4 |      static ref FOO: String = String::new();
  |                    ^^^
```

```
error: Cannot initialize static values using ()
  --> src\main.rs:12:27
   |
12 |      static ref VOID: () = ();
   |                            ^^
```

```
error[E0277]: `*mut u8` cannot be shared between threads safely
 --> src\main.rs:8:20
   |
8 |      static ref NO: *mut u8 = 0 as *mut u8;
  |                     ^^^^^^^ `*mut u8` cannot be shared between
threads safely
   |
  = help: the trait `Sync` is not implemented for `*mut u8`
  = help: see issue #48214
  = help: add `#![feature(trivial_bounds)]` to the crate attributes to
enable
```

You can see that our custom warning and error were emitted. We can now try seeing how one of our static bindings **FOO** looks when it's expanded using the command **cargo expand**:

```
struct FOO;
impl ::std::ops::Deref for FOO {
    type Target = String;
    fn deref(&self) -> &String {
        struct _AssertSync
        where
            String: ::std::marker::Sync;
        struct _AssertSized
        where
            String: ::std::marker::Sized;
        static ONCE: ::std::sync::Once = ::std::sync::Once::new();
        static mut VALUE: *mut String = 0 as *mut String;
        unsafe {
            ONCE.call_once(|| VALUE = Box::into_
```

```
raw(Box::new(String::new()))));
            &*VALUE
        }
    }
}
```

Conclusion

In this chapter, we learned the two different types of macros in Rust that allow general metaprogramming (declarative macros) and complex syntax metaprogramming (procedural macros). In declarative macros, we learned about Rust's different token types such as items, expressions, identifiers, and so on. While in procedural macros, we learned how to parse token streams and use them in a way we see fit.

While metaprogramming plays a big role in Rust, we explore when to and when not to create macros, and how someone can make use of prebuilt attribute macros from the standard library.

Key facts

- If a function can complete the same task as a declarative macro, it is recommended to use the function instead to reduce compile times.

- When creating a procedural macro, it is recommended to look at the documentation of the **syn** crate to see what it offers.

- Always consider how you want the expanded form of the macro to look; this can help decide what is needed and how you will return the final result.

- Declarative macros are created using the **macro_rules!** macro.
  - To make it public, use the attribute **#[macro_export]**

- Procedural macros are created by setting the **proc-macro** field to **true** under the **lib** section in **Cargo.toml**.

- The following syntax is required for each type of procedural macro.
  - Function-like: Use attribute **#[proc_macro]**
    - Fn form: **(input: TokenStream) -> TokenStream**
  - Attribute: Use attribute **#[proc_macro_attribute]**
    - Fn form: **(attr: TokenStream, item: TokenStream) -> TokenStream**
  - Derive: Use attribute **#[proc_macro_derive]**
    - Fn form: **(input: TokenStream) -> TokenStream**

Exercises

1. Create a derive macro **HeapSize** that will return the size a type takes in the heap, using the implemented method, **heap_size()**. This exercise is based on the **heapsize** example inside the **syn** repository found here: **https:// github.com/dtolnay/syn/tree/master/examples/heapsize**.

2. Create an attribute macro, **trace_var** that prints the values of a given variable every time they are reassigned (such as in a recursion function). This exercise is based on the **trace-var** example inside the **syn** repository found here: **https://github.com/dtolnay/syn/tree/master/examples/trace-var**.

Answers

1. The macro we will be creating is called **HeapSize**. It will implement the trait **HeapSize** to each of the fields in a struct, where if the type is implemented, will contain the **heap_size()** method. The **heap_size()** method will return the memory size a type takes inside the heap. If we consider a primitive type like **u8**, it will return 0 since this type takes no space on the heap and lives in the stack. However, if we have a **String**, the memory taken from the heap is equal to the capacity of the **String**, which allocates enough memory up to the string's length.

    To begin this project, we will need to create a new binary project with two libraries inside it. Open your terminal and run the following commands:

    ```
    $ cargo new heapsize_demo
    $ cd heapsize_demo
    $ cargo new --lib heapsize
    $ cargo new --lib heapsize_derive
    ```

    We can now make the following changes to each of the package's **Cargo. toml**:

    ```
    # heapsize_demo/Cargo.toml
    [dependencies]
    heapsize = {path = "heapsize"}


    # heapsize_demo/heapsize/Cargo.toml
    [dependencies]
    heapsize_derive = {path = "../heapsize_derive"}


    # heapsize_demo/heapsize_derive/Cargo.toml
    ```

```
[lib]
proc-macro = true


[dependencies]
proc-macro2 = "1.0.47"
quote = "1.0.21"
syn = "1.0.103"
```

Before we think of working on our derive macro **HeapSize**, let us talk about the new crate we will be using, **proc-macro2**. Since this project requires using **TokenStream** outside a procedural macro function, we will need to use the crate, **proc-macro2** which provides a substitute implementation of **proc-macro**.

Usually, when we create a derive macro, we begin by working on the trait. However, if you will notice, this project does the opposite. Instead of us importing the trait, **HeapSize**, we will instead be re-exporting the macro in the library **heapsize**. Now, we can open **heapsize_derive/src/lib.rs** and add the following imports on the top of the file:

```
use proc_macro2::TokenStream;
use quote::{quote, quote_spanned};
use syn::spanned::Spanned;
use syn::{
    parse_macro_input, parse_quote, Data, DeriveInput, Fields,
GenericParam, Generics, Index
};
```

We will begin with writing the function for our derive macro, **HeapSize**, which will be named **derive_heap_size()** with a parameter **input** that is a **proc_macro::TokenStream** and will return **proc_macro::TokenStream**:

```
#[proc_macro_derive(HeapSize)]
pub fn derive_heap_size(input: proc_macro::TokenStream) -> proc_
macro::TokenStream{
```

With the parameter **input**, we can parse it to a **DeriveInput** using the macro, **parse_macro_input!()** and assign it to the binding **input**. We can get the name or identifier of the data using the field **ident** in **input**:

```
    // parse the input to syntax tree
    let input = parse_macro_input!(input as DeriveInput);
    // get the identifier of the struct
```

```
let name = input.ident;
```

Next, we will need to add our trait **heapsize::HeapSize** to each of the generic bounds in our data. To do this, we will assign the binding **generics** to **add_trait_bounds()** using the **generics** field in our binding **input**. The function **add_trait_bounds()** will be defined by us after this function:

```
// add HeapSize trait to each of the generic bounds
let generics = add_trait_bounds(input.generics);
```

Next, we need to get the **impl** generic statement, type generics and for clause from our binding, type **generics**. This is done using the method **split_for_impl()**. We will need to use these bindings when we expand and create an **impl** statement for whichever **struct** it's derived to.

```
// get the impl generic statement, type generics and where
clause
let (impl_generics, ty_generics, where_clause) = generics.
split_for_impl();
```

The last binding we need to write is **sum** which is an expression to sum up all of the heap sizes of the fields in a **struct**; we will use the function **heap_size_sum()** and borrow **input.data** to get a **TokenStream**. The function **heap_size_sum()** will be defined by us after **add_trait_bounds()**:

```
// get the sum of the heap size for each field
let sum = heap_size_sum(&input.data);
```

If we derive the macro, **HeapSize** onto a struct, **SomeValues**, we expect the expanded form to look like the following:

```
#[derive(HeapSize)]
struct SomeValues<T, K>{
    a: K,
    b: T,
    c: Box<K>
}


// Expanded form:
struct SomeValues<T, K> {
    a: K,
    b: T,
    c: Box<K>,
}
```

```
impl<T: heapsize::HeapSize, K: heapsize::HeapSize>
heapsize::HeapSize
for SomeValues<T, K> {
    fn heap_size(&self) -> usize {
        0 + heapsize::HeapSize::heap_size(&self.a)
            + heapsize::HeapSize::heap_size(&self.b)
            + heapsize::HeapSize::heap_size(&self.c)
    }
}
```

With the expanded form shown to us, we can create the binding **expanded** using the **quote!** macro. We will need to create an **impl** statement, where after the **impl** keyword, we are followed by our **impl_generics** followed by the trait we are implementing. This is **heapsize::HeapSize**.

After the trait name comes the **for** keyword, then our binding **name**, our type generics **ty_generics**, and then our binding **where_clause**. Inside the **impl** block, we need to define the function, **heap_size()** which immutably uses **self** and returns **usize**, inside the function we will put in **sum**. After we create the binding **expanded**, we can return a **TokenStream** using the function **TokenStream::from()** using the binding **expanded**:

```
let expanded = quote!{
    impl #impl_generics heapsize::HeapSize for #name #ty_
generics #where_clause{
        fn heap_size(&self) -> usize{
            #sum
        }
    }
};
proc_macro::TokenStream::from(expanded)
}
```

The next function we need to write is **add_trait_bounds()** which mutably uses the parameter **generics** with type, **Generics** and will return **Generics**. The point of this function is to add the bound **T: heapsize::HeapSize** to every generic type in our input:

```
// add a bound `T: HeapSize` to every type parameter T
fn add_trait_bounds(mut generics: Generics) -> Generics{
```

We will need to iterate through each of the generic parameters and to do this, we will use a for loop to get each **param** in **generics.params**. We will do this mutably (**&mut**). Inside the loop, we will use an **if let** statement to check whether **param** is equal to **GenericParam::Type(ref mut type_param)**. If it does, we can push to **type_param** bounds with the macro **parse_quote!()** with **heapsize::HeapSize** inside. In the end of the function, we can return **generics**:

```
    for param in &mut generics.params{
        if let GenericParam::Type(ref mut type_param) = *param{
            type_param.bounds.push(parse_
quote!(heapsize::HeapSize));
        }
    }
    generics
}
```

The next function we need to write is **heap_size_sum()**, which is responsible to generate an expression, to sum the heap sizes of each field in a **struct**. The function has a parameter **data** that has type **&Data** and returns **TokenStream**.

Consider the three different kinds of structs. How would we write the implementation for each kind? Let us look at an example of a normal struct, **Normal**:

```
#[derive(HeapSize)]
struct Normal<N>{
    a: Box<N>,
    b: N
}
```

We want the implementation to use the function **heap_size()** for each of the struct's field and sum them up. We expect the **impl** block for **Normal** to look like the following:

```
impl<N: heapsize::HeapSize> heapsize::HeapSize for Normal<N> {
    fn heap_size(&self) -> usize {
        0 + heapsize::HeapSize::heap_size(&self.a)
            + heapsize::HeapSize::heap_size(&self.b)
    }
}
```

The next kind of **struct** we need to consider is a tuple struct, as shown:

```
#[derive(HeapSize)]
struct Tuple<T>(Box<T>, T);
```

We want the implementation to use the function **heap_size()** for each of the struct's indexes and sum them up. We expect the **impl** block for **Tuple** to look like the following:

```
impl<T: heapsize::HeapSize> heapsize::HeapSize for Tuple<T> {
    fn heap_size(&self) -> usize {
        0 + heapsize::HeapSize::heap_size(&self.0)
            + heapsize::HeapSize::heap_size(&self.1)
    }
}
```

The last kind of struct we need to consider is an empty or unit struct. Since it has no values inside, it does not take up any space inside the heap. So when we create the implementation for it, the function **heap_size()** will just return 0.

Since we are only considering **structs**, if we are given an **enum** or **union**, we will leave those unimplemented. With all the prelude done, we can start working on the function, **heap_size_sum()**, starting with its declaration:

```
// generate an expression to sum up the heap size of each field
fn heap_size_sum(data: &Data) -> TokenStream{
```

To handle each kind of **Data**, we will use a **match** statement on the parameter **data** dereferenced and have each of the following cases:

```
match *data{
    Data::Struct(ref data) => {
        match data.fields{
            // Named struct like Normal
            Fields::Named(ref fields) => {

            }
            // UnNamed struct like Tuple
            Fields::Unnamed(ref fields) => {

            }
            Fields::Unit => quote!(0)
```

```
            }
        }
        Data::Enum(_) | Data::Union(_) => unimplemented!()
    }
}
```

The first case we need to handle is for **Fields::Named**. We will create a binding **recurse**, which will be an **impl Iterator<Item = TokenStream>**. To do this, we will assign it to **fields.named** and then chain it with the **iter()** method, so it can be an **Iterator**. After the **iter()** method, we can chain it with the **map()** method using the parameter **f** that has type **&Field**. Inside the block, we will create a binding **name** that will be the field's identifier or **f.ident** that will be immutably borrowed. We can then return a **TokenStream** using the macro, **quote_spanned!()**. Thus, we can span out **f** using the **span()** method and have a **TokenStream** of the function **heap_size()** being used on our field, by interpolating the binding **name** after **&self**:

```
let recurse = fields.named.iter().map(|f|{
    let name = &f.ident;
    quote_spanned!(f.span() =>
    heapsize::HeapSize::heap_size(&self.#name))
});
```

Now that we have the binding, **recurse**, we can return the expression **0 (+ ...)** where in the parentheses, it will repeatedly have each expression in **recurse** prefixed with a plus so that they can be summed up. This will all be done using the macro, **quote!()** and using the syntax **#()*** for repetition:

```
quote!(
    0 #(+ #recurse)*
)
```

The last case we need to handle is for **Fields::Unnamed** which is a tuple struct. We will use a similar strategy as **Fields::Named** with a few minor changes. We will create a binding, **recurse** that will be assigned to **fields.unnamed** that will use the **iter()** method, so that it can be an **Iterator**. After the **iter()** method, we will chain it with the **enumerate()** method, so that we can have the current count for the indexes. Then, we will chain it with the **map()** method. With the **map()** method, we will have the parameters as a tuple, **(i, f)** where **i** is the index as a **usize** and **f** is the field as **&Field**:

```
let recurse = fields.unnamed.iter().enumerate().map(|(i, f)|{
```

Inside the **map()** block, we will create a binding **index** that will use the function **Index::from()**. We can thus turn the parameter **i** which is an **usize** into an **Index**. Then, we will do the same as we did before and use the macro, **quote_spanned!()** to span out **f** using the **span()** method and using the **heap_size()** method on **&self** using the **index**. After that, we can return the same **quote!()** that sums each expression in **recurse**:

```
let index = Index::from(i);
quote_spanned!(f.span() =>
heapsize::HeapSize::heap_size(&self.#index))
});
quote!(0 #(+ #recurse)*)
```

With everything written in **heapsize_derive**, we can head over to **heapsize/src/lib.rs** and start creating the trait, **HeapSize** and implement it to a few data types. To begin, add the following import and re-export at the top of the file:

```
use std::mem;
pub use heapsize_derive::HeapSize;
```

The trait **HeapSize** will have one method **heap_size()** that will immutably borrow **self** and return **usize**:

```
pub trait HeapSize{
    fn heap_size(&self) -> usize;
}
```

Now, we can start implementing the trait for a few data types. Let us start with a primitive type such as **u8** that, as discussed earlier, takes no space in the heap, and so, will return 0:

```
impl HeapSize for u8{
    fn heap_size(&self) -> usize {
        0
    }
}
```

The next type we can implement is **String,** where the amount of space it takes in the heap is equal to the string's capacity. So inside the function **heap_size()**, we can return the capacity using the method, **capacity()** which is already **usize**:

```
impl HeapSize for String{
    fn heap_size(&self) -> usize {
```

```
        self.capacity()
    }
}
```

The next type we can implement is **Box<T>** where **T** is not **Sized** and implements the trait **HeapSize**. To determine the amount of space this type takes, we need to sum the size of the inner value and the heapsize of the inner value. To get **T** from **Box<T>**, we will need to double dereference **self**; the reason being the first dereference returns **&T** and then the second will return **T**. To get the size of the value, we will use the function, **size_of_val()** from the **mem** module in the standard library. The final form of the implementation is as follows:

```
impl<T> HeapSize for Box<T>
where T: ?Sized + HeapSize{
    fn heap_size(&self) -> usize {
        mem::size_of_val(&**self) + (**self).heap_size()
    }
}
```

The next type is a slice **[T]** where the type **T** implements the trait, **HeapSize**. To get the sum of the heapsizes for each value in the slice, we will iterate using the **iter()** method, chain it with **map()** that will use the function **HeapSize::heap_size** for each value and then sum it by finishing the chain with the **sum()** method:

```
impl <T> HeapSize for [T] where T: HeapSize{
    fn heap_size(&self) -> usize {
        self.iter().map(HeapSize::heap_size).sum()
    }
}
```

Lastly, we will look at implementing a reference of type, **T** where the type is not **Sized**. Since it's a reference to a value, it takes no space in the heap. Thus, we will return 0:

```
impl <'a, T> HeapSize for &'a T
where T: ?Sized{
    fn heap_size(&self) -> usize {
        0
    }
}
```

In an actual library, you may choose to implement more types, but this is enough for us to make an example. We can now head over to **src/main.rs** and add the following struct we discussed in the beginning:

```rust
use heapsize::HeapSize;


#[derive(HeapSize)]
struct SomeValues<T, K>{
    a: K,
    b: T,
    c: Box<K>
}
```

We can now work on the **main()** function by creating a binding **SomeValues** where we will have the type **T** as an **u8** and **K** as a **String**. After we created our values, we can print the heap size for each field at the end of the sum of the heap sizes, as shown:

```rust
fn main(){
    let some_values = SomeValues{
        a: "some values".to_string(),
        b: 56,
        c: Box::new("wow some more values".to_string())
    };
    println!("a: {}", some_values.a.heap_size());
    println!("b: {}", some_values.b.heap_size());
    println!("c: {}", some_values.c.heap_size());
    println!("Sum: {}", some_values.heap_size())
}
```

We can now run our program and also see if the expanded form of the implementation is as we expected:

```
$ cargo run
a: 11
b: 0
c: 44
Sum: 55


$ cargo expand
```

```
struct SomeValues<T, K> {
    a: K,
    b: T,
    c: Box<K>,
}
impl<T: heapsize::HeapSize, K: heapsize::HeapSize>
heapsize::HeapSize
for SomeValues<T, K> {
    fn heap_size(&self) -> usize {
        0 + heapsize::HeapSize::heap_size(&self.a)
            + heapsize::HeapSize::heap_size(&self.b)
            + heapsize::HeapSize::heap_size(&self.c)
    }
}
```

2. In this exercise, we will create the attribute macro **trace_var** that will trace specified arguments and will print its new value every time it has been changed. Consider the following function, **factorial()** that has a parameter **n** and a binding **p** that returns the final result. Suppose we use the macro, **trace_var** and have **p** and **n** as arguments as shown:

```
#[trace_var(p,n)]
fn factorial(mut n: u64) -> u64{
    let mut p = 1;
    while n > 1{
        p *= n;
        n -= 1;
    }
    p
}
```

If we wanted to calculate **factorial(5)**, then we will get an output like the following:

```
p = 1
p= 5
n= 4
p= 20
n= 3
p= 60
```

```
n= 2
p= 120
n= 1
Answer: 120
```

This is the same as seeing **5*4*3*2*1=120**, so let us create the project **trace-var-demo** and its inner library **trace-var**:

```
$ cargo new trace-var-demo
$ cd trace-var-demo
$ cargo new --lib trace-var
```

We will need to make the following changes to each of the packages' **Cargo.toml**:

```
# trace-var-demo/Cargo.toml
[dependencies]
trace-var = {path = "trace-var"}


# trace-var-demo/trace-var/Cargo.toml
[lib]
proc-macro = true


[dependencies]
quote = "1.0.21"
syn = { version = "1.0.103", features = ["full", "fold"] }
```

We will begin working on **trace-var/src/lib.rs** by importing the following on the top of the file:

```
use proc_macro::TokenStream;
use quote::{quote, ToTokens};
use std::collections::HashSet as Set;
use syn::fold::{self, Fold};
use syn::parse::{Parse, ParseStream, Result};
use syn::punctuated::Punctuated;
use syn::{parse_macro_input, parse_quote, Expr, Ident, ItemFn,
Local, Pat, Stmt, Token};
```

To handle our different arguments, we will create the struct **Args** that will contain the field, **vars** with type **Set<Ident>** where **Set** is an alias for **HashSet**:

```
struct Args{
    vars: Set<Ident>
}
```

First, we need to implement the trait, **Parse** for **Args** so we can use the macro, **parse_macro_input!** to turn a **TokenStream** to **Args**. The trait contains the method, **parse()** with the parameter, **input** having type **ParseStream** and returning **Result<Self>**:

```
impl Parse for Args{
    fn parse(input: ParseStream) -> Result<Self> {
```

To get the different variables identifiers that are separated by a comma, we will use the function **Punctuated::parse_terminated()** using **input** assigned to a binding, **vars**. We will, however, need to use the **turbofish** operator on **Punctuated** as it requires a node type **T**. For us, that is **Ident** and separated by a type **P**, which is **Token![,]**. With the binding, **vars** iterated and collected as a **Set<Ident>** to create new **Args** that will be wrapped in **Ok()** since the function returns **Result**:

```
        let vars = Punctuated::<Ident, Token![,]>::parse_
terminated(input)?;
        Ok(Args { vars: vars.into_iter().collect() })
    }
}
```

We have a few methods we need to write for **Args**, so we can ensure we are able to print an expression or pattern as well as able to assign and print or create a let statement and print.

The first function we will write is **should_print_expr()** that immutably borrows **self** and has the parameter **e** with type **&Expr** and returns a **bool**. To handle the expression **e**, we will use a **match** statement and dereference **e**. Thus, we can handle an **Expr::Path()** or otherwise we return **false**:

```
impl Args{
  fn should_print_expr(&self, e: &Expr) -> bool{
    match *e{
        Expr::Path(ref e) => {

        }
        _ => false
    }
  }
}
```

```
}
```

In our case for **Expr::Path**, we will use the variable **e**, which has type **&ExprPath**. We need to make sure whichever path we have only has one segment, so if there is a leading colon "::", we will return false, or if the segment length is not 1. If we do not have a leading colon and the segment length is 1, and we get the first segment, then check whether the identifier is in **self.vars** and if the arguments in the first segment are empty:

```
if e.path.leading_colon.is_some(){
    false
} else if e.path.segments.len() != 1{
    false
} else {
    let first = e.path.segments.first().unwrap();
    self.vars.contains(&first.ident) && first.
arguments.is_empty()
}
```

The next function we need to write is **should_print_pat()** which immutably borrows **self** and has a parameter **p** that has type **&Pat** and returns a **bool**. The function is simple and uses a **match** statement on **p** and checks whether we have **Pat::Ident(ref p)**. If we do, we will check whether **self.vars** contains the identifier **&p.ident**. For any other kind of **Pat** variants, we will return **false**:

```
fn should_print_pat(&self, p: &Pat) -> bool{
    match p{
        Pat::Ident(ref p) => self.vars.contains(&p.ident),
        _ => false
    }
}
```

When we are tracing bindings, we need to handle when they are reassigned such as **var = init** or **var += value** so that we can turn that statement into **{var = init; println!("{:?}", var)}**. We will write the function, **assign_and_print()** that will mutably borrow **self**, have the parameters **left** (type **Expr**), **op** (type **&dyn ToTokens**) and **right** (type **Expr**) to represent an assignment of a binding and will return an **Expr**:

```
fn assign_and_print(&mut self, left: Expr, op: &dyn ToTokens,
right: Expr) -> Expr{
```

Thus, we will use the function **fold::fold_expr()** on **self** with the node as **right**. After we can use the macro, **parse_quote!()**, we can put in our expression and then we can add a **println!()** statement using the **concat!()** macro so we can use the macro, **stringify!()** on the parameter, **left** along with **" = {:?}"** and have **left** as the parameter for the debug format:

```
// before var = init
// after {var = init; println!("{:?}", var)}
let right = fold::fold_expr(self, right);
parse_quote!({
    #left #op #right;
    println!(concat!(stringify!(#left), " = {:?}"), #left);
})
}
```

The next case we need to handle when tracing bindings is when there is a **let** statement. If that occurs, we need to create a block, assign the pattern to its initial expression, print the identifier with its value debugged, and then return the identifier. To have this make more sense, consider the following:

```
// before:
let mut p = 1;


// expanded:
let mut p = {
    #[allow(unused_mut)]
    let mut p = 1;
    println!("p = {:?}", p);
    p
};
```

In our example, we would identify the pattern as **mut p**, the initial expression as **1** and the identifier as **p**. We will write the function, **let_and_print()** that mutably borrows **self** and has the parameter **local** with type **Local** (represents a local binding) and returns **Stmt** (a Rust statement):

```
fn let_and_print(&mut self, local: Local) -> Stmt{
```

From our parameter **local**, we will assign from the fields in **Local**, **pat** and **init** to get the bindings pattern and initial expression.

To get the inner expression, we will use the method **fold_expr()** that requires an **Expr** that is found by unwrapping **init** and using the second element of the tuple. However, the second element is a **Box<Expr>**, so we will need to dereference it to get **Expr**.

To get the identifier from the pattern, we will use a **match** statement on the binding, **pat** so we can create the binding, **ident**. The binding will handle the following two cases, **Pat::Ident(ref p)** and otherwise which will return the macro, **unreachable!()**. With the case of **Pat::Ident(ref p)**, we will return a borrow of **p.ident** which returns the identifier of the pattern:

```
let Local{pat, init, ..} = local;
let init = self.fold_expr(*init.unwrap().1);
let ident = match pat{
    Pat::Ident(ref p) => &p.ident,
    _ => unreachable!()
};
```

Now, we may return the expanded form which, as seen above, is a **let** statement of our pattern assigned to a block. Inside the block, we will have the attribute **#[allow(unused_mut)]** since we do not use the **mut** inside of the pattern. After the attribute, we will assign our pattern with a **let** statement to the initial expression, after we can print the value using the identifier as well as use it as the final return of our value:

```
parse_quote!{
    let #pat = {
        #[allow(unused_mut)]
        let #pat = #init;
        println!(concat!(stringify!(#ident), " = {:?}"),
#ident);
        #ident
    };
}
```

With our methods written, what's next to write? Well, we have been using the method **fold_expr()** but it does not exist yet, so we need to fix that. We will implement the trait **Fold** for our struct **Args**, so we can write the methods **fold_expr()** and **fold_stmt()** so we can handle traversing through an expression and a statement:

```
impl Fold for Args{
    fn fold_expr(&mut self, e: Expr) -> Expr {
        // TODO
```

```
    }
    fn fold_stmt(&mut self, s: Stmt) -> Stmt {
        // TODO
    }
}
```

The first function we will work on is **fold_expr()**. Using a **match** statement on the parameter **e**, we can check whether we are handling an expression that is either an assignment (=), or an assignment operator (+=, *=, etc.). Otherwise, we use the function **fold::fold_expr()** on **self** and **e** as the node:

```
match e{
    Expr::Assign(e) => {


    }
    Expr::AssignOp(e) => {


    }
    _ => fold::fold_expr(self, e)
}
```

First, we need to handle the case of **Expr::Assign(e)**, where the binding, **e** has type **ExprAssign** which we can use in an **if/else** statement. We will check whether we can print the expression using **self.should_print_expr()** and pass **&e.left** as the expression to evaluate. If we get true, then inside the **if** block, we will assign and print using the method, **assign_and_print()**. If we need not print the expression, then we will return **Expr::Assign()** and inside it, use the function, **fold::fold_expr_assign()** using **self** and **e** as the node:

```
if self.should_print_expr(&e.left){
    self.assign_and_print(*e.left, &e.eq_token, *e.right)
} else {
    Expr::Assign(fold::fold_expr_assign(self, e))
}
```

Lastly we need to handle the case of **Expr::AssignOp(e)** where the binding **e** has type **ExprAssignOp**. We will have the same **if/else** statement, however, in our **else** block we will need to replace **Expr::Assign()** with

Expr::AssignOp() and using the function **fold::fold_expr_assign_ op()** with **self** and **e** as the node instead:

```
if self.should_print_expr(&e.left){
    self.assign_and_print(*e.left, &e.op, *e.right)
} else{
    Expr::AssignOp(fold::fold_expr_assign_op(self, e))
}
```

With the function **fold_expr()** completed, we can now work on **fold_ stmt()**, where we will begin by using a **match** statement on the parameter **s** that has type **Stmt**. In our **match** statement, we will handle the case that we have **Stmt::Local(s)** and otherwise, we will use the function **fold::fold_ stmt()** on **self** and **s** as the node:

```
        match s {
            Stmt::Local(s) => {


            }
            _ => fold::fold_stmt(self, s)
        }
```

In the case of **Stmt::Local(s)** where the binding **s** has type **Local**, we need to check whether the initial expression exists and if we should print the pattern. If these are true, then we can use the method, **let_and_print()** using the binding **s**. If not, then we will return **Stmt::Local()** where inside, we will use the function **fold::fold_local()** using **self** and **s** as the node:

```
if s.init.is_some() && self.should_print_pat(&s.pat){
    self.let_and_print(s)
} else {
    Stmt::Local(fold::fold_local(self, s))
}
```

With the **Fold** trait fully implemented, we can finally start working on the attribute, **trace_var**. We will have the attribute **#[proc_macro_ attribute]** on top of the public function, **trace_var()** so we can declare it as an attribute macro. The function **trace_var()** will have two parameters, **args** and **input** which both have the type **TokenStream** and we will return **TokenStream**:

```
#[proc_macro_attribute]
pub fn trace_var(args: TokenStream, input: TokenStream) -> TokenStream{
```

We will first parse the **input** as an **ItemFn** using the macro **parse_macro_ input!()** since we use this attribute for functions and will assign it to the binding, **input**. We will then parse the list of variables that the users want to print, by parsing the parameter, **args** to **Args** using the macro, **parse_ macro_input!()** and assign to a mutable binding, **args**:

```
let input = parse_macro_input!(input as ItemFn);
// parse the list of variables the user wants to print
let mut args = parse_macro_input!(args as Args);
```

Since our changes to the function are done by traversing through the function with our methods written in the Fold trait, we will get the output by using the method, **fold_item_fn()** from the binding, **args** and using **input**. After we get the output, we can return the function back to the compiler using **TokenStream::from()** with **output** in the macro, **quote!()**:

```
// use a syntax tree traversal to transform the function body
let output = args.fold_item_fn(input);
// hand the result function back to the compiler
TokenStream::from(quote!(#output))
}
```

With the attribute, **trace_var** completed, we can head over to **src/main. rs**, where we will write some recursive functions. In a simple demo, we will write a factorial and dumb exponent function, and in the **main()** function, we will calculate **6!** and **2^6** as shown:

```
use trace_var::trace_var;
#[trace_var(p,n)]
fn factorial(mut n: u64) -> u64{
    let mut p = 1;
    while n > 1{
        p *= n;
        n -= 1;
    }
    p
}
#[trace_var(num)]
fn dumb_exp(mut num: u64, pow: u64) -> u64 {
    let init = num;
    for _ in 0..pow{
```

```
        num *= init
    }
    num
}
fn main(){
    println!("---Factorial---");
    let six_fact = factorial(6);
    println!("6! = {}", six_fact);
    println!("---Dumb Exponent---");
    let two_pow_6 = dumb_exp(2, 6);
    println!("2^6 = {}", two_pow_6);
}
```

If we run our code, we get the following output:

```
$ cargo run
---Factorial---
p = 1
p = 6
n = 5
p = 30
n = 4
p = 120
n = 3
p = 360
n = 2
p = 720
n = 1
6! = 720
---Dumb Exponent---
num = 4
num = 8
num = 16
num = 32
num = 64
num = 128
2^6 = 128
```

If we try to expand our attribute, we will observe the expansion of the functions **factorial()** and **dumb_exp()**. To simplify the expansion, we have replaced the expansion for **println!()**, so that we can focus on the work we created:

```rust
fn factorial(mut n: u64) -> u64 {
    let mut p = {
        #[allow(unused_mut)]
        let mut p = 1;
        println!("p = {:?}", p);
        p
    };
    while n > 1 {
        {
            p *= n;
            println!("p = {:?}", p);
        };
        {
            n -= 1;
            println!("n = {:?}", n);
        };
    }
    p
}


fn dumb_exp(mut num: u64, pow: u64) -> u64 {
    let init = num;
    for _ in 0..pow {
        {
            num *= init;
            println!("num = {:?}", num);
        }
    }
    num
}
```

CHAPTER 10
Project – StdLib for Mufi

Introduction

The toy language written by the author of this book, Mufi-Lang, is written under the tutelage of the book, *Crafting Interpreters* by *Robert Nystrom*, that illustrates how to write an interpreter in Java and a bytecode compiler in C. The language written in the book is called Lox, and in particular, Mufi-Lang is pretty much CLox (C version of Lox), with a few differences of having an integer and float type (Lox only has the **number** type) and the use of a Rust standard library. However, instead of giving you that standard library, we will instead be writing the main difference between these two toy languages. We will need to explore the language of Mufi (which is quite small) and familiarise ourselves with the compiler (in a general sense, this is not a book on compilers).

Although we have written a few projects using C and Rust together, this project shows how Rust can be used in a language written in C. So now, it is C + Rust + Mufi essentially. We will be able to see every bytecode operation in Mufi's debugged mode and observe how our native functions written in Rust will be handled in Mufi's bytecode and garbage collector.

Structure

In this chapter, we will cover the following topics:

- Getting started with Mufi-Lang
- Creating native functions in C
- Creating native functions in Rust
- Benchmarking C vs Rust native functions

Objectives

The objective of this chapter is to allow the reader to gain experience with adding Rust to a pre-existing C project. The language itself runs without the need for Rust, but if a developer would like to write the new features in Rust (which many are currently doing), then we can see what it would look like. While we get to experience with adding Rust to our project, we will also try to answer the question if there is any performance loss to our approach, which is why we will create a benchmark comparing some of our C and Rust native functions for Mufi.

Getting started with Mufi-Lang

To get started with the toy language Mufi-Lang, we have conveniently created a repository that contains the main C compiler and a Makefile to compile the project in its different modes. It is recommended that you do this project under a Linux system whether native, a virtual machine, or something like WSL2; the setup instructions will be for Debian distributions:

```
# Update and upgrade packages
$ sudo apt-get update && sudo apt-get upgrade
# Install necessary dependencies
$ sudo apt install git make python3 clang
# Clone the repository
$ git clone https://github.com/MKProj/Mufi-Template.git
# Optional, rename Mufi-Template to Mufi
$ mv Mufi-Template Mufi
```

If we enter the directory **Mufi**, we will see the following contents:

```
$ cd Mufi && ls
compiler
util
Makefile
```

The **compiler** directory contains all the source C files along with their respective headers. Let us talk about what each of these source/header files does:

- **chunk**: Handles the creation and operations related to the virtual machine's chunks.

- **common.h**: Contains all the commonly used libraries.

- **compiler**: Handles all Mufi's statements and compiles them.

- **debug**: Logs all of the bytecode instructions that the virtual machine emits.

- **main.c**: Executes the compiler either from a file or in a REPL environment.

- **memory**: Handles memory allocation and garbage collection.

- **object**: Handles object values such as classes, strings, functions, and so on.

- **pre**: Functions related to running the program.

- **scanner**: Handles parsing a string into a stream of tokens.

- **table**: A handmade HashMap.

- **value**: Handles what a Mufi value is and how to turn it back into C code.

- **vm:** The virtual machine that runs the Mufi compiler.

The **util** directory contains one python script **debug_prod.py** that alters **compiler/ common.h** depending on whether we want to debug logs or not (**undef** the **DEBUG_*** macros). The last file we need to talk about is **Makefile**, which looks like the following:

```
PY = python3
CC = clang
debug:
    $(PY) util/debug_prod.py debug
    make build
release:
    $(PY) util/debug_prod.py release
    make build
build:
    $(CC) compiler/*.c -Werror -Wall -std=c99 -o mufi
clean:
    rm mufi
```

Depending on the C compiler and the Python command your system uses, you can change the variables **PY** and **CC**. In the **build** option, you will notice that we are using the **c99** standard and the warning flags **error** and **all**. If we try to compile our project right now, you will see the following error:

```
$ make build
clang compiler/*.c -Werror -Wall -std=c99 -o mufi
compiler/vm.c:44:13: error: unused function 'defineNative' [-Werror,-
Wunused-function]
static void defineNative(const char* name, NativeFn function) {
            ^
1 error generated.
make: *** [Makefile:10: build] Error 1
```

The issue we have at the moment is that there are no native functions created. So, the function that we use to define them **defineNative()** is unused. Since we are in a way locked out of using the program, we might as well look into the actual language **Mufi** before we start creating some native functions.

Declaring variables in Mufi

Mufi is a general-purpose, dynamic, object-oriented programming language, which means that our variable can be declared dynamically. To declare a variable, we will use the keyword, **var** along with an identifier. Then, we can assign it to a value which is then completed using a semicolon. The language is quite small and only supports four different data types:

- integers (1, 2, 3)
- float (1.2, 3.4, 5.6)
- strings ("hello", "foo")
- bool (true, false)

While integers, floats, and bool types are considered primitive, strings are objects since they require dynamic allocation and are garbage collected. Mufi also comes with a built-in function or command **print**. So, if we create a variable and want to print it, it would look like the following:

```
var integer = 10;
print integer;
//output: 10
```

Control flow in Mufi

The control flow in Mufi is similar to C, wherein in an **if** statement, you must have parentheses of the condition. In terms of conditional and logic operators, they are all supported by the language. So, a simple control flow in Mufi can look like the following:

```
if ((6 > 7) and (9 < 10)) {
print "true";
} else {
print "false";
}
//output: false
```

Loops in Mufi

Loops in Mufi come in the following two forms, **while** and **for**, where they both follow the same syntax in C. The **while** loop expects a condition in parentheses and will execute the block of code inside as long as the condition remains true. The **for** loop has three parts: an initialization expression (such as **var i = 0**), a condition (such as **i < num**), and an increment or decrement of the value (such as i = i+1). Like a **while** loop, the block of code will execute as long as the condition remains true.

Both loops can be seen as follows:

```
var count = 0;
while(count < 5){
        for (var i = 0; i < count; i = i + 1){
                print i;
        }
        count = count + 1;
}
```

Functions in Mufi

Functions in Mufi are objects and are declared using the keyword, **fun** and are followed by an identifier and then its parameters. The functions do not require a return type (values are just returned with the **return** keyword, and if not, **nil** is returned implicitly) and in terms of parameters, only their identifiers are required. The language also supports recursive functions such as a Fibonacci function like the following:

```
fun fib(n) {
  if (n < 2) return n;
  return fib(n - 2) + fib(n - 1);
}
```

```
print fib(10);
//output: 55
```

Classes in Mufi

It is hard to have an object-oriented programming language without classes, and this is done using the keyword **class** followed by an identifier. Classes in Mufi only consist of methods and all methods inside a class do not use the keyword, **fun**.

The way to have fields in a class is to define them in the **init()** method and have them assigned to **self.*** where glob is the field name. When a new class is created using the class name as a function, we can then access the fields as follows:

```
class Foo{
init(a, b){
        self.a = a;
        self.b = b;
}
update(factor){
        self.a = self.a * factor;
        self.b = self.b * factor;
}
}

var foo = Foo(3, 4);
foo.update(5);
print foo.a;
print foo.b;
// Output:
// 15
// 20
```

Inheritance in Mufi

The last major feature in Mufi is class inheritance and this is done using the **<** operator, followed by another class's name (a class cannot inherit itself). To access the inherited class's bounded methods, you will need to use the **super** keyword. An example of class inheritance in Mufi can be seen as follows:

```
class Foo{
foo(){
        print "This is inherited from foo";
}
}
class Bar < Foo{
bar(){
        print "This is bar";
        super.foo();
}
}
var b = Bar();
b.bar();
// Output:
// This is bar
// This is inherited from foo
```

With the introduction of Mufi completed, it is best to discuss the two different build modes given to us. When we say **debug** and **release** mode, you might think about the Rust compiler's optimization modes. However, for Mufi that is not the case. There is no extra optimization. The difference in these modes lies in **compiler/ common.h** so let us look at it:

```
//> All common imports and preprocessor macros defined here
#ifndef mufi_common_h
#define mufi_common_h
#include <stdbool.h>
#include <stddef.h>
#include<stdint.h>
#include <stdlib.h>
#define DEBUG_PRINT_CODE
#define DEBUG_TRACE_EXECUTION
#define DEBUG_STRESS_GC
#define DEBUG_LOG_GC
#define UINT8_COUNT (UINT8_MAX + 1)
#endif
```

This is how **compiler/common.h** looks when in debug mode, since all the **DEBUG_*** macros are defined and will be used when the compiler runs a program. If we would not like to see the different debugging logging, we need to undefine the macros, and this can be seen as follows, when set in **release** mode:

```
#ifndef mufi_common_h
#define mufi_common_h
#include <stdbool.h>
#include <stddef.h>
#include<stdint.h>
#include <stdlib.h>
#define DEBUG_PRINT_CODE
#define DEBUG_TRACE_EXECUTION
#define DEBUG_STRESS_GC
#define DEBUG_LOG_GC
#define UINT8_COUNT (UINT8_MAX + 1)
#endif


// In production, we want these debugging to be off
#undef DEBUG_TRACE_EXECUTION
#undef DEBUG_PRINT_CODE
#undef DEBUG_STRESS_GC
#undef DEBUG_LOG_GC
```

Creating native functions in C

Native functions are functions built into Mufi's compiler and this section will be written in C but usable in Mufi. Every native function defined by us follows this syntax:

```
Value fooNative(int argCount, Value* args);
```

The integer **argCount** represents the number of parameters in the function and the dynamic array, **args** represents an array of Mufi values. Then, to add our native function into our compiler, we will need to head over to **compiler/vm.c** where in the function **initVM()**, we initialize our virtual machine. We will use the function **defineNative()** to define our different native functions.

But we have not written any native functions yet, so to get started, we will create the new files **compiler/mufi_std_c.c** and **compiler/mufi_std_c.h**. To get started, we will write some simple arithmetic functions before we start getting more complicated, and these functions will be defined in the header **compiler/mufi_std_c.h**:

```
//> Contains native functions written in C
#ifndef mufi_std_c_h
#define mufi_std_c_h

#include "common.h"
#include "value.h"

//> Sums two numbers
Value csumNative(int argCount, Value* args);
//> Multiplies two numbers
Value cprodNative(int argCount, Value* args);
//> Divides two numbers
Value cdivNative(int argCount, Value* args);

#endif
```

To get a better understanding of operations related to the struct **Value** defined in **compiler/value.h**, it is best to take a look at the **struct** itself and the handy macros created for it. The struct **Value** contains the field **type** that has type as **ValueType**, which is the enum shown as follows:

```
typedef enum{
    VAL_BOOL,
    VAL_NIL,
    VAL_INT,
    VAL_DOUBLE,
    VAL_OBJ,
}ValueType;
```

The second field is **as** that is a union which has four fields inside representing each different data type. The fields **boolean**, **num_double**, **num_int**, and **obj** represent a **bool**, **double**, **int**, and **Obj**, respectively. We can see the **Value** as shown:

```
typedef struct{
    ValueType type;
    union {
        bool boolean;
        double num_double;
        int num_int;
```

```
        Obj* obj;
    } as;
}Value;
```

To check whether a **Value** is a Boolean, integer, double, object or nil, we will use the macro **IS_*** where the glob will be for each data type, and the macro will evaluate the **type** field of a **Value** to the respective type in **ValueType**:

```
#define IS_BOOL(value) ((value).type == VAL_BOOL)
#define IS_NIL(value)  ((value).type == VAL_NIL)
#define IS_INT(value)   ((value).type == VAL_INT)
#define IS_DOUBLE(value)  ((value).type == VAL_DOUBLE)
#define IS_OBJ(value) ((value).type == VAL_OBJ)
```

To help with turning a **Value** into a C value, we will use the macro **AS_*** where the glob will be for each data type. These macros will be safe to use when used along with our **IS** macros, so we know that the value has the type we are casting to:

```
#define AS_OBJ(value)   ((value).as.obj)
#define AS_BOOL(value) ((value).as.boolean)
#define AS_INT(value) ((value).as.num_int)
#define AS_DOUBLE(value)  ((value).as.num_double)
```

Lastly, we need to turn our C value back into **Value**, and to do that, we will use the macros ***_VAL**, where the glob will be for each data type. Depending on the type, we will return a **Value** with its respective **ValueType** and in the union, assign the value to the respective field:

```
#define BOOL_VAL(value) ((Value){VAL_BOOL, {.boolean = value}})
#define NIL_VAL         ((Value){VAL_NIL, {.num_int = 0}})
#define INT_VAL(value) ((Value){VAL_INT, {.num_int = value}})
#define DOUBLE_VAL(value) ((Value){VAL_DOUBLE, {.num_double = value}})
#define OBJ_VAL(object)  ((Value){VAL_OBJ, {.obj = (Obj*)object}})
```

Now, we can start working on creating some arithmetic native functions in C and use them in Mufi-Lang. To begin, we will need to work on **compiler/mufi_std_c.c** with the following imports on the top of the file:

```
#include "mufi_std_c.h"
#include<stdio.h>
```

We will then write the **static** function **error()** that requires a string message or **const char*** and returns **Value**. If we encounter an error, we need to print a message to **stderr** using **fprintf()** and return **nil** for Mufi or **NIL_VAL**:

```
//> Writes an error to stderr, and returns nil
static Value error(const char* message){
    fprintf(stderr, "ERROR: %s\n", message);
    // in the end return nil
    return NIL_VAL;
}
```

We can start working on the first function **csumNative()**, and we will begin by checking whether the argument count is 2. If it is not, we will return an error. After the **if** statement, we will create two variables **first** and **second** that represent the first and second elements in **args**:

```
Value csumNative(int argCount, Value* args){
    //check if we only have two arguments
    if (argCount != 2){
        return error("csum() only expects two arguments.");
    }
    Value first = args[0];
    Value second = args[1];
```

Next, to make sure the arithmetic is safe, we will need to use a **switch** statement on **first.type** so that we can evaluate if it is an integer or double, and if not, we will return an error in the default case:

```
    // handle the different data types
    switch (first.type)
    {
    case VAL_INT:{

        break;
    }
    case VAL_DOUBLE: {

        break;
    }
    default:{
        return error("Type not supported in csum() cannot be added.");
        break;
    }
    }
}
```

In the case of **VAL_INT**, we will use an **if/else** statement to check the type of our variable **second**. If it is an integer, we will create an integer variable **sum** that adds the **first** and **second** using the macro **AS_INT** and returns the sum using the macro **INT_VAL**.

If the **second** is a double, we will make the sum a double, and to do this, we will cast the **first** as a double after it turned into an **int** and turn the **second** into a double using the macro **AS_DOUBLE**. We can then return the sum using the macro **DOUBLE_VAL**.

If the **second** is not an integer or a double, we will return an error saying that the second argument cannot be added to an integer:

```
if(IS_INT(second)){
    int sum = AS_INT(first) + AS_INT(second);
    return INT_VAL(sum);
} else if (IS_DOUBLE(second)){
    double sum = (double)AS_INT(first) + AS_DOUBLE(second);
    return DOUBLE_VAL(sum);
} else {
    return error("Second argument in csum() cannot be added to
integer.");
}
```

The next case we need to handle is **VAL_DOUBLE**. As discussed earlier, we will use an **if/else** statement to check whether the **second** is a double and if it is an integer. Otherwise, we will return an error. The conditional looks almost identical to our **VAL_INT** case. However, no matter if the **second** is an integer or double, we will return a double, as shown:

```
if (IS_DOUBLE(second)){
    double sum = AS_DOUBLE(first) + AS_DOUBLE(second);
    return DOUBLE_VAL(sum);
} else if (IS_INT(second)){
    double sum = AS_DOUBLE(first) + (double)AS_INT(second);
    return DOUBLE_VAL(sum);
} else {
    return error("Second argument in csum() cannot be added.")
}
```

Before we start working on **cprodNative()**, you might be wondering why there is no **csubNative()**. The answer to that is because the compiler had issues with negative numbers in functions. So, we will sadly not be writing a function to subtract two numbers, but we can look forward to finding the product. The function **cprodNative()** will follow exactly like **csumNative()** with the difference being that we will find the product, so we can see how similar it looks as shown:

```
Value cprodNative(int argCount, Value* args){
    //check if we only have two arguments
    if (argCount != 2){
        return error("cprod() only expects two arguments.");
    }
    Value first = args[0];
    Value second = args[1];

    // handle the different data types
    switch (first.type)
    {
    case VAL_INT:{
        if(IS_INT(second)){
            int prod = AS_INT(first) * AS_INT(second);
            return INT_VAL(prod);
        } else if (IS_DOUBLE(second)){
            double prod = (double)AS_INT(first) * AS_DOUBLE(second);
            return DOUBLE_VAL(prod);
        } else {
            return error("Second argument in cprod() cannot be
multiplied to integer.");
        }
        break;
    }
    case VAL_DOUBLE: {
        if (IS_DOUBLE(second)){
            double prod = AS_DOUBLE(first) * AS_DOUBLE(second);
            return DOUBLE_VAL(prod);
        } else if (IS_INT(second)){
            double prod = AS_DOUBLE(first) * (double)AS_INT(second);
            return DOUBLE_VAL(prod);
        } else {
            return error("Second argument in cprod() cannot be
multiplied to double.");
```

```
            }
        break;
    }
    default:{
        return error("Type not supported in cprod() cannot be
multiplied.");
        break;
    }
    }
}
```

The next arithmetic function we will write is **cdivNative()**. This function will be simpler than the other ones which will have an **if/else** statement checking whether the bindings **first** and **second** are double or **int**. If so, we will get the quotient and return it. However, if the parameters are not numeric, we will return an error that the type is not supported:

```
Value cdivNative(int argCount, Value* args){
    if(argCount != 2){
        return error("cdiv() only expects two arguments.");
    }
    Value first = args[0];
    Value second = args[1];


    //check if first and second are numbers
    if((IS_INT(first) || IS_DOUBLE(first)) && (IS_INT(second) || IS_
DOUBLE(second))){
        double quotient = AS_DOUBLE(first) / AS_DOUBLE(second);
        return DOUBLE_VAL(quotient);
    } else {
        return error("Type not supported in cdiv() cannot be divided.");
    }
}
```

To see these functions work in Mufi, we will need to head over to **compiler/$ vm.c** and in the function **initVM()**, we will define our native functions at the end. Using the **defineNative(0)** function, we will put the name of the function, and then its identifier:

```
    defineNative("csum", csumNative);
    defineNative("cprod", cprodNative);
```

```
defineNative("cdiv", cdivNative);
```

We are now ready to test our Mufi, whether creating a file or using the built-in REPL. We will start with the REPL and then create a script. To see the bytecode operations and garbage collector tracing, you may use **debug** mode. However, it would be a mess presented in the book and so we will run the code in **release** mode. However, we will surely take a look at the bytecode operations:

```
$ make release
$ ./mufi
Version 0.1.0 (Baloo Release)
(mufi) >> print csum(40.4, 30); print cprod(30, 0.2); print cdiv(3.4,
0.5);
70.4
6
6.8
# Bytecode operations are as shown:
== <script> ==
0000      1 OP_GET_GLOBAL       0 'csum'
0002      | OP_CONSTANT         1 '40.4'
0004      | OP_CONSTANT         2 '30'
0006      | OP_CALL             20008    | OP_PRINT
0009      | OP_GET_GLOBAL       3 'cprod'
0011      | OP_CONSTANT         4 '30'
0013      | OP_CONSTANT         5 '0.2'
0015      | OP_CALL             20017    | OP_PRINT
0018      | OP_GET_GLOBAL       6 'cdiv'
0020      | OP_CONSTANT         7 '3.4'
0022      | OP_CONSTANT         8 '0.5'
0024      | OP_CALL             20026    | OP_PRINT
0027      2 OP_NIL
0028      | OP_RETURN
```

To create a script, we will create a new directory in the root of our project called **scripts** and we will create a new file **fib.mufi** with a Fibonacci function using **csum()** internally:

```
fun fib(n){
    if(n<2) return 1;
    return csum(fib(n-1),fib(n-2));
```

```
}
print "Fib 20:";
print fib(20);
```

To run the script, we will need to add the path after **./mufi** in the command line:

```
$ ./mufi scripts/fib.mufi
Fib 20:
10946
# Bytecode operations are as shown
== fib ==
0000    2 OP_GET_LOCAL        10002   | OP_CONSTANT        0 '2'
0004    | OP_LESS
0005    | OP_JUMP_IF_FALSE    5 -> 15
0008    | OP_POP
0009    | OP_CONSTANT         1 '1'
0011    | OP_RETURN
0012    | OP_JUMP             12 -> 16
0015    | OP_POP
0016    3 OP_GET_GLOBAL       2 'csum'
0018    | OP_GET_GLOBAL       3 'fib'
0020    | OP_GET_LOCAL        10022   | OP_CONSTANT        4 '1'
0024    | OP_SUBTRACT
0025    | OP_CALL             10027   | OP_GET_GLOBAL      5 'fib'
0029    | OP_GET_LOCAL        10031   | OP_CONSTANT        6 '2'
0033    | OP_SUBTRACT
0034    | OP_CALL             10036   | OP_CALL            20038       |
OP_RETURN
0039    4 OP_NIL
0040    | OP_RETURN

== <script> ==
0000    4 OP_CLOSURE          1<fn fib>
0002    | OP_DEFINE_GLOBAL    0 'fib'
0004    6 OP_CONSTANT         2 'Fib 20:'
0006    | OP_PRINT
0007    7 OP_GET_GLOBAL       3 'fib'
0009    | OP_CONSTANT         4 '20'
```

```
0011    | OP_CALL                 10013    | OP_PRINT
0014    | OP_NIL
0015    | OP_RETURN
```

Arithmetic functions are kind of boring, so it is about time we add some more functions that can do more things. We will add a function **ccmd()** to run shell commands, **cexit()** to exit the program with a given exit code, **cerr_print()** to print in **stderr**, **cclock()** for the current time, and **cbench()** to run a batch benchmark. We can add the following functions in **compiler/mufi_std_c.h**:

```
//> Runs a terminal command
Value ccmdNative(int argCount, Value* args);
//> Exits a program with an exit code
Value cexitNative(int argCount, Value* args);
//> Prints a message to stderr
Value cerrprintNative(int argCount, Value* args);
//> Returns current time
Value cclockNative(int argCount, Value* args);
```

The batch benchmark will be used at the end when we will compare using a native C benchmark versus Rust versus Mufi. The benchmark will contain 7 integer fields, where the first one will contain the batch number (how much a batch will run) and the other 6 fields are letters a to f that will be used for a sum. With the structure **benchBatch**, we will need a function **initBench()** to create a new **benchBatch**, given a specified batch number and **runBench()**, given a **benchBatch**:

```
//> A structure to run a batch benchmark
typedef struct{
    int batch_num;
    int a;
    int b;
    int c;
    int d;
    int e;
    int f;
}benchBatch;
//> Initializes a benchmark with a specified bench num
benchBatch initBench(int batch_num);
//> Runs a benchmark
void runBench(benchBatch bench);
```

```
//> Runs runBench in Mufi
Value cbenchNative(int argCount, Value* args);
```

Along with these new functions, we will need to add two new imports that can be placed after the current ones:

```
#include "object.h"
#include<time.h>
```

Now, we can head back to **compiler/mufi_std_c.c** and start with the function **ccmdNative()** after **cdivNative()**. We only expect a string command to be in our function and we will run that using the C function **system()** by turning the **Value** into a **const char*** using the macro **AS_CSTRING()**. After that, we can return an **INT_VAL** of 0 or a simpler way is to just return **NIL_VAL** since internally, they are the exact same thing:

```
Value ccmdNative(int argCount, Value* args){
    if(argCount != 1){
        return error("ccmd() only expects one argument.");
    }
    if (!IS_STRING(args[0])){
        return error("Argument in ccmd() must be string.");
    }
    system(AS_CSTRING(args[0]));
    return NIL_VAL;
}
```

The next function we can create is **cexitNative()** which will expect an exit code which must be an integer. Inside the function, we will use the C function **exit()**. To turn our **Value** into an integer, we will use the macro **AS_INT()** and since we are exiting the program, we will not need to return anything:

```
Value cexitNative(int argCount, Value* args){
    if(argCount != 1){
        return error("cexit() only expects one argument.");
    }

    if (!IS_INT(args[0])){
        return error("Argument in cexit() must be an integer.");
    }

    exit(AS_INT(args[0]));
```

```
}
```

To print to **stderr**, we will write the function **cerrprintNative()** that expects a string and we will use the C function **fprintf()**. With the function **fprintf()**, we will set it to output to **stderr**, and we will format a string where the string is from using **AS_CSTRING**. Then, we will return **NIL_VAL** as shown:

```
Value cerrprintNative(int argCount, Value* args){
    if(argCount != 1){
        return error("cerr_print() only expects one argument.");
    }
    if(!IS_STRING(args[0])){
        return error("Argument in cerr_print() must be a string.");
    }
    fprintf(stderr, "%s", AS_CSTRING(args[0]));
    return NIL_VAL;
}
```

To get the current time, we will create a **static** function **clock_current()** that will return a **double**. This function will return **clock()** from the library **time.h** and be divided by the global, **CLOCKS_PER_SEC** so we can get the current time:

```
static double clock_current(){
    return clock()/CLOCKS_PER_SEC;
}
```

Now, we can write the function **cclockNative()** which expects 0 arguments and return the **Value** of type **double** using the macro **DOUBLE_VAL** and using the function **clock_current()** inside:

```
Value cclockNative(int argCount, Value* args){
    if(argCount != 0){
        return error("cclock() expects 0 arguments.");
    }
    return DOUBLE_VAL(clock_current());
}
```

Now, we can start working on the benchmarking side of our standard library. To begin our benchmarking, we need to initialize the structure **batchBench**. The function **initBench()** expects a parameter **batch_num** to set the batch number we need to do. We will set an uninitialized **benchBatch** variable called **bench**. We will set **bench.batch_num** to the parameter **batch_num** while each of the other fields will be set to 1 after which we can return **bench**:

```
benchBatch initBench(int batch_num){
    benchBatch bench;
    bench.batch_num = batch_num;
    bench.a = 1;
    bench.b = 1;
    bench.c = 1;
    bench.d = 1;
    bench.e = 1;
    bench.f = 1;
    return bench;
}
```

One aspect of this benchmarking is that we can do repeated function calls. So, when we create sums of each field from **a** to **f**, we will do so by a function call, as shown:

```
static int benchA(benchBatch bench){
    return bench.a;
}
static int benchB(benchBatch bench){
    return bench.b;
}
static int benchC(benchBatch bench){
    return bench.c;
}
static int benchD(benchBatch bench){
    return bench.d;
}
static int benchE(benchBatch bench){
    return bench.e;
}
static int benchF(benchBatch bench){
    return bench.f;
}
```

To run the benchmark, we will rely on the function **runBench()** that requires a parameter **bench** with type **batchBench**. We will need to set some variables the **sum** and **batch** will be set to 0, and the **start** will be set to **clock_current()**:

```
void runBench(benchBatch bench){
```

```
int sum = 0;
double start = clock_current();
int batch = 0;
```

We will run a **while** loop run as long as we have the current time (**current_clock()**), minus our variable **start** being less than 10 or have the loop run for 10 seconds. In the **while** loop, we will have a **for** loop to iterate from **0** to **bench.batch_num** and in the **for** loop, we will have **sum** be added by every **bench*()** function. After the **for** loop, we will increment the variable **batch** by 1. Thus, after the **while** loop has been completed, we can print the **sum** and **batch**:

```
void runBench(benchBatch bench){
    int sum = 0;
    double start = clock_current();
    int batch = 0;

    while(clock_current() - start < 10.0){
        for(int i=0; i < bench.batch_num; i++){
            sum += benchA(bench) + benchB(bench) + benchC(bench)
            + benchD(bench) + benchE(bench) + benchF(bench);
        }
        batch++;
    }
    printf("Sum: %d\n", sum);
    printf("Batch: %d\n", batch);
}
```

With the internals of the benchmark written, we need Mufi to be able to use it and that is where the **csbenchNative()** function comes in. It will accept an integer batch number and we will use the macro **AS_INT** to convert the **Value** to an **int,** so we can use **initBench()**. With the new **bench**, we can use the function **runBench()** with **bench** to run the benchmark after we will return **NIL_VAL**:

```
Value cbenchNative(int argCount, Value* args){
    if(argCount != 1){
        return error("cbench() only accepts 1 argument.");
    }

    if(!IS_INT(args[0])){
        return error("cbench() only accepts an integer batch number.");
```

```
    }


    benchBatch bench = initBench(AS_INT(args[0]));
    runBench(bench);


    return NIL_VAL;
}
```

You may see how some of the functions work out like running a command or exiting the program, but we should have some fun with our benchmark function. For a simple comparison, we will write a clone of the benchmark in Mufi and see how it compares to C.

We will write a new script in **scripts/bench.mufi** with the **Bench** class cloned from our C program, and we will run a 10k and 30k batch:

```
class Bench{
    init(batch_num){
        self.batch_num = batch_num;
        self.a = 1;
        self.b = 1;
        self.c = 1;
        self.d = 1;
        self.e = 1;
        self.f = 1;
    }
    bench_a(){
        return self.a;
    }
    bench_b(){
        return self.b;
    }
    bench_c(){
        return self.c;
    }
    bench_d(){
        return self.d;
    }
    bench_e(){
```

```
            return self.e;
        }
        bench_f(){
            return self.f;
        }
        run(){
            var sum = 0;
            var start = cclock();
            var batch = 0;

            while(cclock() - start < 10.0){
                for(var i=0; i < self.batch_num; i = i+1){
                    sum = sum + self.bench_a() + self.bench_b() + self.
bench_c()
                    + self.bench_d() + self.bench_e() + self.bench_f();
                }
                batch = batch + 1;
            }
            print "Sum: ";
            print sum;
            print "Batch: ";
            print batch;
        }
}

print "10k batch: ";
var bench = Bench(10000);
bench.run();

print "30k batch: ";
var bench = Bench(30000);
bench.run();
```

We can then create a new script in **scripts/cbench.mufi** that runs **cbench()** for a 10k and 30k batch:

```
print "10k batch (C): ";
cbench(10000);
```

```
print "30k batch (C): ";
cbench(30000);
```

We can then run both of the scripts to see what results we get. Here are the following results we got:

```
$ ./mufi scripts/bench.mufi
10k batch:
Sum:
57120000
Batch:
952
30k batch:
Sum:
57240000
Batch:
318

$ ./mufi scripts/cbench.mufi
10k batch (C):
Sum: 1903392704
Batch: 103306
30k batch (C):
Sum: 1916112704
Batch: 34506
```

Our main focus is the number of batches we were able to complete, and if we compare the two language's implementation, then we see that the C native function performed ~108 times more batches in both 10k and 30k.

Creating native functions in Rust

We have written a lot of C – close to 300 lines in fact. So, why don't we get back to having things rusty? In the root of our project, we will create a new library like the following:

```
# create library
$ cargo new --lib mufi_stdlib
# enter the library
```

```
$ cd mufi_stdlib
# add the following build depends
$ cargo add --build cc bindgen
# create a build script
$ touch build.rs
```

Inside **mufi_stdlib/build.rs**, we will need to create a new **cc::Build** using the **new()** method chained with the files **../compiler/value.c** and **../compiler/object.c** using the **file()** method. After we can include the headers with the method **include()**, pointing to the directory **../compiler/**. We can then use the **compile()** method to a shared object called **libmufi.so**:

```
use bindgen::Builder;
use cc::Build;
use std::path::PathBuf;
fn main() {
    Build::new()
        .file("../compiler/value.c")
        .file("../compiler/object.c")
        .include("../compiler/")
        .compile("libmufi.so");
```

Next, we need to create our bindings which we will need the headers **../compiler/value.h** and **../compiler/object.h**. We will output the generated bindings to **src/bindings.rs** and after we write this script, we can run **cargo build**:

```
    let bindings = Builder::default()
        .header("../compiler/value.h")
        .header("../compiler/object.h")
        .generate()
        .unwrap();
    let out_path = PathBuf::from("src/bindings.rs");
    bindings.write_to_file(out_path).unwrap()
}
```

Since we also want our C program to access the functions, we publicly **extern**, we need to add the name of our library and the crate type as a C dynamic library, under the **lib** section in **Cargo.toml**:

```
[lib]
name = "mufi_stdlib"
```

```
crate-type = ["cdylib"]
```

So, we can properly link our library to our program. We will need to add a new variable in our **Makefile** and edit the **build** option to accommodate our Rust library:

```
RUST = -lmufi_stdlib -L mufi_stdlib/target/debug

...

build:
    cd mufi_stdlib && cargo build
    $(CC) $(RUST) compiler/*.c  -Werror -Wall -std=c99 -o mufi
```

Since our macros are not available to us, we will need to create our own. However, we can easily recreate them as functions. We will write the file **src/helpers.rs** and as shown in the following, we will see the almost exact clones of our macros.

> **Note: Although not all are used, they were included so you can see how all of them are made:**

```
use crate::bindings::*;
use std::ffi::{c_char, c_int, CString};

pub unsafe fn is_bool(v: &Value) -> bool {
    v.type_ == ValueType_VAL_BOOL
}
pub unsafe fn is_int(v: &Value) -> bool {
    v.type_ == ValueType_VAL_INT
}
pub unsafe fn is_double(v: &Value) -> bool {
    v.type_ == ValueType_VAL_DOUBLE
}
pub unsafe fn is_obj(v: &Value) -> bool {
    v.type_ == ValueType_VAL_OBJ
}

pub unsafe fn as_obj(v: &Value) -> *mut Obj {
    v.as_.obj
}
pub unsafe fn as_bool(v: &Value) -> bool {
    v.as_.boolean
```

```
}

pub unsafe fn as_int(v: &Value) -> c_int {
    v.as_.num_int
}

pub unsafe fn as_double(v: &Value) -> f64 {
    v.as_.num_double
}

pub unsafe fn bool_val(b: bool) -> Value {
    Value {
        type_: ValueType_VAL_BOOL,
        as_: Value__bindgen_ty_1 { boolean: b },
    }
}

pub unsafe fn nil_val() -> Value {
    Value {
        type_: ValueType_VAL_NIL,
        as_: Value__bindgen_ty_1 { num_int: 0 },
    }
}

pub unsafe fn int_val(i: c_int) -> Value {
    Value {
        type_: ValueType_VAL_INT,
        as_: Value__bindgen_ty_1 { num_int: i },
    }
}

pub unsafe fn double_val(d: f64) -> Value {
    Value {
        type_: ValueType_VAL_DOUBLE,
        as_: Value__bindgen_ty_1 { num_double: d },
    }
```

```
}

pub unsafe fn obj_val(o: *mut Obj) -> Value {
    Value {
        type_: ValueType_VAL_OBJ,
        as_: Value__bindgen_ty_1 { obj: o },
    }
}

pub unsafe fn is_string(v: &Value) -> bool {
    is_obj(v) && (*as_obj(v)).type_ == ObjType_OBJ_STRING
}

pub unsafe fn as_cstring(v: &Value) -> *mut c_char {
    (*(as_obj(v) as *mut ObjString)).chars
}
```

The last helper function we will need to write is **as_rs_string()** to help make our life easier by borrowing a **Value** immutably and returning a **String**. First, we will need to turn the **Value** into a C string or ***mut i8** using the function **as_cstring()**. We can then use the raw pointer with **CString::from_raw()** to create the binding **cstr**. Using the **method to_str()** from **cstr**, we can turn the **CString** to an **&str**. However, we will need to use **unwrap()** since **to_str()** returns a **Result**. Then, we can return a **String** using the method **to_owned()**:

```
pub unsafe fn as_rs_string(v: &Value) -> String {
    let c = as_cstring(v);
    let cstr = CString::from_raw(c);
    let str = cstr.to_str().unwrap();
    str.to_owned()
}
```

Now, with all the helper functions written, we can start working on the file **src/lib.rs** and that starts with adding the following imports:

```
mod bindings;
mod helpers;
use bindings::*;
use helpers::*;
use std::ffi::{c_int, CString};
```

```
use std::fs::{read_to_string, File};
use std::io::Write;
use std::ops::Sub;
use std::ptr::read;
use std::time::{Duration, Instant};
use std::process::{Command, exit};
```

To make our life easier in terms of error reporting, we will write a sort of clone to the **error()** function in C by accepting an **&str** message, printing it to **stderr** using **eprintln!()**, and returning nil using **nil_val()**:

```
unsafe fn error(message: &str) -> Value {
    eprintln!("ERROR: {message}");
    nil_val()
}
```

To know what Rust functions we need to write, we will create a new header file in the **compiler** directory called **mufi_std_rs.h** and add the following functions:

```
#ifndef mufi_std_rs_h
#define mufi_std_rs_h

#include "value.h"

//> Executes a shell command
Value rscmdNative(int argCount, Value* args);
//> Exits a program given an exit code
Value rsexitNative(int argCount, Value* args);
//> Prints a string to stderr
Value rserrprintNative(int argCount, Value* args);
//> Reads a file and returns a string
Value readfileNative(int argCount, Value* args);
//> Writes to a file given a path and content
Value writefileNative(int argCount, Value* args);
//> Runs a batch benchmark using Rust
Value rsbenchNative(int argCount, Value* args);
//> Runs a batch benchmark using scoped threads
Value rsbenchThread(int argCount, Value* args);

#endif
```

Now, we can head back to **lib.rs** in the library **mufi_stdlib** and start working on the function **rscmdNative()**. To avoid the name being changed or mangled when compiled down to a dynamic library, we will use the attribute **#[no_mangle]** on top of the function. Since we are interacting with C bindings, almost all our functions will be **unsafe**. To create a function for C, we will need to use prefix our function with **extern "C"**. The C parameters are **argCount** with type **int** which will be **c_int**, and **args** has type **Value*** which is ***mut Value** in Rust. We will then have the function return **Value** like it does in our C header:

```
#[no_mangle]
pub unsafe extern "C" fn rscmdNative(argCount: c_int, args: *mut Value)
-> Value {
```

We expect the function **rscmd()** to only accept one string argument, so that we can use an **if** statement to check whether **argCount** is not 1. If it is, then we return an error:

```
if argCount != 1 {
    return error("rscmd() only expects one argument.");
}
```

To get the first element in the raw mutable pointer of **args**, we cannot just index like we do in C. If you remember when we wrote our own **Vec**, we used the function **read()** from **std::ptr**. The function requires the type to be ***const T**, and so we will need to cast **args** as ***const Value**. Since we only need the first element, we do not need to do anything extra with **args**. After we have our **Value** that will be assigned to the binding **val**, we can check whether it is not a string using the function **is_string()**. If it is not so, we will return an error:

```
let val = read(args as *const Value);
if !is_string(&val) {
    return error("rscmd() only accepts string arguments.");
}
```

Now that we are sure we have a string, we can turn **val** to a **String** using the function, **as_rs_string()**. After we have our string, we can use the function **Command::new()** and passing in our string by borrowing it and spawning it using the method **spawn()** and handling the **Result** using **unwrap()**. After we run our command, we can return **nil_val()** as shown:

```
    let str = as_rs_string(&val);
    let _ = Command::new(&str).spawn().unwrap();
    nil_val()
}
```

The next function we will work on is **rsexitNative()** that will exit a program given an exit code. This function will contain the same function declaration as our previous one.

We will make sure that we only have one argument, and if we do not, we will return an error. Since we are sure we only have one argument, we are safe to read **args** as a ***const Value** and assign it to the binding, **val**. Using the binding **val**, we will check whether it is not an **int**. If **val** is not an integer, we will return an error using the **error()**   function. If it is an integer, we will use the function **exit()** from **std::process** and inside it, use the function **as_int()** to pass in an integer by borrowing **val**:

```
#[no_mangle]
pub unsafe extern "C" fn rsexitNative(argCount: c_int, args: *mut Value)
-> Value {
    if argCount != 1 {
        return error("rsexit() only expects one argument.");
    }
    let val = read(args as *const Value);
    if !is_int(&val) {
        return error("rsexit() only expects an integer value.");
    }
    exit(as_int(&val));
}
```

The function **rserrprintNative()** will require only one argument that must be a string. Once we get the **Value** that will be assigned to **val**, we can turn it into a **String** using **as_rs_string()**. We can then print the **String** using **eprintln!()**, so we output to **stderr** and then return **nil_val()**:

```
#[no_mangle]
pub unsafe extern "C" fn rserrprintNative(argCount: c_int, args: *mut
Value) -> Value {
    if argCount != 1 {
        return error("rserr_print() only expects one argument.");
    }
    let val = read(args as *const Value);
    if !is_string(&val) {
        return error("rserr_print() only expects a string value.");
    }
    let str = as_rs_string(&val);
```

```
    eprintln!("{str}");
    nil_val()
}
```

All the functions we have written so far have been returning **nil_val()** which is kind of boring. However, what if we want to return a string? All of the strings in the Mufi compiler are interned and hashed into a HashMap or table, and so we do not just simply create a new **ObjString** and return that to a **Value**. We have the handy function **copyString()** which expects a string or **char*** and a length, **int**. While in Rust, that function instead needs ***mut i8** and **c_int** for its parameters (pointer to the characters, and the string's length respectively) and will return ***mut ObjString**.

We can now start working on the function **readfileNative()** that only expects a string path to read a file from and return its contents. The first steps will be to check whether we only have one argument, and then we are safe to get the binding **val** by reading **args** as ***const Value**. After that, we can check whether **val** is a string. If it is not a string, we will return an error. Otherwise, we can get the path as a Rust **String** using the function, **as_rs_string()**:

```
#[no_mangle]
pub unsafe extern "C" fn readfileNative(argCount: c_int, args: *mut
Value) -> Value {
    if argCount != 1 {
        return error("read_file() only expects one argument.");
    }
    let val = read(args as *const Value);
    if !is_string(&val) {
        return error("read_file() only expects a string value.");
    }
    let path = as_rs_string(&val);
```

With the path, we can borrow it in the function **read_to_string()** so that we can get a file's contents and to handle the **Result**, we will use **unwrap()**. We need to turn **content** into a C string **content_cstr**, and so we will use the function **CString::new()** by dereferencing **content**. We will then borrow it, and since the **new()** method returns a **Result**, we will handle it with **unwrap()**.

Now, we are ready to create an ***mut ObjString** using the function **copyString()**. We will use the method **as_ptr()** in **content_cstr** to get ***mut i8** or a mutable raw pointer of c characters. We will use the **len()** method from **content** and cast it as **c_int** to return the length of the string. This will be assigned to the binding **obj**.

Now, we can return a **Value**. We will assign the field **type_** as **ValueType_VAL_OBJ** or you may also put in 4. Then, for the **as_** field, we will need to assign the **union Value__bindgen_ty_1**. With the **union**, we will use the **obj** field to assign our binding **obj** and casting it as a ***mut   Obj**:

```
let content = read_to_string(&path).unwrap();
let content_cstr = CString::new(&*content).unwrap();


let obj = copyString(content_cstr.as_ptr(), content.len() as c_int);


Value {
    type_: ValueType_VAL_OBJ,
    as_: Value__bindgen_ty_1 {
        obj: obj as *mut Obj,
    },
}
}
```

If we are able to read a file, should we also not be able to write one? The function **write_file()** will expect a path and content to write to the file; both need to be strings. While we are used to only reading one argument, how do we read the second one? When we want to read the second element for content, we will use the method **add()** in **args** to offset our pointer by a value. We want it to be 1, and then we can cast it as ***const Value**:

```
#[no_mangle]
pub unsafe extern "C" fn writefileNative(argCount: c_int, args: *mut
Value) -> Value {
    if argCount != 2 {
        return error("write_file() only expects two arguments.");
    }
    // write_file(path, content);
    let path_val = read(args as *const Value);
    let content_val = read(args.add(1) as *const Value);
    if !is_string(&path_val) && !is_string(&content_val){
        return error("write_file() only expects string arguments.");
    }
```

We can turn the bindings **path_val** and **content_val** into strings using the function, **as_rs_string()** and assign to the bindings **path** and **content**, respectively. We can then create a new file using the function, **File::create()** using our **path**, and unwrapping the **Result**. Then, we can write to **file** using the method **write_all()** using **content** and the method, **as_bytes()** to turn it into an **&[u8]**. At the end of our function, we will return **nil_val()**:

```
let path = as_rs_string(&path_val);
let content = as_rs_string(&content_val);
let mut file = File::create(&path).unwrap();
file.write_all(content.as_bytes()).unwrap();


nil_val()
}
```

The last functions are **rsbenchNative()** and **rsbenchThread()** which both require us to do some preparation. First, we will need to create the structure, **BenchBatch** which will have the traits, **Debug**, **Clone** and **Clone**, derived onto it. We will have the same fields as we did in **benchBatch** except that the fields are **u64**:

```
#[derive(Debug, Clone, Copy)]
struct BenchBatch {
    batch_num: u64,
    a: u64,
    b: u64,
    c: u64,
    d: u64,
    e: u64,
    f: u64,
}
```

We will need to create some methods for **BenchBatch**; the first would be a **new()** method, similar to **initBench()**. We will need a batch number to set to and the other fields will be 1:

```
impl BenchBatch {
    pub fn new(batch_num: u64) -> Self {
        Self {
            batch_num,
            a: 1,
            b: 1,
            c: 1,
            d: 1,
            e: 1,
```

```
        f: 1,
    }
}
```

Just like how we will use invocations when getting our sum of the different fields, we will do the same with the private functions **bench_*** where glob will be the different alphabetic fields:

```
fn bench_a(&self) -> u64 {
    self.a
}
fn bench_b(&self) -> u64 {
    self.b
}
fn bench_c(&self) -> u64 {
    self.c
}
fn bench_d(&self) -> u64 {
    self.d
}
fn bench_e(&self) -> u64 {
    self.e
}
fn bench_f(&self) -> u64 {
    self.f
}
```

Now, we are ready to create the **run()** method which immutably uses **self** and will be used in the function **rsbenchNative()**. We will need to set the mutable binding **sum** to 0, **start** as the current time using **Instant::now()** and the mutable binding **batch** to 0:

```
pub fn run(&self) {
    let mut sum = 0;
    let start = Instant::now();
    let mut batch = 0;
```

Next, we will create a **while** loop that will get the current time (**Instant::now()**), subtract it by **start** using the method **sub()**, and see if it is less than 10 seconds or **Duration::from_secs(10)**. Inside the loop, we will create a **for** loop iterating from 0 to **self.batch_num** and we will add **sum** to **self.bench_***. After the **for** loop, we will increment **batch** by 1, and once the **while** loop is complete, we can print the sum and batch results:

```
while Instant::now().sub(start) < Duration::from_secs(10) {
    for _ in 0..self.batch_num {
        sum += self.bench_a()
            + self.bench_b()
            + self.bench_c()
            + self.bench_d()
            + self.bench_e()
            + self.bench_f();
    }
    batch += 1;
}
println!("Sum: {sum}");
println!("Batch: {batch}");
}
```

The last method we will write is **run_scoped()** that will immutably use **self** and will be used in **rsbenchThread()**. The aim of this function is to get the highest sum in the least number of batches required. To make this a reality, we will have three mutable bindings, **sum1**, **sum2**, and **sum3** set to 0, and will be the sums used in each scoped thread. We will also have to set **start** to **Instant::now()** and **batch** to 0:

```
pub fn run_scoped(&self) {
    let mut sum1 = 0;
    let mut sum2 = 0;
    let mut sum3 = 0;
    let start = Instant::now();
    let mut batch = 0;
```

We will have the same while loop but inside, we will have a different story. We will use the function **std::thread::scope()** where we will have the parameter **s** of type **&Scope**. Using the parameter **s**, we will use the **spawn()** method in three instances where each one will have our **for** loop for each **sum** binding. Then, we will increase **batch** by 1 and once the **while** loop finishes, we can print the sum (all the sums added together) and the batch:

```
while Instant::now().sub(start) < Duration::from_secs(10) {
    std::thread::scope(|s| {
        s.spawn(|| {
```

```
                for _ in 0..self.batch_num {
                    sum1 += self.bench_a()
                        + self.bench_b()
                        + self.bench_c()
                        + self.bench_d()
                        + self.bench_e()
                        + self.bench_f();
                }
            });
            s.spawn(|| {
                for _ in 0..self.batch_num {
                    sum2 += self.bench_a()
                        + self.bench_b()
                        + self.bench_c()
                        + self.bench_d()
                        + self.bench_e()
                        + self.bench_f();
                }
            });
            s.spawn(|| {
                for _ in 0..self.batch_num {
                    sum3 += self.bench_a()
                        + self.bench_b()
                        + self.bench_c()
                        + self.bench_d()
                        + self.bench_e()
                        + self.bench_f();
                }
            });
        });
        batch += 1;
    }
    println!("Sum: {}", sum1 + sum2 + sum3);
    println!("Batch: {batch}");
    }
}
```

The functions **rsbenchNative()** and **rsbenchThread()** both require only one argument that needs to be an integer. We will use the integer and cast it as a **u64,** so that we can use it to create a new **BenchBatch**. In the case of **rsbenchNative()**, we will use the **run()** method for starting the benchmarking while **rsbenchThread()** will use the **run_scoped()** method. At the end both of the functions, we will return **nil_val()** as we already print the results in the **run** methods:

```
#[no_mangle]
pub unsafe extern "C" fn rsbenchNative(argCount: c_int, args: *mut
Value) -> Value {
    if argCount != 1 {
        return error("rsbench() only accepts 1 argument");
    }
    if !is_int(&args.clone().read()) {
        return error("rsbench() only accepts an integer batch number.");
    }


    let bench = BenchBatch::new(as_int(&args.read()) as u64);
    bench.run();
    nil_val()
}


#[no_mangle]
pub unsafe extern "C" fn rsbenchThread(argCount: c_int, args: *mut
Value) -> Value {
    if argCount != 1 {
        return error("rsbench() only accepts 1 argument");
    }
    if !is_int(&args.clone().read()) {
        return error("rsbench() only accepts an integer batch number.");
    }
    let bench = BenchBatch::new(as_int(&args.read()) as u64);
    bench.run_scoped();

    nil_val()
}
```

All our work will be for naught if we do not define it in **compiler/vm.c** and to do so, we will need to import the header **mufi_std_rs.h**. After we define our headers, we are free to test out some of our functions:

```c
#include "mufi_std_rs.h"
...
void initVM(){
...

    defineNative("rscmd", rscmdNative);
    defineNative("rsexit", rsexitNative);
    defineNative("rserr_print", rserrprintNative);
    defineNative("read_file", readfileNative);
    defineNative("write_file", writefileNative);
    defineNative("rsbench", rsbenchNative);
    defineNative("rsbench_thread", rsbenchThread);


}
```

Since we have our Rust library to link, if we want to try to test out the file operations in the repl system, we need to build the project and then export our library path. This can be seen as follows:

```
$ make release
$ export LD_LIBRARY_PATH=mufi_stdlib/target/debug
$ ./mufi
Version 0.1.0 (Baloo Release)
(mufi) >> write_file("test.txt", "hello this is a test");
$ ./mufi
Version 0.1.0 (Baloo Release)
(mufi) >> var content = read_file("test.txt"); print content;
# Bytecode operations are the following:
== <script> ==
0000     1 OP_GET_GLOBAL      0 'write_file'
0002     | OP_CONSTANT        1 'test.txt'
0004     | OP_CONSTANT        2 'hello this is a test'
0006     | OP_CALL        20008     | OP_POP
0009     2 OP_NIL
0010     | OP_RETURN
```

```
== <script> ==
0000      1 OP_GET_GLOBAL      1 'read_file'
0002      | OP_CONSTANT        2 'test.txt'
0004      | OP_CALL            10006      | OP_DEFINE_GLOBAL    0 'content'
0008      | OP_GET_GLOBAL      3 'content'
0010      | OP_PRINT
0011      2 OP_NIL
0012      | OP_RETURN
```

If we want to see how our function **rscmd()** works out, we can try using it like the following:

```
$ ./mufi
Version 0.1.0 (Baloo Release)
(mufi) >> rscmd("ls");
(mufi) >> compiler  Makefile  mufi  mufi_stdlib  README.md  scripts  test
test.txt  util


# Bytecode are the following:
== <script> ==
0000      1 OP_GET_GLOBAL      0 'rscmd'
0002      | OP_CONSTANT        1 'ls'
0004      | OP_CALL            10006      | OP_POP
0007      2 OP_NIL
0008      | OP_RETURN
```

Lastly, we can have some benchmarking Rust versus Mufi; we already have the Mufi script written in **scripts/bench.mufi**, so now we can create the script, **script/rsbench.mufi**. We will be benchmarking using **rsbench()** and **rsbench_thread()** for 10k and 30k batches:

```
print "10k batch (Rs): ";
rsbench(10000);
print "30k batch (Rs): ";
rsbench(30000);
print "10k batch (Rs thread): ";
rsbench_thread(10000);
print "30k batch (Rs thread): ";
rsbench_thread(30000);
```

Let us run the Mufi bench first and then the Rust bench:

```
$ ./mufi scripts/bench.mufi
10k batch:
Sum:
54900000
Batch:
915
30k batch:
Sum:
53820000
Batch:
299
$ ./mufi scripts/rsbench.mufi
10k batch (Rs):
Sum: 3256620000
Batch: 54277
30k batch (Rs):
Sum: 3274740000
Batch: 18193
10k batch (Rs thread):
Sum: 3340620000
Batch: 18559
30k batch (Rs thread):
Sum: 3355560000
Batch: 6214
```

One thing we can notice is that our scoped thread benchmarking model does indeed work as we expect. We are seeing higher sums with almost 1/3 the batches. In terms of sums, we can notice that we averagely got ~59x compared to the Mufi benchmark, and in terms of batches, we got around 20-60x times the number of batches.

Benchmarking C versus Rust native functions

While thinking of different ways of how benchmarking could be done, such as experimenting with **criterion-rs**, we can refer to the benchmark we have created – it can provide some input to us. The benchmarking we are doing is not something super scientific and should not have an article written about it. It is simply a measure of how many batches can be completed and the sum it produces.

The two values calculated are the sum and batches completed with a specified batch number. For our benchmarking, we will use 10k and 30k batches. With the two values, we can consider the two results we can find, the fastest implementation (highest batch number) and the most efficient implementation (highest sum per batch).

We have already written our benchmark files, but we have only compared Mufi to the other implementation. How about comparing all three? We will run each of the scripts, **bench.mufi**, **cbench.mufi** and **rsbench.mufi**, all located in the **scripts** directory, one at a time.

We will run three trials to see any differences in the sums and batches, as well as seeing if each trial results in the same conclusions.

To begin, let us see the results of Trial 1 as shown in *Table 10.1*:

Function	Batch Num	Sum	Batch	Sum/Batch
bench.run()	10k	58860000	981	60000
	30k	59760000	332	180000
cbench()	10k	1884132704	102985	18295.21
	30k	1905132704	34445	55309.41
rsbench()	10k	3254280000	54238	60000
	30k	3266100000	18145	180000
rsbench_thread()	10k	3310380000	18391	180000
	30k	3271860000	6059	540000

Table 10.1: Trial 1 comparing Mufi, C, & Rust native functions

If we first look at the **Batch** column, we can notice that **cbench()** has the greatest batch number in both 10k and 30k batch numbers. The second result we care about is **Sum/Batch** which we can see **rsbench_thread()** taking the lead in both 10k and 30k batch numbers.

The following results are seen:

- Fastest: **cbench()**
  - o 10k result: 102985
  - o 30k result: 34445
- Efficient: **rsbench_thread()**

- 10k result: 180000
- 30k result: 540000

How fast is **cbench()** compared to our other functions? Let us see the following results:

- Compared to **bench.run()** batch
  - 10k: 105 times faster
  - 30k: 103.75 times faster
- Compared to **rsbench()** batch
  - 10k: 1.9 times faster
  - 30k: 1.9 times faster
- Compared to **rsbench_thread()** batch
  - 10k: 5.6 times faster
  - 30k: 5.7 times faster

How efficient is **rsbench_thread()** compared to our other functions? Let us see the following results:

- Compared to **bench.run()** Sum/Batch
  - 10k: 3 times faster
  - 30k: 3 times faster
- Compared to **cbench()** Sum/Batch
  - 10k: 9.84 times faster
  - 30k: 9.76 times faster
- Compared to **rsbench()** Sum/Batch
  - 10k: 3 times faster
  - 30k: 3 times faster

Why do our results make sense? First, if we consider why C would be the fastest; it is because it has the least amount of latency (running natively, instead of being linked or interpreted). When we run **bench.run()** for example, it first needs to interpret it into bytecode, gets evaluated in C, and then we see the results. The **cbench()** function runs natively in C and has the least number of hoops to hurdle through. Even Rust, while faster than Mufi, still has conversion in its name and will not perform as well as native C.

Why is **rsbench_thread()** the most efficient one? Consider that our goal for this function is to get the highest sum per batch. For every batch, we have three scoped threads running the batches for the sum. While the other implementations run one for loop, our function is running multiple simultaneously in separate threads that are then joined together, but because we are running the same task three times per batch, the function does perform slower than **cbench()** or **rsbench()**.

Let us see the second trial to see if our results stay relatively the same with **cbench()** having the highest batch and **rsbench_thread()** having the highest sum per batch. Refer to *Table 10.2*:

Function	Batch Num	Sum	Batch	Sum/Batch
bench.run()	10k	60540000	1009	60,000.00
	30k	61020000	339	180,000.00
cbench()	10k	1881972704	102949	18,280.63
	30k	1885872704	34338	54,920.87
rsbench()	10k	3242520000	54042	60,000.00
	30k	3263580000	18131	180,000.00
rsbench_thread()	10k	4762980000	26461	180,000.00
	30k	4820580000	8927	540,000.00

Table 10.2: Trial 2 comparing Mufi, C, & Rust native functions

We can notice that our conclusions have not changed, the function **cbench()** still holds the highest numbers in the Batch column, while **rsbench_thread()** has the highest numbers in the Sum/Batch column. With each trial, it is useful to see how much our sums and batches change, so that we can later simplify our data using a mean value or estimate.

The changes for each function compared to Trial 1 can be seen in *Table 10.3*:

Function	Batch Num	Change in Sum	Change in Batch
bench.run()	10k	2.85%	2.85%
	30k	2.11%	2.11%
cbench()	10k	-0.11%	-0.03%
	30k	-1.01%	-0.31%
rsbench()	10k	-0.36%	-0.36%
	30k	-0.08%	-0.08%
rsbench_thread()	10k	43.88%	43.88%
	30k	47.33%	47.33%

Table 10.3: Changes between Trial 1 and 2 results

Except for **rsbench_thread()**, the other functions saw minimal changes with half of them seeing a decrease, while many of the changes were identical between their sums and batches.

Now, we can proceed to see the results for the third trial. Our expectations are the same but another question we can ask is are we going to see any performance gains from trial 2 to 3 or from 1 to 3?

Refer to *Table 10.4:*

Function	Batch Num	Sum	Batch	Sum/Batch
bench.run()	10k	60120000	1002	60,000.00
	30k	59760000	332	180,000.00
cbench()	10k	1839432704	102240	17,991.32
	30k	1881372704	34313	54,829.74
rsbench()	10k	3251340000	54189	60,000.00
	30k	3266820000	18149	180,000.00
rsbench_thread()	10k	4618800000	25660	180,000.00
	30k	4722300000	8745	540,000.00

Table 10.4: *Trial 3 comparing Mufi, C, & Rust native functions*

From the third trial, we can notice that we still have the same results; **cbench()** has the highest batch in the 10k and 30k batch numbers making it the fastest implementation. The function **rsbench_thread()** still has the highest sum/batch in the 10k and 30k batch numbers making it the most efficient implementation.

How does our third trial compare to the first trial? Will we see an overall increase in values or decrease? We can only answer this once we see the results, as shown in *Table 10.5:*

Function	Batch Num	Change in Sum	Change in Batch
bench.run()	10k	2.14%	2.14%
	30k	0.00%	0.00%
cbench()	10k	-2.37%	-0.72%
	30k	-1.25%	-0.38%
rsbench()	10k	-0.09%	-0.09%
	30k	0.02%	0.02%
rsbench_thread()	10k	39.52%	39.52%
	30k	44.33%	44.33%

Table 10.5: *Changes between Trial 1 and 3 results*

Overall, we can see an increase in our values: while the functions **cbench()** and **rsbench()** saw minor decreases in their values, **rsbench_thread()** saw a large increase. These changes are similar to what was seen between trial 1 and 2, so we should look at how trial 3 compares to trial 2. Refer to *Table 10.6*:

Function	Batch Num	Change in Sum	Change in Batch
bench.run()	10k	-0.69%	-0.69%
	30k	-2.06%	-2.06%
cbench()	10k	-2.26%	-0.69%
	30k	-0.24%	-0.07%
rsbench()	10k	0.27%	0.27%
	30k	0.10%	0.10%
rsbench_thread()	10k	-3.03%	-3.03%
	30k	-2.04%	-2.04%

Table 10.6: Changes between Trial 2 and 3 Results

Except for the function **rsbench()**, we can see that overall, there was a decrease in our sum and batch changes, which means that trial 2 was our best trial. However, with each trial we got the same conclusion: we were able to see that **cbench()** was the fastest implementation by having the least amount of overhead compared to the other functions, and **rsbench_thread()** was the most efficient by using a concurrent model.

Conclusion

In this chapter, we learned a practical usage of Rust's **Foreign Function Interface (FFI)** to allow us to build a standard library for the toy language, Mufi. While the library was small, it can be expanded to be a lot larger and the steps taken to integrate Rust into our project can be translated to how you can go about adding Rust into your pre-existing C project.

Key facts

- To create bindings for a project, it is recommended to use the crates **cc** and **bindgen**.

- For the executable to locate the dynamic library, you must use **export LD_LIBRARY_PATH** and assign it to the path where the library is located at.

- It is recommended to use a **Makefile or for cross-platform development CMake**, when building a project integrating Rust and C together, as it helps reduce the work.

- To read a mutable raw pointer, use the function **std::ptr::read()**.
  - o To offset the pointer, use the method **add()** where the value is the amount you want to offset by.

Exercises

1. The library, **mufi_stdlib** contains a lot of duplicate code and some cloning that could be avoided. It would be best to simplify the functions by adding the helper functions, **check_argcount_error()** and **check_type_error()**.

2. Build a install script that allows the user to install Mufi-Lang either in **debug** or **release** mode. (**Note:** Either mode should build **mufi_stdlib** in release mode).

Answers

1. The goal of our helper functions **check_argcount_error()** and **check_type_error()** is to return a **bool** if our expectations are not met. We will have to return **nil_val()** in the function itself, unlike **error()** that did it for us. However, we can also choose to write a macro that reduces our lines of code even more.

   Although we have discussed in *Chapter 9, Metaprogramming*, that macros are best used when functions can do the task, we will accompany our helper functions with their own macro to reduce repetition.

   We can head over to **mufi_stdlib/src/helper.rs**, where we will start working on the first helper function, **check_argument_error()**. In this function, we will have three parameters, **arg_count** which is the argument count given in the function **expected**, which is the expected arguments and **name**, which is the name of the function. We will return a **bool**, where if we have an error, the function returns **true**, and if not, **false**:

```
pub fn check_argcount_error(arg_count: i32, expected: i32, name:
&str) -> bool{
```

   This function is simple; we will use an **if/else** statement to check whether **arg_count** is not equal to **expected**. If it is not equal, we will print an error and return **true**, and if it is equal, we will return **false**:

```
    if arg_count != expected{
        eprintln!("ERROR: {name} expects {expected} arguments,
got {arg_count} instead.");
        true
    } else{
```

```
        false
    }
}
```

Before we work on the next helper function **check_type_error()**, we need to write a function to turn our **ValueType** into a **String**. If we want to report a type error, we cannot be printing out integers, which **ValueType** actually is, and so, we will first write a function **type_to_str()** that takes a **ValueType** and returns **String**. The function is simple and uses a **match** statement to look at each **ValueType** and return its respective string.

> **Note: Since ValueType is a u32, we need to use the exhaustive pattern, which is dedicated to the nil type.**

```
unsafe fn type_to_str(ty: ValueType) -> String{
    match ty{
        ValueType_VAL_BOOL => "bool".to_owned(),
        ValueType_VAL_DOUBLE => "double".to_owned(),
        ValueType_VAL_INT => "int".to_owned(),
        ValueType_VAL_OBJ => "string".to_owned(),
        _ => "nil".to_owned()
    }
}
```

Now, we can write the **function check_type_error()** that returns **bool** and contains three different parameters. The first parameter is **value** that borrows the **Value** we are checking; the second parameter is **expected_type** that we will equate to our value's type, and lastly, the third parameter is **name** which is the name of the function:

```
pub unsafe fn check_type_error(value: &Value, expected_type:
&str, name: &str) -> bool{
```

To get the type of our value as a **String**, we will use the function **type_to_str()** along with **val.type_**. We can then use an **if/else** statement to check whether the value's type is not equal to **expected_type**, and if it is not, we print an error and return **true**. If it is equal, we return **false**:

```
    let ty = type_to_str(value.type_);
    if ty != expected_type{
        eprintln!("ERROR: {name} expected a {expected_type}, got
{ty} instead.");
        true
```

```
    } else{
        false
    }
}
```

It would be annoying to have to rewrite a bunch of **if/else** statements with smaller ones. To try and have **do-not repeat yourself (DRY)** code, we will use our best friend: declarative macros.

As a refresher, to make a macro public, we need to use the attribute, **macro_export** on top of the **macro_rules!** declaration. The macro will also be named our respective helper functions, **check_argcount_error** and **check_type_error** while containing the same parameters. However, these have the type, **expr**. Inside is a simple **if** statement that if the function results to **true**, it will return **nil_val()**, as shown:

```
#[macro_export]
macro_rules! check_argcount_error {
    ($arg_count: expr, $expected: expr, $name: expr) => {
        if check_argcount_error($arg_count, $expected, $name){
            return nil_val();
        }
    };
}
```

```
#[macro_export]
macro_rules! check_type_error {
    ($value: expr, $expected_type: expr, $name: expr) => {
        if check_type_error($value, $expected_type, $name){
            return nil_val();
        }
    };
}
```

Since these macros involve changing all our functions, we will show the new versions of each functions. Since we will create a binding **name** that has our function's name and replace each of the **if** statements. Inside **mufi_stdlib/src/lib.rs**, we can remove the function **error()**, and we will see the rewrites of all of our functions:

```
#[no_mangle]
pub unsafe extern "C" fn rscmdNative(argCount: c_int, args: *mut
```

```
Value) -> Value {
    let name = "rscmd()";
    check_argcount_error!(argCount, 1, name);
    let val = read(args as *const Value);
    check_type_error!(&val, "string", name);
    ...
}
#[no_mangle]
pub unsafe extern "C" fn rsexitNative(argCount: c_int, args: *mut
Value) -> Value {
    let name = "rsexit()";
    check_argcount_error!(argCount, 1, name);
    let val = read(args as *const Value);
    check_type_error!(&val, "int", name);
    exit(as_int(&val));
}
#[no_mangle]
pub unsafe extern "C" fn rserrprintNative(argCount: c_int, args:
*mut Value) -> Value {
    let name = "rserr_print()";
    check_argcount_error!(argCount, 1, name);
    let val = read(args as *const Value);
    check_type_error!(&val, "string", name);
    ...
}
#[no_mangle]
pub unsafe extern "C" fn readfileNative(argCount: c_int, args:
*mut Value) -> Value {
    let name = "read_file()";
    check_argcount_error!(argCount, 1, name);
    let val = read(args as *const Value);
    check_type_error!(&val, "string", name);
    ...
}
#[no_mangle]
pub unsafe extern "C" fn writefileNative(argCount: c_int, args:
*mut Value) -> Value {
```

```
        let name = "write_file()";
        check_argcount_error!(argCount, 2, name);
        // write_file(path, content);
        let path_val = read(args as *const Value);
        let content_val = read(args.add(1) as *const Value);
        check_type_error!(&path_val, "string", name);
        && check_type_error(&content_val, "string", name);
        ...
}


#[no_mangle]
pub unsafe extern "C" fn rsbenchNative(argCount: c_int, args:
*mut Value) -> Value {
        let name = "rsbench()";
        check_argcount_error!(argCount, 1, name);
        let val = read(args as *const Value);
        check_type_error!(&val, "int", name);
        ...
}


#[no_mangle]
pub unsafe extern "C" fn rsbenchThread(argCount: c_int, args:
*mut Value) -> Value {
        let name = "rsbench_thread()";
        check_argcount_error!(argCount, 1, name);
        let val = read(args as *const Value);
        check_type_error!(&val, "int", name);
        ...
}
```

If we run **make release** and try out **mufi**, we can see some of our new error reporting:

```
$ make release
# incase running on new session
$ export LD_LIBRARY_PATH=mufi_stdlib/target/debug
$ ./mufi
Version 0.1.0 (Baloo Release)
```

```
(mufi) >> rscmd(1);
ERROR: rscmd() expected a string, got int instead.
(mufi) >> rscmd();
ERROR: rscmd() expects 1 arguments, got 0 instead.
```

2. When writing a programming language, it is nice to be able to install it and not have to constantly remember to export the library every time we create a new session. Our install script is not perfect; a more portable solution is a bash script. However, using a Rust script will be more relevant for this book. Before we continue, we need to do a quick alteration in our **Makefile** and change our **cargo build** to **cargo build --release** and our C compiler using the **-o3** flag for optimizations. If the user is going to install our language, we may as well have the binaries compiled in the highest optimizations:

```
build:
    cd mufi_stdlib && cargo build --release
    $(CC) $(RUST) compiler/*.c  -Werror -Wall -std=c99 -o3 -o mufi
```

When we are writing our install script, we need to consider the following:

- **mufi_stdlib** path: **/usr/local/lib/Mufi/**

- **mufi** path: **/usr/local/bin/**

- Appending **~/.bashrc** with the export command

As you may notice, our programming language will only be supported by Unix systems such as MacOS or Linux systems. Another observation is that we will need our script to be run by the super user because we need to access **/usr** and that is only accessible by the super user. Since we are running the script as **sudo**, we cannot use the **$HOME** variable to get the home path to access **~/.bashrc**. Thus, we will need to ask the user to enter the path to finish the installation.

In the root of our project, we can create the file, **install.rs** and add the following imports at the top of the file, along with constants **INFO** and **CMD** that will be displayed at the beginning of the installation. The constant **INFO** will be used to explain the difference between the two modes, **debug** and **release**. The constant **CMD** will be used to append our export command to our bash file:

```
use std::io::{stdin, Result, Write, Read};
use std::fs::{File, create_dir,copy, OpenOptions};
use std::process::Command;
use std::path::Path;
```

```
const INFO: &str = r#"MUFI-LANG INSTALL MODES:
- Debug: Shows bytecode logs and garbage collector tracings
- Release: Only shows results from interpreter
"#;
```

```
const CMD: &str = "\nexport LD_LIBRARY_PATH=/usr/local/lib/Mufi";
```

In our **main()** function which will return **Result<()>**, we will print our **INFO** and ask the user to enter which mode to install. Using that mode, we will run the respective **make** command. However, we will not spawn it and just use the **output()** method in **std::process::Command**:

```
fn main() -> Result<()>{
    println!("{INFO}");
    println!("Please choose install mode: ");
    let mut input = String::new();
    stdin().read_line(&mut input)?;
    input = input.trim().to_lowercase();


    let _ = Command::new("make").arg(&input).output()?;
```

Now, the first step is copying our shared object library to **/usr/local/lib/Mufi**. Firstly, we need to create the directory if it does not already exist:

```
// create directory /usr/local/lib/Mufi
let lib_path = Path::new("/usr/local/lib/Mufi");
if !lib_path.exists(){
    println!("Creating directory: {:?}", lib_path);
    create_dir(lib_path)?;
}
```

Now, with the directory created, we can proceed to define the source path of our library and the destination path. With the destination path, we can create an empty file, and then we can copy the contents from our source file to the destination, while letting the user know what we are doing:

```
// handle copying libmufi_stdlib.so
let lib_src = Path::new("mufi_stdlib/target/release/libmufi_
stdlib.so");
let lib_dest = lib_path.join("libmufi_stdlib.so");
// create empty file in lib destination
```

```
let _ = File::create(&lib_dest)?;
// copy src to destination
println!("Copying Mufi Standard Library to /usr/local/lib/
Mufi");
copy(lib_src, &lib_dest)?;
```

Now, we can proceed to do the same thing, except for our **mufi** binary. We will copy the binary from the root of our project to **/usr/local/bin/**. We will need to create an empty file, then copy the contents from our source to the destination, while letting the user know:

```
// handle copying mufi binary
let bin_src = Path::new("mufi");
let bin_dest = Path::new("/usr/local/bin/mufi");
// create empty file in bin destination
let _ = File::create(bin_dest)?;
// copy src to destination
println!("Copying Mufi binary to /usr/local/bin");
copy(bin_src, bin_dest)?;
```

As mentioned earlier, when we are appending to **~/.bashrc** or whatever is the equivalent, we need the user to enter this path as its hard for us to access it. After this, we can create a new path using the input (trimmed to remove any unnecessary whitespace). We can open our file using **OpenOptions::new()** with the **read()** method set to **true** and **append()** method set to **true**. Then, we can complete the chain with the **open()** method using our path:

```
// get home path
let mut input = String::new();
println!("Please enter path to .bashrc or equivalent to finish
installation: ");
stdin().read_line(&mut input)?;
let bashrc_path = Path::new(input.trim());
// open ~/.bashrc as append only, we do not want to overwrite
it
let mut bashrc = OpenOptions::new().read(true).append(true).
open(&bashrc_path)?;
```

It would be annoying if we keep appending this command to the file. Thus, before we do so, we will read the file and check whether it's already there, and if it is, we are done. However, if it is not present, we will write the command to our file and let the user know we are doing so, and once that is completed, we are done:

```
let mut contents = String::new();
bashrc.read_to_string(&mut contents)?;
// if the file already contains it we don't want to add it
again
if contents.contains(CMD){
    println!("Installation completed!");
} else {
    println!("Adding export to {}", bashrc_path.display());
    bashrc.write_all(CMD.as_bytes())?;
    println!("Installation completed!");
}
Ok(())
}
```

With our installation script written, let us try running it and afterwards, we can add it to our **Makefile**:

```
$ rustc install.rs
$ sudo ./install
MUFI-LANG INSTALL MODES:
- Debug: Shows bytecode logs and garbage collector tracings
- Release: Only shows results from interpreter


Please choose install mode:
release
Copying Mufi Standard Library to /usr/local/lib/Mufi
Copying Mufi binary to /usr/local/bin
Please enter path to .bashrc or equivalent to finish installation:
/home/mustafif/.bashrc
Installation completed!

# if we try to run without sudo
$ ./install
MUFI-LANG INSTALL MODES:
- Debug: Shows bytecode logs and garbage collector tracings
- Release: Only shows results from interpreter
```

```
Please choose install mode:
debug
Error: Os { code: 13, kind: PermissionDenied, message:
"Permission denied" }
```

Now, we can add an **install** option to the **Makefile** and add the **install** binary to our **clean** option:

```
install:
    rustc install.rs && sudo ./install
clean:
    rm mufi install
```

With everything written, not only have we written a standard library for a programming language written in C, but also learned how we can allow a user to install it and have it work on their system (granted it is a Unix system).

CHAPTER 11

Project – App in Tauri

Introduction

In *Chapter 7, Project – GTK App*, we built a desktop app using the crate **gtk** and while we were able to build a desktop app for Linux systems, it was not the best experience. When building a desktop app, it would be nice to be able to port it to as many systems as possible, and it would be easier for a developer if that is done in one codebase. So, we need to use a cross-platform framework that can be built for different systems. There is already a popular framework for that and that is Electron!

However, there are also issues with Electron, which makes quite a few people use Tauri instead, to write a simple desktop app, to showcase open-source books written in **mdbook**. Electron is a JavaScript framework that uses chromium to build a cross-platform app that can be built to a Windows **MSI** file, macOS **DMG** file, or a Linux **AppImage** file (or **deb** for Debian distros). The problem with Electron is the word *chromium*. Having chromium essentially built into the app, causes it to be a memory hog (depending on what the app does, for example, **vscode**) and have large file sizes (our simple app was ~1GB). While Tauri may still be a relatively new framework that uses Rust as its backend, and because Rust can sometimes output binaries smaller than the input, you can get the relatively same experience, while having much smaller executables (our simple app became a few megabytes).

For more information about the Electron framework, check out their official documentation: **https://www.electronforge.io/**. If you want more information about the Tauri framework, you may also check their documentation **https://tauri.app/**.

Structure

In this chapter, we will cover the following topics:

- Getting Started with Tauri
- Getting familiar with Svelte
- Overview of the application
- Creating the application
- More with Tauri
- Challenges with Tauri development

Objectives

This chapter aims to enable the reader to use their knowledge in Rust to build a desktop app alongside a JavaScript framework, Svelte, to build cross-platform apps with Tauri. We will also learn how to use our desktop app alongside a web server that we will build to show how to send requests, process them, and send back the results to our desktop app.

Getting started with Tauri

To set up Tauri, we will need to make sure we have the dependencies of the appropriate system, and we will discuss the different ways to create a project, while we will use the **Cargo** method to simplify our lives.

Systems dependencies

We will need Rust installed in all the different systems. In a Windows system, we will need to have the Microsoft Visual Studio C++ Build tools installed. The easiest way to do this is by installing *Build Tools for Visual Studio 2022* from **https://visualstudio. microsoft.com/visual-cpp-build-tools/** and ensuring that "C++ *build tools*" and the Windows SDK are selected. Tauri also heavily depends on **WebView2**, while in Windows 11, it is preinstalled; if you are running Windows 10, you will need to download and install the Evergreen Bootstrapper from Microsoft's website, **https:// developer.microsoft.com/en-us/microsoft-edge/webview2/#download-section**.

In a macOS system, you will need to make sure that **CLang** and development dependencies installed are installed. Then, you will need to run the following command on a terminal:

```
$ xcode-select –install
```

To install on Linux, we will focus on Debian and Arch distributions. For Debian, you will need to run the following commands on the terminal:

```
$ sudo apt update
$ sudo apt install libwebkit2gtk-4.0-dev \
    build-essential \
    curl \
    wget \
    libssl-dev \
    libgtk-3-dev \
    libayatana-appindicator3-dev \
    librsvg2-dev
```

For Arch distributions, you will need to run the following commands on the terminal:

```
$ sudo pacman -Syu
$ sudo pacman -S --needed \
    webkit2gtk \
    base-devel \
    curl \
    wget \
    openssl \
    appmenu-gtk-module \
    gtk3 \
    libappindicator-gtk3 \
    librsvg \
    libvips
```

There are different ways to start creating a Tauri app. Using the **create-tauri-app** utility, you can choose to use **Bash**, **PowerShell**, **Cargo**, **npm**, **yarn**, and **pnpm** to run the utility.

For Bash, you need to run the following command on the terminal:

```
$ sh <(curl https://create.tauri.app/sh)
```

For PowerShell, you will need to run the following command:

```
PS C:\> iwr -useb https://create.tauri.app/ps | iex
```

For Cargo, we will need to install the utility and then run it using **cargo**:

```
$ cargo install create-tauri-app
$ cargo create-tauri-app
```

For **npm yarn** and **pnpm**, they have the same command depending on which package manager you decide to use:

```
$ {pm} create tauri-app
```

We will use the **cargo** method throughout this chapter. However, you are free to choose any method shown above.

Hello World in Tauri

We can practice using this utility by creating a hello world application with a Vanilla template (no JS framework). When we run the utility, **create-tauri-app**, we are asked for a project name. We will name the project **hello_world**. Then, you have to choose a package manager; for a Vanilla UI template, **cargo** is fine, but to use a JS framework (we will use Svelte later), we will need to use **yarn**, **npm** or **pnpm**.

> **Note: You have two different UI templates when using the cargo package manager. The first is vanilla while the second is yew, which involves WebAssembly:**

```
$ cargo create-tauri-app

✓ Project name · hello_world
✓ Choose your package manager · cargo
✓ Choose your UI template · vanilla
```

Please follow **https://tauri.app/v1/guides/getting-started/prerequisites** to install the needed prerequisites, if you have not already done it.

You also need to install the following:

```
tauri-cli (cargo install tauri-cli)
```

Once done, run the following:

```
cd hello_world
cargo tauri dev
```

At the end of the installation, we are told to install **tauri-cli** if it is not already installed. Let us install it now:

```
$ cargo install tauri-cli
```

To run the desktop app and see how it looks like, we need to use the following commands:

```
$ cd hello_world
$ cargo tauri dev
```

When we run the application, we will see the following window, as shown in *Figure 11.1*:

Figure 11.1: *Greeting window from hello_world*

Let us go under the hood to see what the Tauri framework has provided us. If we look at the project structure from **hello_world**, we can see the following:

```
$ ls
README.md  src  src-tauri

$ ls src
assets  index.html  main.js  style.css

$ ls src-tauri
build.rs  Cargo.lock  Cargo.toml  icons  src  target  tauri.conf.json
```

We can notice the following from the project structure:

src: This folder contains all the front-end of the application. This involves HTML, CSS and JS files.

src-tauri: This folder contains all the back-end of the application.

Inside **src-tauri/Cargo.toml**, we will use the following crates:

tauri: Provides APIs that our front-end can use (we will checkout later).

serde: For serialization and deserialization.

serde_derive: Provides the derive macros for the **serde** crate.

Now, we are ready to look at **src-tauri/src/main.rs** and see what magic brews for us there:

```
#![cfg_attr(
    all(not(debug_assertions), target_os = "windows"),
    windows_subsystem = "windows"
)]


// Learn more about Tauri commands at https://tauri.app/v1/guides/features/command
#[tauri::command]
fn greet(name: &str) -> String {
    format!("Hello, {}! You've been greeted from Rust!", name)
}


fn main() {
    tauri::Builder::default()
        .invoke_handler(tauri::generate_handler![greet])
        .run(tauri::generate_context!())
        .expect("error while running tauri application");
}
```

You can see that the text we were greeted in *Figure 11.1* can be seen in the **greet()** function and is handled by an invocation handler in the method **invoke_handler()**, using the **tauri::generate_handler!** macro.

To see how the **greet** command is brought to the front end, we need to look at **src/main.js** where we asynchronously wait for the function to be invoked. We can then create an event listener that will select the greet input and greet message, and when we click on the button, we run **greet()**:

```
const { invoke } = window.__TAURI__.tauri;

let greetInputEl;
let greetMsgEl;

async function greet() {
  // Learn more about Tauri commands at https://tauri.app/v1/guides/
features/command
  greetMsgEl.textContent = await invoke("greet", { name: greetInputEl.
value });
}

window.addEventListener("DOMContentLoaded", () => {
  greetInputEl = document.querySelector("#greet-input");
  greetMsgEl = document.querySelector("#greet-msg");
  document
    .querySelector("#greet-button")
    .addEventListener("click", () => greet());
});
```

To see where the queries are taking place, we need to look at **src/index.html** where these inputs, buttons, and text are defined:

```
<p>Click on the Tauri logo to learn more about the framework</p>
<div class="row">
  <div>
    <input id="greet-input" placeholder="Enter a name..." />
    <button id="greet-button" type="button">Greet</button>
  </div>
</div>
<p id="greet-msg"></p>
```

The whole point of using a cross-platform project such as Tauri is to be able to build the same application for different operating systems and to start, we need to look at **src-tauri/tauri.conf.json**.

Inside the **bundle** key in the JSON file, we can see the different kinds of operating systems and options for them, such as for *macOS, Windows* and *deb*. To build the project, we need to change the identifier, and so we will change it to something simple such as **com.hello.world**. When you are building the Tauri project, depending on what operating system you are building on, Tauri will bundle the system-specific executable.

At the time of writing, the project is running on POP_OS! and as such, when we build the project, we will get a **.deb** file and a **.AppImage** file. The Debian file is used for any **.deb** based Linux distributions, while other distributions can use the **.AppImage** file.

Let us build the project using the command line tool **tauri-cli**:

```
# make sure to be in hello_world
$ cargo tauri build
# in my case we will see the bundles for Linux
$ ls src-tauri/target/release/bundle
appimage  deb
# lets check what is in the appimage folder
$ ls src-tauri/target/release/bundle/appimage
build_appimage.sh  hello-world_0.0.0_amd64.AppImage  hello-world.AppDir
# lets check what is in the deb folder
$ ls src-tauri/target/release/bundle/deb
hello-world_0.0.0_amd64  hello-world_0.0.0_amd64.deb


# to run you can do the following:
$ cd src-tauri/target/release/bundle/appimage
$ ./hello-world_0.0.0_amd64.AppImage


# to install you can do the following:
$ cd src-tauri/target/release/bundle/deb
$ sudo dpkg -i hello-world_0.0.0_amd64.deb
```

Getting familiar with Svelte

In our actual project, we will not be using a Vanilla template but rather, use the **npm** package manager so that we can use the Svelte JS framework for our UI template. The Svelte framework first became popular with the news that it was planning to rewrite its compiler in Rust with the aim of reducing output size (possibly smaller than the input) and for better performance. Svelte's JavaScript has quite an intuitive syntax.

For our example, make sure to have **nodejs** installed and the package manager **npm**. If you want to use **yarn** or **pnpm**, then you should be able to use it by replacing **npm** with your package manager in the given commands. You may download **nodejs** from its official website: **https://nodejs.org/en/download/**.

To get familiar with Svelte, we will create a project using **SvelteKit** that gives us a project using **Svelte** and a better experience for experimenting. We will create the project **svelte_fun** with the following commands:

```
$ npm create svelte@latest svelte_fun
✓ Which Svelte app template? › Skeleton project
✓ Add type checking with TypeScript? › Yes, using TypeScript syntax
✓ Add ESLint for code linting? … No / Yes
✓ Add Prettier for code formatting? … No / Yes
✓ Add Playwright for browser testing? … No / Yes


$ cd svelte_fun
$ npm install
$ ls src
app.d.ts  app.html  routes
```

If we look into the **src** directory inside **svelte_fun**, we can notice the directory **routes** which will contain all our **.svelte** files. We will focus on working in the **routes** directory, so that we can show off the general syntax of the language.

Note: There is a Svelte plugin for vscode that provides syntax highlighting.

To begin, remove everything in **routes/+page.svelte** which represents our index path and we will replace it with a more standard layout for a Svelte file. The layout of a Svelte file contains three components: the first is the **script** tag which is where we will have all our JavaScript code or in our case typescript; the second component is the HTML code; and the last component is the **style** tag for any CSS styling. This can all be seen as follows:

```
<script lang="ts">

</script>


<!--HTML-->


<style>

</style>
```

What happens if we want to create a counter that is displayed and handles the following two events. The first event will handle incrementing the counter which will be done using the "Add Counter" button. The second event will handle decrementing the counter which is done using the "Decrease Counter" button.

To start with, we will work on the **script** section and create a global variable **counter** with the type **number** and initialize it with the value 0. We can then create the function, **add_counter()** by using the keyword **function**. We will have 0 parameters and inside the block, we will increment **counter** by 1. After **add_counter**, we will write **min_counter()** which will decrease **counter** by 1 inside its block:

```
let counter: number = 0;
function add_counter(){
    counter++;
}
function min_counter(){
    counter--;
}
```

Now, we can start working on the HTML side of things and that starts with displaying our counter. This will be done inside a **<p>** tag. In Svelte, to interpolate a value from the **script** tags inside HTML, they must be inside the brackets. We can then create two buttons using the **<button>** tag and inside it, we will use **on:click{}** that handles the event when a user clicks on the button. To use the functions we created, we will put the functions inside the brackets of **on:click{}** for their respective button:

```
<p>Count: {counter}</p>


<button on:click={add_counter}>Add Counter</button>
<button on:click={min_counter}>Decrease Counter</button>
```

Keep in mind that we could have done this entirely without our functions, if we replaced the event with an empty parentheses, followed by a matching arm and then our action. This can be seen done as follows:

```
<button on:click={() => counter++}>Add Counter</button>
<button on:click={() => counter--}>Decrease Counter</button>
```

To test our program, we can run the following command that will open our project on the browser in localhost:

```
$ npm run dev -- --open
```

However, what if we wanted to do some control flow in the path **/flow**, how would we go about it? Well, that is an easy enough job. We create a new directory **flow** in

routes and we will create a file **+page.svelte** that will act as the index file for that path.

On this page, we will have a counter that will have two buttons: one to double its count and another to reset it back to 1. We will declare the variable, **counter** and set it to 1 and have two functions **double()** and **reset()** inside the **script** tags, as follows:

```ts
<script lang="ts">
    let counter: number = 1;
    function double(){
        counter *= 2;
    }
    function reset(){
        counter = 1;
    }
</script>
```

What if we want a message to be displayed to the user to keep doubling the count as long as the counter is less than 10? We will need to use the tag **{#if <condition>}** and have it end using the **{/if}** tag. Once the count is equal to or greater than 10, we want to tell the user the count is too high and they need to reset it. This is done using the **{:else if <condition>}** tag, as follows:

```
{#if counter < 10}
    <h1>Welcome to Double the Counter!</h1>
    <p>Keep doubling the count!!!</p>
{:else if counter >= 10}
    <h1>Woah the count is high!!!!</h1>
    <p>RESET!!!!!!!!</p>
{/if}
```

Now, we can create our text to display the count and the buttons to double and reset it using the **on:click{}** property we used earlier:

```
<button on:click={double}>Double Counter</button>

<br>

<button on:click={reset}>Reset Counter</button>
```

The last thing we need to do is allow the user to go to this path from our homepage. We will use an anchor tag to let them be sent to the **flow** path. Add the following after the buttons in **routes/+page.svelte**:

```
<br>
<a href="/flow">Go to Flow</a>
```

Overview of the application

We have talked about Tauri and Svelte and getting a basic view in both frameworks. However, it is now time to put them together and help it create our application. What is our desktop application even about? Creating a login application is still kind of boring and so to have fun and also simplify our lives, let us create a zodiac sign application instead.

A zodiac sign application? What does that even mean? Here's the plan: a user enters their zodiac sign; we read it and output the results of the zodiac sign, which is a programming language that represents it and a funny short description of why they got the language.

Let us look at the different zodiac signs and the programming languages that can represent it, given the attributes each sign has. Keep in mind that this is all for fun and you should not take these languages with zodiac signs seriously.

- **Aries**: March 21 – April 19
    - Loves to be #1
    - Python

- **Taurus**: April 20 – May 20
    - Loves to be relaxed
    - Swift

- Gemini: May 21 – June 21
    - Loves to be curious, wishes to clone themselves
    - Kotlin

- **Cancer**: June 22 – July 22
    - Highly Intuitive
    - Golang

- **Leo**: July 23 – August 22
    - Loves to be in the spotlight
    - C++

- **Virgo**: August 23 – September 22
    - Loves to be a perfectionist
    - TeX

- **Libra**: September 23 – October 23
  - o Loves to be at equilibrium
  - o JavaScript

- **Scorpius**: October 24 – November 21
  - o Elusive and mysterious
  - o Assembly

- **Sagittarius**: November 22 – December 21
  - o Always on the quest for knowledge
  - o WebAssembly

- **Capricorn**: December 22 – January 19
  - o Loves to be patient
  - o C

- **Aquarius**: January 20 – February 18
  - o Wants to make the world better and is innovative
  - o Rust

- **Pisces**: February 19 – March 20
  - o Intuitive, sensitive and empathetic
  - o Java

In terms of what we can see in the Rust code, we will need a general structure **Zodiac** that needs fields to contain the name of the zodiac sign, the description of its personality, and its respective programming language. It can look like the following:

```
pub struct Zodiac{
    name: String,
    description: String,
    language: String
}
```

How will this interact with the frontend of the application? Well, we will ask the user to input their zodiac sign. We will have a method for each zodiac sign and a **to_string()** method that returns a **Vec<String>**. You may wonder why we are returning a vector of strings and not a **String**, and that is because of problems with newlines. If we try to return a **String** with newlines formatted into the string, when we return that into JavaScript, we will still have "\n" in the string.

How about embedding the **
** tag in the string; that must work right? Sadly, no. It is the same issue as "\n", so what we do instead is return a vector of strings in the right order. With the vector in Svelte, we can use the **{#each}** tag, so that we can iterate through the vector and have them in HTML.

Creating the application

While we were discussing the overview of the application, we started to discuss some of the code involved and while that may be nice to consider, it's better for us to start the project. To begin, make sure to have **npm** installed, and once that is done, we will install the **yarn** package manager. We can then create our project with the following options, as follows:

```
$ npm install -g yarn
# create project
$ cargo create-tauri-app
✓ Project name · zodiac_app
✓ Choose your package manager · yarn
✓ Choose your UI template · svelte-kit


Done, Now run:
  cd zodiac_app
  yarn
  yarn tauri dev
```

After we create our project, we will follow the given instructions:

```
$ cd zodiac_app
# installs all dependencies
$ yarn
# test out the application
$ yarn tauri dev
```

The greeting application already built for us will be useful since our core frontend will be using it. For now, we will not touch it because we have more pressing issues to handle and that is our backend. The Rust code is placed in the directory **src-tauri** and the inside **src-tauri/src**, we will create the file **zodiac.rs**. This file will handle all our code related to zodiac signs and we can begin by writing the **Zodiac** struct:

```
#[derive(Debug, Clone)]
pub struct Zodiac{
    name: String,
    description: String,
```

```
    language: String
}
```

The first method we need to write for **Zodiac** is a **new()** method that expects the zodiac sign's name, a description of it, and its respective programming language. All the parameters will be **&str** and we will turn them into a **String** for each field using the **to_string()** method:

```
impl Zodiac{
    pub fn new(name: &str, description: &str, language: &str) -> Self{
        Self{
            name: name.to_string(),
            description: description.to_string(),
            language: language.to_string()
        }
    }
}
```

When we described each zodiac sign in our overview, we had already been given a description and a programming language for each sign. We will use our given information to create a method for each zodiac sign as follows:

```
    pub fn aries() -> Self{
        Self::new("Aries", "Loves to be #1!", "Python")
    }
    pub fn taurus() -> Self{
        Self::new("Taurus", "Loves to be relaxed!", "Swift")
    }
    pub fn gemini() -> Self{
        Self::new("Gemini", "Loves to be curious!", "Kotlin")
    }
    pub fn cancer() -> Self{
        Self::new("Cancer", "Highly Intuitive!", "Golang")
    }
    pub fn leo() -> Self{
        Self::new("Leo", "Loves to be in the spotlight!", "C++")
    }
    pub fn virgo() -> Self{
        Self::new("Virgo", "Loves to be a perfectionist!", "TeX")
    }
    pub fn libra() -> Self{
```

```
        Self::new("Libra", "Loves to be at equilibrium!", "JavaScript")
    }
    pub fn scorpius() -> Self{
        Self::new("Scorpius", "Loves to be mysterious!", "Assembly")
    }
    pub fn sagittarius() -> Self{
        Self::new("Sagittarius", "Always on the quest for
knowledge!","WebAssembly")
    }
    pub fn capricorn() -> Self{
        Self::new("Capricorn","Loves to be patient!","C")
    }
    pub fn aquarius() -> Self{
        Self::new("Aquarius","Wants to make the world better!","Rust")
    }
    pub fn pisces() -> Self{
        Self::new("Pisces","Intuitive, sensitive and empathetic","Java")
    }
```

The next method we need to write is **to_string()** that will immutably use **self** and return a **Vec<String>**. Inside the method, we will have three bindings: **sign**, **why**, and **lang** that represents the formatted text for the zodiac sign's result, a description of why the language represents it, and the programming language. We will then return a vector with the order of **sign**, **lang**, and **why**, as follows:

```
    pub fn to_string(&self) -> Vec<String> {
        let sign = format!("Results of zodiac sign: {}",&self.name);
        let why = format!("Why: {}", &self.description);
        let lang = format!("Your programming language: {}", &self.language);
        vec![sign, lang, why]
    }
}
```

What if the user enters a zodiac sign that does not actually exist? We need to handle that case and to do so, we will implement the **Default** trait to **Zodiac**, and we will return a **Zodiac** with a lot of question marks:

```
impl Default for Zodiac{
    fn default() -> Self {
        Self::new("????", "What zodiac sign is that?", "Fortran???")
    }
}
```

Now, we can head over to **main.rs** and replace it with the following:

```
#![cfg_attr(all(not(debug_assertions), target_os = "windows"),
    windows_subsystem = "windows"
)]
mod zodiac;
use zodiac::Zodiac;


#[tauri::command]
fn get_zodiac(zodiac: &str) -> Vec<String>{
    // TODO
}
fn main() {
    tauri::Builder::default()
        .invoke_handler(tauri::generate_handler![get_zodiac])
        .run(tauri::generate_context!())
        .expect("error while running tauri application");
}
```

As you can see, we have the function **get_zodiac()** that will expect an input of the user's zodiac sign and we will return a **Vec<String>**. To not worry about whether the user entered the zodiac sign with an uppercase or all lowercase, we will create a binding **zodiac** that will turn the parameter **zodiac** into a lowercase using the **to_lowercase()** method. We can then use a **match** statement on the binding, **zodiac**. However, since it is a **String**, we will use the **as_str()** method to turn it into an **&str**:

```
fn get_zodiac(zodiac: &str) -> Vec<String>{
    let zodiac = zodiac.to_lowercase();
    match zodiac.as_str(){
        _ => Zodiac::default().to_string()
    }
}
```

We can use a matching arm to handle each zodiac sign, using the respective method in **Zodiac**, chained with the **to_string()** method, so that we return a **Vec<String>**. This can be seen done in the following code:

```
    match zodiac.as_str(){
        "aries" => Zodiac::aries().to_string(),
        "taurus" => Zodiac::taurus().to_string(),
```

```
    "gemini" => Zodiac::gemini().to_string(),
    "cancer" => Zodiac::cancer().to_string(),
    "leo" => Zodiac::leo().to_string(),
    "virgo" => Zodiac::virgo().to_string(),
    "libra" => Zodiac::libra().to_string(),
    "scorpius" => Zodiac::scorpius().to_string(),
    "sagittarius" => Zodiac::sagittarius().to_string(),
    "capricorn" => Zodiac::capricorn().to_string(),
    "aquarius" => Zodiac::aquarius().to_string(),
    "pisces" => Zodiac::pisces().to_string(),
    _ => Zodiac::default().to_string()
}
```

With the **get_zodiac()** function finished, we are ready to start handling the frontend of our application and that begins with the appearance of the page. We need to edit the file **src/routes/+page.svelte** by adding in our own title, replacing the images with our own, changing the lib file/class tag and the subtitle. Any picture from Google will work, and a height of 200px is suitable:

```
<script>
  import Zodiac from "$lib/Zodiac.svelte";
</script>


<h1>Welcome to Programming Zodiacs!</h1>
<div class="row">
  <img src="/ProgrammingIllustration.png" height="200px">
</div>
<p>Please enter your zodiac sign... </p>
<div class="row">
  <Zodiac/>
</div>
<style>
  .logo.vite:hover {
    filter: drop-shadow(0 0 2em #747bff);
  }
  .logo.svelte:hover {
    filter: drop-shadow(0 0 2em #ff3e00);
  }
</style>
```

You can delete the file **lib/Greet.svelte** and create the new file **lib/Zodiac. svelte**. We will begin by worrying about the **script** portion of our file. Firstly, we need to import the **invoke()** function from **@tauri-apps/api/tauri**, and then, we can create a variable **zodiac_msg** that will be assigned an array with an empty string (will contain the strings from **get_zodiac()**). After we create **zodiac_msg**, we can also create the variable **zodiac**, which will be an empty string (will contain the zodiac sign input). Lastly, we need a way for **zodiac_msg** to be assigned the result of **get_zodiac()** and that is done in the asynchronous function **handle_zodiac()**. Inside it, we will assign **zodiac_msg** to **invoke()** (being awaited using the **await** keyword) with the string *"get_zodiac"* and using the variable **zodiac** wrapped in brackets:

```
<script>
    import { invoke } from "@tauri-apps/api/tauri"
    let zodiac_msg = [""];
    let zodiac = ""
    async function handle_zodiac(){
      zodiac_msg = await invoke("get_zodiac", {zodiac})
    }
</script>
```

Now, we can work on the HTML portion of our Svelte program. Firstly, we will need to create an **input** tag that uses the proper **bind:value={zodiac}** to assign **zodiac** to whatever value is in the input:

```
<div>
  <div class="row">
    <input bind:value={zodiac} placeholder="Libra...">
  </div>
```

After that, we can create a button using the **button** tag and use the property **on:click={handle_zodiac}** to trigger the function **handle_zodiac()**, when we click on the button. This property is equivalent to using an event listener on the button by querying its ID:

```
<button on:click={handle_zodiac}>Enter</button>
```

Once the user presses the button, the variable **zodiac_msg** is loaded with our strings that we need to output to the user in some way. In the overview, we discussed using the tag **{#each}**, which is like a **for-each** loop where we will use the array **zodiac_ msg** and have each element be the variable **z** and placed inside a **<p>** tag:

```
  {#each zodiac_msg as z}
  <p>{z}</p>
  {/each}
</div>
```

With the frontend completed, we are free to test out our application using the following command. The application window is shown in *Figure 11.2*:

```
$ yarn tauri dev
```

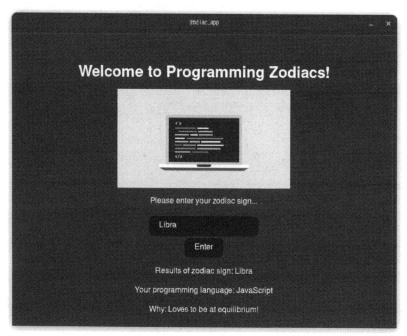

Figure 11.2: *Results of Libra with zodiac_app*

We have built our application and it is worth trying to build the application, so that we can install it. However, we cannot simply run **yarn tauri build**; we need to edit the application's identifier found in the file **src-tauri/tauri.conf.json**. Change the identifier from **com.tauri.dev** to **app.zodiac** or any name you would like to use to identify the project. We are now ready to build our project as follows:

```
$ yarn tauri build

# when building on POP_OS!

Finished 2 bundles at:

zodiac_app/src-tauri/target/release/bundle/deb/zodiac-app_0.0.0_amd64.
deb

zodiac_app/src-tauri/target/release/bundle/appimage/zodiac-app_0.0.0_
amd64.AppImage

# when building on Windows (use latest stable rust compiler, currently
1.65.0)

Finished 1 bundle at:

C:zodiac_app\src-tauri\target\release\bundle/msi/zodiac_app_0.0.0_x64_
en-US.msi
```

For those wondering how large these files are (a reason one would choose Tauri against Electron), here are the sizes for each of the files we have built in Linux and Windows:

- zodiac-app_0.0.0_amd64.deb
    - 5.2 MB

- zodiac-app_0.0.0_amd64.AppImage
    - 78.3 MB

- zodiac_app_0.0.0_x64_en-US.msi
    - 3.3 MB

Overall, the install files we have built are relatively small, with the **deb** and **msi** files being a few megabytes and the **AppImage** being close to 75 megabytes. These are better than Electron's 700 MB - 1GB average.

More with Tauri

The application we built is fairly simple and did not require us to do too much in terms of conversion between Rust and JavaScript. However, let us talk about a few situations in which you will need to do more with Tauri.

Error handling

The first thing that comes to one's mind when creating a new application is error handling. It is really difficult to create a complex application without using error handling. So how do you use **Result** in Rust and use that in JavaScript? Consider the following function:

```
// divides two numbers
#[tauri::command]
fn divide(numerator: &str, denominator: &str) -> Result<f32, String>{
    // turn the numerators to integers so we can match it
    let numerator: f32 = numerator.trim().parse().unwrap();
    let denominator: f32 = denominator.trim().parse().unwrap();
    // use if/else statement to check denominator
    if denominator == 0.0{
        Err(format!("Error: Cannot divide {numerator} by 0"))
    } else{
        Ok(numerator/denominator)
    }
}
```

We expect the user to input two numbers and when they click on a button, they are presented with the result. However, what happens if the denominator is 0? You cannot divide a number by 0, and you do not want to crash the program if this happens. So instead, we will let JavaScript handle this error and this is done using the .**then()** and .**catch()** methods.

The .**then()** method handles our **Ok** value and evaluates when the function does not throw an error. But what if it does? The .**catch()** method handles our **Err** value and is evaluated when the function throws an error and we catch it and do something with it.

How do we go about the Svelte frontend? To begin with, we will need to create variables for the numerator and denominator (variables **num** and **dem** respectively) and initialize them with an empty string. After that, we need a way for the frontend to know an error occurred, and so we will create the variable **error** with initial value **false**. If an error occurs, we will store the error message in the variable **err_msg** that is initialized as an empty string. If the result has no errors, we need to store the result, and that is contained in the variable **result** that has an initial value **0.0**:

```
<script>
    import { invoke } from "@tauri-apps/api/tauri"
    // numerator
    let num = "";
    // denominator
    let dem = "";
    // checks if we have an error
    let error = false;
    // if we do have an error, this contains the message
    let err_msg = "";
    // contains the result
    let result = 0.0;
```

Now, we need to write an asynchronous function to handle the event when the user needs to calculate their result. We will need to use the function **invoke()** along with **await**. Inside **invoke()**, we will have the command **divide** and the parameters be wrapped in brackets with the parameters **numerator** assigned to the variable **num** and **denominator** assigned to the variable **dem**:

```
    async function divide(){
        await invoke("divide", {numerator: num, denominator: dem})
```

If the user does not put the denominator as 0, then we should get the result of the division. So, we will use the **then()** method to handle assigning **result** to the **Ok** value:

```
// if we don't divide by 0, we get a result
// assign the variable result to the value, r
.then((r) => result = r)
```

However, if the user does decide to divide by 0, then we need to make sure to assign the error message to **err_msg** and turn the error flag on, or assign **error** to **true**:

```
// if we divide by 0, assign the error message to err_msg
// and make the error flag to true
.catch((msg) => {err_msg = msg; error = true})
}
</script>
```

The HTML code is very straightforward. We create inputs for the numerator and denominator and use the property **bind:value={}**. To calculate the result, we will have a button that says **Calculate** and uses the property **on:click={}** with the function, **divide**.

Now, in terms of displaying either the result or error message, we will make use of our flag **error** and use the **{#if }** tag. If we do have an error, we display the error message and if we do not have one, we will display our result. This can all be seen as follows:

```
{#if error}
  <p>{err_msg}</p>
{:else}
  <p>{result}</p>
{/if}
</div>
```

We can see the different kinds of results as shown with a proper input in *Figure 11.3*:

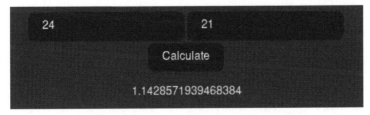

Figure 11.3: *Display of Ok value from divide()*

We can see the displayed error message when there is an error due to division by zero in *Figure 11.4:*

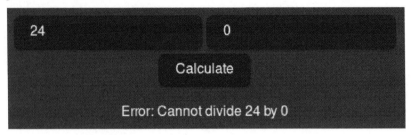

Figure 11.4: *Display of Error Message from divide()*

Nesting each loops

While developing the exercise program in this chapter, an issue was found with nesting each loop in Svelte, where each value will happen multiple times. We will consider the situation where you have an element that must include iterations from multiple arrays, and an important note is that all of these arrays have the same length.

To begin with, we will consider an application that contains a table that has three columns, a number, the number squared, and the number cubed. For our purposes, we will consider an array from 1 to 25. To keep our code DRY, we will create a function called **num_pow()** that goes from 1 to 25 and pushes it to a vector to the power that is given. This can be seen as follows:

```rust
fn num_pow(pow: u32) -> Vec<u32>{
    let mut vec = Vec::new();
    for i in 1..=25 as u32{
        vec.push(i.pow(pow))
    }
    vec
}
```

Now, we can create our commands using this function given their respective exponent:

```rust
#[tauri::command]
fn numbers() -> Vec<u32>{
    num_pow(1)
}
#[tauri::command]
fn numbers_squared() -> Vec<u32>{
```

```
        num_pow(2)
}
#[tauri::command]
fn numbers_cubed() -> Vec<u32>{
        num_pow(3)
}
```

Inside the frontend, we want to be able to create a table with each row having the numbers, its respective square, and cubed values in the next columns. We will go through the wrong way to approach nesting each loop, and how it causes the loop to iterate multiple times and a simple way through which we can fix this using indexes.

Before we get ahead of ourselves, let's begin by creating the **script** portion of the Svelte frontend by initializing our arrays with a 0 inside. After that, we will create asynchronous functions for their respective **tauri** command. For all these functions to happen at once, we will create the function **load()** that asynchronously executes each of our functions using **await**:

```
<script>
  import { invoke } from "@tauri-apps/api/tauri";
  let num = [0];
  let num_sq = [0];
  let num_cubed = [0];

  async function numbers() {
    num = await invoke("numbers");
  }
  async function numbers_squared() {
    num_sq = await invoke("numbers_squared");
  }
  async function numbers_cubed() {
    num_cubed = await invoke("numbers_cubed");
  }
  async function load() {
    await numbers();
    await numbers_squared();
    await numbers_cubed();
  }
</script>
```

The HTML is fairly simple; we will require a button and a table, and the button will use the property **on:click={}** with the function **load()**, while the table will contain three columns, **N**, **N^2**, and **N^3**:

```
<div>
  <div class="row">
    <button on:click={load}> Load </button>
  </div>
  <div class="row">
    <table>
      <tr>
        <th>N</th>
        <th>N^2</th>
        <th>N^3</th>
      </tr>
```

When you are thinking of nesting each loop tags, you might try to have each of the tags handle one of the arrays, something like what is shown as follows:

```
        {#each num as n_1}
          {#each num_sq as n_2}
            {#each num_cubed as n_3}
              <tr>
                <td>{n_1}</td>
                <td>{n_2}</td>
                <td>{n_3}</td>
              </tr>
            {/each}
          {/each}
        {/each}
      </table>
  </div>
</div>
```

This is a similar to a nested for loop in a different language. For example, in C, you might do something like this:

```
for(int i =0; i < length; i++){
    for(j=0; i < length; j++){
        for(k=0; l < length; k++){
            /* Do something */
```

```
        }
    }
}
```

However, even if it might work as you would expect in C, you cannot expect the same in Svelte, and this can be seen if we run the application and see the mess we created, as shown in *Figure 11.5*:

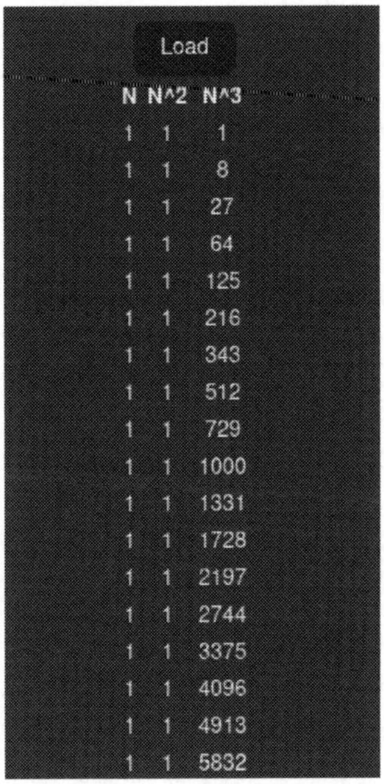

Figure 11.5: Nested Each Loop Unexpected Behavior

To fix this issue, we will consider the fact that the **{#each}** tag has a second argument that will take account of the indexes. Instead of trying to go through each value, we will use the indexes, reducing our need for each loop, from 3 to 1. Keep in mind that this will work as long as the arrays have the same length, or you may get index out of bounds errors.

A fix to our code can be seen as follows where you use the variable **i** to be the index of our arrays:

```
{#each num as _, i}
<tr>
  <td>{num[i]}</td>
  <td>{num_sq[i]}</td>
  <td>{num_cubed[i]}</td>
</tr>
```

```
    {/each}
  </table>
 </div>
</div>
```

If we run the application and load the numbers, we can see that it works as we expected. This can be seen in *Figure 11.6*:

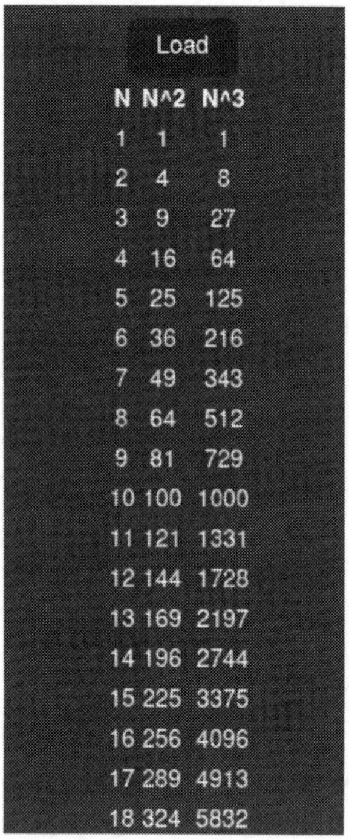

Figure 11.6: *Nested Each Loop Expected Behaviour*

Challenges with Tauri development

The Tauri development is an amazing framework compared to using alternative ways to create desktop apps such as Electron and GTK. However, like other frameworks, Tauri also has a good number of unexpected challenges that can make life a lot harder.

The first challenge encountered when writing different ideas for this chapter was the weird behavior of Tauri with other crates – some work, some do not. The problem with this issue is that you do not know until you start writing the base of your application and find out that the core component just does not work. One such example is when you try to write an encryption program and use the crate **magic-crypt**. Another crate that did not work was the tex engine, **tectonic**, which is one way of taking latex input from the user and returning a pdf sounded good, but that had not been able to work due to the issues in tectonic's C bindings.

Another challenge is that Tauri apps are read-only and that can be an issue if you have a program that needs to write files because here, you cannot. The problem is that you do not know this issue until you build the program and get this error. So imagine writing a whole application only for the program to be read-only.

You can still try changing the permissions in Linux using **chmod**. Even when you write new files in the development environment using something like **yarn tauri dev**, when a new file is found in **src-tauri**, the whole project is rebuilt which can be really annoying.

Conclusion

The Tauri framework helps making a developer's life easier by using a JavaScript framework frontend UI and Rust as a backend language. Instead of wasting time trying to build an UI with Rust types, it is a lot easier when created using HTML, and with the help of the Svelte framework, using JavaScript has made life a lot easier. In conclusion, we have seen how we can create a desktop app using the Tauri framework alongside the SvelteKit framework.

Key facts

- When using Svelte, try to use the various tags and properties to help simplify the JavaScript experience.

- When returning a **Result** in a Tauri command, use the methods, **then()** and **catch()** in JavaScript:
  - **then()** handles the **Ok** value of the **Result**.
  - **catch()** handles the **Err** value of the **Result**.

- To create a new command in Tauri, use the attribute **#[tauri::command]**.
  - Make sure to add the identifier in **tauri::generate_handler![]**.

- For the best experience with Tauri, make sure to use the latest Rust compiler and the latest **npm** or **yarn** version.
  - For Windows build, recommended to use Windows 11.

- Recommended using **vscode** with the **Tauri** plugin and **Svelte** plugin for the best development experience.

- The best resource when building an application with Tauri is using their official guide: **https://tauri.app/v1/guides/**.

Exercises

1. Create an application that shows the top 25 stories from an RSS feed, make sure to include the article's title (the link embedded in it) and the published dates.

Answers

1. In this exercise, we will show the top 25 stories from the news site **https://www.phoronix.com/** that has many articles about the latest happenings in the Linux kernel/community. The site conveniently provides the **rss** feed of the website using the link, **https://www.phoronix.com/rss.php**. We can easily use the **reqwest** crate to send a get request to the link and read the XML file from the request's bytes.

   To begin the exercise, it is best that we create the project, **rss_app** using the **cargo create-tauri-app** command, as follows:

```
# create app rss_app
$ cargo create-tauri-app rss_app
✓ Choose your package manager · yarn
✓ Choose your UI template · svelte-kit


Done, Now run:
  cd rss_app
  yarn
  yarn tauri dev


# enter into the project
$ cd rss_app
# install dependencies
$ yarn
```

   We will first focus on the Rust backend and that begins with adding in the necessary crates for our application. To send requests to phoronix, we will need to use the **reqwest** crate and to read the XML file, we will use the **rss** library. To add the crates, we will use the **cargo add** command:

```
$ cd src-tauri
$ cargo add rss reqwest
```

Inside **main.rs**, we will need to import **Error** from **std::error** and the type **Channel** from **rss**. Aside from our imports, we will also need to define a **const** binding, **LINK** that will contain the rss link of phoronix:

```
#![cfg_attr(
    all(not(debug_assertions), target_os = "windows"),
    windows_subsystem = "windows"
)]
use std::error::Error;
use rss::Channel;
const LINK: &str = "https://www.phoronix.com/phoronix-rss.php";
```

We can then create the structure **Feed** that will contain the three fields, **titles**, **dates**, and **links** which will all have type **Vec<String>**. The reason we are keeping the titles, dates, and links in separate vectors is because we cannot properly format strings with newlines from Rust to JS, but rather, we will need to return each vector separately:

```
#[derive(Debug, Clone)]
struct Feed{
    titles: Vec<String>,
    dates: Vec<String>,
    links: Vec<String>
}
```

If there is an error with loading our stories, we will just return an empty Feed; an improvement that can be made is to replace this with a proper error system. However, let us keep our program simple and not have to try and find out which field had an error. We will just implement the **Default** trait to **Feed** which will return **Feed** with empty vectors for each field:

```
impl Default for Feed{
    fn default() -> Self {
        Feed{titles: vec![], dates: vec![], links: vec![]}
    }
}
```

Before we try and create a **new** method for **Feed**, we will need to create the function **get_feed()** that will send a get request to our link and return the **Channel**. However, because we want to handle the errors, we will be returning **Result<Channel, Box<dyn Error>>**, and since we need to send a request the function, it will be asynchronous:

```
async fn get_feed() -> Result<Channel, Box<dyn Error>>{
```

To create a **Channel**, we need to read an array of bytes so that we will need to use the function **reqwest::get()** using **LINK** to send a response. After that, we will need to chain it with the **bytes()** method to turn it into the type **Bytes** which we can read from. Do note that between using the **bytes()** method and **await**, we will need to use **await** and the **?** operator to handle the **Future** of the asynchronous function and the error, respectively:

```
let content = reqwest::get(LINK)
.await?
.bytes()
.await?;
```

To create a new **Channel**, we will use the function **Channel::read_from()** where we will borrow the binding **content** and slice it with **[..]**. After this, we can return our channel wrapped with **Ok** as shown as follows:

```
let channel = Channel::read_from(&content[..])?;
Ok(channel)
}
```

Now, we are ready to create a **new()** method for **Feed** which will be asynchronous and return **Result<Self, Box<dyn Error>>**:

```
impl Feed{
    pub async fn new() -> Result<Self, Box<dyn Error>>{
```

The first step is to get our **Channel** using the function **get_feed()**, which we will need to use **await** and the **?** operator, to handle the future and error. After that, we can have mutable bindings for the titles, publish dates and links for the channel, and initialize them using **Vec::new()**:

```
let channel = get_feed().await?;
let mut titles = Vec::new();
let mut dates = Vec::new();
let mut links = Vec::new();
```

We will create a binding **items** that will contain the different articles in the **rss** feed using the method **items()** from the binding **channel**:

```
let items = channel.items();
```

To get the latest 25 stories, we can create a **for** loop that iterates from 0 to 25, uses the index to iterate through **items**, and push the fields to its respective vectors. After that, we can return **Self** using the vectors **titles**, **dates** and **links** as shown:

```
        for i in 0..25{
            titles.push(items[i].title.clone().unwrap());
            dates.push(items[i].pub_date.clone().unwrap());
            links.push(items[i].link.clone().unwrap())
        }
        Ok(Self { titles, dates, links})
    }
```

To get the inner **Feed**, we will have a separate method called **load()** which will also be asynchronous and return **Feed** by using a **match** statement on **Feed::new()**. In the **Ok** case, we will return the value which will be **Feed**, while in the **Err** case, we will ignore the error and choose to return **Feed::default()**:

```
pub async fn load() -> Self {
    match Self::new().await {
        Ok(f) => f,
        Err(_) => Self::default(),
    }
}
```

Now, we can create Tauri commands using the attribute **#[tauri::command]** for the functions **get_titles()**, **get_dates()**, and **get_links()** that will return a **Vec<String>**, and will use the function **Feed::load()** to get their respective field. Another important note about these functions is that they will all be asynchronous, and by default, they will run on a separate thread. If you would like it to be on the same main thread, you will need to use the attribute **#[tauri::command(async)]**:

```
#[tauri::command]
async fn get_titles() -> Vec<String> {
    Feed::load().await.titles.clone()
}


#[tauri::command]
async fn get_dates() -> Vec<String> {
    Feed::load().await.dates.clone()
}
#[tauri::command]
async fn get_links() -> Vec<String> {
```

```
        Feed::load().await.links.clone()
}
```

Now, we are ready to create our **main** function that will use the function **tauri::Builder::default()**. After that, we will need to chain it with the method, **invoke_handler()** that will allow us to use the **invoke()** function in JavaScript for our tauri command. Inside **invoke_handler()**, we will use the declarative macro, **tauri::generate_handler![]** and include our functions from above. Next, we will chain the method **run()** with the function **tauri::generate_context!()** inside, and since **run()** returns a **Result**, we will end the chain with the **expect()** method:

```
fn main() {
    tauri::Builder::default()
        .invoke_handler(tauri::generate_handler![get_titles, get_
dates, get_links])
        .run(tauri::generate_context!())
        .expect("error while running tauri application");
}
```

Now, we can start working on the frontend and that begins with editing some of our files in **src**. This begins with **src/app.html**, where we will add the **w3.css** stylesheet. The reason we added this is so we can use the class **w3-table** and **w3-bordered**, and so we can see the entirety of **src/app. html** as the following:

```
<!DOCTYPE html>
<html lang=»en»>
  <head>
    <meta charset="utf-8" />
    <link rel="icon" href="%sveltekit.assets%/favicon.png" />
    <link rel="stylesheet" href="https://www.w3schools.com/
w3css/4/w3.css">
    <meta name="viewport" content="width=device-width" />
    %sveltekit.head%
  </head>
  <body>
    <div>%sveltekit.body%</div>
  </body>
</html>
```

Next, we need to edit **src/routes/+page.svelte** where we will need to import **Rss** from our file **Rss.svelte** that we will create next, and edit the title and subtitles of the application. The entirety of the file can be seen as follows:

```
<script>
  import Rss from "$lib/Rss.svelte";
</script>


<h1>Welcome to RSS News App!</h1>


<p>Press the refresh button for the latest stories</p>


<div class="row">
  <Rss/>
</div>


<style>
  .logo.vite:hover {
    filter: drop-shadow(0 0 2em #747bff);
  }


  .logo.svelte:hover {
    filter: drop-shadow(0 0 2em #ff3e00);
  }
</style>
```

Now, we can create the file **src/lib/Rss.svelte** and we will begin with the **script** portion. We will need to import the **invoke** function from **@tauri-apps/api/tauri** and initialize the arrays **titles**, **dates** and **links** using an array with an empty string inside:

```
<script>
    import { invoke } from "@tauri-apps/api/tauri"
    let titles = [""]
    let dates = [""]
    let links = [""]
```

We will create the asynchronous function **get_feed()** that will asynchronously assign each of the arrays using **invoke()** with their respective tauri command:

```
async function get_feed(){
  titles = await invoke("get_titles")
  dates = await invoke("get_dates")
  links = await invoke("get_links")
}
</script>
```

In terms of the HTML side of our Svelte file, we will need to begin with creating a refresh button that will use the property **on:click={}** with the function **get_feed()** inside:

```
<div>
  <div class="row">
    <button on:click={get_feed}>Refresh</button>
  </div>
<br>
```

Now, we are able to create a table with two headers, **Title** and **Publish Date**. Note that we use the **w3.css** classes **w3-table** and **w3-bordered** for our table:

```
<div class="row">
  <table class="w3-table w3-bordered">
    <tr>
      <th>Title</th>
      <th>Publish Date</th>
    </tr>
```

To iterate through all our arrays, we will use the fact that all of them have the same length. Thus, if we use the indexing part of the **{#each }** tag, we can iterate through them without any weird behavior. This is something we did in the **More Tauri** section as follows:

```
{#each titles as _, i}
  <tr>
    <a href="{links[i]}"><td>{titles[i]}</td></a>
    <td>{dates[i]}</td>
  </tr>
{/each}
```

```
    </table>
  </div>
</div>
```

With the frontend completed, we are done writing our application and that means we can choose to try it out using **yarn tauri dev** or build it using **yarn tauri build**. Let us build the project and before we do so, we will need to change the identifier of our project, which is found in **src-tauri/tauri.conf.json**. We changed it to **app.rss**; however, if you had an organization, it would be best to have it related to that (for example, **com.mkproj.rss_app**).

Now, we are able to build our project and try it out like the following:

```
# note that this is being built in POP_OS!
$ yarn tauri build
# we will run the appimage executable
$ cd src-tauri/target/release/bundle/appimage
$ ./rss-app_0.0.0_amd64.AppImage
```

We can see our application running in *Figure 11.7*:

Figure 11.7: *Top Articles from Phoronix displayed on the RSS News App*

If the user would like to read the article, they may click on the link and read the article directly on the app, as shown in *Figure 11.8*:

rss_app — ✕

Linux 6.1-rc7 Released Following A Busy Thanksgiving Week

Written by Michael Larabel in Linux Kernel on 27 November 2022 at 04:55 PM EST. Add A Comment

Linus Torvalds just christened the Linux 6.1-rc7 kernel as what is now expected to be the second to last release candidate before Linux 6.1 is officially released in December.

Linux 6.1 has seen an uptick in changes this cycle compared to where Torvalds prefers seeing the patch flow slow down. He's been teetering the past few weeks on whether the v6.1 cycle will be drawn out by an extra week. As it stands now, he's leaning towards indeed declaring Linux 6.1-rc8 next week before issuing the stable Linux 6.1 kernel the following week. So Linux 6.1 stable will be out on 11 December unless this next week ends up being extremely quiet that would lead Linus to instead go straight to v6.1.

Linus commented in the 6.1-rc7 announcement:

Another week has gone by. It started quietly, and I was fairly sure that it being Thanksgiving week here in the US would mean that it would continue fairly quietly too.

But I was wrong. The end of the week was the usual "people send me their stuff on Friday", and the weekend hardly slowed people down. And so the stats for this week look almost exactly the same as they did for the previous two weeks.

And it's not just the statistics - everything feels very similar. There is really

Figure 11.8: *Latest Article displayed on RSS News App*

Index

Printed in Great Britain
by Amazon

40187580R00253